D0629996

Critical Essays on Margaret Atwood

Critical Essays on
World Literature

Robert Lecker, General Editor
McGill University

Critical Essays on Margaret Atwood

Judith McCombs

G. K. Hall & Co. • Boston, Massachusetts

Library of Congress Cataloging in Publication Data

Critical essays on Margaret Atwood / Judith McCombs [editor].
p. cm. — (Critical essays on world literature)
Bibliography: p.
Includes index.
ISBN 0-8161-8840-8 (alk. paper)
1. Atwood, Margaret Eleanor, 1939– —Criticism and interpretation. I. McCombs, Judith. II. Series.
PR9199.3.A8Z58   1988
818'.5409 — dc19   87-30869
                                                          CIP

This publication is printed on permanent/durable acid-free paper
MANUFACTURED IN THE UNITED STATES OF AMERICA

CONTENTS

INTRODUCTION

Margaret Atwood is, perhaps, three writers: the Canadian poet whose first real book, the 1966 *Circle Game*, won the Governor General's Award, whose pioneer *Journals of Susanna Moodie* evoked Canadian history, whose *Power Politics* and *You Are Happy* continue to attract international scholarship, and whose *Selected Poems II, 1976–1986*, has just appeared. Margaret Atwood is also the internationally read, translated, and critiqued fiction writer whose six novels, from the 1969 *Edible Woman* through *Surfacing, Lady Oracle, Life Before Man*, and *Bodily Harm* to the 1985 *Handmaid's Tale*, have established her as one of the very best women writing in English, and one of the world's most original contemporary novelists. Margaret Atwood is also the forthright critic whose thematic guide to Canadian literature, *Survival*, has survived, after brief but intense 1973 controversy, as Canada's best-selling and most influential work of literary criticism, and has become, as a side-effect, a key guide to her own work; and whose collected 1982 *Second Words* range from Canadian poetry and women's writing to international human rights.

And, as George Woodcock presciently saw, in 1969, the connections between Atwood's diverse genres are capillary;[1] the works correspond to and resonate with one another, so that the serious reader is drawn, book by book, further into Atwood's allusive and metamorphic territory.

Atwood has been, since the mid-1970s, Canada's most studied contemporary writer; the secondary work is extensive, international, and contagiously proliferating: there are now four critical books on Atwood, four collections of original essays, and a fifth forthcoming, and other books in progress. This volume is based on over a thousand reviews and essays, which represent a comprehensive gathering and analysis of the English-language Canadian and U.S. journal work, through mid-1987, including feminist and small press work, with some coverage of newspapers and of work in other countries, chiefly British and Commonwealth. The Alan J. Horne 1979–81 annotated bibliographies and checklist, which cover several hundred secondary items and which are still the indispensable starting points for Atwood research, are, in 1987, much in need of updating. Meanwhile, the extensively footnoted introduction here, which is as detailed as this series permits, will provide for the general reader and researcher a current guide to the North American scholarship.[2]

Readers in Canada, or in Canadian studies programs, may recognize certain well-known Canadian essays, collected and reprinted here in their original forms, along with less accessible, new, and U.S. commentaries. Readers outside Canada, who, in the United States, must often rely on very limited Canadian studies library holdings, will find most of the major Canadian literary journals represented here, and many of the major Canadian poets, novelists, and critics who have assessed and reassessed Atwood's work. My only conscious quota has been to limit works to one per author, and one per journal, except where a great deal of essential Atwood work has appeared in one journal; this means that certain writers are represented here by only one of the possible choices, and that certain journals — *Canadian Literature* and *Essays on Canadian Writing* in particular — have been proportionately represented, or perhaps underrepresented. Given the abundance of key periodical work, and the difficulties of obtaining it outside Canada, very little work from books and collections still in print has been included; the serious Atwood reader will want to obtain those books. That over two-thirds of the selections, and more of the pages, come from Canada indicates Atwood's earlier and more extensive publication there, as well as the seriousness with which Canadians take their literature, including poetry, and their contemporary writers. That about three-fifths of the selections, and pages, come from women may seem low, or high, to readers familiar with, perhaps, only the work by American feminists, or by Canadian men; my first and conscious choice has been to reprint the range of the best obtainable and still-key Atwood criticism, from whichever country, persuasion, or gender.

As the selections here suggest, most of the major Atwood work to date has focused on themes and patterns of social criticism; feminism and women's literature; Canadian literature; Gothic and popular genres; re-enacted or transformed myth and, lately, folklore. The linguistic, formal, structuralist, postmodern, and manuscript approaches have been fewer, but will no doubt increase. Most of the key Atwood work comes after 1972, for several reasons: by the early 1970s counter-cultural, feminist, and Canadian issues had become prominent, and could be recognized in Atwood's writing; the 1972 *Surfacing* had simultaneously written Atwood's themes large and established her as a major North American novelist, worth serious scholarship; and the 1972 *Survival* had named and defined the Canadian tradition that, critics could then infer, underlay her own work. Hindsight sees, in fact, that Atwood's own work has consistently anticipated, articulated, coincided with, and created the cultural and critical perceptions that are later applied to it.

Atwood's first real book, the 1966 *Circle Game* poems, appeared at a time when English-speaking writers in Canada took the vocation of the poet very seriously, but the most influential models were imported: Robert Graves and T. S. Eliot; the British classic and Victorian poetry tradition, which Atwood was taught at Victoria College; the American moderns and Black Mountain writers. *Circle*'s early, first-book reviews, in the leading Canadian journals and the U.S. *Kayak* and *Poetry*, were generally perceptive and very positive New Critical appreciations: *Circle* was a work of art, perhaps a strange one, but vivid, evocative, disciplined, and complete in itself, and connected to the classic European myths that were, in the sixties, presumed universal. Though the photograph, journey, carved animal, and survivor poems that would later be identified as Canadian were often singled out and praised, their Canadian themes went unmentioned; the poet was praised as an autonomous creator, writing out of her own unique sensibility and poetic discipline. Michael Ondaatje, a poet who himself excels in bringing the violence of mythology into the present, gave *Circle* the most detailed and romantic praise, as a "fully realised imaginative world" of the poet's "personal mythologies," written out of her own mysterious, violent, demanding, even cannibalistic desire to know all; his vivid appreciation is reprinted here from the *Canadian Forum*, the first real journal to publish Atwood's poetry and sequences.[3]

With the 1968 *Animals in That Country*, which won first prize in the Centennial Contest and moved Atwood's poetry from Canadian small presses to the Canadian Branch of Oxford University Press, and to its first U.S. publisher, the Canadian literary reviews moved from first-book celebrations to recognition of Atwood's growing status, intimations of later Atwood criticism, and high but almost always ambivalent praise for her exciting, controlled, but disquieting and rather cold poetry. Robert Gibbs's still-valuable discussion of the structured and controlled Jamesian horror in *Animals* anticipates later Gothic studies. Poet Tom Marshall, who seems to be the first to note, in parentheses, Canadian themes, found her poems "beautifully made and always intelligent, but a little inhuman." Writer David Helwig, whose thoughtful, honest *Queen's Quarterly* review is reprinted here, put his qualified admiration most disarmingly: he respected Atwood's poetry more than he could like it, and, sentimentalist or not, he wanted more of *Animals*'s warm love poems. Senior poet A. W. Purdy put his responses most dramatically, finding "tremendous, soul-stirring, awesomely analytical, penetrating," complicatedly simple poems from a "Poet Besieged" or, in "Arctic Syndrome," a metamorphosed Peggy-animal who "attacks the man-animal. . . . Perhaps she is too terrified of the Indians (animals, dammit!) on the outside of her stockade (skin)."[4]

Clearly, feminism had not yet arrived, and Atwood's poetry was running counter to traditional assumptions that a woman should provide warmth and stability; both Purdy and the American Mona Van Duyn, who may have been the first woman poet to review Atwood, began by complimenting *Animals* as "not 'women's poems' " and "nothing 'feminine.' " Van Duyn's *Poetry* review, however, differs from the Canadian men's reviews in concluding with identification and empathy, "as one guilty trapper to another," for a poet who compulsively distrusted man's imagination and works, even the poem and her own love.[5]

Because *The Edible Woman*, though written in 1965, was not published until 1969, its reviews came soon after *Animals's*; the most influential of these, by George Woodcock, acclaimed Atwood as a perceptive and realistic social observer, comparable to Jane Austen, and found *Edible Woman's* emotional cannibalism to be generically and symbolically true. Woodcock is a poet, critic, founding editor of *Canadian Literature*, and Anglophone Canada's pre-eminent man of letters; his fall 1969 acclaim, for the poetry as well as the novel, is reprinted here, mostly verbatim, as part of his landmark 1975 essay, "Poet as Novelist."[6]

In Canada, England, and the United States, those who accepted *Edible Woman's* anti–consumer-society thesis tended to praise its satire and affirm its hero's protest; Canadian men's reviews generally followed Woodcock in seeing the hero's symptoms as literally improbable, but metaphorically true. Two women's reviews saw Marian and the other characters as more literally true: Canadian novelist Agnes Montagnes presciently named and defined not only Marian's anorexia nervosa, but also *Edible Woman's* part in "the inception of a Canadian national identity." In the *New York Times*, Millicent Bell was perhaps the first to identify the novel as "feminist black humor," with woman as product and man as media-programmed *Playboy* consumer; *Edible Woman's* situation-comedy elements, Bell argued, served wacky, sinister, surreal ends; and its "truth-telling dementia" symbolically answered "lying sanity."[7]

Others, chiefly men, who in all three countries reviewed *Edible Woman* as an example of women's work — which by 1969–70 had become an issue — found the themes misleading, or the humour too strange or self-deprecating, or the characters too peculiar, stock, or ordinary. Poet Robin Skelton argued the problem most eloquently, in genre terms: though his review praised *Edible Woman* as a fable and a Swiftian "sexual satire," entitled by definition to unreal characters, still he found the book disquieting, and lacking in human presence and tenderness.[8]

In spring 1970, less than a year after Woodcock's acclaim, *The Journals of Susanna Moodie* appeared in Canada, with Atwood's evocative collages and eloquent Canadian identity "Afterwood," which argued that her divided, fearful, schizophrenic pioneer hero embodied the way Canadians still lived, as fearful immigrants, exiles, and invaders in a country too big to possess. Later in 1970, Atwood's fourth book of poetry, *Procedures for Underground*, appeared in Canada and the United States.[9]

The three 1971 reviews reprinted here suggest the range of serious praises each book received: Robin Skelton, who gave the highest praise to both, ranked the young poet internationally and read her Canadian vision as universal; Skelton was apparently the first to identify Atwood's haunting, Kafkaesque literary gothic. Poet Peter Stevens, who was the most positive for *Procedures* and the most negative toward *Journals*, congratulated Atwood on breaking out of the repressive, inhibited circle, and shaking off the restrictive Moodie voice, for a tentative but affirming end. A. W. Purdy's much-cited, ambivalently favorable "Atwood's Moodie" wrestled with issues of voice, gender, history, and a dearth of love in author or character; Purdy was apparently the first to identify Atwood as a "subjective Martian" and the final Atwood-Moodie persona as a "corn-mother-spirit." And the foremost critic Northrop Frye, whose definitive 1965 *Literary History* essay on the Canadian imagination had profoundly shaped the then-emerging literary nationalism, and Atwood's work, praised the *Journals*'s Canadian sensibility, titling his 1971 Anansi essays *The Bush Garden*, after a *Journals* poem.[10]

Power Politics, which began as Atwood's most controversial poetry, was also published by Anansi — not Oxford — in 1971. From 1971–72, Canadians reviewed it as Atwood's fifth book of poetry, and agreed in praising highly its particularly modern truths, its power, and its craft; but disagreed whether readers aesthetically could, or ethically should, like such poetry. Most reviewers had done at least one earlier Atwood book: for both genders, those strongly attached to *Procedures* found *Politics* too cool and cruel; those open to *Journals* welcomed *Politics*.

Poet Elizabeth Brewster, who had acclaimed *Journals* more than *Procedures*, spoke for many in finding *Politics* not quite attractive, but a powerful and disturbing whole; Brewster's prescient reading of the "you's" real and mythic manifestations, which is one of the first to follow clues from Atwood's own criticism, is reprinted here. Peter Stevens, who had acclaimed *Procedures*'s warmth, saw *Politics*'s "Deep-Freezing" as modern, Laingian truths and very dexterous poetry, but withdrew from the hard, cool language. Joan Harcourt, who had praised *Procedures*'s haunting nightmares, found a *Politics* so nightmarishly real, so strewn with emotional corpses, that even hysteria would be better than its desolating futility. George Woodcock's very different response was to champion *Politics*, finding in its cactus poem Atwood's personal poetic and survival ethic; his prescient July 1972 essay, written before he knew of *Surfacing* or *Survival*, is reprinted here, again mostly verbatim, as part of his 1975 "Poet as Novelist."[11]

II

Until mid-1972, then, almost all the secondary Atwood work consists of the serious reviews, mainly from Canadians, men and poets, that recognized Atwood as a major young Canadian poet with a promising first novel. Then, in fall 1972, the book that was to establish Margaret Atwood as a Canadian best-seller and major North American writer appeared: *Surfacing*.

The immediate Canadian acclaim was widespread and almost unanimous. In the popular press, *Maclean's* editor Christina Newman spelled out most thoroughly the Canadian literary nationalism that *Surfacing* (and the not-yet-published *Survival*) embodied: Newman's review, reprinted here, hailed Atwood as the champion of a new Canadian consciousness, rooted in its own place and realities, rejecting the unreal and mentally colonized internationalism of elder writers. In the literary review reprinted here from *Quarry*, the pre-eminent Canadian novelist Margaret Laurence championed *Surfacing*'s themes and levels, almost without reservation; Laurence's choice to read the novel's inner journey as breakthrough, ritual descent, and archetypal quest, rather than breakdown or madness, outlined many later essays.

From 1972–73, Canadians hailed *Surfacing* as a mythic and Canadian landmark; the few negative responses disallowed the mythic, or found *Survival*'s victim thesis — to be discussed below — constricting the novel. And, though praise and complaint came from both genders, it is worth noting that, for *Surfacing*, two-thirds of the Canadian literary journal reviewers were women, and perhaps particularly keen to hail a woman's work.

In the United States, where Canadian national identity and *Survival* were less visible, but the reawakened feminism and resistance to it were more visible, *Surfacing* was praised by both genders as a major feminist or wilderness novel, and often paired with Sylvia Plath's *Bell Jar*; the few negative reviews, again from both genders, found Atwood's novel too poetic, or too feminist.[12]

The key United States recognition, for *Power Politics* as well as *Surfacing*, came from American feminists who in 1973 aligned in hailing Atwood as a major modern writer, but diverged, aesthetically and politically, in reading her work as literary breakthrough, ecological advocacy, or partial escape from victimhood. This author's comprehensive *Moving Out* analysis read *Politics* as an inevitable, woman-centered breakthrough in love poetry, and as multiple, permuting victor/victim power games, between author/lover/beloved.[13] The two most influential 1973 assessments are reprinted here: poet Joan Larkin's *Ms.* acclaim justified the Surfacer's and *Politics*'s seeming coldness as a passionate human advocacy of all our planet's life, and the Surfacer's seeming madness as a Laingian inner voyage of vision and discovery; Larkin's quest for affirmation focused on *Politics*'s "hostile nations" poem as a lovers' politics of shared survival, as Woodcock had focused on its cactus poem as the writer's individual survival ethic. Writer Marge Piercy's *American Poetry Review* essay, which was the first to assess all Atwood's work in the light of *Survival*'s victim positions, welcomed the women's consciousness, struggle, and social criticism so far as they went, but wanted alternatives more real than the inner, individual-solution endings of the novels, *Journals*, and *Politics*.

Survival: A Thematic Guide to Canadian Literature, which was to become Canada's most popular and most influential work of literary criticism, and Atwood's most controversial book, was published by Anansi in 1972, shortly after *Surfacing*. The two Canadian assessments reprinted here come from the last months of an intense 1973 *Survival* controversy, and are both from writers who had reviewed *Survival* before it became that year's cause célèbre.

Critic Phyllis Grosskurth's October 1972 review, which was part of the first wave of enthusiastic nationalist identification, had acclaimed *Survival* "the most important book ever to come out of this country. . . . [*Survival*] has seized me, a Canadian, by the shoulders and forced me to look unflinchingly into the mirror."[14] By August 1973, the invaluable capsule history–overview that Grosskurth prepared for English readers, reprinted here from the *New Statesman*, tempered praise with the widespread criticism of *Survival*'s overgeneralized victim thesis and omitted authors; most important, Grosskurth documented the emerging Canadian identity, Anansi's nationalist mission, and Atwood's immense popularity, especially among the young, throughout the controversy.

A detailed replay of the 1973 *Survival* polemics is beyond the scope of this introduction, but the salients are as follows: in early 1973, both George Woodcock and Gloria Onley had reacted with serious ambivalence to the victim-survival thesis that fit, yet failed to fit, so much of Canadian literature. Meanwhile, in the winter 1972–73 *This Magazine*, Robin Mathews's impassioned political indictment had charged that *Survival* ignored Canadian works of community and struggle to focus on a literature of victims and surrender; *Survival*, he argued, was part of a Northrop Frye–George Grant–D. G. Jones colonial establishment tradition of supposedly nonevaluative exclusions, class-biased alienation, and liberal individual anarchism.[15]

A host of mixed and negative reviews, fence sittings, and defenses, had followed; as the critics polarized on ethical, political, literary, and generational grounds, re. Atwood, Frye, Anansi, et al., *Survival* became the Canadian best-selling cause célèbre of 1973. Senior editor Malcolm Ross put most eloquently the elders' case against Anansi's "sophisticated trickeries of word-play" and the "dank 'garrison mentality' " that had maligned or ignored Canada's two hundred years of "profound and iron stoicism." Don Gutteridge's two similar literary-ethical critiques detailed the case against a powerful and dangerous thesis book whose "contrived politico-psychological matrix" had neglected and victimized Canadian writers' complex experience of the land, God, Necessity, guilt, and courage. The most influential literary attack came from Frank Davey, who in his summer 1973 *Open Letter* journal charged *Survival* with overemphasizing Anansi and Ontario WASP writers, "suppressing" writers outside its victim thesis and distorting others, practicing Frye's unfortunate, nonevaluative thematic criticism while ignoring distinctive Canadian form, and "culture-fixing," here and in Anansi's advertised "Survival II" anthology, "an untouchable canon of CanLit according to Atwood."[16]

Meanwhile, in the May-June *This*, Atwood had replied to Mathews, at the editors' request, in a debater's essay assessing the range of *Survival* reactions, defending the victim thesis as characteristically Canadian and a working hypothesis, not dogma, and charging that Mathews had misread *Survival*'s evidence, particularly on the historic *Wacousta*, and had claimed more Canadian struggle literature than existed.[17]

Woodcock's considered July 1973 defense, reprinted here almost verbatim as part of his 1975 "Poet as Novelist," rose above the controversy to find in *Survival*'s mildly exasperating polemic the same personal ethic of defensive strength shown in the poetry; *Survival*, he argued, should be seen as tactical and salutory for Canada, and, for Atwood, as a journey into her culture's darkness and small, meaningful lights.[18]

The *Survival* controversy, then, peaked in 1973 with Mathews's political indictment and Davey's literary attack, and subsided into occasional flare-ups thereafter;[19] Anansi's back-cover advertised "Survival II" was never published. In contrast to the 1972–73 *Surfacing* acclaim, led by Canadian women, Canadian men, and American women, the 1973 *Survival* polemics were conducted primarily, but not exclusively, by Canadian men, who polarized, sometimes extremely negatively. Those few non-Canadians who had obtained Anansi's *Survival* tended, as in Piercy's essay here, to accept the insights as given for Canada, while using them as a key to Atwood's own works.

Conciliatory reviews were appearing by 1974, along with the negative ones: Walter E. Swayze's most diplomatic assessment compared *Survival* to T. S. Eliot's youthful, dogmatic, and highly influential criticism; Davey's 1974 *From There to Here* guidebook, which was not enthusiastic about Atwood's limited, fearful themes and cold personae, recognized that *Survival* had been useful, as a layman's guide. And T. D. MacLulich's irreverent but highly relevant overview of Canadian literary criticism dramatized the "*Survival* Shoot-Out" as the lady versus the gunslingers, while pointing out that a real literary or cultural refutation had yet to be written.[20]

By 1974, Margaret Atwood was widely recognized as English Canada's foremost writer; *Surfacing* and *Survival* had written her themes large, and had impelled as well as coincided with nationalist, feminist, and counter-cultural movements. In the newly burgeoning fields of women's studies and Canadian studies, which countered New Criticism by proclaiming the personal and the literary as the political and the national, Atwood's works were evaluated not as unique or peculiar artistic creations, but as voicing the hitherto-suppressed truths of women's and Canadians' lives.

Gloria Onley's groundbreaking "Power Politics in Bluebeard's Castle," reprinted here from the spring 1974 *Canadian Literature*, linked Atwood's

Politics and fiction to feminist and dissident, Laingian critiques of a depersonalizing, alienating, patriarchal Western society; similarly, in the United States, Karen F. Stein's and Annette Kolodny's 1975 feminist critiques set the Surfacer in a newly defined tradition of women's truth-telling "madness." Meanwhile, writer Robert Kroetsch's influential post-modern speculations reached parallel conclusions about the Canadian writer's need to *de*mythologize a British- or American-defined language and experience, and argued that in *Surfacing* "The terror lies not in her going insane but in her going sane." And Susan Wood Glicksohn's tracing of the science fiction themes in Atwood's poetry, which is the first popular culture study, affirmed Atwood's truth-telling metaphors of the alien being in a world perceived as alien.[21]

Other mid-1970s essays found a healing journey of the divided self who moved through Laingian alienations to reintegration and, as the key Gibson interview of 1972–73 had put it, "some kind of harmony with the world": see Catherine McLay on *Surfacing*; Gary Ross on *Circle Game* and on *Animals*; and, in the United States, Susan Fromberg Schaeffer's kindred reading of *Surfacing* as a mortal's healing quest for her lost parents, particularly her mother.[22]

Acclaim for the new star of Canadian literature was not, of course, unanimous: in spring 1974, a crude octopus satire of Atwood appeared in *Canadian Forum*, along with George Galt's rave overview of *Surfacing*'s reception; in *Canadian Literature*, alongside the recognition from Onley and Ross, Linda Rogers's intensely poetic "Margaret the Magician" found only cold, dead love in the books, and a hypnotizing ice-woman in their author's cover photos.[23]

The 1974–75 Canadian reviews of the *You Are Happy* poems, which precede the 1976 surge of *Surfacing* scholarship and the major 1977 poetry essays reprinted here, replayed already polarized responses to Atwood's star status, plus the womanly warmth and power aspects of *Animals*'s and *Politics*'s reviews: fans praised the transformations; almost everyone de-lighted in the final warm love poems; a number found the animals negative and Circe's powers displeasing. Alan Pearson, who reviewed a "snaky-haired Medusa" he saw on an Atwood poster and a Brontëan specter he envisioned, found the poems forceful but icy, sour, puzzling, and bleak. Poet George Amabile, who speculated that Atwood's prose success had driven her poetic consciousness into ambush, found the book uneven, the animals gimmicky, the "Circe/Mud" poems best, but Circe herself "the archetypal bitch," filled "with sexual coldness and intellectual savagery."[24]

Conversely, Christopher Levenson affirmed the shrewd hits against man's arrogance, and the final journey of equals; Andrew Scott's mytho-poeic appreciation praised most the subtle "Mirrors" and bitingly satiric "Circe/Mud," but found the animal metamorphoses glib, and the closing love poems perhaps artificially placed. And editor Ken Norris, who had previously disliked the Ice-Mother antiromanticism in Atwood's poetry, now, after *Surfacing*'s deep feeling and *Survival*'s Canadian ethics, praised her journey, as woman and writer, from *Circle*'s struggles to *You Are Happy*'s culminating, commingled feeling.[25]

The Canadian backlash against Atwood's poetry was all but suspended in reviews of the 1976 *Selected Poems*, which were favorable and very favorable indeed, seldom negative; most welcomed the *Selected Poems* as Atwood's milestone, approved her qualities and progress, and singled out her best work as the *Journals*, *Politics*, or parts of *You Are Happy* — especially "Siren," the animal "Songs," and the final love poems. The chronological *Selected Poems* did favor *You Are Happy*'s mythic and personal transformations, reprinting its "Songs" and "Circe/Mud" intact, and its final love poems at the culminating end; *Politics*'s darker images and original three-part structure were obscured by cuts; *Journals*'s poems were reprinted intact, but without the evocative collages or the defining Canadian identity "Afterwood."[26]

The year 1977 was a milestone one for Atwood criticism, and, in the poetry, for *You Are Happy*, which most critics treated, explicitly or implicitly, as Atwood's culminating book: in January 1977 the first formal analysis of Atwood's poetry, Robin Skelton's "Timeless Constructions," appeared with poet Eli Mandel's "Atwood's Gothic" in the first collection of Atwood criticism, the indispensable but out-of-print *Malahat Review: Margaret Atwood: A Symposium*, edited by Linda Sandler. In spring 1977 "Circe/Mud" entered the feminist canon, as critics on both sides of the border celebrated women's empowering themes and radically transformed female mythologies; and before the year was out two other landmark essays, by Frank Davey and John Wilson Foster, summed up what hindsight sees as Atwood's first stage in poetry.[27]

Poet Eli Mandel's "Atwood's Gothic," which followed clues from *You Are Happy*'s "Mirrors" and "Gothic Letter" poems, has been the most influential in directing critical attention from Atwood's much-discussed social concerns to the static literary genre underlying her work, including *Survival*, which he read as a ghost story disguised as literary criticism. Though Mandel is not the first to discuss Atwood's ghosts or gothic elements, he is the first to link her work, especially "Frankenstein," the *Surfacing* abortion, and *Survival*, to the taboo births of Ellen Moers's 1976 "Female Gothic"; both Sandler's key *Malahat* interview and Atwood's 1976 *Lady Oracle*, which is not mentioned in Mandel's "Gothic," confirmed many of his genre speculations, reprinted here from *Malahat* and his *Another Time*.[28]

Conversely, in feminist criticism, *de*mythologizing became what would later be termed *re*mythologizing: in the United States, Jane Lilienfeld gave the highest praise to "Circe/Mud" as women's anger and power transforming traditional love to new, more equal modes; her "Circe's Emergence," reprinted here, is apparently the first to explicate Odysseus' moonmarks, and forms a basis for Estella Lauter's 1984 "Remythologizing Circe." Simultaneously, in Canada, Carolyn Allen, who cited Atwood's own 1975 statement on transforming the mythology, acclaimed a partially but progressively transformed female mythology in *Journals, Surfacing,* and "Circe/Mud." And, in the *American Poetry Review*, Valerie Trueblood upheld Circe's, and Atwood's, female kinship with the vulnerable natural world.[29]

Frank Davey's elegantly argued "Atwood's Gorgon's Touch," reprinted here, is the basis for his 1984 *Margaret Atwood: A Feminist Poetics*; Davey, who like Skelton returned to Atwood's forgotten 1961 *Double Persephone* chapbook, and who like Mandel focused on static and re-enacted, underlying patterns in Atwood's poetry, found their source, however, to be an irresolvable, modernist-rooted aesthetic and ethical opposition between fixed form versus kinetic, subversive process, and between space versus time; Atwood's artist-woman-transformer, he argued, is a Medusa, turning life and love to stony art.

Mandel and Davey, then, treated *You Are Happy* implicitly as Atwood's culminating poetry; Lilienfeld and Allen treated its "Circe/ Mud" explicitly as Atwood's culminating transformations. Between their essays and the *Selected Poems*'s cuts and order, it would appear that *You Are Happy* had, by 1977, replaced *Power Politics* as Atwood's stellar work — a replacement that rested, in great part, on assumptions of chronological progress toward wished-for happy ends of warmth, equality, and love.

It is John Wilson Foster's pioneer tracing of archetypal Canadian literary forms, reprinted here, that first and definitively recognized *The Journals of Susanna Moodie* as Atwood's poetic masterpiece, by going back to Canadian history and by reading the other books in *Journals*'s light. Though Foster searched like Mandel and Davey for underlying forms, he found not stasis but a primordial and metamorphic universe where, as implied in Woodcock's capillary correspondences, "Nothing is destroyed . . . it simply assumes another shape, another form."[30]

A number of Canadian critics have since followed Foster's lead in treating *Journals* as a Canadian archetype and Atwood's best poetry: of these, see especially R. P. Bilan's perceptive 1979 explication of structure, imagery, and form; and Sherrill Grace's 1980 *Violent Duality* discussion of the *Journals*'s evocative collages, Gravesian Triple Goddess and Reaney-esque myths, which proclaimed *Journals* a Canadian classic and Atwood's best. Lorraine Weir, 1981, and Diana M. A. Relke, 1983, then followed Grace in their analyses of *Journals*'s iconic collages and imagery, doubled form and voice.[31]

Meanwhile, concurrent with the 1977 poetry essays reprinted here, a remarkable 1976–78 surge of literary, feminist, and theological scholarship confirmed *Surfacing*'s essential place in the new Canadian and feminist canons: in 1976 alone, nine major essays from Canada and the United

States assessed *Surfacing*'s victim, alien, and feminist ethics; its Gothic and ghost story genres; its languages; its national, feminist, and archetypal myths. Of particular interest are Keith Garebian's psychological and genre discussion of its Jamesian ghosts, which preceded Eli Mandel's gothic speculations; Nancy E. Bjerring's very perceptive analysis of four of its language groups, from the Americanized social chatter to the visionary meta-language; and Carole Gerson's very useful explication of the Quebec elements that are, for the Anglophone Surfacer, simultaneously home ground and foreign territory.[32]

The three 1977–78 *Surfacing* assessments reprinted here are linked to the landmark *Surfacing* work of 1976: Rosemary Sullivan's "Breaking the Circle," reprinted from the January 1977 *Malahat: Atwood*, complements her 1976 comparison of national mythologies in *Surfacing* and *Deliverance*, which found in Atwood a Canadian vision and responsibility that went beyond James Dickey's American nostalgic, machismo cult of violence. Sullivan, who followed Frye's Canadian identity metaphors in both essays, was in 1976 the first to explicate the Surfacer's Eliade shaman stages; the 1977 "Circle," which reprints those stages, remains the most cogent critique of Atwood's visionary insights as ultimately evasive, alienated, and circumscribed by logic.[33]

Meanwhile in the United States, in autumn 1976, Roberta Rubenstein's definitive, multilevel analysis of the Jungian, archetypal quest in *Surfacing* and certain poems had identified Atwood's Joseph Campbell, Conrad, Dante, and Eliade sources — and set the precedent for the two mythic essays reprinted here, Josie P. Campbell's 1978 archetypal "Woman as Hero" and Russell Brown's 1980 "Atwood's Sacred Wells." And the winter 1976 *Signs* had featured Atwood: theologian Carol P. Christ's landmark "Surfacing of Women's Spiritual Quest and Vision" replied to Piercy's 1983 essay by defining a women's spiritual, not social, quest; Judith Plaskow's "Theological Reflections" thereon had debated the Surfacer's potentially oppressive woman/nature connection, pregnancy, and abortion. See also, in the same *Signs*, Atwood's laconic "Reply" to both Christ and Plaskow, which commented on United States versus Canadian perceptions and on the logic of storytelling.[34]

In July 1977, writer Francine du Plessix Gray's highly influential "Nature as the Nunnery," reprinted here from the *New York Times Book Review*, followed Christ and archetypal heroes' quests to define and celebrate *Surfacing*'s tradition of female visionary novels. In the spring 1978 *Mosaic*, Josie P. Campbell, who followed remarks from Gray and Rubenstein, challenged the social quest, ghost story, and *Survival*-victim readings as inadequate to Atwood's radically woman-centered mythic process, and demonstrated that the novel's structure recapitulates the three stages of Joseph Campbell's mythic quest.

Together with the essays of Allen, Lilienfeld, Christ, Gray, and Rubenstein, Campbell's landmark "Woman as Hero," reprinted here, belongs to that golden late-1970s feminist celebration of women's suddenly reclaimed, transformed, empowering religious and archetypal energies. Similarly, this author's 1978 "Nature Concepts" defined an emerging women's nature myth in *Surfacing* and the poetry; and Barbara Hill Rigney's highly influential 1978 *Madness and Sexual Politics*, which followed *Signs* and recast Laing to feminist psychoanalytic ends, celebrated the Surfacer's quasi-religious, thereaupeutic descent.[35]

From the 1976 *Lady Oracle* on, *Surfacing*'s triumphs meant more North American reviews, and immediate scholarly recognition, for Atwood's later novels. In Canada, where Atwood was most seriously reviewed, almost everyone found *Oracle* a very entertaining comedy, and an accurate satire of Toronto's literati and Canadian nationalists; a minority of the literary reviews tempered praise with ethical or emotional complaints for the author or her earlier novels, and a few women's reviews in the Toronto press were extremely negative about Atwood's successes. In the United States, reviewers were generally very pleased with *Oracle*'s skill, wit, and humor; a very few found it too feminist.[36]

Those who recognized *Oracle*'s older genres took it seriously from the beginning: Karl Miller's knowledgeable *New York Review of Books* essay set *Oracle* in a tradition of self-imagined, multiple-identity orphans that included Radcliffe, the Brontës, Stevenson, and Beckett; Miller also identified a very likely plot antecedent in British MP John Stonehouse's faked drowning escapade. In Canada, Patricia Morley's multilevel "Gothic as Social Realism" appreciated most thoroughly the straight and parody Gothic, and the Toronto and Reaneyesque realism; Clara Thomas, in the first of several assessments, followed Ellen Moers's 1976 *Literary Women* to define *Oracle* as self-dramatizing and self-pitying heroinism, not self-defining feminism.[37]

Susan J. Rosowski's "Fantasy and the Modern Gothic Novel," reprinted here in its 1978 paper form, has resolved the Gothic-parody-realism levels most elegantly, by reading *Oracle* as a reversed Gothic where the horror is located not outside but within our social mythology: compare the parallel but unconscious Gothic in Robert Kroetsch's 1974 remark on *Surfacing*: "The terror resides not in her going insane but in her going sane."[38]

Rosowski's essay, like Mandel's, is part of the 1970s rediscovery of the Gothic and discovery, through Ellen Moers, of female Gothic; so far, the most valuable of the kindred genre essays have come from Catherine Sheldrick Ross, whose 1979 "Calling Back the Ghost of the Old-Time Heroine" in Canadian women's romantic novels was apparently the first to discuss *Oracle*'s parallels to *Anne of Green Gables*; Clara Thomas, whose culminating 1981 "Fool-Heroine" invented a new Moers category; and Lucy Freibert, whose landmark 1982 "Artist as Picaro" set *Oracle* in an episodic rogue's tradition that included *Moll Flanders* and *Felix Krull*.[39]

Other 1977–80 Canadian essays read *Oracle*, often with *The Edible*

Woman and *Surfacing*, as a portrait of the artist, a realistic social satire, or a search for identity; the similarities of theme and characters in all three novels were now generally perceived as strengths, or stages, not faults. The particularly valuable realistic criticism includes novelist Jane Rule's influential *Malahat: Atwood* "Pursuit of Normalcy"; Arnold E. and Cathy N. Davidson's 1978 witty essay on the "Psuedo-Artist as Escapist and Apprentice Seer"; Wildred Cude's several perceptive, although intensely moral, 1977–80 assessments of *Oracle* as a didactic satire; and Leila G. Mitchell's 1980 acute appreciation of Atwood's use of clothing, appearance, and setting to create characters. Frank Davey's 1980 realistic genre reading, which rejected Atwood's "anti-comedy" remarks to Gibson and Sandler as misleading, affirmed in all three novels a contemporary optimism and a comic structure that progressed from alienation to reintegration of the self, equivalent to Shakespearean comedy and Freudian catharsis; Davey's influential essay complements his 1977 poetry analysis reprinted here, and with it forms the basis for his 1984 *Atwood: A Feminist Poetics*.[40]

Surfacing's triumphs, then, had brought Atwood's first novel into the Canadian canon; a process that had begun in 1973, when Alan Dawe's indispensable introduction to the reissued *Edible Woman* laid the groundwork for a number of Canadian essays on the hero's choices, the *Alice in Wonderland* parallels, and the doubled characters. John Lauber's most perceptive "Alice in Consumer Land," for example, followed the mainstream of Dawe and Woodcock on *Edible Woman*, and the Laingian interpretations of *Politics* and *Surfacing*, to discuss *Edible Woman* as a realistic comic novel of sexually stereotyped identities in a depersonalizing consumer society. Other 1974–80 essays set *Edible Woman* in a tradition of realistic Canadian women's writing: see especially Elizabeth Brady's 1975 Marxist-feminist analysis of Marian as a worker alienated from work, love, and reproduction; and Lorraine McMullen's 1980 discussion of complementary accepting/rebelling women characters, from Frances Brooke through *Edible Woman*'s Marian and Ainsley to Audrey Thomas.[41]

T. D. MacLulich's interdisciplinary and innovative 1978 "Adult Fairy Tale," reprinted here from *Essays on Canadian Writing*, went beneath the realistic surfaces of Atwood's first novel to argue that its haunting images and "uneasy appeal" came from its folkloric transformations of motifs from fairy tale and children's story; MacLulich's essay is the first to deviate from the mainstream validations of *Edible Woman*'s realism, and to discover in *Edible Woman* the transformed popular and preliterary structures that parallel the genre and mythic structures Mandel, Campbell, Rosowski, and others were simultaneously finding in Atwood's other works.

Russell Brown's retrospective 1980 meditations on "Atwood's Sacred Wells," reprinted here in perforce-shortened form, go beneath the surfaces of Atwood's alienated, mass-culture–inundated world to reveal the tenuous but recurrent glimpses into numinous and sacred depths; Brown's original essay, which is the most comprehensive of the mystic interpretations of Atwood's first creative stage, provides a model of how to read *through* Atwood's ironic surfaces to the depths below, particularly in his explication of the two 1977 *Dancing Girls* stories, "The Resplendent Quetzal" and the metafictive, visionary "Giving Birth."

The retrospective 1977 Canadian *Dancing Girls* collection is, as Brown's Atwood preface in the 1983 Oxford *Anthology of Canadian Literature in English* makes clear (and as the usually sexual-politics-preoccupied Canadian reviews of 1977–78 did not), the end of a first stage in Atwood's writing; Brown's Oxford selections, and his 1980 "Sacred Wells" essay, ensure the survival of *Dancing*'s otherwise-overlooked "Resplendent Quetzel" story, and favor Atwood's mystic poems while scanting the sexual *Power Politics*. Note that Brown's essay refers to the original 1977 *Dancing Girls*, published in Canada only, which begins with the sterile, divided-self "War in the Bathroom," and has the funny-sad office worker's monologue on "Rape Fantasies" as its sixth story: those two stories are omitted from the 1982 U.S. and British *Dancing Girls*, which was marketed after *Bodily Harm*, and which includes two later stories, "Betty" and "The Sin Eater," in second and penultimate place.[42]

III

As the first book of Atwood criticism, Sherrill Grace's 1980 *Violent Duality* first suggested, Atwood's second creative stage begins with the 1978 Canadian *Two-Headed Poems* and the 1979 *Life Before Man*. As is now apparent, this second stage ends with the 1986 Canadian *Selected Poems II*; in between come two more novels, three more books of poetry and prose poems, one book of criticism, and one of stories (in two versions, like *Dancing Girls*). That this second, more realistic, and more political stage — which might be called the Open World as opposed to the first, Gothic, Drowned World — mirrors the first should now be obvious.[43] Meanwhile, from 1979–80 on, Atwood criticism — which one would hope mirrors the works being criticized — has also reached a second stage, where the newer works are fitted into an existing canon; the first critical books have appeared; and another late–1980s group is emerging.

Poet Douglas Barbour's 1979 review of *Two-Headed Poems*, reprinted here, is the most thorough of the somewhat mixed but generally appreciative Canadian reviews of a book that seemed the old Atwood, yet newly familial, and newly political: as Barbour pointed out, *Two-Headed Poems* reran Atwood's familiar Gothic ambiguity and too-true paranoia, but nonetheless moved toward greater hope and a more humane compassion, both in the daughter/grandmother poems and the political "Footnote to the Amnesty Report" — a much-praised poem that was cut from the 1986 *Selected Poems II*.

The definitive recognition of *Two-Headed Poems*'s new elements came from Jerome H. Rosenberg, whose key 1979–80 explication of the 1976 Julian Jaynes *Origin of Consciousness* bicameral theories underlying the title sequence, the pivotal "Right Hand Fights the Left," and the "Daybooks I: After Jaynes" is reprinted in his 1984 *Margaret Atwood*; and from Lorna Irvine, whose 1981 article celebrated Atwood's first female book, where, after so many books of danger, suffering, and negative generation, the matriarchal generations at last connect and the child becomes at last real and welcome.[44]

Recognition of the new realism in the widely reviewed 1979 *Life Before Man* was immediate and almost unanimous, both from those who, in the *New York Times Book Review* and *Ms.*, hailed *Life* as Atwood's first true novel, and therefore her best; and from those who found its characters too bleakly pessimistic, or its author too much praised. As Woodcock, Grace, and almost everyone perceived, *Life's* social and domestic realism had displaced the fantasy and romance conventions of Atwood's first three novels; of the 1979–80 reviews, apparently only Michael Hurley's "Dance of Death in Toronto the Good" saw through *Life's* realistic surfaces to the powerful Southern Ontario Gothic nightmares below.[45]

Recognition of the new Jaynesian elements in *Life* came much later, in Ildikó de Papp Carrington's 1986 "Demons, Doubles, and Dinosaurs," reprinted here, which is the first full analysis to go beneath *Life's* realistic, ironic surfaces to the romance structure, demonic doubles, and Jaynesian theories of conscious man's split-off, god-severed life. Though *Life's* godless world was linked to Joseph Campbell's disempowered myths in the Davidsons' key 1981 analysis, their emphasis is on *Life's* relentless evolutionary realism; Carrington's analysis is, in fact, much closer to certain critiques of *Edible Woman*: especially Catherine McLay's essential 1981 analysis of the disguised Frygian romance and divided selves beneath *Edible Woman's* seeming comic surfaces; and Carrington's own landmark 1982 explication of its Conradian, "Secret Sharer" doubles.[46]

Meanwhile, concurrent with the 1979 *Life*, the first critical Atwood books were appearing: Alan J. Horne's indispensable 1979–80 annotated primary and secondary bibliographies made Atwood the first writer doubly recognized, for prose and poetry, in ECW Press's *Annotated Bibliography of Canada's Major Authors*. Sherrill Grace's 1980 *Violent Duality* provided the first, and, though sometimes deceptively casually worded, still the most germinal assessment of Atwood's work, from the early journal-published sequences through *Life*. Atwood's double vision, Grace argued, is rooted in the old subjective-objective dualities — we both see, and, in seeing, create our world and our art — and in Atwood's concept of the self as no fixed ego, but a place where things happen, which is changed by things happening in it — as, literally, in the Surfacer's visions. In this book and in her 1983 structuralist analysis of Atwood's dialectic processes, Grace most directly challenged *Survival's* critics, and

Davey's 1977 Gorgon oppositions, by finding Atwood's dualities valid, fluid, and a source of dynamic aesthetic tension.[47]

The 1981 *Art of Margaret Atwood*, edited by Arnold E. Davidson and Cathy N. Davidson, built, like Grace, on the major late-seventies work to cover Atwood's several genres most comprehensively, through *Life:* see, in addition to the work already cited, Sandra Djwa's essential explication of the poetry's Canadian sources; and this author on the haunting Gothic elements in *Circle*, the *Journals*, and *Politics*.[48]

Art's editors had in 1979 followed and anticipated Annis Pratt on the problem of the Surfacer, as a female hero, returning to society at the end of the Frygian archetypal plot. Pratt's culminating Green World and Rebirth Journey essay, in the 1981 *Art* and Pratt's *Archetypal Patterns in Women's Fiction*, followed Carol P. Christ to celebrate a radical, ancient goddess quest that could transform Atwood's hero and reader, if not society. Conversely, Robert Lecker's 1981 *Art* essay followed Sullivan and Mandel to argue that in all three novels the heroines' affirmations remained ambivalent, and the ritual patterns powerless, in a duplicitous and secular modern culture.[49]

Anthropologist Marie-Françoise Guédon's very interesting source study, in the structuralist 1983 *Margaret Atwood: Language, Text, and System*, edited by Sherrill E. Grace and Lorraine Weir, came to much the same conclusion, finding the Surfacer's Amerindian and shamanic visions unsustainable in her fragmented, godless culture. See, also in *Language*, Linda Hutcheon's structuralist analysis of the first four novels, especially *Life;* and Robert Cluett's striking computer-generated syntactic profile of *Surfacing*. For overviews of the continuing debates on the Surfacer's transformation or powerlessness, which go back to the 1973 Laurence and Piercy work reprinted here, and continue through Grace, Rosenberg, and Davey, and thereafter, see William James's conscientious 1981 affirmation, and Philip Kokotailo's elegant 1983 modern/postmodern synthesis.[50]

Meanwhile, in 1981, Atwood's overtly political, Amnesty International poetry and novel appeared in Canada: *True Stories* in the spring, followed by the closely linked *Bodily Harm* in the fall. *True Stories* was very favorably reviewed in Canada — more so than either *Two-Headed Poems* or the 1984 *Interlunar* — the consensus being that Atwood had created not only new personal affirmations, but also, ranging beyond her earlier work, responsible and truthful poetry out of the political horrors of torture and oppression. Ann Mandel's 1982 appreciation, reprinted here, is the most politically acute and thorough of the contemporary reviews; linking Atwood's work to Foucault's theories of politicization, Mandel demonstrates (as others did not) the essential unity of the book's personal, poetic, and political stories.

Though, as the 1986 *Selected Poems II* makes clear, Atwood's second-stage poetry is much less extensive than her first, most of the 1983–85 criticism has favored, for diverse reasons, the personal poems of *Two-*

Headed Poems and *True Stories* over their political poems and the first-stage poetry. In the 1983 *Language*, Anglican priest Barbara Blakeley, whose feminist political analysis parallels Ann Mandel's, focused especially on *Two-Headed Poems*'s culminating female bloodlines and consecrated bread; and George Woodcock's "Metamorphosis and Survival," which complements his 1975 essay reprinted here, read *True Stories* as the end of a cycle of poems of personal contentment and Hesiod-like country life begun in *You Are Happy* and most evident in *Two-Headed Poems*. Rosenberg's 1984 *Atwood*, which is the first book to assess Atwood's literary career in detail, traced her evolving politics from *Animals* through *True Stories*, critiqued the *Journals*'s "cold community," and praised most the enlarged love, warmth, and compassion of *Two-Headed Poems*. Davey's 1984 *Atwood*, which followed Atwood's recurrent themes and images, and his earlier spatial/temporal, female/male oppositions, discussed the increasing male violence from *Two-Headed Poems* on, but avoided ranking the poetry. The most comprehensive poetry analysis so far, Jean Mallinson's landmark 1985 appreciation of form and theme, from the pre-*Circle* poems through *True Stories*, gave high but brief praise to *Journals*'s flawless mask lyrics; and, building on Mallinson's own 1978 essay and Gordon Johnston's 1980 essay, read the "Circe/Mud" maneuvers and ruthless Homeric story as prelude to the dailiness, ease, and immanence of the final *You Are Happy* poems which, Mallinson argued, begin the partly changed, more real, less Gothic, sometimes shared epiphanies that are most fully realized in *True Stories*.[51]

Meanwhile, *Bodily Harm* had appeared in fall 1981 in Canada, and in spring 1982 in the United States. The Canadian reviews, which ranged from favorable to mixed, were, as usual, more serious and more critical than those in the United States; some in both countries found *Bodily Harm* too bleak, or anti-men. Novelists Audrey Thomas and Clark Blaise vouched for the authenticity of *Bodily Harm*'s homemade revolution and Toronto characters; see also Diana Brydon's discussion of tourists as the new imperialists. A number of reviewers were sure that the hero, Rennie, returned to Canada to bear witness; Frank Davey, who found *Bodily Harm* fit both the Shakespearean green world and Virgilian descent patterns of Atwood's female comedies, was perhaps the first to explain the end as an ambivalent future/fantasy.[52]

Two kindred essential essays have since appeared: Ildikó de Papp Carrington's 1983 structural explication, which read *Bodily Harm* as a *Surfacing*-like descent into a knowledge of human suffering and compassion; and Roberta Rubenstein's 1983–85 feminist existential analysis, reprinted here, which pulled together the novel's personal, female, and political victimizations and responsibilities. Both essays ably assessed *Bodily Harm*'s unifying doubled characters, hands, and faces; see also Sharon R. Wilson's 1985 discussion of *Bodily Harm*'s pervasive camera imagery; and Lorna Irvine's 1986 decoding of its politically subversive female body-text.[53]

Atwood's two 1982 books, the Anansi *Second Words: Selected Critical Prose* and the *New Oxford Book of Canadian Verse in English*, received a fair but not large number of Canadian reviews, mostly favorable, and almost none outside Canada; the negative responses to both books usually involved *Survival*.[54] The tongue-in-cheek, left-liberal, feminist-humanist review reprinted here appears to align itself with the general reviewers' consensus, that *Second Words* was a minor book by a major writer; the reviewers' urban sprawl and caddis fly metaphors, though not poetical, may contain essential truths of Atwood's creative processes.

The consensus of reviewers praised Atwood's 1982 Oxford anthology as a thoughtful and comprehensive updating of A. J. M. Smith's classic text; Mark Abley's most knowledgeable review, which, alas, space precludes reprinting here, traced the historic development of Canadian English poetry, and found Atwood's trenchant introduction and selections the best guide available, for readers outside Canada, to the new Canadian poetry.[55]

The spring 1983 *Murder in the Dark: Short Fictions and Prose Poems* was published by Coach House Press of Toronto, and drew a fair number of generally appreciative reviews in Canada, almost none elsewhere. Elspeth Cameron's perceptive reading, reprinted here, links Atwood's aesthetics to the nature images and the sexual "Iconography," as well as to the obviously literary pieces; Cameron's first discussion of *Murder*'s not-obvious structure and unity anticipates a forthcoming deconstructive analysis by Lorna Irvine.[56]

The original *Bluebeard's Egg* appeared in Canada in fall 1983; the reviews were generally favorable, praising especially the warm, reminiscent parental stories that opened and closed the collection; but at the time only Magdalene Redekop's eloquent appreciation, reprinted here, went beneath the much-complimented contemporary Toronto surfaces to Atwood's specific craft and elder elements — the sliding present tense, the demonic depths versus flattened characters, and the ghostly, haunting storyteller's voice. More recently, in the summer 1986 *Canadian Literature*, Barbara Godard appreciatively discussed *Bluebeard*'s embedded folk narratives, anecdotes, and legends; and Frank Davey compared its ironic, iconic, unarticulated alternate stories to those of Audrey Thomas.[57]

Atwood's *Interlunar*, published in Canada in 1984, has had somewhat fewer, briefer, and more mixed reviews than her other second-stage poetry; the few women, and about half the men, affirmed Atwood's characteristic voice and worldview, which about half the men found too bleak, dark, and cold. For serious and thorough appreciations, see Ronald B. Hatch, 1985, on *Interlunar*'s transcendent and Canadian myths; George Woodcock on its almost-animist empathy; and Anne Blott's 1985

"Journey to Light," reprinted here, which reads the book as a cyclic whole, where mythic descent is part of the process of encounter and re-emergence, and life is on a continuum with death and rebirth.[58]

Atwood's sixth novel, *The Handmaid's Tale*, was published in fall 1985 in Canada, where it won the Governor General's Award, and in spring 1986 in the United States, where first the hardcover and then the spring 1987 paperback soon became Atwood's first U.S. best-sellers. Feminists and liberals in both countries found its *1984* speculative fictions frighteningly plausible; more conservative reviewers and, most notably in the United States, the writer Mary McCarthy, found it incredible and dogmatic. Conversely, Canadian novelist Sarah Sheard appreciated its wicked games and prison-novel realism; writer John Updike found it both a spirited Canadian caricature of the States and a feminist liberal's "lovely subversive hymn to our ordinary life"; and writer Catharine R. Stimpson praised its political realism and responsibility.[59]

Lucy M. Freibert's ground-breaking essay on "The Politics of Risk" in *The Handmaid's Tale*, written for this book, sets Atwood's speculative fiction in its literary, biblical, and feminist contexts; as Freibert shows, Atwood's multilevel satire demystifies and deconstructs Western phallocentricism while, at the same time, testing the viability of French feminist theories of women's reconstructive risk-taking and storytelling. Freibert's essay justly apprehends Atwood's position of feminist speculator and, simultaneously, questioning realist — and incurable satirist and punster.

Two very perceptive explications, complementing Freibert's study, have just appeared: from Michele Lacombe, 1986, on certain of *Handmaid's* essential literary and critical feminist allusions; and from Amin Malak, 1987, on its inclusive feminist politics and dystopian tradition.[60]

For the just-beginning archival scholarship, it is hoped that Carol L. Beran's exemplary and germinal 1987 study of the *Lady Oracle* drafts will serve as model. For two landmark comparative essays, see Roslyn Jolly's 1986 assessment of the colonial Caliban versus Ariel archetypes in Atwood's *Journals* and *Surfacing*; and Annis Pratt's 1986 celebration of the Medusa stone/woman archetype in Atwood and other Canadian poets; see also Sharon R. Wilson's first discussion of Atwood's unpublished and hitherto little-known watercolors.[61]

The late–1980s surge of secondary work on Atwood includes two more just-published 1987 books, plus two 1987 fiction studies, making this a new milestone year for Atwood criticism: Barbara Hill Rigney's essential *Margaret Atwood* is just appearing in England and the U.S.; Beatrice Mendez-Egle's *Margaret Atwood: Reflection and Reality* becomes the third book (and fourth collection) of critical essays on Atwood; Roberta Rubenstein's *Boundaries of the Self* provides an extensive discussion of Atwood's novels through *Handmaid's Tale*; and Ilkdikó de Papp Carrington's *Canadian Writers* fiction essay provides an indispensable analysis of Atwood's doubles in novel and story, from *Edible Woman* through

Bluebeard's Egg. A comprehensive collection, *Margaret Atwood: Vision and Forms*, edited by Kathryn Van Spanckeren and Jan Garden Castro, is due in spring 1988; much other Atwood work is in progress and imminent in the United States and Canada.[62]

I am grateful to the Canadian Embassy for the Senior Fellowship under which this book was begun, and to the Center for Creative Studies for an extended leave of absence; to Marian Burghardt for immediate and excellent research; to Margaret Atwood, who provided certain reviews; and especially to Dr. Roberta Buchanan, Martha Muzychka, Alan J. Horne, and Carole L. Palmer, who have provided bibliographies, advice, and encouragement.

Judith McCombs

Center for Creative Studies
College of Art and Design

Notes

1. In his 1969 *Edible Woman* reviews, Woodcock used a Siamese twins metaphor for the connections between Atwood's poetry and fiction; cf. the title sequence of Atwood's 1978 *Two-Headed Poems*. The Siamese twins first became the capillary metaphor in his 1972 *Literary Half-Yearly* essay, 236; which was incorporated into his 1975 "Poet as Novelist," reprinted here. See note 6.

2. See Carol Fairbanks, "Margaret Atwood: A Bibliography of Criticism," *Bulletin of Bibliography* 36, no. 2 (1979):85–90, 98, 290 items, unannotated; as well as Alan J. Horne, "Margaret Atwood: An Annotated [Primary and Secondary] Bibliography (Prose)," in *The Annotated Bibliography of Canada's Major Authors*, vol. 1, ed. Robert Lecker and Jack David (Downsview, Ont.: ECW Press, 1979), 13–46; and "Margaret Atwood: An Annotated [Primary and Secondary] Bibliography (Poetry)," in *The Annotated Bibliography of Canada's Major Authors*, vol. 2, ed. Robert Lecker and Jack David (Downsview, Ont.: ECW Press, 1980), 13–53. Horne's 1979 prose "Bibliography" annotates 139 secondary items, and his 1980 poetry "Bibliography" 128; some are listed twice, under prose and under poetry, for a total of fewer than 267 items. See also Alan J. Horne, "Margaret Atwood: A Checklist of Writings By and About Margaret Atwood," in *The Art of Margaret Atwood*, ed. Arnold E. Davidson and Cathy N. Davidson (Toronto: Anansi, 1981), 243–85, 242 secondary items, briefly annotated.

The present research covers, in addition to literary and humanistic publications, reviews in Canadian journals such as *Books in Canada* and *Quill & Quire*, and in the British *Books and Bookmen*, but has only glanced at the brief notices in American trade journals such as *Best Sellers*, *Kirkus Reviews*, and *Library Journal*. Systematic newspaper coverage is limited to the major Canadian newspapers as indexed in the *Canadian Index to Periodicals and Documentary Films*, *Canadian News Index*, and the *Canadian Periodical Index*; in the United States, to the *Washington Post Book World* and the *New York Times*; in Britain, to the *London Times*, *Manchester Guardian*, and several others. Coverage of other newspapers is occasional. I have consulted the standard Canadian and American indexes, and searched the Canadian journals, for comprehensive coverage of the essays there; the basic research was completed mid-1986, then updated through mid-1987.

I am especially grateful to Martha Muzychka and Dr. Roberta Buchanan, who provided a copy of Muzychka's "Semi-Critical Bibliography of Margaret Atwood," prepared for Dr. Buchanan's English 490 A class, Memorial University of Newfoundland, 15 December 1981, Holograph, 1–135, 528 secondary items, including American trade journals, which the published bibliographies ignore; to Alan J. Horne, who in November 1982 provided a copy of his holograph-updated bibliographies; and to Carole L. Palmer, who provided essential bibliographic advice.

Palmer's "Current [Primary and Secondary] Atwood Checklist, 1987" of 127 secondary items, some annotated, is distributed with the *Newsletter of the Margaret Atwood Society*, no. 4 (1987), ed. Kathryn Van Spanckeren, English Department, University of Tampa, Florida. An annotated secondary bibliography is now in preparation, coauthored by Judith McCombs and Carole L. Palmer.

3. See especially Peter Stevens, "On the Edge, on the Surface," *Canadian Literature*, no. 32 (Spring 1967): 71–72; Roger Seaman, review of *The Circle Game* and *Naked Poems* by Phyllis Webb, *Quarry* 16, no. 4 (Summer 1967):40–42; Samuel Moon, *Poetry* 112 (June 1968): 204–5; and Vern Rutsala, "An Authentic Style," *Kayak*, no. 12 (1967): 63–65; *Kayak* is the journal that first published Atwood's most-studied poem, *The Circle Game*'s "This Is a Photograph of Me."

4. Robert Gibbs, "*The Animals in That Country*," *Fiddlehead*, no. 79 (March/April 1969):117–18. Tom Marshall, review of *The Animals in That Country, The Dumbfounding*, by Margaret Avison, *Winter of the Luna Moth*, by Joe Rosenblatt, *Civil Elegies*, by Dennis Lee," *Quarry* 18, no. 3 (Spring 1969): 53–54, quoted 53; cf. the end of chapter 18 in Atwood's 1972 *Surfacing*. A. W. Purdy, "Poet Beseiged," *Canadian Literature*, no. 39 (Winter 1969): 94–96, quoted 95, 96.

5. Purdy, "Poet Beseiged," 94; Mona Van Duyn, "Seven Women," *Poetry* 115 (March 1970):432–33, quoted 432, 433.

6. George Woodcock, "Are We All Emotional Cannibals?" *Toronto Star*, 13 September 1969, 13; and "The Symbolic Cannibals," *Canadian Literature*, no. 42 (Autumn 1969):98–100. In 1972, in the *Literary Half-Yearly* of Mysore, India, Woodcock incorporated his 1969 *Edible Woman* reviews into his "Margaret Atwood," 13, no. 2 (July 1972): 233–42, which he then incorporated into "Margaret Atwood: Poet as Novelist," in *The Canadian Novel in the Twentieth Century*, ed. George Woodcock (Toronto: McClelland and Stewart, 1975), 312–27. The 1975 essay, lightly revised, became part 1 of his "Margaret Atwood: Poet as Novelist," in *The World of Canadian Writing: Critiques and Recollections*, ed. George Woodcock (Vancouver: Douglas & McIntyre, 1980; Seattle: University of Washington Press, 1980), 149–73.

7. George Jonas, "A Choice of Predators," *Tamarack Review* 54 (Winter 1970): 75–77; Julian Symons, "An Extremely Funny First Novel," *Sunday Times* [England], 31 August 1969; and Melvin Maddocks, "That Consuming Hunger," *Time*, 26 October 1970, 116 (U.S.); 82 (Can.). Anne Montagnes, "Two Novels that Unveil, Maybe, a Coming Phenomenon, the Species Torontonensis," *Saturday Night* 84, no. 11 (November 1969): 54, 56, 58; quoted 56; and Millicent Bell, review of *Edible Woman*, *New York Times*, 18 October 1970, 51.

8. Robin Skelton, review of *Edible Woman*, *Malahat Review*, no. 13 (January 1970): 108–9.

9. Atwood, *Journals of Susanna Moodie*, 62–64.

10. Northrop Frye, *The Bush Garden* (Toronto: Anansi, 1971), x; his 1965 "Conclusion to a *Literary History of Canada*" is reprinted there, 213–51.

11. Elizabeth Brewster, "Dream Gave Life to Atwood Poems," *Edmonton Journal*, 10 April 1970, 61; and "Poetic Dreams in a City Park," *Edmonton Journal*, 4 September 1970, 55; Peter Stevens, "Deep-Freezing a Love's Continual Small Atrocities," *Globe Magazine [Globe and Mail]*, 24 April 1971, 16; and Joan Harcourt, review of *Procedures for Underground*, *Quarry* 20, no. 1 (Winter 1971):52–53; and review of *Power Politics*, *Quarry* 20, no. 4 (1971):70–73. George Woodcock, "Margaret Atwood," *Literary Half-Yearly*, July 1972, cited in note 6 above; and "Surfacing to Survive: Notes of the Recent Atwood," *Ariel* 4, no. 3 (July 1973):16–17. Cf. Katherine E. Waters, "Margaret Atwood: Love on the Dark Side of the Moon," in *Mother Was Not a Person*, compiled by Margret Andersen (Montreal: Black

Rose Books, 1972),102–19; Waters's poetry-*Surfacing* essay anticipates much later criticism on Atwood's sexual politics and commitment to a more human survival.

12. See especially Canadian resident Paul Delany's "Clearing a Canadian Space," *New York Times Book Review*, 4 March 1973, 5; David H. Rosenthal, "And the Shoe Fits, Worse Luck," *Nation*, 19 March 1973, 374–75; Margaret Wimsatt, "The Lady as Humphrey Bogart," *Commonweal* 98, no. 20 (7 September 1973), 483–84; and George Galt's laudatory overview, "*Surfacing* and the Critics," *Canadian Forum* 54 (May–June 1974):12–14.

13. Judith McCombs, "*Power Politics*: The Book and Its Cover," *Moving Out* 3, no. 2 (1973):54–69.

14. Phyllis Grosskurth, "Truth—and a Major Talent," *Globe and Mail*, 28 October 1972, 33.

15. G[eorge] W[oodcock], "Horizon of Survival," *Canadian Literature*, no. 55 (Winter 73): 3–6; Gloria Onley, "Margaret Atwood: Surfacing in the Interests of Survival," *West Coast Review* 7, no. 3 (January 1973): 51–54; and Robin Mathews, "Survival and Struggle in Canadian Literature: A Review of Margaret Atwood's *Survival*," *This Magazine Is about Schools* 6, no. 4 (Winter 1972–73):109–24.

16. Malcolm Ross, review of *Survival*, *Dalhousie Review* 53 (Spring 1973):159–60, quoted 159; Don Gutteridge, review of *Survival*, *Canadian Forum* 53 (May 1973):39–41; and "Surviving the Fittest: Margaret Atwood and the Sparrow's Fall," *Journal of Canadian Studies* 8 (August 1973):59–64, quoted 60; and Frank Davey, "Atwood Walking Backwards," *Open Letter*, a journal edited by Frank Davey, Second Series, no. 5 (Summer 1973):74–84, quoted 84, 83.

17. Margaret Atwood, "Mathews and Misrepresentation," *This Magazine* 7, no. 1 (May–June 1973): 29–33; reprinted in her *Second Words*, 129–50; see also, in *Second Words*, "Part II," 105–6, and "Canadian-American Relations," a fall 1981 address, 385–88.

18. George Woodcock's "Surfacing to Survive: Notes of the Recent Atwood," *Ariel* 4, no. 3 (July 1973):16–28, is reprinted, virtually word-for-word, here as part of his 1975 "Margaret Atwood: Poet as Novelist, which cut from the 1973 "Surfacing to Survive" only its circumstantial introduction.

19. Jerome H. Rosenberg's *Margaret Atwood*, Twayne's World Authors Series, Canadian Literature, ed. Robert Lecker (Boston: Twayne Publishers, 1984), 139–43, provides a fuller account of the *Survival* controversy. After 1974, Davey and Mathews continued to publish objections; the most important are Davey's "Surviving the Paraphrase," *Canadian Literature*, no. 70 (Autumn 1976): 5–13, a principled, formalist attack on the antievaluative, thematic criticism of Frye, Jones, Atwood, and Moss; and Mathews's "Margaret Atwood: Survivalism," in *Canadian Literature: Surrender or Revolution* (Toronto: Steel Rail Educational Publishing, 1978), 119–30, which is his 1973 "Struggle" essay, substantially cut and revised in response to Atwood's 1973 "Mathews" essay. Davey's *Margaret Atwood: A Feminist Poetics* (Vancouver: Talonbooks, 1984), 153–56, amplified his 1973–74 thesis.

The most important counter-arguments have come from Jean Mallison, whose "Ideology and Poetry: An Examination of Some Recent Trends in Canadian Criticism," *Studies in Canadian Literature* 3, no. 1 (Winter 1978): 93–109, argued that it was Davey's own 1973–74 unsupported, hostile, ideological misreadings of Atwood and other women writers that could create an excluding, Davey-judged canon of Canadian literature; Eli Mandel, in his "Atwood Gothic," reprinted here, and "Criticism as Ghost Story," *Impulse* 3, no. 2, 1–6; reprinted in *Another Time* (Erin: Porcepic, 1977), 146–50; and Sherrill Grace, who defended *Survival*'s struggle for affirmation and its dialectic processes; see her *Violent Duality* (Montreal: Véhicule, 1980), 1–6, and "Articulating the 'Space Between': Atwood's Untold Stories and Fresh Beginnings," in *Margaret Atwood: Language, Text, and System*, ed. Sherrill E. Grace [*sic*] and Lorraine Weir (Vancouver: University of British Columbia Press, 1983), 1–16.

20. Walter E. Swayze, "Survey and Survival," *Journal of Canadian Fiction* 3, no. 1 (Winter 1974):112–13; Frank Davey, *From There to Here: A Guide to Our English Literature*

Since 1970, Our Nature—Our Voices II (Erin, Ontario: Press Porcepic, 1974), 30–34—see note 19; and T. D. MacLulich, "The *Survival* Shoot-Out," *Essays on Canadian Writing*, no. 1 (Winter 1974):14–20.

21. Karen F. Stein, "Reflections in a Jagged Mirror:Some Metaphors of Madness," *Aphra* 6, no. 2 (Spring 1975):2–11; Annette Kolodny, "Some Notes on Defining a 'Feminist Literary Criticism,'" *Critical Inquiry* 2, no. 1 (Autumn 1975):75–92; Robert Kroetsch, "Unhiding the Hidden: Recent Canadian Fiction," *Journal of Canadian Fiction* 3, no. 3 (1974):43–45, quoted 43; and Susan Wood Glicksohn, "The Martian Point of View," *Extrapolation* 15, no. 2 (May 1974):161–73.

22. Graeme Gibson, "Margaret Atwood," in *Eleven Canadian Novelists*, interviewed by Graeme Gibson (Toronto:Anansi [1973]), 5–31, quoted p. 27; Catherine McLay, "The Divided Self:Theme and Pattern in Margaret Atwood's *Surfacing*," *Journal of Canadian Fiction* 4, no. 1 (1975):82–95; reprinted in *The Canadian Novel: Here and Now*, ed. John Moss (Toronto: N.C. Press, 1978), 32–44. Gary Ross, "The Circle Game," *Canadian Literature*, no. 60 (Spring 1974):51–63; and Gary Ross, "The Divided Self," [sic] *Canadian Literature*, no. 71 (Winter 1976):39–47. Susan Fromberg Schaeffer, "'It Is Time that Separates Us,'" *Centennial Review* 18 (Fall 1974):319–37.

23. "The Lady of the Lake:or How the Octopus Got Its Tentacles," *Canadian Forum* 54 (May–June 1974):68–69; Galt, note 12; and Linda Rogers, "Margaret the Magician," *Canadian Literature*, no. 60 (Spring 1974):83–85.

24. Alan Pearson, "A Skeletal Novella in Plain Diction. A Bestiary under Iron Grey Skies," *Globe and Mail* 28 September 1974, 33; and George Amabile, "Consciousness in Ambush," *CV/II* 1, no. 1 (Spring 1975):5–6, quoted 6. Mallinson, "Ideology and Poetry" (cited in note 19), argued that Amabile misread the Circe character and Atwood's ironic subversions of the heroic stance.

25. Christopher Levenson, review of *You Are Happy*, *Queen's Quarterly* 82 (Summer 1975):297–98; Andrew Scott, "The Poet as Sorceress," *Essays on Canadian Writing*, no. 3 (Fall 1975):60–62; and Ken Norris, "Survival in the Writings of Margaret Atwood," *Cross Country*, no. 1 (Winter 1975): 19–29.

26. The U.S. reviews came later, and varied: poet Carolyn Forche, "*Selected Poems*," *New York Times Book Review*, 21 May 1978, 15, 42, found a disturbing romanticizing of the wilderness and of madness; see also the accompanying interview by Joyce Carol Oates, 15, 43–45, and Alan Williamson's discussion of Atwood's modern ambivalence toward civilization, in "'Fool! Said My Muse to Me . . .'" *Poetry* 133, no. 2 (November 1978):102–3.

See also the perceptive *Selected Poems* discussions by Pat Sillers, "Power Impinging: Hearing Atwood's Vision," *Studies in Canadian Literature* 4, no. 1 (Winter 1979):59–66; and Linda Wagner, "The Making of *Selected Poems*, the Process of Surfacing," in *The Art of Margaret Atwood*, 1981, 81–94.

27. Robin Skelton, "Timeless Constructions: A Note on the Poetic Style of Margaret Atwood," *Malahat Review: Margaret Atwood: A Symposium*, ed. Linda Sandler, no. 41 (January 1971):107–20.

28. Linda Sandler, "Interview with Margaret Atwood," in her *Malahat: Atwood*, 7–27; the first Atwood Gothic essay is Margot Northey's "Sociological Gothic: 'Wild Geese' and 'Surfacing,'" in her *Haunted Wilderness: the Gothic and Grotesque in Canadian Fiction* (Toronto: University of Toronto Press, 1976), 62–69.

29. Estella Lauter, *Women as Mythmakers: Poetry and Visual Art in Twentieth-Century Women* (Bloomington: Indiana University Press, 1984), 62–78, 192–94; see also Lilienfeld's "Silence and Scorn in a Lyric of Intimacy: The Progress of Margaret Atwood's Poetry," *Women's Studies* 7, 1–2 (1980):185–94. Carolyn Allen, "Power of Transformation," *Essays on Canadian Writing*, no. 6 (Spring 1977): 5–17; and Valerie Trueblood, "Conscience and Spirit," *American Poetry Review* 6, no. 2 (March–April 1977):19–20.

30. Foster, "The Poetry of Margaret Atwood," quoted p. 8.

31. R. P. Bilan, "Margaret Atwood's *The Journals of Susanna Moodie*," *Canadian Poetry* 2 (Spring–Summer 1978):1–12; Grace, *Violent Duality*, 33–44; Lorraine Weir, "Meridians of Perception: A Reading of *The Journals of Susanna Moodie*," in *Art* 1981, 69–79; and Diana M. A. Relke, "Double Voice, Single Vision: A Feminist Reading of Margaret Atwood's *The Journals of Susanna Moodie*," *Atlantis* 9, no. 1 (Fall 1983):35, 37–48.

32. Keith Garebian, "*Surfacing*: Apocalyptic Ghost Story," *Mosaic* 9, no. 3 (Spring 1976):1–9; Nancy E. Bjerring, "The Problem of Language in Margaret Atwood's *Surfacing*," *Queen's Quarterly* 83, no. 4 (Winter 1976): 597–612; and Carole Gerson, "Margaret Atwood and Quebec: A Footnote on *Surfacing*," *Studies in Canadian Literature* 1 (Winter 1976):115–19. See also theologican Peter Slater, whose "Individual Transformations" *Surfacing* discussion followed William James, *Survival*, and Laing, in Slater's *Dynamics of Religion: Meaning and Change in Religious Traditions* (San Francisco: Harper and Row, 1978), 113–33, 147–49.

33. Rosemary Sullivan, "*Surfacing* and *Deliverance*," *Canadian Literature*, no. 67 (Winter 1976):6–20. But see her winter 1987 "Margaret Atwood and *Wacousta* [:] the Forest and the Trees" (*Brick*, no. 29:43–46), which reconsiders and acclaims *Surfacing*'s culture-limited visions.

34. Roberta Rubenstein, "*Surfacing*: Margaret Atwood's Journey to the Interior," *Modern Fiction Studies* 22, no. 3 (Autumn 1976):387–99; Carol P. Christ, "Margaret Atwood: The Surfacing of Women's Spiritual Quest and Vision," *Signs* 2, no. 2 (Winter 1976):316–30; reprinted, lightly revised, as "Refusing to Be Victim," in Carol P. Christ, *Diving Deep and Surfacing: Women Writers on Spiritual Quest* (Boston: Beacon Press, 1980),41–53. Also in *Signs* 2, no. 2: Judith Plaskow, "On Carol Christ on Margaret Atwood: Some Theological Reflections," 331–39; and Margaret Atwood, "A Reply," 340–41.

35. Judith McCombs, "Atwood's Nature Concepts," *Waves* 7, no. 1 (Fall 1978):68–77; and Barbara Hill Rigney, *Madness and Sexual Politics in the Feminist Novel: Studies in Brontë, Woolf, Lessing, and Atwood* (Madison: University of Wisconsin Press, 1978), 91–127.

36. Marian Engel, "She Who Laughs Last. . . ," *Tamarack Review* 69 (Summer 1976):94–96; I. M. Owen, "Queen of the Maze," *Books in Canada* 5 (September 1976):3–5; and Brigid Brophy, "A Contrary Critic Takes a Crack at *Lady Oracle*," *Globe and Mail*, 9 October 1976, 33.

37. Karl Miller, "Orphans and Oracles: What Clara Knew," *New York Review of Books*, 28 October 1976, 30–32; Patricia Morley, "The Gothic as Social Realism," *Canadian Forum*, December–January 1977, 49–50; and Clara Thomas, "Feminist or Heroine?" *Essays on Canadian Writing*, no. 6 (Spring 1977):28–31.

38. See note 21 for Kroetsch, "Unhiding the Hidden," quoted p. 43.

39. Catherine Sheldrick Ross, "Calling Back the Ghost of the Old-Time Heroine: Duncan, Montgomery, Atwood, Laurence, and Munro," *Studies in Canadian Literature* 4, no. 1 (Winter 1979):43–58; Clara Thomas, "*Lady Oracle*: The Narrative of a Fool-Heroine," in *Art* 1981, 159–75; and Lucy M. Freibert, "The Artist as Picaro: The Revelation of Margaret Atwood's 'Lady Oracle,'" *Canadian Literature*, no. 92 (Spring 1982):23–33. Cf. Sybil Korff Vincent, "The Mirror and the Cameo," in *The Female Gothic*, ed. Juliann E. Fleenor (Montreal: Eden Press, 1983), 153–63, a Freudian feminist reading that also finds a new Moers category, the comic/Gothic.

40. Jane Rule, "Life, Liberty and the Pursuit of Normalcy: The Novels of Margaret Atwood," in the *Malahat: Atwood*, 42–49; Arnold E. Davidson and Cathy N. Davidson, "Margaret Atwood's *Lady Oracle*: The Artist as Escapist and Seer," *Studies in Canadian Literature* 3 (1978):166–77. Wilfred Cude, "The Truth Was Not Convincing," *Fiddlehead*, no. 112 (Winter 1977):133–37; reprinted, lightly revised, as "Bravo Mothball! An Essay on *Lady Oracle*," in *The Canadian Novel*, ed. John Moss, 1978 (cited in note 22), 45–50; and "Nobody Dunit: The Loose End as Structural Element in *Lady Oracle*," *Journal of Canadian Studies* 15, no. 1 (Spring 1980): 30–44. Leila G. Mitchell, "The External World in the Novels

of Margaret Atwood," *Journal of Canadian Studies* 15, no. 1 (Spring 1980):45–55; and Frank Davey, "*Lady Oracle's* Secret: Atwood's Comic Novels," *Studies in Canadian Literature* 5, no. 2 (Fall 1980):209–21.

41. Alan Dawe, Introduction to *The Edible Woman* (Toronto: New Canadian Library, 1973), no. 93 [ii–vii]; John Lauber, "Alice in Consumer-Land: The Self-Discovery of Marian MacAlpine," [sic] in *The Canadian Novel*, ed. John Moss, 1978, 19–31; Elizabeth Brady, "Towards a Happier History: Women and Domination," in *Domination: Essays for the University League for Social Reform*, ed. Alkis Kontos (Toronto: University of Toronto Press, 1975), 17–31; and Lorraine McMullen, "The Divided Self," [sic] *Atlantis* 5, no. 2 (Spring 1980):52–67.

42. Russell Brown, "Margaret Atwood," in *An Anthology of Canadian Literature in English*, vol. 2, ed. Donna Bennett and Russell Brown (Toronto: Oxford University Press, 1983), 454–91; Brown confirmed, in a 12 May 1987 conversation with the author, his writing the "Atwood" preface.

43. Grace, *Violent Duality*, 135; building on Grace's *Violent Duality* and Brown's "Atwood's Sacred Wells" and "Margaret Atwood," Judith McCombs's "Atwood's Fictive Portraits of the Artist: From Victim to Surfacer, from Oracle to Birth," *Women's Studies* 12, 1 (1986):69, 69–88, first defined a "Stage I, Closed, Divided, Mirroring World" and a "Stage II realistic, Open World."

44. Jerome Rosenberg, " 'For of Such is the Kingdom . . . : Margaret Atwood's *Two-Headed Poems*," *Essays on Canadian Writing*, no. 16 (Fall–Winter 1979–80):130–39; reprinted in Rosenberg, *Margaret Atwood*, 83–94; and Lorna Irvine, "One Woman Leads to Another," in *Art* 1981, 95–106.

45. Marilyn French, "Spouses and Lovers," *New York Times Book Review*, 3 February 1980, 1, 26; Katha Pollitt, "Margaret Atwood Finally Surfaces as a Major Novelist," *Ms.*, March 1980, 27–29; George Woodcock, "Victor — or Victim," *Canadian Literature*, no. 86 (Autumn 1980):136–38; Grace, *Violent Duality*, 135–38; and Michael Hurley, "Dance of Death in Toronto the Good," *Journal of Canadian Studies* 15, no. 1 (Spring 1980):122–23.

46. In *Art* 1981: Cathy N. Davidson and Arnold E. Davidson, "Prospects and Retrospect in *Life Before Man*," 205–21; and Catherine McLay, "The Dark Voyage: *The Edible Woman* as Romance," 123–38. Ildikó de Papp Carrington, " 'I'm stuck': The Secret Sharers in *The Edible Woman*," *Essays on Canadian Writing*, no. 23 (Spring 1982):68–87; see, for a different Doppelganger study, Susan E. Lorsch, "Androgyny and the Idea of the Double: Margaret Atwood's *The Edible Woman*," *Dalhousie Review* 63, no. 3 (Autumn 1983):464–74.

47. Grace, *Violent Duality*, 1–3, 86, 106; and "Articulating the 'Space Between,' " in *Language* 1983, 1–16, cited in note 19.

48. In *Art* 1981: Sandra Djwa, "The Where of Here: Margaret Atwood and a Canadian Tradition," 15–34; and Judith McCombs, "Atwood's Haunted Sequences: *The Circle Game*, *The Journals of Susanna Moodie*, and *Power Politics*, 35–54.

49. Arnold E. Davidson and Cathy N. Davidson, "The Anatomy of Margaret Atwood's *Surfacing*," *Ariel* [University of Calgary] 10, no. 3 (July 1979): 38–54; Annis Pratt, "*Surfacing* and the Rebirth Journey," in *Art* 1981, 139–57; and Annis Pratt with Barbara White, Andrea Loewenstein, and Mary Myer, *Archetypal Patterns in Women's Fiction* (Bloomington: Indiana University Press, 1981), 135–66, especially 157–61. Lorelei Cederstrom, "The Regeneration of Time in Atwood's *Surfacing*," *Atlantis* 6, no. 2 (Spring 1981):24–37, similarly celebrated the feminine unconscious and the ancient, archetypal Inanna quest. Robert Lecker, "Janus through the Looking Glass: Atwood's First Three Novels," in *Art* 1981, 177–203.

50. In *Language* 1983: Marie-Françoise Guédon, "*Surfacing*: Amerindian Themes and Shamanism," 91–111; Linda Hutcheon, "From Poetic to Narrative Structures: The Novels of Margaret Atwood," 17–31; and Robert Cluett, "Surface Structures: The Syntactic Profile of

Surfacing," 67–90. William James, "Atwood's 'Surfacing,'" *Canadian Literature*, no. 91 (Winter 1981):174–81; and Philip Kokotailo, "Form in Atwood's *Surfacing:* Toward a Synthesis of Critical Opinion," *Journal of Canadian Studies* 8, no. 2 (Summer 1983):155–65.

51. In *Language* 1983: Barbara Blakeley, "The Pronunciation of Flesh: A Feminist Reading of Atwood's Poetry," 33–51; and George Woodcock," Metamorphosis and Survival: Notes on the Recent Poetry of Margaret Atwood," 125–42. Rosenberg, *Margaret Atwood*, 29–39, provides the personal and political background to read *Animals* as an ecological treatise, and the best thematic analysis of the book as a whole; quoted p. 50. Davey, *Margaret Atwood*, esp. 27–28; and Jean Mallinson, "Margaret Atwood," in *Canadian Writers and Their Works*, Poetry Series, vol. 9, ed. Robert Lecker, Jack David, and Ellen Quigley, introduced by George Woodcock (Toronto: ECW Press, 1985), 17–81; Mallinson, "Ideology and Poetry," cited in note 19; and Gordon Johnston, " 'The Ruthless Story and the Future Tense' in Margaret Atwood's 'Circe/Mud Poems,' " *Studies in Canadian Literature* 5, no. 1 (Spring 1980):167–76.

52. Audrey Thomas, "Topic of Cancer," *Books in Canada* 10, no. 8 (October 1981): 11–12; Clark Blaise, "Tale of Two Colonies," *Canadian Literature*, no. 95 (Winter 1982): 110–12; Diana Brydon, "Caribbean Revolution & Literary Convention," *Canadian Literature*, no. 95 (Winter 1982):181–85; and Frank Davey, "Life After Man," *Canadian Forum*, December/January 1981, 29–30.

53. Ildikó de Papp Carrington, "Another Symbolic Descent," *Essays on Canadian Writing*, no. 26 (Summer 1983): 45–63; Roberta Rubenstein, letter to the author, 16 July 1986, indicates that her *Bodily Harm* essay was written in late 1982, accepted July 1983, but not published until spring 1985 — a not uncommon chronology. Sharon R. Wilson, "Turning Life into Popular Art: *Bodily Harm*'s Life-Tourist," *Studies in Canadian Literature* 10, nos. 1 & 2 (1985):136–45; and Lorna Irvine, "Atwood's Parable of Flesh," in *Sub/version* (Toronto: ECW Press, 1986), 37–53.

54. See Lee Thompson, review of *Second Words*, *World Literature Written in English* 22, no. 2 (Autumn 1983):290–92, for the most thorough and appreciative analysis; and W. J. Keith, "Atwood as (Infuriating) Critic," *Canadian Forum*, February 1983, 26–28, for the most thorough negative response.

55. Mark Abley, "Hating the Beautiful Trees," *Times Literary Supplement*, 27 April 1984, 460.

56. Lorna Irvine, "Murder and Mayhem: Atwood Deconstructs," accepted August 1986, forthcoming *Contemporary Literature* 1988; Davey, *Margaret Atwood*, 28, 166–67, after insisting that "Liking Men" "demanded to be read as blaming individual men," praised highly *Murder*'s prose metafictions and foregrounded syntax.

57. The 1983 Canadian *Bluebeard's Egg* has "Betty" and " The Sin Eater " as the fifth and tenth of its twelve stories; these two, which had appeared in the second, 1982 U.S. and English *Dancing Girls*, are replaced in the second, 1986 U.S. *Bluebeard's Egg*, which was marketed after the 1986 *Handmaid's Tale*, by "Two Stories about Emma: 'The Whirlpool Rapids' and 'Walking on Water,' " and the parental "In Search of the Rattlesnake Plaintain," as the fifth and tenth of twelve.

In *Canadian Literature*, no. 109 (Summer 1986): Barbara Godard, "Tales within Tales: Margaret Atwood's Folk Narratives," 57–84; and Frank Davey, "Alternate Stories: The Short Fiction of Audrey Thomas and Margaret Atwood," 5–14.

58. Ronald B. Hatch, "Towards Transcendence: The Poetry of Judith Fitzgerald, Margaret Atwood and Ted Hughes," *West Coast Review* 19, no. 4 (April 1985):47–59; and George Woodcock, "Metamorphosis and Survival: Notes on the Recent Poetry of Margaret Atwood," in his *Northern Spring: The Flowering of Canadian Literature* (Vancouver/ Toronto: Douglas & McIntyre), 1987, 266–84; the *Interlunar* section, 280–84, expands his 1983 *Language* essay.

59. Atwood's novels had been Canadian best-sellers since *Surfacing; The Handmaid's*

Tale was fifteen weeks on the *New York Times Book Review*'s "Best Sellers" lists in hardback, twenty-three weeks in paperback.

See also English biographer Victoria Glendinning, "Lady Oracle," *Saturday Night*, January 1986, 39–41; Mary McCarthy, "Breeders, Wives and Unwomen," *New York Times Book Review*, 9 February 1986, 1–35; Sarah Sheard, "Captives and Keepers," *Brick*, no. 25 (Fall 1985): 24–26; John Updike, "Expeditions to Gilead and Seegard," *New Yorker*, 12 May 1986, 118–23, quoted 123; and Catharine R. Stimpson, "Atwood Woman," *Nation*, 31 May 1986, 764–67.

60. Michele Lacombe, "The Writing on the Wall: Amputated Speech in Margaret Atwood's *The Handmaid's Tale*," *Wascana Review* 21, no. 2 (Fall 1986):3–20; and Amin Malak, "Margaret Atwood's 'The Handmaid's Tale' and the Dystopian Tradition," *Canadian Literature*, no. 112 (Spring 1987):9–16.

61. Carol L. Beran, "George, Leda, and a Poured Concrete Balcony: A Study of Three Aspects of the Evolution of 'Lady Oracle,' " *Canadian Literature*, no. 112 (Spring 1987): 18–28; Roslyn Jolly, "Comparative Transformations of Caliban and Ariel: Imagination and Language in David Malouf, Margaret Atwood and Seamus Heaney," *World Literature Written in English* 26, no. 2 (1986): 295–330; Annis Pratt, "Medusa in Canada," *Centennial Review* 31, no. 1 (Winter 1987):1–32; and Sharon R. Wilson, "Bluebeard's Forbidden Room: Gender Images in Margaret Atwood's Visual and Literary Art," *American Review of Canadian Studies* 16, no. 4 (Winter 1986):385–97.

62. Barbara Hill Rigney, *Margaret Atwood*, Women Writers, ed. Eva Figes and Adele King (Houndmills, Basingstoke, Hampshire RG21 2XS and London: Macmillan Education, 1987; Totowa, New Jersey: Barnes & Noble Books, (1987). Beatrice Mendez–Egle, ed., *Margaret Atwood: Reflection and Reality*, Living Author Series No. 6, ed. James M. Haule (Edinburg, Texas: Pan American University, 1987); Roberta Rubenstein, "Escape Artists and Split Personalities: Margaret Atwood," in *Boundaries of the Self: Gender, Culture, Fiction* (Urbana: University of Illinois Press, 1987), 63–122; and Ildikó de Papp Carrington, "Margaret Atwood and Her Works," in *Canadian Writers and Their Works*, Fiction Series, vol. 9, ed. Robert Lecker, Jack David, and Ellen Quigley, introduced by George Woodcock (Toronto: ECW Press, 1987), 23–116.

Articles and Essays

[Review of *The Circle Game*] Michael Ondaatje*

Three of the best books of poetry in 1966 were by women: Gwen
MacEwen's *Breakfast for Barbarians*, Margaret Avison's *The Dumbfounding*, and, perhaps the liveliest of the three, Margaret Atwood's *The Circle
Game*. Unlike Gwen MacEwen, Margaret Atwood does not need to make
forays, now and then, into the world of mythology, for her book is full of
her own personal mythologies. The people she creates, or the poses she
assumes for herself, are aspects of a well-rounded fully realised imaginative world. Private and traditional worlds blend into one. Heroes in her
poems are not distant figures but her friends. One of them

> blew
> his arm off in a cellar
> making bombs
> to explode the robins
> on the lawns.

And she has her very own sibyl ("every woman should have one") who lives
in her ovaltine jars.

When Margaret Atwood does use myth she gives it such immediacy
and humanity that we scarcely recognize it. In one of her best poems,
" 'After the flood, we,' " she describes the drowned world: "fish must be
swimming/down in the forest beneath us,/like birds from tree to tree," and
then brings into the poem Pyrrha and Deucalion, herself and a friend,
who parody the myth of recreation by casual movements:

> You saunter beside me, talking
> of the beauty of the morning, . . .
> tossing small pebbles
> at random over your shoulder
> into the deep thick air, . . .

Her worlds have the form and violence of mythologies but none of the
expected grandeur and costume. In the poem, "Playing Cards," she

*From *Canadian Forum*, April 1967, 22–23. Reprinted by permission of the journal.

captures vividly the royalty in a deck of cards—with those Queens who hold ". . . a golden flower/with five petals, ordered/and unwilting," and these cards seem to taunt the players, as her sibyl does, for being neither brilliant nor timeless:

> You have nothing
> that serves the function of a sceptre
> and I have
> certainly
> no flowers.

Her people play in this world of archaic machinery but use the legends casually or with banality. Her sister, in "An Attempted Solution for Chess Problems," "ponders her next move/the arrangement of her empire/(cross-legged on the floor)." The idea is best seen in a section from the long poem, "The Circle Game," where she describes children being read stories:

> When we read them legends
> in the evening
> of monstrous battles, and secret
> betrayals in the forest
> and brutal deaths,
> they scarcely listened;
> one yawned and fidgeted; another
> chewed the wooden handle
> of a hammer;
> the youngest one examined
> a slight cut on his toe, . . .

Opposed to this world of monstrous battles is the ordered, too-clean world which Margaret Atwood pits herself against like an arsonist, well armed with "remnants of ancestors / fossil bones and fangs." There are perhaps too many poems which describe the objectionable order. She tends to see people as mechanical too quickly ("On the Streets, Love"; "Totems"[1]); or she gives a hackneyed description of suburbia with the "rational whine" of power mowers etc. She is better in poems like "The Circle Game" where she sees the "prisoning rhythms" more subtly engrained in us.

The reason for the breaking of the rhythms, circles, and the order is to get at the meat in others. This desire is stated seriously and humorously in several poems. She is the quiet Mata Hari, the mysterious, violent figure who never explains why her suitcase contains

> soiled clothing, plastic bottles,
> scissors, barbed wire
> and a lady
> and a man.

She knows there will always be "some other face or evidence/to add to the/

collection in my suitcase." In "A Meal" she talks of this desire for collecting in her:

> feeding
> on other people's leavings
> a furtive insect, sly and primitive
> the necessary cockroach. . . .

And this causes her to demand everything of her friends. Just as she is not satisfied with the orange on the table, she objects to "orange silences" in people:

> I'd crack your skull
> like a walnut, split it like a pumpkin
> to make you talk, or get
> a look inside.

This is why we are fully prepared for the last two poems (which are the best) in the book. "The Explorers" describes two dying people who will be dead when the rescuers come, but the two, she being one, have destroyed themselves. It has been a battle of man and woman with talk of survivors — but survivors of their own battle, not survivors for the rescuers to find. The violence of exploring others results in destruction:

> (they won't be able
> to tell . . .
>   from these
> gnawed bones,
> which was the survivor)

Margaret Atwood brings all the violence of mythology into the present world. Her exceptional imagery and discipline survive each other, and her imagination can lend itself well to humor, as in "This is a Photograph of Me." The book is also well edited: there are no tangents into themes which do not fit the book, and no bad poems — a relief after the total exposure, good and bad, of poets like Layton and Cohen.

Above all the book displays the awesome furniture of the mind which motivates the cannibalistic speaker who demands to know everything of the people around her: those with her in train stations, and those marooned with her on islands. As she herself shows, there is too much in others to overlook:

> (there are mountains
> inside your skull
> garden and chaos, ocean
> and hurricane; certain
> corners of rooms, portraits
> of great-grandmothers, curtains

of a particular shade;
your deserts; your private
dinosaurs; the first
woman).

Notes

1. Ed. note: "Some Objects of Wood and Stone, i) Totems."

[Review of *The Animals in That Country*]

David Helwig*

This is Margaret Atwood's second collection of poetry. Her first, *The Circle Game*, first published by Contact Press, then reprinted by The House of Anansi, won the Governor-General's Award for poetry and established her reputation as one of the most exciting young Canadian poets. The poems in her new book are in general similar to her earlier work, highly disciplined, dry, even astringent, centred around certain obsessive images, and showing a cerebral interest in violence.

The poems depend heavily on paradox and tend to multiply paradoxes into a surreal country of "signs without motion, red arrows / pointing in no direction."

He stood, a point
on a sheet of green paper
proclaiming himself the centre,

with no walls, no borders
anywhere; the sky no height
above him, totally un-
enclosed
and shouted:

Let me out!
("Progressive insanities of a pioneer")

Once again, as in *The Circle Game*, Margaret Atwood is concerned with forms, especially the oppressiveness of form as a limitation, with central images of freezing, encirclement, maps, masks. In her world, "unstructured / space is a deluge," but structured space is a trap.

*From *Queen's Quarterly* 76 (Spring 1969):161–62. Reprinted by permission of the author.

> Burn down
> the atlases, I shout
> to the park benches; and go
>
> past the cenotaph
> waving a blank banner
> across the street, beyond
> the corner
>
> into a new land cleaned of geographies,
> its beach gleaming with arrows.
> ("The reincarnation of Captain Cook")

The patterns imposed by the brain are both feared and clung to, and the feelings are often feelings about what has been thought: "Aren't there enough words / flowing in your veins / to keep you going."

In this book, as in *The Circle Game*, my personal response to Margaret Atwood's poems is not usually enthusiastic. I respect them more than I can like them. Their emotional temperature is too far from my own. But in one way, I find this book more appealing. The love poems here are warmer as are some of the poems about animals.

> I touch you, I am created in you
> somewhere as a complex
> filament of light
>
> You rest on me and my shoulder holds
>
> your heavy unbelievable
> skull, crowded with radiant
> suns, a new planet, the people
> submerged in you, a lost civilization
> I can never excavate.
> ("I was reading a scientific article")

Here the senses and emotions reach out, undeterred by chaos or inhibiting form. The mind expresses feeling rather than interfering with it.

And at the risk of being dismissed as a sentimental old softy, I must say, I prefer it that way.   [1969]

[Review of *The Journals of Susanna Moodie* and *Procedures for Underground*]

Robin Skelton*

In an Afterword to *The Journals of Susanna Moodie* Margaret Atwood says of Canada:

> We are all immigrants to this place even if we were born here: the country is too big for anyone to inhabit completely, and in the parts unknown to us we move in fear, exiles and invaders. This country is something that must be chosen — it is so easy to leave — and if we do choose it we are still choosing a violent duality.

In saying this Miss Atwood has perhaps indicated the way in which the "Canadian experience" can be related to universal themes. She herself, certainly, in *The Journals of Susannah* [*sic*] *Moodie* and in *Procedures for Underground*, while utilizing her strong sense of place and her ambiguous feelings about the culture of her own country, has produced poetry which directs our attention to more than local or national predicaments. The Canada she portrays is a state of mind, a poise, a questioning; it is haunted, disturbed, wary; it is a vision of the human condition. One is tempted to assert that neither of these books could have been written anywhere other than Canada, as *Candide*, let us say, could not have been written anywhere but in France; nevertheless they make of their place of origin a spiritual environment as unshackled to time and space as Kafka's *Castle* or Walpole's *Otranto*. There is, indeed, more than a touch of Kafka in Miss Atwood's procedures, and a certain gothic enjoyment of the unnameable terror and the hallucinations of solitude. These elements are, however, essential aspects of her vision and not merely decorative affectations. Miss Atwood is a subtle, but not an affected writer. Her language is spare, direct, and elegant. Her images are precise. Her perceptions are acute and her thought is often profound. She has made full use of her understanding of her country, as Cervantes made full use of his, and, like Cervantes, she has constructed from local and inimitable materials a vision which crosses all territorial boundaries. It is this capacity to create not merely a number of good poems, but a coherent poetic system capable of continual development and enrichment that separates the major talents from the minor. It is this which (among other things) sets Wallace Stevens apart from, for example, e.e. cummings and it is this that sends one scurrying to the bookstore to discover the latest enlargement of the canon of Robert Lowell. From her first small pamphlet, through *The Circle Game* of 1966, and *The Animals in that Country* of 1968 to these two latest collections, Margaret Atwood has steadily intensified and elaborated

*From *Malahat Review*, no. 17 (January 1971):133–34. Reprinted by permission of the author.

her poetic vision; she must now certainly be regarded as one of the very few important poets under forty that are writing in English.

Powerful Poetry [*Power Politics*]   Elizabeth Brewster*

Margaret Atwood's newest book of poems is powerful, if somewhat disturbing. A sequence of poems addressed by an "I" to a "you," it might at first sight appear to be a book of love poems.

A closer reading would seem to indicate that the "love" of the poems is mixed with something very like hate. Also, "I" is fairly clearly not the individual Margaret Atwood, and "you" (if he is an individual) is a very strange individual indeed.

"You" makes his first appearance rising (as in a nightmare) from a snowbank with three heads. In a later poem, he hangs, rather like Superman, "suspended above the city/in blue tights and a red cape."

In another poem, he is a mixture of Christ and drunken lover, with wine mist forming a halo around his head.

He is, in some ways, an everyman, with the unpleasant characteristics of twentieth century man:

> You thrive on smoke; you have
> no chlorophyll; you move
> from place to place like a disease
> Like mushrooms you live in closets
> and come out only at night.

Yet he is sometimes nostalgic for a better past: "You want to go back/ to where the sky was inside us."

He is "ordinary." He is also sick and unhappy. He is not in possession of himself, is becoming "slowly more public." He is the one who is responsible for the evils of the time, "who started the countdown." He is cauterizing his senses, turning himself into "an impervious glass tower." "I" seems to represent the whole female sex (if not also the earth) when she says to him,

> How long will you demand I love you?
> I'm through, I won't make
> any more flowers for you
> I judge you as the trees do
> by dying

*From *Edmonton Journal*, 16 April 1971, 60. Reprinted by permission of the author.

But "I," if she is everywoman, the mate of everyman, also fails in love. She loves "you" as if he were a machine, only "by sections and when you work." She is cold:

> You asked for love
> I gave you only descriptions
> Please die I said
> so I can write about it

The world which "you" and "I" inhabit has become sterile, does not favour the growth of flowers or children. (If love, as the cliche has it, makes the world go round, the lack of love deadens it.) "You" and "I" are engaged in a struggle for power, and this struggle ("sexual politics"?) is repeated in the larger world, where nations are at war and fists dominate over language. The attempt to dominate, to exercise "power politics," over individuals or over nature, must end in disaster.

"You" does not always seem to be everyman. Once or twice he seems to be divinity or muse, birdlike or reptilian, who occupies the personality of the poet. Margaret Atwood has herself written, in an article on Gwendolyn MacEwen in a recent issue of *Canadian Literature*, "There are several male Muses about, even in Canadian poetry; often when the reader comes across an unnamed 'you,' he would be better employed searching for the Muse than for someone with a birth certificate and a known address."

But "you" as Muse is not much more attractive than "you" as everyman. He is demanding, "the sun in reverse" who absorbs the energy of the writer. Something has gone wrong with the whole creative force of the universe, the force behind both artistic creation and sexual love.

"You" appears in the final poem "carrying a new death." He cannot be slowed or speeded up. He brings death in the shape of a glass paperweight, inside which are "a man and woman, hands joined and running." He is a menacing figure; yet he strides "towards firm ground and safety." He seems to be a different "you" from the "you" of the earlier poems (who has more in common with the running man in the paperweight).

Much of the imagery is chosen to reflect the mechanical and sterile nature of relationships.

But there is also contrasting imagery from the animal world. Her lover's body is "tentative as moths." His back is rough "like a cat's tongue." He is a wounded, trapped animal. He is a bird digging his claws into her heart.

As a sustained group of poems, unified by theme and imagery, this book is a remarkable accomplishment. I do not find it quite as attractive a book, on first sight, as *Susanna Moodie* or *Procedures for Underground*; but it is certainly an important one, with reverberations of meaning. A significant step in the development of one of our major poets.

Dark Mouth [*Procedures for Underground*]

Peter Stevens*

Much of what Margaret Atwood says in this volume she has said in her previous books. She presents a world of peripheries, under-surfaces, divisions and isolation similar to the one in *The Circle Game*, but it would be a mistake to think that *Procedures For Underground* is simply a repetition of her earlier work. Certainly the surface of these poems remains the same; many of the images of drowning, buried life, still life, dreams, journeys, and returns recur and the book is locked into a very repressive and inhibited atmosphere, even though the time-scope of the book is large, covering the chronological stretch from pre-history to the present. As in *The Circle Game*, personal relationships offer only minimal hope, yet most of the second half of this book expresses a promise of breaking-out that did not occur in the earlier work.

Even the title suggests that people need not be trapped or buried in stasis but that they can take action: there are motions that will push life and the individual forward. This volume moves in its second half more and more to the notion that words can break the authorities and inhibitions that fetter us and even a cry of agony is worth shouting, for it expresses that deep underside with its mouth "filled with darkness." This howl may be an automatic response to fear or pain, simply uttering itself, but it is a statement, and, as such, is preferable to the blankness of "a white comic-strip balloon / with a question mark; or a blank button."

People still live on the edge in these poems, surrounded by flux, impermanence and repression, haunted by bad dreams, menaced by objects but

> in fear everything
> lives, impermanence
> makes the edges of things burn
>
> brighter.

In our present pre-historic state of human relationships we are at least evolving; "we are learning to make fire." Flux and disintegration continue but the poet has the means of preserving experience — "Over all I place / a glass bell." This attempt at preservation does not necessarily have the effect of a dead hand. In one poem a swimmer dives, is lonely in the lake but the marks on paper that the poem makes about the swimmer are words which "move outwards." Art may be "the link between / the buried will and the upper / world of sun." Things may frighten man but he is a creator; he may in fact create his own fears, his own divisions, his own dreams and

*From *Canadian Literature*, no. 50 (Autumn 1971):91–92. Reprinted by permission of the author.

nightmares, but the act of creation, in particular the act of poetry, becomes an important procedure.

The volume progresses from the opening poem presenting a picture of entrapment with parents inside a fantasy zoo created by the I figure within the poem to the closing poem about those parents dancing. There is still entrapment within the circle of the dance but that circle is constantly "forming, breaking." The dance continues "transformed / for this moment / always"; it "goes / on in a different / time (because / I say it)."

"Because I say it"—that's the important triumph in the end. The progression in the book is towards a fundamental belief in the prerogatives of poetry in a threatening, tense world. Even the lining of the poems, still the usual broken, tentative expression she has used before, somehow sounds firmer, playing some kind of strength against the details of violence, repression, doubt and fear, finally emphasizing the courage of coming to terms with that lower layer where "you can learn / wisdom and great power, / if you can descend and return safely."

Margaret Atwood has returned safely, broken the circle, shaken off the persona of Susanna Moodie which to my mind was a restriction on her own personality as a poet. Her own clear voice rings out from this book to give us her best collection to date.

Atwood's Moodie [*The Journals of Susanna Moodie*]
A. W. Purdy*

Susanna Moodie was an English emigrant to Canada in 1832. She settled with her husband in Douro Township, near Peterborough, and her book, *Roughing It in the Bush*, is one of the basic pioneer documents of Canada.

Margaret Atwood says in the Afterword to her own book that "These poems were generated by a dream. I dreamt I was watching an opera I had written about Susanna Moodie. I was alone in the theatre: on the empty white stage, a single figure was singing." And later, about her poems: "I suppose many of these were suggested by Mrs. Moodie's books, though it was not her conscious voice but the other voice running like a counterpoint through her work that made the most impression on me."

Well, that "other voice" is also the one that makes the poems impressive. Perhaps it is Atwood's own voice, or perhaps it is Susanna Moodie herself singing Atwood's opera. The duality is there. But I think Margaret Atwood has always had this duality in herself, a quality that she suggests is Canadian, a kind of "paranoid schizophrenia" which enables

*From *Canadian Literature*, no. 47 (Winter 1971):80–84. Reprinted by permission of the author.

her to be a ghostly observer peering over the ghostly shoulder of Susanna Moodie. In spite of hard physical details (fire and plague, dead children, trees, emigrants, etc.), these poems make a strange slightly-off-from-reality impression on the reader: and browsing through *Roughing It in the Bush*, I don't think Moodie's 19th century prose has this ingredient. The poems' impact is in this strangeness: as if Atwood were from Mars and Moodie an Englishwoman of "gentle" birth. And Atwood is not talking to a possible reader; she is an entirely subjective Martian.

The Journals of Susanna Moodie has many of the qualities of fictional biography: the reader knows very well (the Canadian reader, anyhow) that Moodie was a real person, and reading the poems both the Moodie and Atwood personae are inescapable. John Berryman did something similar in *Homage to Mistress Bradstreet*, assuming the persona of a long-dead American woman of pioneer days. A similar authoritative and undeniably once-actual personage takes over in both books: Moodie and Bradstreet, with Atwood and Berryman as shadow manipulators coming to life in the publishers' blurbs. The puppets steal the show (but not the royalties): and this to me, is fiction.

Another advantage of using a once-living protagonist is the cohesive and intensive quality that a single viewpoint—or time or geographic area—gives a book of poems. (Bowering's *Rocky Mountain* is another example of the latter.) But there is a sub-basic quality in the poet's self that cannot be conveyed by speaking in another person's voice. Because, in its finest expression, the poet's voice is for everyman, not just a single person. And I think it's a very debatable point whether a poet can occupy another body and mind and still retain the sub-basic qualities of himself or herself. That is, Atwood as Atwood strikes me as authentic, but Atwood as Moodie is a very fine tour de force. But the latter is entirely legitimate, valuable and, in this case, rather marvellous fiction.

Peggy Atwood said to me about three weeks ago that a reviewer (that's me) should seek to fathom the author's (that's her) intent, implying that marks should be given, according to how close the author came to achieving that intent. This I disagree with in Atwood's absence, almost completely—unless the reviewer, knowing the intent, feels it was achieved and is, in addition, impressive as hell.

Re intent, I prefer Earle Birney's opinion (also verbal, though maybe he's written it somewhere too): that whatever meaning or levels of meaning the reader "extracts" from the work, this meaning is legitimate and valid. Because (my own comment as well as Birney's) there is something in a writer's head which causes him or her to incorporate meanings and possible interpretations he (or she) doesn't even know are there. Writers are generally a bit stupid—and I cite my own case particularly—feeling that too much knowledge and accumulation of literary debris in their heads can be a handicap: this apart from straight intelligence. Of course that's an alibi on my part, as I'm aware.

What I'm getting at: I'm not really interested in what Atwood is trying to do in her opinion: I'm interested in what she succeeds in doing — in my opinion. The two may be identical. I think they probably are in this book, but I'm far too cautious to say what I think she's trying to do, even though she more or less says what that is in the book's Afterword. And I guess that sounds pretty convoluted and involved.

Well, I've held certain opinions about writing poems for a long time, but these opinions have changed recently. For instance: consistency of tone and metre. I've thought previously that inconsistency was the best way to write poems, in fact the only way for myself. Part of the reason for that opinion has been that critics seemed to demand consistency. Well — well, I still hold to the view that consistency of tone and metre would be a bad thing for me, for *me* — but not necessarily for others. Particularly in a book like the Moodie poems where a related and integrated outlook on the author-persona's part appears to make the poems more believable. In fact, I think Atwood's book has caused me to change my mind on this point. And I do think the Moodie poems are that impressive.

But looking at Atwood's books, I believe they all have this consistent and distinctive tone. And that's okay for her: what's sauce for the goose is not for the gander, and the difference in gender is not unintentional. For I believe that my personal outlook on life is markedly inconsistent: I may be temperamentally up one hour and down the next; I may be happy, I may be sad; I may be in love with life and all women, I may not. I want to convey these human inconsistencies in poems, and I try. But of course, I say all this after I look at my own poems and know (think) that they do reflect these attitudes.

In Atwood's poems I see no humour other than satire, very little love for anything (exept possibly the Atwood-Moodie dead children in "Death of a Young Son by Drowning"); I do see subjective navel-watching and analysis, a hard cold look at the human condition. In the past I've said these shortcomings were a bad thing in any writer. But now I cannot transplant my own hangups into Atwood. If she lacks these things (and I think she does), it does not in any way lessen her poems. I would say they were just short of magnificent — except, that's another quality I don't think she has. One can cite a mixed bag of poets — say Yeats, Eliot, Layton and Birney: Yeats has magnificence, satire and no humour: Eliot, satire, magnificence and no humour: Layton the same: only Birney has genuine selfconscious humour as well. But I should add joy to this catalogue, for Layton does have that.

In John Glassco's *Memoirs of Montparnasse*, here's what Ford Madox Ford said about joy: "All modern effusions of joy are definitely unbalanced. Very well. Now, if poetry expresses the reality of existence — as I believe, along with Willie (jesus!) Yeats, it does, and as I hope you will too, my young friend — it follows that the experience of joy is in the nature of a fever, of hysteria, and not a well-founded natural human experience or condition. Therefore we can say: joy itself is hysteria, a drunkenness, an unnatural state."

It doesn't follow at all: joy isn't an unnatural state, even in the human-animal. And add that drunkenness (of the spirit, not artificially induced) is natural. Joy is part of the *condition humaine*, which isn't all terror and foreboding, can't be that or we'd all collapse damn quick under the psychic weight. Three of the people mentioned above whom I know (Layton, Birney and Atwood) all have joy personally, but Atwood has not communicated the feeling in poems and probably has not wanted to. Again, I must not read my own preoccupations re how to write poems into Atwood. For I think she is a marvellous poet, perhaps the only one right now in Canada whose poems I look forward to reading with tremendous anticipation each time a book of hers appears. And she is what she is, without what I say to be shortcomings or weaknesses being shortcomings or weaknesses. Therefore, I say I have been wrong in my opinions that certain human life-qualities are necessary poem-qualities. (They were pretty naive opinions anyway.) At least, not for her, as not for Yeats and Eliot.

Having said what Atwood does not have, it devolves on me to say what she does. And, sticking to the Moodie book, I *believe* in Atwood-Moodie. I think the Moodie conveyed by Atwood is scared to death of life, but is nevertheless a real person. Moodie is also afraid of the rough and tough pioneer forest of early Canada, but what nice sweet well-bred and bedded English gentlewoman wouldn't be?

In "The Wereman":

> My husband walks in the frosted field
> an X, a concept
> defined against a blank;
> he swerves, enters the forest
> and is blotted out.

Why, that Moodie bitch! I say. There isn't a scintilla, not a jot or milligram of affection for anyone but herself (Moodie) in the poem (in *Roughing It in the Bush* she calls her husband "Moodie"!) This I say, knowing Atwood meant to convey something quite different. I think she meant to say that humans are undefined as such, that they waver into hate and love like ghosts and things of mist in other people's minds. She meant (perhaps) to convey human inconsistency, as I have said her writing did not. Whereas I, becoming a vicarious female while reading the poem, growl soprano-bass that Moodie should have rushed after her husband into the dark forest, at least she should have if she gave a single damn. But she didn't, and that's one reason why Moodie is not quite human, was only worried about herself in the poem, was absolutely solipsistic. (Which is one of Atwood's strengths.)

On the other hand, I guess most Victorian women felt themselves to be only sexual objects (or so books tell me, and also certain Victorian female survivals), individuals only privately and partly, in their fears and hates but not their loves.

However, the Atwood-Moodie persona crosses me up in "Death of a Young Son," about whom she/they say: "I planted him in this country/like a flag." The line has multiple meanings, none of which I intend to mention. Unless to say that sons were loved but husbands were not, which interpretation should come from the whole book, not this one poem.

Here's an example of Atwood's verbal virtuosity: "After we had crossed the long illness/that was the ocean. . . ." No ordinary pioneer woman would say that, and neither would Victorian-literary Moodie: but Atwood-Moodie might and did. Here I believe both. And briefly I see hundreds of mile[s] of ocean vomit. I see sickness of the spirit and endurance. I believe. (Hallelujah!)

For the first few years in Canada the historical Susanna Moodie hated the new country (Canada), hated it like hell and the devil: but in later years came up with phony-sounding eulogies for the country that don't ring true. Along those lines, Atwood makes Moodie come to love the country as well. But I don't think Moodie ever really did. But Atwood does, and that's probably the most love lifting out of these pages of print. For the Moodie-Atwood persona becomes some kind of primitive corn-mother-spirit that sits in a modern bus along St. Clair Ave. in Toronto, embodying the ghostly citified barbarism of this country. I don't believe that double-love, only Atwood's.

Well, I could go on and on with these poems, tearing them apart, figuring them out, the radar echoes between them and me bouncing back and forth, back and forth, hypnotically boring. But if I'm talking to anyone here, I hope they carry this review farther than I am energetic enough to take it.

I disagree with most of Atwood's viewpoints wholeheartedly, and the circumstances will never arrive when I can say the rest of this review to her personally (besides, she's a woman, even though very intelligent), because she wouldn't listen to such confused and partly intuitive arguments. I've said here that she lacks many things in her poems which I think desirable (and I retract nothing), such as magnificence which she has not got in single poems. Taking the whole book though, she mysteriously does have that quality. Also clarity of intellect (if the reader will read hard, and give the poems at least the attention of a personal monetary transaction). The country itself is the Atwood-Moodie children (hail, corn-mother!) who never had a chance to grow to adulthood and be what the actual country too may never become.

What I'm saying is that this book will stand in any company, despite what I call shortcomings that are not shortcomings in Atwood. I can think of no comparisons for the book. Which seems to me a high compliment. Atwood may even deserve it.

In Search of a Native
Tongue [*Surfacing*]

Christina Newman*

Ever since Margaret Atwood published her first collection of poetry, *The Circle Game*, in 1966 (and won the Governor General's medal for it) there has been a certain concord in the nervous circles of the literati in this country that she is special, a contender for the championship, maybe even deserving of those accolades that have always been the highest honor we can bestow on an artist — "worthy of international recognition" or "remarkable by any standards," meaning the standards of London and New York.

This fall she's publishing a book called *Surfacing*, her second novel, which should command her an audience beyond the universities and the publishing houses and the poetry reading audiences in high school auditoriums because it is quite simply superb, the product of a talent that's maturing inexorably out of its own internal authority.

The book is a journey, backward in time, northward in space, taken by the narrator, a woman in her late twenties who tries to go home again not because she thinks she can but because she feels she must. She's been summoned to the island in the Quebec bush country where she grew up by a letter from a French-Canadian neighbor telling her that her father, a reclusive biologist, has disappeared, leaving the door of his cabin open and his boats tied up at the dock. She's brought with her three city friends, a couple who own the old shark-finned car that takes them there and her lover, a man who makes pottery that doesn't sell and has a head like the buffalo's on the U.S. nickel, hairy, small-eyed and impenetrable. The men are making a film (they've never made one before but they're "the new Renaissance Men, you teach yourself what you need to know"). The other woman, who's called Dorothy [sic] and who wears white bell-bottoms because she figures jeans make her look fat, is along for the ride, singing *Lilli Marlene* in a voice she hopes is throaty, talking incessantly out of a mind she thinks is hip or at least responsive to "flow."

They spend a week caught in the isolation of the bush while the narrator searches for her father in the undergrowth and for herself in the numbness of her mind. ("The trouble other people have being German I have being human.")

The ways in which the novel is remarkable are many. It moves from the plain perceptions of the opening chapters onto the knife edge of madness and fantasy that are characteristic of Atwood's vision. Only Margaret Drabble and Doris Lessing are as good at conveying what goes on in the mind of a woman trying to deal with the little brutalities inflicted on her body and spirit by the harsh politics of sex.

*From *Maclean's*, September 1972, 88. Reprinted by permission of the journal.

But what makes the book so important is the way in which Atwood is able to deal with the country that made her. When she writes about passing the highway signs at the edge of the trees (Thé Salada, Blue Moon Cottages ½ Mile, Buvez Coca Cola, Jesus Saves) or describes the Americans flying in by seaplane to fish out a lake, slapping at mosquitoes ("next year we'll go to Florida"), bugging the hired guides with their Elvis Presley haircuts, duck-ass at the back, to produce more and bigger pike, she's dealing with what we know about ourselves straight on. She writes with the ease of total acceptance from right inside the culture, authenticating our experience, holding up a mirror so that the image we get back is not distorted by satire or made unreal by proselytizing, not disguised as "universal" for the export market, not aimed at the Leacock medal but real — as real, say, as the Chicago of Nelson Algren. It's this space, this place, an answer to the famous Northrop Frye question, Where Is Here? Here is where we've been and when we go again it'll be different, clearer because Atwood's written about it.

Now I can't think of another country where this would be described as an unusual feat because what she's doing, of course, is fulfilling the novelist's function. But to know how remarkable it is in this country that's been colonized so long in its own mind, where the poets have been able consistently to get at our reality but the novelists have not, you have only to take a look at the work of the current champion novelist, Mordecai Richler.

Richler also has a new book out this fall, called *Shovelling Trouble*. It's not a novel but a collection of his magazine pieces from the *Nation*, *Saturday Night* and *Commentary*. Still, Richler is Richler, whether he's writing novels as a social critic or social criticism as a novelist, he's the same old Mordecai, witty, acerbic, brilliant, sick with angst but "cunning," as he says, "someone with a use for everything, even intimacies" — and even (or especially) his own pained embarrassment at having been born Canadian. In these pieces he talks about how he writes, why he writes, which writers he envies, where he writes, how he learned to write, and there is something chokingly familiar about all of it, like the boiled buttered cabbage your father used to make you swallow, not just because so much of it is twice-cooked material (Richler invented recycling) but because the attitudes it expresses have grown cold and stale.

What's real to Richler is his own pain. What's important to him is that he's probed this pain in other places, London, Paris, Surrey, far from where it was inflicted. What's unreal is his country and his countrymen.

In Richler-land, Canadians are objects, no more motivated or animated than mooseheads — louts, bores, fools, people suffering from the unforgivable failure of not having been born American. (New York, New York. The Big Time.) Every attitude he expresses springs out of his impossible yearning to be something or somebody else so that in the end he becomes a parody of a classic type — the provincial who's been to Rome, who can't resist coming back again to boast of the wonders he has seen, to dazzle with his gossip, his standards and his style, thereby denying his engagement in the absurdities he left behind. ("Gently I let on that Terry Southern and I were old friends / E. M. Forster asked me the questions he always asked young Americans / Cocteau was across the room / *Time* applauded me / *Newsweek* bowed / even though I was something of a country cousin" and on and on.)

What's disturbing about all this is that Richler once seemed to me and my friends, people now in their advancing thirties, to be a kind of spokesman for us; what's heartening is that he now seems so remote and so bound into the ideas he took with him to Europe 20 years ago.

Richler is 41. Atwood is 32. But so much happened here between the time he left in the Fifties and she began writing in the Sixties, there could be half a century between them. They've both become archetypes. He represents the old consciousness, she represents the new. He's still trying to exorcise his past, our past, she's searching through it to find our roots.

[Review of *Surfacing*]   Margaret Laurence*

I read a great many novels, a fair number of which I find interesting. A few I find extremely interesting and worthwhile. And occasionally, very very rarely, I come across a novel which will continue to inhabit my head, a novel so striking that I become evangelical about it. Margaret Atwood's second novel is such a book. It is excellent in so many ways that one cannot begin to do justice to it in a review. It has to be read and experienced.

The novel's central character, a woman whose name we never learn, goes back to the cabin in the northern Quebec forests where she spent most of her childhood. Since the death of her mother, her father has lived there alone and he has now disappeared. She does not believe he is dead, and she goes — with a kind of hopeless determination — to look for him. She is accompanied by a couple, David and Anna, and by her own current lover, Joe. She feels painfully separated in spirit from all these people, and her return to the cabin and the bush, the great good place of her earlier life, serves only to confirm and underline this sense of alienation, of living among strangers.

David and Joe are making a trendy spontaneous film, in the course of which they begin to play psychologically sadistic games with Anna. The woman, the central character, watches, realizing that David and Anna, far from being the happy couple she had imagined, are locked together in mutual destruction. Anna resents, as well she might, the constant put-downs she suffers from David, but either out of fear of losing him or

*From *Quarry* 22, no. 4 (Spring 1973):62–64. Reprinted by permission of the journal.

because she has been irrevocably brain-washed, she goes along with his image of her, applying a load of makeup each day with painstaking care. The woman (it works well within the novel to have her un-named but it makes it damned difficult for reviewers; novelists, however, can scarcely be expected to take this into consideration) finds herself more and more repelled by Anna's false cosmetic face and by the unseen but nonetheless real false faces (real and false? yes) of all of them, herself included, the masks of cameraderie, of enlightened thinking, of politeness, perhaps even of love. What is real and where can she find some core of reality within herself? She goes over her past — her happy childhood, her unhappy marriage and divorce. Her parents were both scientists, both rationalists, yet now she is living in a world increasingly irrational, a world in which Reason does not seem to supply the answers. Have her parents been wrong, and is there some reality, some truth, to be found only in a journey into un-reason, or as it might be termed, madness?

This is what does occur. She finds herself growing closer and closer to the answer of what happened to her father. The clues are bizarre. Had her father really found some ancient Indian cave paintings, as the drawings in his study finally lead her to believe? She sets out, accompanied by the other three, guided by her own interpretation of her father's maps, but all that is discovered is a dead bird — a great blue heron, senselessly killed by senseless American hunters. (These "American" hunters, incidentally and vitally, turn out to be Canadians. Margaret Atwood [has] used the word "American" in a symbolic way which is probably unfair to your actual Americans, or at least to some of them, but which within the novel is enormously effective — the new barbarians, of whom we are a part to the precise extent that we slaughter trees, birds, and rivers, to name only a few.) Later, the woman goes alone and dives into the water, certain the ancient and runic drawings exist there. She returns to the cabin, ostensibly and outwardly the same person, not telling the others what she has found, but when the boat arrives to take them all back to (you should pardon the expression) civilization, she runs away and hides. They leave without her.

She has in fact (and in myth) discovered what happened to her father, but not why. Now begins her inner journey, which can be seen as a breakdown, a breakup or a break-through. I myself opt for the last expression. She is now convinced that she is pregnant from her last coupling with Joe. She becomes convinced, also, that she has offended the forest and the ancient gods and that the only way to live in the world, as it is becoming, is to return to the sources of life, to turn away from the cabin and the tinned food, to eat only what grows in the forest. She will become an animal-woman, and her child, who will be a god-child, will be born with fur as its natural protection.

The descent into madness (as one might call it, although I am not among them) also leads her into a true confrontation with her own past. We begin to realize that she has been fictionalizing it all along, to herself and possibly to others as well. She had not in fact been married. She had become pregnant by a man she cared about, who cared about her just enough to pay for the abortion which to her was a mind-searing experience.

The dust-jacket of *Surfacing* contains a curious sentence, saying that the novel ends on "an unexpected note of hope." Personally, I did not think that the note of hope (and it is a very qualified hope) was unexpected at all. No one, I would have thought, who knows the meaning of rites de passage or who has read even fragments of *The Golden Bough, Beowulf* or, somewhat more recently, Amos Tutuola's *The Palmwine Drinkard*, to name only a few out of zillions, could think so. For it is the ancient Quest which is the journey here, the descent into the dark regions, where some special knowledge is gained, some revelation, before the return to the world of known creatures. The woman does return, and will go back to the world of humans, but she has been given a knowledge of her own power, a power which had frightened her and which she had therefore denied, and a knowledge of her previous willingness to be a victim, a willingness which had of course also victimized others. She has also, I think, been given another knowledge — the ancient gods of forest and lake are by no means dead; they are there, and attention must be paid.

The woman's journey will, of course, be seen by the others as a breakdown in response to the discovery of what happened to her father. The "American" hunters, ironically enough, have in their bulldozer fashion also discovered what happened, and must publicize it, bring everything out, literally, in a detestable fashion. But even this violation to the spirit of the dead cannot in the end damage the woman's newfound self, for the truth is that she has gone into the deepest places, the deepest lakes of the mind, and has surfaced.

The skilful language of this novel reminds one of the beautifully sparse language and many-layered quality of Margaret Atwood's poetry. It is an incredibly short novel (192 pages) to convey so much. The images of animals, birds, fish, trees, water, act on several levels simultaneously — yes, as symbols, but as symbols rooted in living breathing things.

The themes are many, and the nature of reality is one of the most interesting. Some of the themes concern our most burning contemporary issues — the role of women, the facts of urban life, and most of all, the wounding and perhaps killing of our only home, Earth. Margaret Atwood is one of the very few novelists writing today who can deal with these issues without ever writing propaganda. Perhaps she has been able to do this partly because she has interwoven all these themes with the theme which is central to our mythology, our religions, our history and (whether we know it or not) our hearts — humankind's quest for the archetypal parents, for our gods, for our own meanings in the face of our knowledge of the inevitability of death.

Soul Survivor [*Surfacing* and *Power Politics*]

Joan Larkin*

Surfacing, a novel which is simply one of the best around, and *Power Politics*, a strong and startling book of poems—both published in the United States this spring—are the work of a young Canadian writer named Margaret Atwood. In her early thirties, Atwood has already published a skillful first novel, *The Edible Woman*, and four books of verse. She has been compared to such unalike talents as Sylvia Plath, Leonard Cohen, and Doris Lessing; but her voice is entirely her own, that of a woman, a Canadian, and above all a human being, one who attempts to speak even for earth and water, plants and animals—for all that is still alive on the planet.

The title of Atwood's new novel, *Surfacing*, suggests its theme: a swimmer surfaces so that air, not water, will fill her lungs. Surfacing, then, is a metaphor for rebirth, awakening, return. But one cannot come up without first diving down; and most of the novel is concerned with the downward movement. An unnamed woman, the narrator and central character, dives into human history, into her personal past, and into her own psyche. From concealed depths of the self, from a level of feeling beyond the reach of words or reasons—from a place the world calls madness—the woman emerges into the world with a new vision of herself and of her powers as a human being.

The narrator is looking for her father who has silently disappeared from an island cabin in the desolate bush of Northern Quebec where he lived alone. Is he dead? mad? There is a mystery to be solved, and the novel builds in excitement like a detective thriller, while the meanings of the search widen to include more of the truth—psychological, political, religious—than such a comparison usually implies. We follow the narrator in her search, never knowing more than she does, watching with her as events unfold, diving with her into her memories and feelings as she comes upon the things of her past, and finally identifying with her completely—living the pages in which she evokes her "madness"—so that, like her, we see the world with new eyes at the end of the novel.

It would be a great mistake to read the novel as a standard story of the alienated young, though at first it seems to be assembling the typical cast of restless characters: David, amateur filmmaker putting together a movie called "Random Samples," whose speech is made up of automatic sexual humor and routine anti-Americanisms ("David says 'Bloody fascist pig yanks' as though he's commenting on the weather"); David's wife, Anna, a natural victim, who in one of the cruelest scenes of the novel submits to becoming one of the "random samples," a pornographic object of the camera's dehumanizing lens; Joe, the narrator's lover, unconscious and ordinary, a failed potter. But the narrator is something else again. She has survived an affair with a married teacher, an abortion, a loveless marriage, and the birth of a baby (never really hers, because it had been forced on her by a husband wishing to gratify his ego); but the price of survival has been a feeling of amputation. She lives as though anesthetized. While Joe has nightmares filled with enemies, she has no dreams, no feelings: "When he suggested we should live together, I didn't hesitate. It wasn't even a real decision, it was more like buying a goldfish or a potted cactus plant, not because you want one in advance but because you happen to be in the store and you see them lined up on the counter." She compares him to David: they both have "atrophy of the heart."

But it would be truer to call her "brokenhearted," a human soul in need of mending: ". . . I'd allowed myself to be cut in two. Woman sawn apart with a wooden crate, wearing a bathing suit, smiling, a trick done with mirrors. I read it in a comic book; only with me there had been an accident and I came apart. The other half, the one locked away, was the only one that could live; I was the wrong half, detached, terminal. I was nothing but a head, or no, something minor like a severed thumb; numb. At school they used to play a joke, they would bring little boxes with cotton wool in them and a hole cut in the bottom; they would poke their finger through the hole and pretend it was a dead finger."

The ten days this group spends together on the island are like litmus, revealing essences of character: Anna surfaces as a helpless doll, and David, bumbling but cruel, as an inept but real usurper and abuser of life; Joe remains the "average" with "its needless cruelties and lies" — even here, he pressures the narrator to label their relationship "love." But for the narrator, the wilderness is the way back to self, the reintegration of feeling and behavior, the undoing of adjustment to a destructive civilization. Her understanding of plants, animals, and water comes back to her, separating her from the others. The techniques of conservation and survival she learned as a child now become ritual acts of respect, reconnecting her with the nonhuman forms of life from which we civilized beings have severed ourselves.

The island holds a series of epiphanies, unforgettable images that momentarily arrest and illuminate the story. Some of these images come from the inner stream, the narrator's memory: a semi-drowned child, a crude drawing of female genitals, the city's "zero mouthed toilets in their clean tiled cubicles," an aborted fetus. Others occur in the present action: a frog used as bait, a caught fish, a killed heron, a terrifying underwater shape of something dead (her father's corpse?), and things left behind by her parents, which she takes for spiritual guides: maps of the sites of paintings by a vanished Indian culture, places where powerful or protective spirits lived (still live, perhaps, for one able to admit them); and her own childhood drawing of herself as an unborn baby gazing out of the womb at a God with horns and a tail, a God that has attributes of the Devil. Death and evil, the narrator comes to realize, are not to be written off as exclusive properties of the Hitler she remembers from childhood or the Americans of the present—"them." All humans are involved; none of us is exempt.

She elects, then, to become unhuman (not "inhuman," as, ironically, the others label her), to reject the language, food; and furniture of civilized human beings, to reconnect herself with nature. Alone on the island, she experiences an episode some would call psychotic. She accepts direction from the gods, smashes and burns the contents of the cabin, strips herself naked and waits for her body to grow fur, gnaws the earth for wild food, and sleeps in a lair in the earth. After relentlessly eliminating all that represents her history as a human being, she purifies herself in the "multilingual water."

It is in these final chapters that the novel, already a masterpiece of unified imagery and spare, crystal-clear language, becomes something of a miracle. The pace quickens, the sentence rhythms suggest breathlessness, the language reflects the narrator's identification with animals ("dung," "droppings," "lair," "blood egg"). Somehow the prose calls forth from us an extraordinary degree of empathy with the narrator, so that instead of seeing her experience objectively, we participate in her "madness" as a voyage of discovery, much like the trip into inner space and time that R. D. Laing described in *The Politics of Experience* as a natural healing process: "This journey is experienced as going further 'in,' as going back through one's personal life, in and back and through and beyond into the experience of all mankind, of the primal man, of Adam and perhaps even further into the beings of animals, vegetables, and minerals." And like some of the schizophrenic "explorers" described by Laing, Atwood's narrator completes her voyage of discovery by her return to the normal world, with insights previously unavailable to her: "This above all, to refuse to be a victim. Unless I can do that I can do nothing. I have to recant, give up the old belief that I am powerless and because of it nothing I can do will ever hurt anyone. A lie which was always more disastrous than the truth would have been. The word games, the winning and losing games are finished; at the moment there are no others but they will have to be invented, withdrawing is no longer possible and the alternative is death."

Like *Surfacing, Power Politics*—a small group of extraordinary lyrics about the disintegration of what is usually termed a "love affair"— explores the theme of victimization:

> you fit into me
> like a hook into an eye
>
> a fish hook
> an open eye

The voice in these poems is unique, clear, perilously close to experience. It is unpretentious, deceptively simple, speaking in short well-crafted lines: "you aren't sick & unhappy / only alive and stuck with it." (Atwood once with characteristic humor attributed her rhythms to the cold air that makes Canadians unable to open their mouths very wide.)

The title, *Power Politics*, at first seems a curious one for a book of poems about an intimate human relationship. Atwood, in a note to her American publisher, explains, "The title was a phrase from a letter written by a friend. I saw the same phrase the next day in a newspaper, and for me that's where the poems exist: in that space where the personal and the public overlap." Thus she can describe herself and her lover as hostile nations, who "touch as though attacking," whose kindnesses to each other are maneuvers in a struggle for power. Their love, like the planet with its "fading animals" and "the sea clogging, the air / nearing extinction," may yet live, if they can give up their war games:

> Put down the target of me
> you guard inside your binoculars,
> in turn I will surrender
>
> this aerial photograph
> (your vulnerable
> sections marked in red)
> I have found so useful

Atwood reveals that human language is political, debased by our misuses of it: "We are hard on each other / and call it honesty," and "If I love you / is that a fact or a weapon?" Is it only language that is corrupt? How is erotic experience to be taken?

> Does the body lie
> moving like this, are these
> touches, hairs, wet
> soft marble my tongue runs over
> lies you are telling me?

Beginning again becomes more difficult:

> regrowing the body, learning
> speech again takes
> days and longer
> each time/too much of
> this is fatal

Our language invents the other person ("How can I stop you / Why did I create you"), who then exists for us only insofar as we can put her or him to our own use: "Please die I said / so I can write about it." Margaret Atwood's own use of language attempts to resist the corruption of human speech that is one of her themes. The diction is modest, the sentences unadorned, stripped of adjectives; language is reduced to what seems to be its essence. The power of Margaret Atwood's voice comes from her understatement; after the shock at the end of each poem, one rereads— each time finding new ironies in the quiet lines.

In a statement to the American publisher of *Power Politics* (it was first published in Canada in 1971), Atwood denies that her themes come out of Women's Liberation. This was a common assumption about her first novel, *The Edible Woman*, written in 1965 but not published until 1969 (1970 in the United States): "Incredible as it may seem, the publisher misplaced the manuscript for two years; but because of this delay it was assumed by some that the novel was a product of what is commonly termed the Women's Movement. It wasn't, and neither is *Power Politics*. I see both books as amplifications of themes that have been present in my work since I first started writing and publishing. To say this is not to disparage anyone's politics. It is merely to indicate that parallel lines do not usually start from the same point, and that being adopted is not, finally, the same as being born.

"If the Women's Movement had little to do with the composition of *Power Politics*, however, it had a lot to do with its reception. In general, response divided rather neatly along sex lines, women greeting the book with recognition, men with fear; ten years ago women would probably have ignored and men dismissed it. Women, both critics and ordinary readers, spoke of the book as though it was about them, about the way it was; for them it was realistic. Men tended to use adjectives like 'cruel' and 'jagged' and to see it either as a display of perversity on my part or as an attack, a conspiracy, a war or an inhumane vivisection of Love, nasty and unfair as cutting up a puppy."

But *Power Politics* is none of these things. If Margaret Atwood's voice at times seems cold, the coldness serves a passionate purpose: to demystify the word "love" and expose the violence humans to do one another in its name. One's sense of the importance of her theme grows with each rereading of these poems: it is nothing less than the survival of life on this planet, and the threat to it posed by our perverted language and by the destructive games, public and private, which we play in the attempt to control one another.

Margaret Atwood: Beyond Victimhood [*Survival, The Edible Woman, Surfacing,* and five books of poetry]

Marge Piercy*

Margaret Atwood is an extraordinarily good writer who has produced widely different books: so far, two novels, five books of poetry, and a critical guide to Canadian literature. She possesses an unusual combination of wit and satiric edge, a fine critical intelligence, and an ability to go deep into the irrational earth of the psyche. Her books are varied in genre yet through everyone of them run victor/victim and quest for self themes, a set of symbols, and a developing underlay of theory. Some themes she shares with other Canadians, and others are characteristic of our developing women's culture. All are vital and juicy. Technique she has in plenty; what I want to look at is her matter.

In *Survival: a Thematic Guide to Canadian Literature,* Atwood finds throughout a preoccupation with survival; survival in a bare and hostile place; survival in crisis — shipwreck, snowstorm; cultural survival for the French; survival as obsolescence (those who consider Canada a relic); survival in the face of economic take-over by the United States. Considering Canada as a colony, she finds this obsession with the obstacles to physical and/or spiritual survival unsurprising. She outlines what she calls the Basic Victim Positions.

1. Deny that you're a victim. Direct anger against your fellow victims.

2. Acknowledge victimhood but explain it as God's will, history, fate: you may play it out as resigned or rebellious, but of course you will lose. The explanation displaces the cause of oppression to something too vast to change.

3. Acknowledge victimization but don't accept it as inevitable. This dynamic position can slide back to no. 2 or attempt to move on to no. 4. Here you can make real decisions about what can be changed and what can't; anger can be directed against what is oppressing you.

4. Be a creative nonvictim. She describes this as almost impossible in an oppressive society. I would conclude from her work that basically position 4 is achievable in moments from which insight can be brought back to the normal life of struggle and confusion in no. 3.

Survival is an extremely canny and witty book, but I am using it, or misusing it, not for its insight into Canadian literature, but for what it tells us about Atwood's ideas. I find in *Survival* a license to apply it to her

*From *Parti-Colored Blocks for a Quilt*, Poets on Poetry, by Marge Piercy (Ann Arbor: University of Michigan Press, 1982), 281–99; first published in *American Poetry Review* 2 (November–December 1973): 41–44. Copyright © 1982 by The University of Michigan. Used by permission of the University of Michigan Press.

own work, as she argues that discovery of a writer's tradition may be of use, in that it makes available a conscious choice of how to deal with that body of themes. She suggests that exploring a given tradition consciously can lead to writing in new and more interesting ways. I think her work demonstrates that a consciousness of Canadian themes has enriched her ability to manipulate them.

In both *The Edible Woman* and *Surfacing*, the protagonist is a woman who becomes aware she has lost her identity—her self—who comes to experience herself as victim, and finally to reject that state. Although a lacing of terror runs through *The Edible Woman*, especially in the chase scenes in which Marian tries quite literally to escape her lawyer fiancé, it is a comic novel, clever in details and language—the endless playing on the metaphor of eating and food—and successful as slapstick. Although *Surfacing* has a satirical side (the description of the fashionably mindless and exploitative film making of Random Samples), it is in effect and intent a grim, desperate novel. In yet another narrative, *The Journals of Susanna Moodie*, Atwood uses a series of poems to embody a historic nineteenth-century Englishwoman who moved to Canada and did keep journals of her experiences as an immigrant. Atwood follows her through a sense of loss and alienation into an even more bizarre transformation than we'll find in the novels, into a kind of local ghost or chthonic presence.

In *The Edible Woman* Marian, who works for a market research firm at a job she finds unreal among women she cannot relate to (the office virgins decorating themselves to snare, passively, the man who will become their lives), agrees against all her stronger impulses to marry her boyfriend. Although a Canadian lawyer, Peter is a type Atwood identifies elsewhere as an American, whether or not he is born and bred in Ontario: slick, ambitious, empty, laden with expensive gadgets that give him a sense of power (fancy camera, fancy guns, the accoutrements of the business-man playing sportsman), conscious of his image and locked into his head, alienated from his body, his sexuality, his emotions, whatever they may be, most happy when he is destroying something or consuming something.

Marian tries to tell herself she is happy and lucky, moving inexorably toward marriage and only thinking beyond in advertising images. Her head does not save her; but her body rebels. She stops being able to eat first meat (animal victim), then fish, then vegetables, and finally anything at all. She slowly identifies more and more with things consumed. Marian's breakout comes at a party at Peter's. Under pressure from him she has had herself "done" until she feels even further alienated from what remains of her sense of self; uncomfortable exotic dress, hair processed, face altered, scent manufactured. The moment when Peter prepares to consume her image with his camera, for the second time she runs from him, this time successfully.

In "Camera" from Atwood's first book, *The Circle Game*, we find what bothers her in the use of photographs as an attempt to control reality and fix it in stasis.

> You want this instant:
> nearly spring, both of us walking,
> wind blowing . . .
>
> you want to have it and so
> you arrange us:
>
> in front of a church, for perspective,
> you make me stop walking
> and compose me on the lawn;
>
> you insist
> that the clouds stop moving
> the wind stop swaying the church
> on its boggy foundations
> the sun hold still in the sky
>
> for your organized instant.
>
> Camera man
> how can I love your glass eye?

The speaker escapes into the distance "at almost the speed of light."

Marian bakes a cake in the form of a woman and ices it carefully and cosmetically. "You look delicious. . . . Very appetizing. And that's what will happen to you; that's what you get for being food." When Peter comes she serves him the cake. "You've been trying to destroy me, haven't you," she said. "You've been trying to assimilate me. But I've made you a substitute, something you'll like much better."

What bothers me in *The Edible Woman* is, first the lack of awareness written into the character of Marian *or* the novel itself, about the programming inside her that makes her cooperate so neatly with Peter in her consumption. Second, the relationship with Duncan, sloppy self-centered graduate student, who is presented as the opposite of the perfectly packaged playboy prince, strikes me as no great leap forward. The relationship into which Marian seems headed is surely not conventionally bourgeois but conventional in the subculture and basically about as masochistic. He may not consume her, but use her he certainly will.

In both the novels, the women quit or are about to quit unreal jobs (the protagonist in *Surfacing* illustrates books and has learned to compromise before she starts drawing) but there is not much indication what on earth (what in Toronto) they are going to do next: where the real work that presumably will replace the alienated labor is going to come from.

The awareness of programming I miss in *The Edible Woman* is present in the title poem of *The Circle Game*, where children move in circles on a lawn:

> We can see
> the concentration on
> their faces, their eyes
> fixed on the empty
> moving spaces just in
> front of them.
>
> We might mistake this
> tranced moving for joy . . .
>
> . . . the whole point
> for them
> of going round and round
> is (faster)
>   slower)
> going round and round

The poem shuttles between a man and woman in a room who are not communicating, who play mirror games, control games; and children learning fear from the adults, learning defenses and weapons, learning to keep others at a distance, learning to need to control, define, keep out, destroy. The poem ends: "I want the circle / broken." The circle of protection, lying, custom, fear, gamesplaying, roles that keep people "neither / joined nor separate." Atwood's latest book of poetry, *Power Politics*, explores the area of victor, victim games, pain and loss games, the confined war in intimacy between a woman and a man. The conception of the book and individual poems are brilliant:

> you fit into me
> like a hook into an eye
>
> a fish hook
> an open eye

Between the first and the fifth book of poetry, she has gained enormously in compression, daring, shape of the poem, precision of language. Here is a poem about the game of mutual losers admiring each other's style:

> My beautiful wooden leader
> with your heartful of medals . . .
> you long to be bandaged
> before you have been cut.
>
>   . . . General, you enlist
> my body in your heroic

struggle to become real:
though you promise bronze rescues

you hold me by the left ankle
so that my head brushes the ground,
my eyes are blinded,
my hair fills with white ribbons. . . .

Magnificent on your wooden horse
you point with your fringed hand;
the sun sets, and the people all
ride off in the other direction.

Love, in Atwood, is often an imitation of the real: an aquarium instead of the sea, in one poem. Rather than communicating her people evade each other, are absent in their presence, try to consume, manipulate, control. By saying, "in Atwood" or "her people" I'm not implying I find such behavior unusual. What she describes is dismally familiar; only the precision and the very shaped often witty anguish of the descriptions make them unusual.

. . . pretending to love
the wrong woman some of the
time, listening to your brain
shrink . . .

Still I find both *The Journals of Susanna Moodie* and *Procedures for Underground* finally more successful as total books. Few of the poems have individual titles, and we are clearly to find *Power Politics* not a collection but a book. Why does the shape of the book, especially toward the end, bother me? When she says, "In the room we will find nothing/In the room we will find each other," why do I not believe? Perhaps the language does not change enough, the terms of the struggle deepen mythologically but do not change in any convincing way from the conventional power struggle. Some fear seems to prevent her breaking through in this book as she breaks through with her protagonist in *Surfacing*. To put it another way, she doesn't seem able to imagine the next stage, and a book that remains caught in its first terms while seeming to suggest that it will transcend them, is frustrating, but brilliantly so. It is still a strong and good sequence and a far more satisfying book as a book than 90 percent of the poetry collections I read. Only in reading her work I have come to want more than that. A talent like hers needs to transcend its own categories, to integrate the preconscious and conscious materials, the imagery and ideas. Her wit can lead her into trivia; just as her passion for the omen can lead her to see the portentous in grains of sand and jam jars, as in "Two Visions [sic] of Sweaters" (*Procedures for Underground*).

At one point in *Survival*, she applies her chart of victim positions to

attitudes toward nature. Meaningful connection with the environment is
important in her values. In position no. 1, the writer goes on about
Beneficient Nature the sublime while sinking in a mosquito-ridden bog (in
Surfacing Atwood describes the sound of love in the North as a kiss and a
slap). Canada was too hard for Wordsworthian sentiments to last. Next the
harshness of the land is admitted and nature is seen from dead and
indifferent to downright nasty. Nature becomes the enemy. Often the will
to lose merges with a willing of the role of the victim in a hostile universe.
From there, one can decide to "win the war against nature." Since success
in that war has brought us to ecological disaster, one can then identify
with weak nature, attacked by man.

Atwood posits that in position no. 4 nature exists as itself "not as a
collection of separate and inert objects; rather it exists as a living process
which includes opposites, life and death, 'gentleness' and 'hostility' . . .
man himself is seen as part of the process. . . . He can accept his own
body, including its sexuality. . . ."

Her immigrant heroine Susanna Moodie, experiences the new land at
first as a loss of self. She:

> entered a large darkness.
>
> It was our own
> ignorance we entered.
>   "Further Arrivals"

She knows "fears hairy as bears." She needs to become different in order to
communicate with the land, in order to live with this new place. At first
she holds on to her identity with all her strength and loss is all disaster and
attack. But when she leaves the wilderness she realizes she is losing
something she did not yet have, that she needs:

> There was something they almost taught me
> I came away not having learned.
>   "Departure from the Bush"

They: the alien animals, plants, beings of the real woods.

> I need wolf's eyes to see
> the truth.

In "The Immigrants" Atwood encompasses a depth of the personal and
social, the historical realized as living pain, that is breathtaking and leaves
me wondering why I can't think of an equally powerful American poem
on what should surely be a common topic. Here is a little of it:

> I see them coming
> up from the hold smelling of vomit,
> infested, emaciated, their skins grey
> with travel; as they step on shore

> the old countries recede, become
> perfect, thumbnail castles preserved
> like gallstones in a glass bottle, the
> towns dwindle upon the hillsides
> in a light paperweight-clear.
>
> They carry their carpetbags and trunks
> with clothes, dishes, the family pictures;
> they think they will make an order
> like the old one, sow miniature orchards,
> carve children and flocks out of wood
>
> but always they are too poor, the sky
> is flat, the green fruit shrivels
> in the prairie sun, wood is for burning; . . .

Susanna visits an insane asylum and there she experiences again that glimpse of the other place, the reality she craves:

> The landscape was saying something. . . .
>   . . . the air
> was about to tell me
> all kinds of answers.
>   "Visit to Toronto, with Companions"

Susanna is trying to love the land, but something is wrong. Not what seemed wrong at first, that it wasn't a great good friendly place. Something else is going rotten. She curses

> the invaders of those for whom
> shelter was wood,
> fire was terror and sacred
>
> the inheritors, the raisers
> of glib superstructures . . .
>   "Alternate Thoughts from Underground"
>
> god is not
> the voice in the whirlwind
>
> god is the whirlwind
>
> at the last
> judgement we will all be trees.
>   "Resurrection"

Susanna scorns those who think "[w]e will build / silver paradise with a bulldozer" and returns after her death as a demon of the place: a crazy old lady on a bus. She has finally "changed" and she is at home, prophesying.

In Atwood there is the old dichotomy between the city as a place of artifice (associated with being armored, becoming a machine or a thing), a hollow place as Edmonton is seen:

> a tight surface covering
> panic or only more
> nothing than I've ever seen
>   "84th Street, Edmonton,"
>   *Procedures for Underground*

And the cabin in the woods as a place where reality is approachable, where the self can be reintegrated. Yet she has none of the romanticism about nature that usually goes with such a dichotomy. Her rabbits are very much rabbits, they have real fur and bones and fleas and use their hind legs to give warning. Her blue jays and herons are more alive than those often overly symbolic props in writers — names, exotica, stuffed feathers inhabited by bits of human psyche and projection. She contrasts the two herself in the title poem of *The Animals in That Country*, and in another way in *Surfacing*, where the protagonist and her brother as children pretend there are "good leeches and bad leeches."

Yet finally her animals too are something else in their alien and irrational aliveness, as is the landscape itself. Both are at once themselves and transmitters of energy, the doorways to another level of reality at once alien and inner. The source of integration of the self, the reservoir of insight in Atwood lie deep in a wild and holy layer of experience usually inaccessible in modern life — in how her characters make a living, how they act with each other, how they respond or fail to respond to birth, death, loss, passion, how they permit themselves to live out of touch with what they want and what they feel. The landscape of the psyche in Atwood tends to be a cabin in the Canadian woods, on a lake, on a river — the outpost of contact between straight lines (roads, houses, gardens) and natural curves (trees, deer, running water): the imposed order and the wild organic community.

Every place the fundamental fact of being alive is being eater or being eaten. "[T]he food rolls over on my plate" ("Creatures of the Zodiac"). The authentic way of approaching this revelation involves experiencing the reality of the victim you are consuming. Both her heroines go through a sense of the awfulness of taking life to eat. Some of this is, especially in *Surfacing*, a function of animals as totems. But the vegetable world is also sacred with life:

> . . . potatoes curled
> like pale grubs in the soil
> the radishes thrusting down
> their fleshy snouts, the beets
> pulsing like slow amphibian hearts . . .
> When I bent

> to pick my hands
> came away red and wet . . .
>   "Dream 1: The Bush Garden,"
>   *Journals of Susanna Moodie*

In *Surfacing* the protagonist thinks of the green blood of weeds.

This strand in Atwood is an emerging theme of women's culture, I believe, for women have been forced to be closer to food, to know more of where it comes from and what it looks like raw (I think of a poem I saw in *Off Our Backs* in which a woman sees herself in the plucked chicken ready for the oven, sprawled on its back with a large hole between its legs from which its guts have been torn out), and where the garbage goes afterward. Perhaps societies in which meat comes sanitized in the supermarket wrapped in transparent plastic and advertised by Disney pigs in aprons offering with big grins to be eaten, produces more vegetarians finally than societies in which everybody has seen a pig carried squealing to be slaughtered and the disemboweling of its warm carcass.

In killing too there is a proper natural and an improper and inauthentic attitude in her work. For instance the invaders, in their costumes as hunters, are seen with that terrible naive deadpan stare she can muster (somehow I think of Breughel, then of Bosch): the hunters are dressed up in their red suits for a ritual occasion, though obviously an unsuccessful one.

> They must be waiting
> for the god to appear,
> crossed in the sights of their rifles . . .
>   "The Festival,"
>   *The Animals in That Country*

In *Journals*, Brian the Still-Hunter embodies the other way. When he hunts, he says "I feel / my skin grow fur / my head heavy with antlers." Like an Indian he feels kinship with what he eats. Unlike the tourist sportsmen in *Surfacing*, he enters the animal imaginatively and risks death: he has a "white scar made by the hunting knife / around his neck."

Those "holy and obsolete symbols," gods, are best perceived (as the Egyptians, or more to the point, the Indians grasped them) as creatures emerging through and of the animal, like ourselves. In "Dream: Bluejay or Archeopteryx," a woman kneeling on rock by lakeside sees herself in the water, a bluejay reflected, then:

> in the water
> under my shadow
> there was an outline, man
> surfacing, his body sheathed
> in feathers, his teeth
> glinting like nails, fierce god
> head crested with blue flame

If the god does not surface, you may dive. Drowning occurs again and again in Atwood, appearing to represent going down and not coming up like insanity with which it is sometimes linked. In "Death of a Young Son by Drowning" (*Journals*) drowning is entry to "a landscape stranger than Uranus / we have all been to and some remember." In the title poem of *Procedures for Underground* are the instructions for such a "trip": the other reality there is the country beneath the earth, inherent in nature and in your head at once. It's impossible to read this after Castaneda without making connections, but never in Atwood are there guides, old men, or sorcerers, no wise old women even, only the enigmatic dead, as we will see in *Surfacing*, and the individual vis-à-vis the ground of being as never unsavage nature:

> The country beneath
> the earth has a green sun
> and the rivers flow backwards;
>
> the trees and rocks are the same
> as they are here, but shifted.
> Those who live there are always hungry;
>
> from them you can learn
> wisdom and great power,
> if you can descend and return safely. . . . .
>
> For this gift, as for all gifts, you must
> suffer. . . .

As she makes clear in *Survival*, Atwood is aware of Indians in literature as victims, avatars, symbols useful to whites. She uses Indian materials very sparsely in an overt way, but I feel under the surface of her work a lot of material learned from Indian sources, Indian thinking, Indian religion and mythologies and practice. The procedures for getting in touch with the power in a place that can connect you with the power in yourself in Atwood include openness to knowledge received from other living creatures, fasting, and usually physical exposure, a respect for the earth, a concern with taking only what you need, respect for dream and vision as holy and instructive. In Atwood the trip to be taken is something like this: you go into the forest, the natural and wild ground that is the past inside, the deep collective mostly unconscious past not knowable with the logical controlling brain, the ground of being, food and terror, birth and death: you experience the other which is yourself, your deeper nature, your animal and god half. The experience of transcendence is the gift of the totem animal and the god who is both human and animal and something else, energy perhaps. The procedures by which the protagonist in *Surfacing* finally comes to her vision would be familiar to just about any forest or plains Indians who inhabited the area Canada and the U.S. were carved

out of. I wonder if the protagonist in *Surfacing* has no name because she
has not, till the end of the novel, earned one. In *Surfacing* ancient
pictographs provide the link between the generations, the dead father and
the "dead" daughter.

In *Surfacing* of course the primary metaphors are of a descent
through space, time and water, and then a hazardous return to the
surface.[1] The protagonist returns to a cabin where she spent the heart of
her childhood, to look for her father who has disappeared there. Lacking a
car, with a typically female inability to drive, she has got home by
persuading two friends to bring her and the man she's living with. Though
her mother has died recently in a hospital, she has not been back to the
lake since she left abruptly under circumstances she does not remember
herself till she can force herself to remember — pregnant by a married man
who was her teacher and who manipulated her into an abortion. She
drifted into a plastic marriage, then "running off and leaving my husband
and child, my attractive full-color magazine illustrations, suitable for
framing." The couple, David and Anna, praise marriage but are busy
throughout torturing each other, role playing (he says constantly he
married her for her ass, humiliates her by forcing her to strip for the
camera, then complains she is not smart enough). Joe, the protagonist's
boyfriend, is a loser. "That's how he thinks of himself, too: deposed,
unjustly. Secretly he would like them to set up a kind of park for him, like
a bird sanctuary." Their relationship is a cipher best summed up by the
fact that the first time she went to bed with him, he was impressed by her
cool, that she showed no emotion. But she felt none. "Perhaps it's not only
his body I like, perhaps it's his failure; that also has a kind of purity."

Thus the relationships are empty; the aesthetics of the two men
making a faddish movie are empty; the politics of David are empty. Anti-
American, he posits guerrilla warfare against imperialism but as soon as
the protagonist becomes interested and asks him how, he says "Organize
the beavers." "Now we're on my home ground, foreign territory," the
protagonist thinks as they cross into Montreal. The setting is a colony
inside a colony, marginal economically. The lake will or will not be
flooded on the decision of a presumably American-owned power company: "my country, sold or drowned, a reservoir; the people were sold
along with the land and the animals. . . ." *Surfacing* is so carefully put
together it would be rewarding to follow through any of the strands, what
she does with water, fishing, the notion of pictures, from pictographs to
childhood drawings (personal pictographs), the camera, the illustrations
the heroine does for pseudo-European fairy tales.

The protagonist lost herself at some point, she is not sure when. The
secret must be in her past. "I have to be more careful about my memories,
I have to be sure they're my own and not the memories of other people
telling me what I felt, how I act, what I said." She has become
disassociated from her history, emotions, body. Part 2 begins:

> The trouble is all in the knob at the top of our bodies. I'm not against the body or the head either; only the neck, which creates the illusion that they are separate. . . . If the head extended directly into the shoulders like a worm's or a frog's . . . they wouldn't be able to look down at their bodies and move them around as if they were robots or puppets. . . .

Much later she realizes, "At some point my neck must have closed over . . . shutting me into my head; since then everything had been glancing off me. . . ."

At first she believes her father has gone crazy; she interprets the bizarre drawings she finds as proof. She imagines him "bushed" lurking on the island watching them, potentially dangerous. Then finding a letter from an archeologist thanking him for photographs and drawings of ancient pictographs, she put that together with a map studded with crosses and decided he has left something there for her. She becomes obsessed with decoding the gifts that each of her parents, strong in love and integrity, must have left for her. She has always been good at survival — recognizing edible plants, knowing how to catch a fish and kill it — but survival alone is not enough when all that survives is a remote cold head. She dupes her companions into an expedition to a mark on the map, where she should find a pictograph; the quest is futile. She has forgotten that the land was flooded years before and the ancient shore drowned. On route she finds a dead heron hung up by "Americans" who turn out to be Canadian Met fans. Why did they kill a creature that could not harm them, that they could not eat? "To prove they could do it, they had the power to kill. Otherwise it was valueless; beautiful from a distance but it couldn't be tamed or cooked or trained to talk, the only relation they could have to a thing like that was to destroy it." This is her turning point. She does not find proof of her father's sanity, a legacy of connection she must have; but she identifies herself as dead victim. She begins a social withdrawal, refusing to continue the social and sexual games. She will not tell Joe she loves him and then stops sleeping with him, will not placate him.

She goes alone to another map entry and dives into the cold deep waters of the lake. There she encounters something: not the pictograph but a figure at once her dead father and the dead fetus: the abortion she did not want that cut her off from herself, turned her from lover to object. After the failure of logic, terror accompanies vision. The spot marked by her father is a sacred place where she may learn her truth, how she died. Here presumably is where her father drowned, as she senses he wanted to, the heavy camera pulling him down. His body finally surfaces.

Now she needs to make herself alive again, to heal together her animal and conscious selves. She has sex with Joe for the specific purpose of conceiving a child to replace: 1) the dead fetus, 2) the dead experience of giving birth to an actual child who was the property of her husband.

Just as dying was stolen from her mother by the hospital, so the hospital stole from her the experience of giving birth. She goes through the pain she could not feel before, into the primitive and irrational, into the inhuman in order to be born again as a self. She hallucinates, i.e., enters another more integral reality for her in which she experiences her body as part of the landscape (Atwood's position no. 4) and then sees each of her parents again. Each gives her the gift of presence. She then assents in their deaths and transformations. They cease to be the vehicles for her self exploration and become the people they were in their own now ended lives. She relinquishes them.

From her ritual of integration she returns to daily life. Cannily she looks at Joe, who has come back after the others have left. She decides they must do better, they must learn to communicate. "But he isn't an American . . . he is only half formed, and for that reason I can trust him." She is going back to Toronto, presumably pregnant with the child she wants, and what she has in her teeth she sums up like this:

> This above all, to refuse to be a victim. Unless I can do that I can do nothing. I have to recant, give up the old belief that I am powerless and because of it nothing I can do will ever hurt anyone. . . . The word games, the winning and losing games are finished; at the moment there are no others but they will have to be invented, withdrawing is no longer possible and the alternative is death.

One trouble I have here and I think Atwood still has, is how to translate this particular rhetoric into any kind of action. What will the protagonist do? If position no. 4 involves being no more a victim or victor, how does one get there in an oppressive society except as a stance in one's head? To remain in the inner landscape is to drown, not to surface — to go mad or die. Can a victim cease being one except through some victory? Easily she renounces the victor games; she has never been anything but a victim. Atwood says yes, but I wonder even in her own terms. Women dislike the idea of winning, of gaining power, even of trying to grasp power as a stage to freedom. Yet her heroine cannot stay in the woods. She can choose a man who opts to be a loser rather than a winner at her expense, but how does *she* stop being a loser after deciding to? Atwood distrusts the glib merely fashionable politics of David, but provides no alternatives. The totems stay in the water, the woods, the base of the spine; the modern woman will go back to the city. No one except her heroines is even faintly likeable in these novels. Susanna Moodie may in death become Canada, but a crazy old lady on a bus has little to offer even if she had a hand grenade in her purse, and Atwood hasn't even given her that.

To cease to be a victim, each of her protagonists fights an entirely solitary battle. Their only allies are the dead, the forces in nature and the psyche, their own life energies. Yet they must live among others. Somehow the next step is missing. I don't believe one woman can single-handedly leave off being a victim: power exists and some have it. Atwood seems to me still to rest in an untenable coyness about what it will mean in the daily world to attempt to take charge of one's life—as a Canadian, as a working person (none of her protagonists have money), and as a woman.

Atwood is a large and remarkable writer. Her concerns are nowhere petty. Her novels and poems move and engage me deeply, can matter to people who read them. As she has come to identify herself consciously, cannily, looking all ways in that tradition she has defined as literature of a victimized colony, I hope that she will also come to help consciously define another growing body to which her work in many of its themes belongs: a women's culture. With her concern with living by eating, with that quest for the self that Barbara Demming has found at the heart of major works by women from the past 150 years (*Liberation*, Summer 1973),[2] with her passion for becoming conscious of one's victimization and ceasing to acquiesce, with her insistence on nature as a living whole of which we are all interdependent parts, with her respect for the irrational center of the psyche and the healing experiences beyond logical control, her insistence on joining the divided head and body, her awareness of roleplaying and how women suffocate in the narrow crevices of sexual identity, she is part of that growing women's culture already, a great quilt for which we are each stitching our own particolored blocks out of old petticoats, skirts, coats, bedsheets, blood, and berry juice.

Notes

1. Compare the metaphor in Adrienne Rich's "Diving into the Wreck."
2. "Two Perspectives on Women's Struggle."

Survival Kit   Phyllis Grosskurth*

Canadians are not as optimistic, as volatile, as imaginative, as experimental, as assertive, as egotistic or as energetic as the Americans. Those who are have often become Americans.

So wrote A. R. M. Lower, the dean of Canadian historians, in a 1958 book called *Canadians in the Making*. Well, if we aren't any of these interesting things, who is it who can tell us who we are? Not even, apparently, Northrop Frye, who believes that the question is further compounded by a more paradoxical problem: Where is *here*?

For Canadians, identity and independence have tended to be inter-

*From the *New Statesman*, 24 August 1973, 254–55. Reprinted by permission of the editor.

changeable—and equally elusive. People in other countries—at least any who have given us a passing thought—regarded us once as an appendage of Britain, and later as a satellite of the United States. Quite right they were, too. In *O Canada*, Edmund Wilson wrote: "I always thought of Canada as an inconceivably limitless extension of the wilderness—the North Woods—of upstate New York." A few years ago, when forced to spend some months here while engaged in his farcical battle with the US Department of Internal Revenue over his refusal to pay income tax, Wilson acted like a conquistador who had discovered an unknown country. No one likes to be ignored, but it is hardly flattering to be treated as an archaeological curiosity—although, admittedly, not as exotic an artifact as the Dead Sea Scrolls. Canadians, consistent in their humility, reasoned that if this is how really important people view us, perhaps we might define ourselves by certain negative characteristics. We kept telling ourselves that we were less materialistic, less loud-mouthed, less domineering than the Americans.

Yet even the humble can feel resentment, and while there have been abortive attempts at self-assertion in the past, only in the last decade has the whole country given voice to a spirit of passionate nationalism. The reasons are varied and complex. The explosive separatist sentiment in Quebec has undoubtedly been a major catalyst. Added to this, a number of hard-nosed young economists have launched a series of disclosures on the stranglehold of American companies on our economy. Anti-Americanism has been fed by Vietnam and Watergate. In our universities—badly hit by falling enrolments—there has been mounting resentment against the number of tenured American academics when our own PhDs can't get jobs. On the literary scene, writers have been agitating about the fact that "our" publishing houses are simply branch plants of absentee owners—distributing agents, in fact—whose lists have included a perfunctory batch of Canadian titles. The situation has become a heated political issue.

About five years ago there sprang up a crop of tiny independent publishing houses motivated by the rash hope of encouraging Canadian writing. The best known of these are the House of Anansi and New Press, both founded by Dave Godfrey, whose novel, *The New Ancestors*, won the Governor-General's Award in 1971. Jack McClelland, president of McClelland & Stewart (one of our few large indigenous publishing firms) was frankly sceptical of their chances of survival. "Anyone can start a publishing firm," he remarked, "but let them try to keep it going." Most of them would certainly have perished without government intervention. The Independent Publishers' Association was founded as a pressure group, and through their efforts the federal and provincial arts councils came to the rescue with subsidies, which in turn enabled them to establish credit with the banks. Government assistance is continuing with the opening this October of Canadian book centres in New York, London, and Paris. As

Shirley Gibson of Anansi puts it, "We are no longer an underground cottage industry." Budgets are still so tight that the fledgling firms cannot afford to advertise, but they do receive a certain amount of free publicity since our two genuinely national magazines have established a policy of reviewing only Canadian books.

The public mood, then, was receptive last autumn for a small critical book entitled *Survival* (Anansi). Its author, Margaret Atwood, was already something of a cult figure with her five books of poetry and an intriguing novel, *The Edible Woman*. By now there are few Canadians who are unfamiliar with photographs of this enigmatically beautiful young woman.

Survival purports to be a descriptive rather than an evaluative study of persistent themes running through Canadian literature. Her approach, she informs her readers, will be to treat the books discussed "as though they were written by Canada." Based on the premise that the literature of each country is pervaded by an informing symbol (in the US it is the frontier, in Britain the island), Atwood claims that victimisation has been the striking characteristic of our own literature through its relatively brief history. (While the political implications are not discussed at length, she leaves no doubt in her readers' minds that the victim/victimiser syndrome exists because Canada has always been at the mercy of an exploiting power.) Examining by turn the literary treatment of nature, animals, native peoples, explorers and settlers, families, immigrants, artists, and women, she sees them collectively as born losers; not Leonard Cohen's "Beautiful Losers" but creatures whose vitality is consumed in futile suffering which can lead neither to glory nor redemption. This picture of unrelieved gloom is enlivened only by Miss Atwood's elegant style and wry humour.

Few books published in this country have aroused so much interest. A first printing was rapidly sold out, and a further printing will be ready shortly. Curiosity was further stimulated by the simultaneous publication of her second novel, *Surfacing*, a mythopoeic study of a girl in search of her ancestral roots. (It is curious that in England *The Edible Woman* was well received as an ironical study of manners, whereas the brief notices of *Surfacing*, published by André Deutsch, indicated an uneasy incomprehension of its theme.)

Miss Atwood has candidly admitted that her victimisation thesis is not particularly original. Her chapter on nature as a hostile force, for example, is strongly indebted to Northrop Frye, one of her former teachers. The uniqueness of her book lies in the fact that it is the first time anyone has synthesised the disparate patterns of Canadian literature; and it was written on the assumption that Canadian literature was worth discussing. In an interview, Miss Atwood has said, "For a long time Canada was regarded as the sticks, not only by people outside the country, but by people in it." The view may not be attractive, she implies, but at least a good hard look at how and why we see ourselves as we do might be an aid to self-understanding and self-respect.

Students have been Miss Atwood's most avid fans. Here again she reinforced rather than created a movement. Can. Lit. courses have become increasingly popular during the past few years, and indeed *Survival* was originally written very rapidly as a thematic study for such courses. As a personality, Margaret Atwood has caught the imagination of the young. Her frequent poetry readings are jammed. They like her blunt manner, casual dress, and intense nationalism. According to publishers, her book has had a remarkable effect on the older generation as well. An amazing number of first novels by people over 40 have begun flowing in to small firms, often accompanied by letters claiming that Atwood had given them the confidence to write.

But the reaction has not been unalloyed enthusiasm. The novelist Margaret Laurence has described *Survival* as "brilliant," but has objected that victimisation is only one of several themes in our literature. Others have added that it is obviously a significant theme in the literature of other countries. Morley Callaghan, who has always been irritated by talk about Canadian literature per se, was moved to a state of jubilant truculence over *Survival*: "Am I as a writer to understand that survival is the big new theme? Under the dreadful United States pressure, we are all supposed to be victims and losers trying to survive. The theme is said to run all through our literature. What literature? Well, I was never a victim or a loser, and no lady with a survival kit for academic misfits is going to make me feel I need such ministrations."

Callaghan was once described by Edmund Wilson as "perhaps the most unjustly neglected novelist in the English-speaking world," and he went on to upbraid Canadians for their scepticism that "a writer whose work may be mentioned without absurdity in association with Chekhov's and Turgenev's can possibly be functioning in Toronto." Whatever one's estimate of Callaghan, he has not been a formidable influence on our younger writers, apart from Alice Munro, whose simple deft rendering of character clearly owes much to him. Certainly his Plain Style could not be more different from the complex, poetic expression of *Surfacing*. Nevertheless, *Survival's* cursory references to Callaghan are puzzling, particularly since his work is filled with little people struggling ineffectively against overwhelming odds. Margaret Atwood has justified her exclusions on the grounds that her book would have run to a thousand pages if she had included "everybody." But she has in fact included an extraordinary number of examples culled from undistinguished and insubstantial writers, while some of the omissions are startling. The most glaring of these is the total absence of Robertson Davies, whose two recent novels, *Fifth Business* and *The Manticore*, are receiving international attention. It could be argued, I suppose, that Davies's vitality and versatility would resist any attempt at superimposed classification.

Perhaps, too, Davies is omitted because he is basically a comic writer—a comic writer, moreover, in the long Canadian tradition of humorous irony stretching from Haliburton through Leacock to Farley Mowat. Significantly, the only one of Mowat's works which Miss Atwood chooses to speak about is *The People of the Deer*, the story of an Eskimo's destruction. Mowat can be a very, very funny man—but one would never know it from reading *Survival*. Perhaps laughter can be justified as a form of survival just as effective as grim tenacity.

In any event, it's exciting to see Canadians getting excited about their own literature. Robertson Davies has actually stated that in *Fifth Business* he was trying to "record the bizarre and passionate life of the Canadian people." Even Canadians are now becoming convinced he may be right.

Power Politics in Bluebeard's Castle [*Power Politics, The Edible Woman, Surfacing, Survival, Procedures for Underground, and "Polarities"*]

Gloria Onley*

Is it possible for men and women to stop mythologizing, manipulating, and attacking one another?

Margaret Atwood, 1971

If the "argument" of Sidney's *Astrophel and Stella* is "Cruel Chastity," the argument of Atwood's *Power Politics* is cruel sexuality. The cover design[1] pictures a knight in armour from whose extended arm and gauntleted hand depends, like a game trophy, the body of a woman, torso swathed in mummylike bandages, head down, hair trailing on the ground at the knight's feet. This inversion of the traditional posture of *homo erectus*—a deliberate echoing of The Hanged Man of the Tarot pack—is repeated in the novel *Surfacing* with David's sadistic upending of his wife, " 'twatface' " Anna. In *Power Politics*, as in Atwood's two novels, the unrequited love of courtly myth gives way to its equally frustrating modern form, a hedonistic, yet somehow mechanical union. The woman in *Power Politics* feels that her being is lacerated and her capacity for vision destroyed by subjection to a sadomasochistic sexual love:

> you fit into me
> like a hook into an eye

*From *Canadian Literature*, no. 60 (Spring 1974):21–42. Reprinted by permission of the author.

a fish hook
a open eye

Atwood's ironic inversion of courtly love connects her art with the revelations of McLuhan, Millett, Roszak, and Chesler about the social mythology of Western culture. Romantic obsession with lover or husband is presumed to provide the woman with her most satisfying form of existence. "To a man, love and life are things apart. To a woman, love is life itself," preaches The Sensuous Woman, echoing Byron.[2] The compulsively exact male/female polarity of "doing" and "being" implied by Atwood's sardonic conversion of garment fastener into deadly weapon expresses the conviction of the female prisoner of the machismo love structure that romantic love, in its modern version, is a devastating mode of existence. "Have to face it I'm / finally an addict," the "hooked" woman in *Power Politics* concludes. In "an air stale with aphorisms", a unique relationship that is sustaining yet liberating and joyous does not develop and, through a painful succession of claustrophobic encounters, Atwood suggests that maybe her female persona is looking for something that just doesn't exist.

Recent studies of the situation of women in our patriarchal society have established that the essential female traits are considered to be passivity, masochism, and narcissism.[3] Atwood's "fish hook . . . open eye" image perfectly condenses this cultural definition of "normal" female personality and emotional capacity and hurls it at the complacent romantic sensibility. Hence the poet Robert Read writes of "Atwood as acupuncture"; her manipulations anaesthetize his persona so that she may gulp his heart down her "icy throat" (*The Canadian Forum*, Dec., 1972, 9). But Atwood is also aware of the basic victor/victim patterning she explores in *Survival* (1972), her thematic guide[4] to Canadian literature, as a vicious circle. The woman in *Power Politics* can proclaim with an ironic self-awareness that verges on compassion: "Night seeps into us / through the accidents we have / inflicted on each other / Next time we commit / love, we ought to / choose in advance what to kill."

To Atwood, the love-aggression complex is an historical-personal fact. The cover of *Power Politics* expresses the predicament of women in the sexist society:

My love for you is the love
of one statue for another: tensed

and static. General, you enlist
my body in your heroic
struggle to become real:
though you promise bronze rescues

> you hold me by the left ankle
> so that my head brushes the ground,
> my eyes are blinded . . .
>
> There are hordes of me now, alike
> and paralyzed . . .

The theme of *Power Politics* is role-engulfment: "You refuse to own /
yourself, you permit / others to do it for you. . . ." The self is lost to the
social role of romantic lover, warrior, wife, superman: fulfilment means
incarnation within the archetype: ". . . through your own split head / you
rise up glowing; / the ceiling opens / a voice sings Love Is A Many /
Splendoured Thing / you hang suspended above the city / in blue tights
and a red cape, / your eyes flashing in unison." Self-emergence is as
difficult as pacifism in a world of war: "If you deny these uniforms / and
choose to repossess / yourself, your future / will be less dignified, more
painful, death will be sooner. . . ." Beyond the mask of social role lies the
paradox of Western culture: a postulated uniqueness of self that may not
exist, or perhaps cannot be known, if it does exist:

> You drift down the street
> in the rain, your face
> dissolving, changing shape, the colours
> running together
>
> My walls absorb
> you, breathe you forth
> again, you resume
> yourself, I do not recognize you
>
> You rest on the bed
> watching me watching
> you, we will never know
> each other any better
> than we do now.

The antithesis of the mask is the "face corroded by truth, / crippled,
persistent," asking "like the wind, again and again and wordlessly, / for the
one forbidden thing: / love without mirrors and not for / my reasons but
your own." Poised on the brink of a metaphysical negation of individuality,
the disillusioned female lover is possessed by a harsh nostalgia. At the same
time there is a continuation of a previous movement in Atwood's poetry
towards accepting the visitation of archetypal presences as a substitute for
authentic interknowledge of the selves, as in "your jewelled reptilian / eye
in darkness next to / mine" or "you descend on me like age / you descend
on me like earth." But the implicit quest is always for some alternative to
the sadistic penetration and destruction of the "fish hook-open eye"
relationship, for some "reality" behind the engulfing political role, and for

some communion with that "reality." *Power Politics* confronts us with an entropic modern world in which a formerly solar masculinity now operates as a suction pump to exhaust and destroy the environment:[5]

> You are the sun
> in reverse, all energy
> flows into you and is
> abolished; you refuse
> houses, you smell of
> catastrophe, I see you
> blind and one-handed, flashing
> in the dark, trees breaking
> under your feet, you demand,
> you demand
>
> I lie mutilated beside
> you; beneath us there are
> sirens, fires, the people run
> squealing, the city
> is crushed and gutted,
> the ends of your fingers bleed
> from 1000 murders

The imagery in Atwood's novels also expresses mechanization and destruction, but there the woman's helpless suffering or retaliation changes into an urgent desire for liberation.[6] In *The Edible Woman*, where social intercourse proceeds by means of "finely adjusted veneers," and the dominant aesthetic is conformity to the consumer ideal ("I love you especially in that red dress") images express role-engulfment as an omnipresent fate shared by everyone from the protagonist, Marian, a reluctant market researcher, to the "office virgins." To Marian, her fiancé's very clothes "smugly [assert] so much silent authority," she fears they would be warm, if touched. Dickens' caricatures and Bergson's essay on mechanization as a principle of comedy seem to underlie Atwood's satirical description of character and behaviour. Despite the humour, sex role mechanization is associated with death, until Marian finally sees Peter as a "dark homicidal maniac with a lethal weapon." A conditioned product of his consumer society, Peter is preoccupied with establishing, perpetuating, and worshipping himself within the glossy confines of the urban male image: a *Playboy* bachelorhood followed in due time by a *House and Garden* marriage. The "lethal weapon" with which he tracks and attempts to capture Marian is, of course, a camera; escaping from its focussing eye, Marian runs away from aggressive consumption and towards selfhood, rejecting the role of "soapwife" in a never-ending soap opera.

Deciding to remain an individual involved in a variety of human relationships, Marian defeats the shaping power of the sexist consumer society. Making a surrogate self out of cake and then eating it in a comic parody of ritual cannibalism, she both destroys a false image and reabsorbs her culturally split-off female self. This form of magic, a self-assertive process of encoding and eliminating what she is *not*, looks forward to the ritual destruction of false images of the self at the end of *Surfacing*; it is a comic anticipation of the magic more seriously practiced by the schizoid personality to restore its connection with the world.

Marian's fiancé refuses to eat her cake body; unable to liberate himself from consumerhood by comic communion, he rejects even the possibility of self-knowledge. Peter's social world is luxurious, totally artificial, self-consciously sensual; the mirrored spaces of his apartment lobby epitomize the glittering surfaces of urban reality: the world of technological hedonism founded on industrial technology. The "high electric vibration of this glittering space," is the concept of the ego as consumer — the grossly inflated ego extending itself in voluptuous narcissism through its glittering "made-up" surfaces: images of chrome and glass, arranged interiors, iced cakes, elaborate hairdos, face-makeup, sequinned dresses, ritualized, mechanized social behavior. It is in reaction to this world of surfaces that Marian slowly becomes unable to eat anything at all. Psychoanalytically, the ego of the cultural personality is shown as being in a state of fixation at the level of oral aggression, an infantile state of consciousness in which "the good" is the consumable or edible, including other people. Marian's consumption of the "edible woman" is a transformation ritual to get her outside of this one-dimensional social nexus, in which the potential self is condemned to collective narcissism as an alternative to genuine interaction with others.

In *Power Politics*, sexual love is imaged several times as a shattering of the ego that seems to be epitomized in the collision between mirrors of "They travel by air": "your / body with head / attached and my head with / body attached coincide briefly / . . . we hurtle towards each other / at the speed of sound, everything roars / we collide sightlessly and / fall, the pieces of us / mixed as disaster / and hit the pavement of this room / in a blur of silver fragments." In the semantic universe of technological man, what ought to be separate modes of existence somehow mirror each other through the shaping effect of myth. Hence velocity and violence enter into personal relationships. The woman cries to her lover, "I lie mutilated beside / you . . . How can I stop you? / Why did I create you?" [sic] Men and women are political prisoners of the sexist society, trapped as victors/victims in their own reflections of the world and of each other. Only in orgasm ("a kick in the head . . . sharp jewels / hit and my / hair splinters") or in fantasied death do the mirrors shatter.[7]

A persistent strain in Atwood's imagery, appearing in the poetry as well as in *Surfacing*, is the head as disconnected from, or floating above, the body.

> But face it, we have been
> improved, our heads float
> several inches above our necks
> moored to us by
> rubber tubes and filled with
> clever bubbles, . . .
>
> (*Power Politics*)

Often the imagery describes the body as a mechanism remotely controlled by the head; sometimes the neck is sealed over; always the intellectual part of the psyche is felt to be a fragment, dissociated from the whole. The "head" of Atwood's schizoid persona is the "Head" described in Michael McClure's "Revolt" (reprinted in Roszak's *Sources*,) the Head that "quickly . . . fills with preconception and becomes locked in a vision of the outer world and itself. . . . The Head [that] finally may act by self-image of itself, by a set and unchanging vision that ignores the demands of its Body."[8] We think of Anna in *Surfacing*, locked into her *Playboy* centrefold stereotype, her soul trapped in a gold compact, her capacity for love locked into a sadomasochistic pattern. The narrator describes her:

> Rump on a packsack, harem cushion, pink on the cheeks and black discreetly around the eyes, as red as blood as black as ebony, a seamed and folded imitation of a magazine picture that is itself an imitation of a woman who is also an imitation, the original nowhere, hairless lobed angel in the same heaven where God is a circle, captive princess in someone's head. She is locked in, she isn't allowed to eat or shit or cry or give birth, nothing goes in, nothing comes out. She takes her clothes off or puts them on, paper doll wardrobe, she copulates under strobe lights with the man's torso while his brain watches from its glassed-in control cubicle at the other end of the room, her face twists into poses of exultation and total abandonment. . . .

Anna conforms; therefore, she is. The narrator inhabits her own cartesian hell. Locked into a sex role herself by the conspiracy of her friends, pursued by "geometrical sex" as "an abstract principle," her past "marriage" and "baby" a fantasy rationalization or restructuring of the personal history she cannot live with, she is clearly intended to be a representative schizoid personality: "I realized I didn't feel much of anything, I hadn't for a long time. . . . At some point my neck must have closed over, pond freezing or a wound, shutting me into my head; since then everything had been glancing off me, it was like being in a vase. . . ."

During the course of her search for her father, a biologist living in isolation near the Quebec-Ontario border who has mysteriously disappeared, she becomes painfully aware of "what circuits are closing" in her friends' heads and in her own. Responsible for the group's survival in the wilderness setting, she finds the mandatory sexual "liberation" of her lover and friends depressing and alienating. For her, it depersonalizes them into cartoon figures or rock drawings, linear caricatures of humanity. "Shadowing" her along the trail to where she is pragmatically contemplating, not the "names," but the "forms" and "uses" of the various plants and fungii, Anna's husband David imposes his one-dimensional, linear, or "phallic" thrust on nature:

> [The Death's Angel] sprang up from the earth, pure joy, pure death, burning, white like snow.
> . . . "Hi, watcha doin'?" he said . . .
> . . . it was like trying to listen to two separate conversations, each interrupting the other. "A mushroom," I said. That wouldn't be enough, he would want a specific term . . . "Amanita."
> "Neat," he said, but he wasn't interested. I willed him to go away but he didn't; after a while he put his hand on my knee. . . . His smile was like a benevolent uncle's; under his forehead there was a plan. . . .
> "How about it?" he said. "You wanted me to follow you." . . . He reached his arm around me, invading . . . I twisted away and stood up . . . "You're interfering." I wiped at my arm where he had touched it.
> He didn't understand what I meant, he smiled even harder. "Don't get uptight," he said, "I won't tell Joe. It'll be great, it's good for you, keeps you healthy." Then he went "Yuk, yuk," like Goofy.

Through the perceptions of her narrator, Atwood records again the pathology of a sexual relationship in which the male asserts his masculinity by inflicting physical or psychological pain:

> . . . then [Anna's] voice began . . . a desperate beggar's whine, *please, please* . . . She was praying to herself, it was as if David wasn't there at all. *Jesus jesus oh yes please jesus.* Then something different, not a word but pure pain, clear as water, an animal's at the moment the trap closes. It's like death, I thought . . .

> "He's got this little set of rules. If I break one of them I get punished, except he keeps changing them, so I'm never sure. He's crazy, there's something missing in him, you know what I mean? He likes to make me cry because he can't do it himself . . ."

Echoing Laing's description of the depersonalized alienated personality — "Bodies halfdead: genitals dissociated from genitals" — the narrator conceives a mental ideogram for David's kind of love: "it would be enough for him if our genitals could be detached like two kitchen appliances and copulate in mid-air, that would complete his equation." Her sudden vision of David as "an imposter, a pastiche," relates him to the "creeping Americanism"[9] that she feels is moving up into Canada, destroying the landscape, the animals, and the people. "He didn't even know what language to use, he'd forgotten his own, he had to copy. Second-hand American was spreading over him in patches . . . He was infested, garbled . . . it would take such time to heal, unearth him, scrape down to where he was true." At her worst moment of alienation, she sees those around her as evolving, "half-way to machine, the left-over flesh atrophied and diseased."

The cultural link between depersonalized sex and modern technology is suggested by George Steiner in *In Bluebeard's Castle: Notes Towards a Redefinition of Culture*.[10] Steiner comments on the significance of the "maniacal monotony" of de Sade:

> . . . that automatism, that crazed repetitiveness, . . . directs us to a novel and particular image, or rather silhouette, of the human person. It is in Sade . . . that we find the first methodical industrialization of the human body . . . Each part of the body is seen only as a part and replaceable by "spares". In . . . Sadian sexual assaults, we have a brilliantly exact *figura* of the division of labour on the factory floor.

Throughout *Surfacing*, as in Sadian fantasy, sex is linked with mechanization, coercion, and death:

> . . . I didn't want him in me, sacrilege, he was one of the killers . . . he hadn't seen, he didn't know about himself, his own capacity for death.
>
> "Don't," I said, he was lowering himself down on me, "I don't want you to."
>
> "What's wrong with you?" he said, angry; then he was pinning me, hands manacles, teeth against my lips, censoring me, he was shoving against me, his body insistent as one side of an argument.

Anna's compulsive need to conform to male expectations makes it impossible for her, despite a degree of self-knowledge, to view other women as friends ("she resented me because I hadn't given in [to David], it commented on her,") and fills her with unconscious self-loathing. As Anna's relationships with others seem to fall almost totally within a general sadomasochistic tendency, and as her love for David seems to be a kind of death, so detective stories are her "theology."

To repulse David's attack, the narrator is able to use magically her awareness of his golem quality:

> His wrist watch glittered, glass and silver: perhaps it was his dial, the key that wound him, the switch. There must be a phrase, a vocabulary that would work, "I'm sorry," I said, "but you don't turn me on."
>
> "You," he said, searching for words, not controlled any more, "tight-ass bitch."

Obviously, David is projecting. In David, and to a lesser extent in Joe, Atwood creates a parody of the mighty hunter:

> [They] appeared . . . one at either end of a thinnish log. They were proud, they'd caught something. The log was notched in many places as though they'd attacked it . . . David . . . wanted some footage . . . for *Random Samples* . . . In the end they stuck the axe in the log, after several tries, and took turns shooting each other standing beside it, arms folded and one foot on it as if it was a lion or a rhinoceros.

Their film, a development from the camera imagery of *The Edible Woman*, is an aimless stockpiling of randomly chosen images—a linear, mechanical imitation of natural flux that is the equivalent in art of their other male activities. Just as ineffectual hacking at the log is rationalized as male strength, so a total lack of vision becomes creative spontaneity when David decides that the film "might be even better if it was out of focus or over-exposed, it would introduce the element of chance, it would be organic." In both novels, Atwood satirizes a general tendency to rationalize—or transcendentalize—conformity to unsatisfactory behaviour patterns.

In connection with their posturing for the film, the narrator senses again the vicious yet pathetic narcissism of David and of her lover, Joe: "He didn't love me, it was an idea of himself he loved and he wanted someone to join him, anyone would do. . . ." Fear and hatred of the repressed "female" element of personality erupts in David's conversation: "None of that Women's Lib," David said, his eyes lidding, "or you'll be out in the street. I won't have one in the house, they're preaching random castration, they get off on that, they're roving the streets in savage bands armed with garden shears." To Atwood's intuitively psychoanalytical consciousness of human nature, engulfment in the sexual role, as she satirically exposes it in *Surfacing*, means that the ego of the cultural personality tends to become fixated at the stage of anal-sadism, condemned to the hellish circle of self-definition through violence, in which each man kills the thing he loves, in one way or another.

The end of Chapter 18 brings the sexual politics of *Surfacing* to a ritual climax of judgment and rejection by the peer group:

> "She hates men," David said lightly. "Either that or she wants to be one. Right?"
>
> A ring of eyes, tribunal; in a minute they would join hands and dance around me, and after that the rope and the pyre, cure for heresy
> . . .
>
> "Aren't you going to answer?" Anna, said, taunting.
> "No," I said.
> Anna said, "God, she really is inhuman," and they both laughed a little, sorrowfully.

Rejecting her assigned sex role, Atwood's protagonist becomes the modern equivalent of the heretic or witch—the mentally ill or "inhuman" person, the deviant by means of whose existence "normal" values are asserted and maintained. At this point, the expulsion/escape or the unfeminine wilderness guide begins. Skulking animal-like beyond the clearing until her friends have abandoned her (as she wishes), she approaches and returns from the verge of total madness.

Alone in the house her father built, she reflects: "Logic is a wall, I built it, on the other side is terror." Starting to groom herself, she feels a "surge of fear," knows the brush is "forbidden," knows why: "I must stop being in the mirror. I look for the last time at my distorted glass face: . . . reflection intruding between my eyes and vision. Not to see myself but to see. I reverse the mirror so it's towards the wall, it no longer traps me, Anna's soul closed in the gold compact, that and not the camera is what I should have broken." She then destroys all the "artifacts" of her past life: among other symbols, her childhood drawings, "the rabbits and their archaic eggs"; the "confining photographs" of her family heritage; her own false art, the "bungled princesses, the Golden Phoenix awkward and dead as a mummified parrot." Her ritual destruction of all falsely defining images of her self and others, her temporary rejection of all linear structures (house, fence, even garden), her reversion to primitive survival by eating roots and mushrooms, leads her to an hallucinatory identification with the matrix of nature, in which the artificial structures of language and culture dissolve for a moment, and she becomes a microcosm of the biosphere:

> The forest leaps upward, enormous, the way it was before they cut it, columns of sunlight frozen; the boulders float, melt, everything is made of water, even the rocks. In one of the languages there are no nouns, only verbs held for a longer moment.
> The animals have no need for speech, why talk when you are a word
> I lean against a tree, I am a tree leaning
>
> I break out again into the bright sun and crumple, head against the ground
> I am not an animal or a tree, I am the thing in which the trees and animals move and grow, I am a place

As Atwood notes in the Introduction to *Survival*, Northrop Frye suggests that in Canada "Who am I?" at least partly equals "Where is here?" Here, in *Surfacing*, is the liberated naked consciousness, its doors of perception symbolically cleansed: the "place" is the Canadian wilderness, which becomes the new body or rediscovered original body of the psychosomatic human. The radiant plurality of the organismic realm into which the narrator descends is epitomized in the image of the frog: "A frog is there, leopard frog with green spots and gold-rimmed eyes, ancestor. It includes me, it shines, nothing moves but its throat breathing." The fairy-tale theme of metamorphosis is present: the narrator transforms herself from a schizoid personality into a basic human creature by going down into forest, swamp, and water, into a primitive Edenic reality where frogs, no longer revolting or worthless, become fellow creatures of the biosphere — breathing, shining kinfolk of the human. The basic metaphor of descent and surfacing is itself a transformation of Atwood's inherited romantic image of death by drowning. The last part of the novel is thus a paradigm of descent into and ascent from the fluid ego boundary state of schizophrenia.[11] But it is a carefully controlled, artistically simulated descent, of therapeutic purpose and value within the psychoanalytic dimension of the novel. The ego core (or inner self) of the narrator always retains its integrity, except for a fleeting moment during the peak experience of hallucinatory oneness with nature where Atwood seems to be synthesizing a primitive state of mind analogous to Lévy-Brühl's "participation mystique." Like Laing, Atwood seems to believe that schizophrenia is a form of psychic anarchy: a usually involuntary attempt by the self to free itself from a repressive social reality structure. John Ayre quite rightly terms her a "psychic iconoclast."[12]

In *Surfacing* and *The Edible Woman*, it is as if Atwood had inferred from the glittering surfaces of our social images the Freudian theory of personality as narcissistic, accomplishing self-definition through various forms of aggression, ranging from overt coercion to the subtle forms of unconscious "induction" revealed by Laing. At the end of *Surfacing*, when the wilderness guide returns to the cabin where she had at the beginning of her descent into madness turned the mirror to the wall, symbolically rejecting the feminine image represented by Anna's gold compact, she turns the mirror around again and regards herself as she has become:

> . . . in [the mirror] there's a creature neither animal nor human, furless, only a dirty blanket, shoulders huddled over into a crouch, eyes staring blue as ice from the deep sockets; the lips move by themselves. This was the stereotype, straws in the hair, talking nonsense or not talking at all. To have someone to speak to and words that can be understood: their definition of sanity.
>
> That is the real danger now, the hospital or the zoo, where we are put, species and individual, when we can no longer cope. They would never believe it's only a natural woman, state of nature, they think of that as a tanned body on a beach with washed hair waving like scarves; not this, face dirt-caked and streaked, skin grimed and scabby, hair like a frayed bathmat stuck with leaves and twigs. A new kind of centrefold.

Beneath this ironic transformation of Narcissus' mirror lies Szasz's concept of the "mentally ill" person as political prisoner of the social reality structure of his society, as enforced by institutional psychiatry, Laing's "mind police." A fusion of many literary forms, Menippean satire, diary, wilderness venture, even the Canadian animal story, *Surfacing* is the classic human animal story: the wilderness guide as social deviant becomes a scapegoat, driven out of the technological society for her sexist peers so that they may define themselves by their rejection of her.

By the end of the psychological quest, it is clear why, as Atwood stated earlier in *The Circle Game*, "Talking is difficult" and why in *Surfacing* "language is everything you do." The difficulty in human relations, metaphored in *Surfacing* as exile from the biosphere, is metaphysically related to the exploitative use of language to impose psychological power structures. The need for communion in *Power Politics* is paralleled by the realization that language tends to warp in the hand from tool to weapon: "The things we say are / true; it is our crooked / aims, our choices / turn them criminal," and there is a corresponding recognition of the value of silence: "Your body is not a word, / it does not lie or / speak truth either. / It is only / here or not here."

In "Hesitations outside the door", Bluebeard's castle is the place where "you twist all possible / dimensions into your own"; it is the house "we both live in / but neither of us owns." As the self defines itself in relation to others, so Bluebeard cannot be himself without a victim / wife. Each induces the other to participate in the structuring of the myth. There is a surrealistic sense in which language itself, because it is habitually and unconsciously used to erect and impose false structure, is Bluebeard's castle. The "wife" cries to "Bluebeard" "Don't let me do this to you, / you are not those other people, / you are yourself / Take off the signatures, the false / bodies, this love / which does not fit you / This is not a house, there are no doors, / get out while it is / open, while you still can. . . ." To use language at all is to risk participation in its induction structure; to define is to risk committing or inciting violence in the name of love.

Why this should be so is suggested by George Steiner in his analysis of the current barbarisms of Western culture: there is a sense in which the grammars themselves "condescend or enslave."

> Indo-European syntax is an active mirroring of systems of order, of hierarchic dependence, of active and passive stance . . . The sinews of Western speech closely enacted . . . the power relations of the Western social order. Gender differentiations, temporal cuts, the rules governing prefix and suffix formations, the synapses and anatomy of a grammar — these are the *figura*, at once ostensive and deeply internalized of the commerce between the sexes, between master and subject. . . .

For Atwood, the basis of the victor/victim patterning she sees in human relations in *Survival* and reflects in the male/female relations of her own literary structures is also psycholinguistic — that is, inherent in the monotheistic, patriarchal social reality structure of Western culture, within which man habitually defines himself by aggression and which has reached a pinnacle of alienation in sexist, technological society, the "America" of the alienated self. The narrator of *Surfacing* remembers her brother's childhood obsession with "wars, aeroplanes and tanks and the helmeted explorers," and realizes that his sadistic treatment of his experimental animals and his military interests are intimately related to his adult habit of imposing moral categories upon nature: "Below me in the water there's a leech, the good kind with red dots on the back, undulating along like a streamer held at one end and shaken. The bad kind is mottled grey and yellow. It was my brother who made up these moral distinctions, at some point he became obsessed with them, he must have picked them up from the war. There had to be a good kind and a bad kind of everything."

In Atwood's poem "Hesitations outside the door," Bluebeard in his castle is both the suffering Christ, the emergent masochistic half of the sadomasochistic Judeo-Christian tradition, and the culturally defined sadistic male, participating with his wife in the melancholy inevitable fusion of Eros and Thanatos:

> What do you want from me
> you who walk towards me over the long floor
>
> your arms outstretched, your heart
> luminous through the ribs
>
> around your head a crown
> of shining blood
>
> This is your castle, this is your metal door,
> these are your stairs, your
>
> bones, you twist all possible
> dimensions into your own.

The myth is a destructive one: it defines love as sacrifice and suffering, and consummation as death. As in *Surfacing*, the sadistic male uses women mechanically as keys to self definition by aggression:

> In your pockets the thin women
> hang on their hooks, dismembered
>
> Around my neck I wear
> the head of the beloved, pressed
> in the metal retina like a picked flower.

If men possess and use women as keys, women have been conditioned to worship men as icons (the Victorian locket, the religious medal). These interlocking attitudes have had the effect of fragmenting and destroying for Atwood's persona the perhaps mythical but longed-for natural order ("women . . . dismembered": "the head of the beloved . . . like a picked flower"). The concept of ownership or romantic "possession" resulting in exploitation by the man and idealization and obedience by the woman is found throughout *Power Politics* in many of its versions and inversions of the basic prisoner or victim of love theme. In "After the agony in the guest / bedroom," the would-be lover, resting in the woman's arms in a parody of the *pietà*, "wine mist rising / around you, an almost– / visible halo," asks "do you love me" and is answered by cruciform manipulation:

> I answer you:
> I stretch your arms out
> one to either side,
> your head slumps forward.

followed by a further relocation and another kind of purgation:

> Later I take you home
> in a taxi, and you
> are sick in the bathtub.

Atwood's delineation of the lovers' agonizingly compulsive tendency to relate primarily through suffering, brutally exposes the sadomasochistic nexus of the monotheistic, patriarchal society. The woman of *Power Politics* brings to her love relationships the advantage of intellectual enlightenment, but her analytical approach serves only to invert the power structure:

> I approach this love
> like a biologist
> pulling on my rubber
> gloves & white labcoat
>
> You flee from it
> like an escaped political
> prisoner, and no wonder . . .
>
> Please die I said
> so I can write about it

She is aware of her own propensity toward sadistic sublimation.

In Atwood's exploration of sexual politics within the patriarchal value structure, orgasm becomes "a kick in the head, orange / and brutal, sharp jewels / hit and my / hair splinters," a redemption by death of the self: "no / threads left holding / me, I flake apart / layer by / layer down / quietly to the bone." There is great ambivalence. The desired ego-transcendence, with its suggestion of a joyous return to a mythic primitive state of consciousness where the "skull / unfolds to an astounded flower," is also dangerous, for "learning / speech again takes / days and longer / each time / too much of / this is fatal." In Atwood's poetry, the psychological basis and the value in human relationships of the individualism of Western man is very much in question: partly by reference to her sense of self-definition by violence explored in the transactional social worlds of the two novels, where individualism becomes a potent carrier of death; and partly by reference to a presumed primitive, non-linear, and pluralistic state of being which functions as a mythic reference in most of her poetry from the earliest work on, emerging in *Surfacing* as a utopian alternative to alienation. In the love poems the tension between individuality and isolation, on the one hand, and loss of identity and sexual fulfilment on the other, is extreme and cannot be resolved. Imagistically it is an anguished oscillation within the *either/or* psycholinguistic structures of Western man,[13] the existentialist trap the wilderness guide describes as the "walls" of "logic." An oscillation between the polarities of civilized/primitive, individual/generic, male/female (in terms of Atwood's camera imagery, focussed/unfocussed), in which reciprocity of being, psychosomatic wholeness, and a sense of genuine communion, as *integrated qualities of experience*, remain mythic states forever beyond reach. The channels of communication and action are patriarchal almost beyond redemption. ". . . you rise above me / smooth, chill, stone- / white . . . you descend on me like age / you descend on me like earth." In her earlier poem, "Dream: Bluejay or Archeopteryx," there is an attempt to invert the hierarchic structure: "in the water / under my shadow / there was an outline, man / surfacing, his body sheathed / in feathers, his teeth / glinting like nails, fierce god / head crested with blue flame" (*Procedures for Underground*).

Atwood suggests that the end of sexual politics might come only with the end of civilization, as in "The accident has occurred, . . . we are alone in . . . / the frozen snow," when problems of physical survival would replace problems of psychic survival. Images of desert, ocean, and tundra are attractive in that they presume a settler-like equality of the sexes, working together, an absolute need for compassion; but repellent in that they are places of isolation from humanity where the known forms of self-definition and of personality, however unsatisfactory, are absent. The isolation and limitation of romantic love is mirrored everywhere in the landscape of Atwood's poetry; the couple marooned on the island, stranded in the car, or in the house in a snowstorm, surviving the holocaust, and, finally, buried together. The couple-structure of love is opposed by the community of the dance, "the circle / forming, breaking, each / one of them the whole / rhythm . . . transformed / for this moment . . ." (*Procedures for Underground*); by the circle or flux of playing children; and by the dissolving of the ego-structure into sleep or into landscape as celebrated in "Fragments: Beach." "In the afternoon the sun / expands, we enter / its hot perimeter . . . light is a sound / it roars / it fills us / we swell with it / are strenuous, vast / rocks / hurl our voices / we / are abolished . . . the sleepers / lose their hold on shore, are drawn / out on a gigantic tide / we also make the slow deep / circle / until / the sea returns us / leaves us / absolved, washed / shells on the morning beach" (*Procedures for Underground*).

Throughout her work Atwood speaks of other languages: "multilingual water" and "the jays, flowing from tree to tree, voices semaphoring, tribal" of *Surfacing*. In *Procedures for Underground*, she tells of learning "that the earliest language / was not our syntax of chained pebbles / but liquid." *Surfacing* abounds with examples of oral aggression or the sadistic use of language for self-definition. Linguistic channels of communication are felt to be analytic, dissecting, futile, impelling the narrator to break out of her received mental categories by psychic anarchy. To the alienated self, linear, logical thought structures operate like knives on the body of love. The narrator remembers her abortion in imagery that is a paranoid echoing of Sadian mechanization: "Nobody must find out or they will do that to me again, strap me to the death machine, emptiness machine, legs in the metal framework, secret knives." Imagining her future child, her "lost child surfacing within her," by reference to her utopian organismic realm, as "covered with shining fur, a god," she decides, "I will never teach it any words."

The anguished lack of communion between the lovers in *Power Politics* is, for Atwood, the inability of the alienated self to break through the thought structures of Western culture. In Atwood's story "Polarities" (*The Tamarack Review*, No. 58, 1971), overt demands for what the American poet Gary Snyder calls "inter-birth" — self-fulfilment through participation in a web of inter-relationships — are regarded as symptoms of madness. The protagonist Louise, who is isolated, even from her intellectual peers, by her deviance from the typical feminine role, tries to create a sense of wholeness by manipulating her friends into a literal acting-out of the title of Atwood's earlier book of poems, *The Circle Game*. Louise has a vision of the city as a topographical image of human relations: "The city is polarized north and south; the river splits it in two; the poles are the gas plant and the power plant. . . . We have to keep the poles in our brains lined up with the poles of the city, that's what Blake's poetry is all about." Her disorientation from conventional reality causes her friends to take her to the hospital where she is put into a chemical straitjacket.

Later, her colleague Morrison wants to rescue her, but is finally disgusted by his ability to achieve masculine self-definition only in response to drug-induced tellurian femaleness: "He saw that it was only the hopeless, mad Louise he wanted, . . . the one devoid of any purpose or defence. . . . a defeated formless creature on which he could inflict himself like shovel on earth, axe on forest, use without being used, know without being known." Morrison realizes that Louise's description of him is essentially accurate: "Morrison refuses to admit his body is part of his mind." He has a sudden perception of human warmth as the only answer to "futile work and sterile love," and of the impossibility of achieving it through mechanical means, either technological ("the grace of the power plant and the gas plant") or magical ("the circle game"). The eyes "yellowish-grey," "alert, neutral" of the wolves in the pen at the game farm where he has gone after leaving the hospital, foreshadow the wolf's eyes of the hallucinatory image of the father in *Surfacing*. Without human communion, Morrison realizes, leaning against the wolf pen, "dizzy with cold," there is only "the barren tundra and the blank solid rivers, and beyond, so far that the endless night had already descended, the frozen sea." Morrison's spatial co-ordinates accurately symbolize his psychic predicament.

Louise attempts to create a body of love by substituting the paleologic of children and primitive peoples[14] for the unsatisfactory social syllogisms of the patriarchal reality structure. Mapping the repressive social polarities onto the landscape, she practices a form of primitive magic to overcome the collective insanity of communal isolation in "apartments." To read Atwood's description of insanity by social definition and of psychic iconoclasm in "Polarities" and *Surfacing* in conjunction with contemporary works which analyze the social construction of reality is to realize that what Atwood calls "mythologizing" is usually a conscious or unconscious enforcement of the sexual "polarities" inherent in the myths of romantic love, nuclear marriage, the machismo male, and the "feminine" woman. As an intelligent woman and a poet, Atwood indicates that we must somehow escape from this alienating cultural definition of personality and human relations. In *Surfacing*, the schizoid personality's magic ritual accomplishes her mental escape from role-engulfment into the personal eclectism or search for new forms spoken of by Steiner.

> I . . . step into the water and lie down. When every part of me is wet I take off my clothes, peeling them away from my flesh like wallpaper . . .
>
> My back is on the sand, my head rests against the rock, innocent as plankton; my hair spreads out, moving and fluid in the water. The earth rotates, holding my body down to it as it holds the moon; the sun pounds in the sky, red flames and rays pulsing from it, searing away the wrong form that encases me, dry rain soaking through me, warming the blood egg I carry. I dip my head beneath the water, washing my eyes . . .
>
> When I am clean I come up out of the lake, leaving my false body floated on the surface . . .

In *Survival*, Atwood distinguishes between Nature's order, "labyrinthine, complex, curved," and the order of Western European Man, "squares, straight lines, oblongs." The Canadian settlers having a strong preconception of order as inherent in the universe, build their "straight-line constructions, but kill something vital in the process . . . often Nature in the form of a woman." In Atwood's poem "Progressive Insanities of a Pioneer," the settler who fails to impose order on nature has his head invaded by "the Nature which he has identified as chaos, refusing to recognize that it has its own kind of order." The interplay between images of fence/garden, vegetable/weeds in *Surfacing*, and the narrator's voluntary exclusion from the fenced-in garden as part of her magic ritual, are an obvious development from this earlier exploration. Atwood also comments that the pioneer's final state of insanity may be a progressive development from an implicit earlier state, since "suppression of everything 'curved' may itself be a form of madness."

In *Surfacing*, the final hallucinatory vision is of the father, the scientist, the man who has both imposed intellectual order on nature and, presumably, taught his daughter the skills of survival in the wilderness. At first she projects on to the father, whose back is to her, her own realization of the limitations imposed by linear structures: "He has realized he was an intruder; the cabin, the fences, the fires and paths were violations; now his own fence excludes him, as logic excludes love. He wants it ended, the borders abolished, he wants the forest to flow back into the places his mind cleared: reparation." But then she progresses through her "insanity" to a further stage of enlightenment:

> He turns towards me and it's not my father. It is what my father saw, the thing you meet when you've stayed here too long alone . . . it gazes at me for a time with its yellow eyes, wolf's eyes, depthless but lambent. . . . Reflectors. It does not approve of me or disapprove of me, it tells me it has nothing to tell me, only the fact of itself.
>
> Then its head swings away with an awkward, almost crippled motion: I do not interest it, I am part of the landscape, I could be anything, a tree, a deer skeleton, a rock.
>
> I see now that although it isn't my father it is what my father has become.

The dissolution of all mental structures returns man completely to nature: *he* becomes *it*. By first experiencing a dissolving of the ego into landscape and then objectifying in the human figure with wolf's eyes the consequences of maintaining this "participation" as a state of consciousness, the narrator is able to visualize the furthest limits to which the dissolution of mental structures can be pushed without the permanent merging with the landscape that occurs in insanity, when the ego appears to dissolve into a totally schizophrenic state from which there is no returning.

Thus the father becomes a "protecting spirit" embodying both the vital anarchic impulse of the self, the husk-dissolving creative spirit, and the essential conservative element. As in the suspended animation of the final hallucination, the fish jumping, turning into a primitive artifact or rock drawing in mid-air, hanging there suspended, "flesh turned to icon," then softening and dropping back into the water, an "ordinary fish" again, there is a sense of all life as a temporary configuration of psychic energy, part of a greater flux of what earlier poets like Pratt thought of as cosmic energy structuring itself in personality and through work.[15] For Atwood, despite the apparent oscillation between ideal and real implied by the image of the fish leaping, integrity of form resides primarily in the natural structure, not in the imposed social form or myth; thus being has a biological rather than a transcendental authority.

The narrator of *Surfacing* returns to sanity with the realization that she can refuse to participate in the destructive "mythologizing" of her society: "This above all, to refuse to be a victim. . . . The word games, the winning and losing games are finished; at the moment there are no others but they will have to be invented, withdrawing is no longer possible and the alternative is death." Arising renewed from the non-evaluative plurality of nature, the wilderness guide comprehends that reality is, as William James said, a "multi-dimensional continuum." For the first time she understands and has compassion for the subjective dimensions of others.

She realizes "the effort it must have taken [her father] to sustain his illusions of reason and benevolent order," and how her mother's "meticulous records" of the weather "allowed her to omit . . . the pain and isolation." Her perception of her lover is altered: "he isn't an American, I can see that now . . . he is only half-formed, and for that reason I can trust him." She has escaped her former sense of total closure, thus achieving a liberated self and a basis for action within the world.

Atwood's sense of "participation mystique" as an alternative to alienation plays its numinous part in a personal dialectic of myths, restoring to sanity the wilderness guide of *Surfacing*. However authentic or inauthentic her concept of the primitive may be outside of the world of her alienated women, it manifests the search for new forms of reality spoken of by Steiner. The last chapter of *Surfacing* makes essentially the same statement as Birney's lines: "No one bound Prometheus / Himself he chained," but makes it within the new context of awareness supplied by such fields as cultural anthropology, the sociology of knowledge, and environmental studies. Interdisciplinary insights are leading us quickly towards what Atwood might term an ecology of human energy, a bioethic to replace what Steiner calls "the blackmail of transcendence."[16] Atwood's poems and stories are not resigned and "graceful" sublimations of what is usually referred to as the human condition. Rather they are frighteningly precise image structures, iconoclastic keys to getting mentally outside of Bluebeard's Castle.

Notes

1. By William Kimber for the Anansi edition. Kimber's design appears again on the jacket of the first American edition, Harper & Row, 1973.

2. "J," *The Sensuous Woman* (New York, 1969).

3. Phyllis Chesler documents *Women and Madness* (New York, 1972) by reference to these studies.

4. In my review article "*Surfacing* in the Interests of *Survival*" (*West Coast Review*, January, 1972), I suggest that *Survival* is really an ethical treatise presented as a thematic guide to Canadian literature. The present article, accepted for publication in March, 1973, is a development from this previous consideration of Atwood's work in relation to the psychology of R. D. Laing.

5. Atwood's vampire story, "The Grave of The Famous Poet," *72 New Canadian Stories*, ed. David Helwig and Joan Harcourt (Oberon Press, Canada, 1972), should be read in conjunction with *Power Politics*. As in *Power Politics*, the lovers form a closed system, a deadly dyadic field characterized by violence and exhaustion. See references to Atwood in my review article, "Breaking Through Patriarchal Nets to The Peaceable Kingdom," *West Coast Review*, January, 1974.

6. The movement from bondage to liberation is not a chronological development of theme. *The Edible Woman* was written in 1965 (letter, Atwood to Onley, Dec. 30, 1972).

7. The mirror is one of Atwood's favorite images. See "Tricks with Mirrors," in *Aphra*, Fall 1972. "Mirrors / are the perfect lovers, / . . . throw me on the bed / reflecting side up, / fall into me, / it will be your own / mouth you hit, firm and glassy, / . . . You are suspended

in me / beautiful and frozen, I / preserve you, in me you are safe. / . . . I wanted to stop this, / . . . this life of vision only, split / and remote, a lucid impasse. / I confess: this is not a mirror, / it is a door / I am trapped behind / I wanted you to see me here, / say the releasing word, whatever / that may be, open the wall. / Instead you stand in front of me / combing your hair." *Cf. Surfacing*, 175 and 190.

8. New York, Harper Colophon Books, 1972.

9. For the narrator of *Surfacing*, "American" signifies not a national identity but a mode of existence. See Chapter 15.

10. New Haven, Yale University Press, 1971.

11. *Cf.* R. D. Laing's description of Julie in *The Divided Self*, Chapter 11.

12. *Saturday Night* (November, 1972), 26. "Atwood plays the role of psychic iconoclast, pulling the categories of existence apart and presenting a broken, confused reality that her readers must often [put] back into order for themselves. . . . she demands uncomfortable mental confrontations that most people would obviously prefer to avoid."

13. According to the cultural anthropologist Melville J. Herskovitz, the tendency to dichotomize experience by using thought structures based on polarities is characteristic of Euroamerican culture. *Cultural Relativism: Perspectives in Cultural Pluralism* (New York, 1972), 238–239.

14. Before his death Lévy-Brühl came to realize that there is in fact no difference between primitive mentality and our own. As Herskovitz comments, all human beings think "prelogically" at times (*op. cit.*, 28–29). Louise is not thinking and acting in terms of objectively provable causation, hence to the Euroamerican mind she appears to have regressed to a childish or "primitive" mode of thought. Much of our thinking and behaviour is similarly based on questionable premises, but if there is a consensus of opinion that the premises are valid, then the behaviour is held to be reasonable or "sane."

15. Sandra Djwa, "E. J. Pratt and Evolutionary Thought: Towards an Eschatology," *Dalhousie Review* (Autumn, 1972), 417.

16. Weyland Drew, in "Wilderness and Limitation," (*The Canadian Forum*, February, 1973), suggests that the real strength of the ecological movement lies in its association with the Romantic and libertarian traditions – "traditions which have respected the subconscious and the primitive" (18). His observation that "the only context in which Canadian nationalism can be acceptable is in the service of the ecological movement . . . as a responsibility to the land" seems to apply to the wilderness guide's dread of "creeping Americanism" in *Surfacing*, and to her pragmatic yet mystical relationship to the Canadian wilderness.

Margaret Atwood: Poet as Novelist [*Power Politics, The Circle Game, The Edible Woman, The Journals of Susanna Moodie, The Animals in That Country, Survival,* and *Surfacing*]

George Woodcock*

The most recent of Margaret Atwood's six books of verse is a collection of poems of sexual communion — for it is a relationship too acrid to be called *love* in the ordinary sense that she describes — entitled with mordantly analogical appropriateness *Power Politics.* The opening poem is a terse and tense pair of couplets that not only set the acerbic tone of the volume itself, but also present an image that takes one by an amazingly short cut to the very heart of Atwood's kind of poetry and — what is largely the same thing — her kind of perception:

> you fit into me
> like a hook into an eye
>
> a fish hook
> an open eye

It is as sharp and disillusioned an expression as one could expect of the cruel inevitabilities of love: that what is so appropriate (fitting) should also be so painful. But look farther: Margaret Atwood is no mere black romantic, delighted only to uncover the horrors in what the polite world likes to dismiss as fortunate because it cannot be escaped. At least three essential characteristics of her poetic nature emerge from a closer look at this veritable caltrop of a poem — spiny in whatever direction you turn it.

First, there is her skill at the poetic booby trap — the sharp ironic inversion by which such an image of domestic bliss as the Victorian hook-and-eye — so secure a fastening until welcome hands undo it — is suddenly transformed by a shift to a related image which shuts out any thought of bliss, shuts it out like an eyelid, with its evocation of a pain one feels with an almost physical twinge, in one's own mind's eye.

But there is another, more intellectual kind of inversion involved: the poet proceeds from the metaphorical to the literal use of an image — that of the eye — and in this way reminds us of that world of resonant correspondences, of shading meanings and relationships in which our mental patterns as well as our physical perceptions exist. And yet, in that complex of symbolic relationships, our attention is still held by that vital

*From *The Canadian Novel in the Twentieth Century*, edited by George Woodcock (Toronto: McClelland and Stewart, 1975), 312–27. Reprinted by permission of the author.

image, the eye itself which holds so much that is significant in Margaret Atwood's poetry. For the eye sees, and is hurt, and so perception and feeling merge into each other.

Margaret Atwood—perhaps more than any other Canadian poet of the younger generation—combines an extraordinary visual sensibility, the first requirement of any good poet, with a spare and laconic intellectual discipline. There is hardly a slack word in the whole corpus of her five most recent volumes, thin and rigorously selected; there are no vague thoughts—everything is honed to sharpness; there is no avoidable obscurity. To make a comparison (which is not meant to be invidious in either direction) with another poet of comparable technical ability and intellectual power, one never finds in Atwood the essential difficulty of Margaret Avison's poetry, perhaps because Atwood's is a world where the complexities which exist are not spiritual. There is ambiguity indeed, but with the terms always clearly perceptible for those who have learnt her language; there is tortuosity of emotion, not of thought or expression. And always that limpidity of tone which tempts one to adapt a phrase of Orwell and talk, in relation to Atwood, of verse like a window pane.

It is a question of poetic objectivity, for in the aspects that count Margaret Atwood is essentially an objective poet. This of course is not a matter of personality being absent; it is hard to imagine a poet's personality more astringently present than Atwood's is in *Power Politics*. But personality, and personal experience, while they shape the content of her poems and infuse the style, in no way opacify the verbal surface; it is everywhere translucent, and if among modern Canadian poets there is in spirit a true descendant of the Imagists, it is Margaret Atwood. For her, as for all the really important modern poets, the visible world exists; her poems are, as all good poems must be, intensely visual, and it is through this quality that the pervading mind and sensibility express themselves. It is precisely, also, because Margaret Atwood is so accurately conscious of the proper relationship between this visual sensibility—blending into the tactile and the aural perceptions—which dictates the substance of poetry, and the mental processes that shape its intent, that she is so remarkably good a critic, as her individual essays and her idiosyncratic survey of Canadian literature, *Survival*, have shown.

So much for general reactions—the qualities abstracted from Margaret Atwood's poems which make one welcome the progress that has brought her in a decade to a position of recognition as one of the established Canadian poets—and, in terms of current production, one of the best among them. Her first volume was a thin leaflet, now almost forgotten, and certainly never mentioned, entitled *Double Persephone*, which a little press brought out in 1961. For the next five years she published sparingly in little magazines; then, in 1966, appeared *The Circle Game*, a collection which served notice that a poet of stature had emerged. It won the Governor-General's Award for that year, and, perhaps a surer sign of its genuine quality, A.J.M. Smith included no less than eleven pages from this volume — about a seventh of its entire length — in the definitive anthology, *Modern Canadian Verse*, which he published in 1967.

Having found her compass point, Margaret Atwood has proceeded with great assurance and as great achievement to publish, since *The Circle Game*, four books of verse, *The Animals in That Country, The Journals of Susanna Moodie, Procedures for Underground* and the already mentioned *Power Politics*. Her affinities are complex; her highly articulate verses continue the tradition of sophisticated poetic utterance one associates with the poets who came into prominence in the Fifties, with Eli Mandel and Jay Macpherson, and, in another way, with Phyllis Webb. Her short-lined stanzas look superficially like those of the breath-counters and Black Mountain grunters who have won and lost so much attention in the past decade, but in fact they are the products of a very tense technical discipline in which the qualities of sound and statement are balanced tightly. It is poetry that — as true poetry must — stays on the page and in the mind when the voice has echoed into silence. Yet there are ways in which Atwood shares a great deal with the poets who came into prominence at the same time, those of her own age like George Bowering and John Newlove, and also the late-blooming Al Purdy, for like them she is conscious of the Canadian land and of the Canadian past in a way the generation of the Fifties, with the notable exception of James Reaney, was not.

But before I enlarge on these aspects of her poetry, I think it is illuminating to consider her first novel, *The Edible Woman*, which appeared in 1969. It is a good novel, articulate, sophisticated, turning phrases and collating images in prose with the same assurance as Atwood does in verse. It is as pungently expressive of a tantalisingly defensive individuality as any of its author's poems.

Some poets who turn novelists show a curiously divided literary personality, and vice verse; one might be excused, for example, for failing to recognize that the same man wrote Roy Fuller's poems and his less well-known novels. But there is none of this kind of division in Margaret Atwood. The capillary links between her poetry, her fiction, her criticism, are many and evident. Indeed, the identity between the poems and *The Edible Woman* is so close that it was with a sense of *déjà vu* that I read *Power Politics* not long after a second reading of the novel, for both concern the cruelties of love, the Proustian impenetrability it encounters, and when I try to think of a quick way of saying what *The Edible Woman* is about, a verse from *The Circle Game* comes immediately to my mind.

> These days we keep
> our weary distances:
> sparring in the vacant spaces
> of peeling rooms

and rented minutes, climbing
all the expected stairs, our voices
abraded with fatigue,
our bodies wary.

The Edible Woman, too, is about the distances and defences between human beings. The distances and defences are necessary — the suggestion is not even skin deep — because human beings are predatory. *The Edible Woman* is a novel about emotional cannibalism.

This is the significance of the title, which also names the central image. The edible woman is a cake shaped like a woman and carefully iced for verisimilitude, which the heroine — Marian McAlpin — eats at the key point of the novel, when she is released from the doggedly normal life she has insisted on pursuing.

Having, cannibalistically, trapped a highly normal young man into a proposal of marriage, Marian has felt herself becoming in turn the victim of his emotional anthropophagy. Seeking escape with a graduate student she meets in a laundromat, she finds that he too, if not exactly a cannibal, is a more insidious kind of parasite, a lamprey battening on her compassion to feed his monstrous self-pity.

Marian's recognition of her situation takes the form of a symbolic neurosis. She finds her throat closing first against meat, as she vividly associates a steak with the living animal. There comes the stage when she peels a carrot and imagines the soundless shriek as it is pulled from the earth. But this point, when she seems doomed to starvation, coincides with the point of climax in her personal relationships, when she runs away from her engagement party to sleep with Duncan, the man from the laundromat, and, having discovered that there is no external solution, no solution in escape, to her problem, returns and bakes the edible woman which, having offered it in vain to her outraged fiancé, she proceeds to eat. She has, of course, eaten herself, and in consuming the artificial "normal" being she tried to become, she is cured.

Such an account does far less than justice to a novel that is full of verbal and situational wit, and equally of ironic observation of human motives; as a comedy of manners the novel has to be read in detail to be completely appreciated. But it does suggest the capable way in which Margaret Atwood uses the element of fantasy which has become so important a component of the New Fiction. She has indeed made Marian's improbable condition extremely plausible, and beside her handling of the fantastic, that of the average novelist seems crude and uncraftsmanly. One has only to compare *The Edible Woman* with the oafish obviousness of the fantasy in a second-rank Richler novel like *Cocksure* to realize this. But Margaret Atwood is a poet, and Richler most clearly is not; evidently, a training in the poetic handling of images and myths gives an enormous advantage to any writer who aspires to fantasy fiction.

The virtuosity of Atwood's achievement becomes completely evident when one considers the other, more mundane aspect of *The Edible Woman*. For it is, among many other things, a social novel of high perceptiveness, and indeed, on second reading, I found the dense patterning of observed detail of human behaviour and of its physical setting perhaps more significant in relation to the writer's poetry than the more obvious "poetic" element in the central fantasy. For here that pained eye of *The Power Game* [*sic*] is at constant agonized play, and the narrator— whether it is Marian herself in the first and last parts of the novel, or the objective third person of the middle section, seems an extension of that lover in the poems whose mind is constantly playing over her emotions and her mental condition, like the "third in the narrow bed" of A.S.J. Tessimond's poem of the Thirties.

Marian moves in a straight world of—to quote the author as quoted on the dust jacket—"ordinary people who make the mistake of thinking they are ordinary." By her occupation as a market researcher, she is kept in constant contact with the vast world of the unswingers (rarely celebrated in contemporary writing) who want nothing more than sheltered normality: the platinum blonde virgins who are more numerous than the sophisticated assume; the young men whose ambitions are bounded by a horizon of suburban retirement; the casualties of the graduate schools, obsessed by the detritus of scholarship; the inhabitants of the world of laundromats and supermarkets. In her own way, and for her own time and place, Atwood has done the kind of thing Jane Austen did for similar people a century ago; not that she is another Jane Austen nor, I imagine, would want to be. Except. . . .

And here one takes a necessary leap back to the poems, for one volume of them extends temporally as well as analogically the web of correspondences that makes Margaret Atwood's imaginary world. In that collection where a modern poet seeks to enter the mind of a pre-Victorian woman, *The Journals of Susanna Moodie*, we are in fact taken back to an English writer of a generation very close to Jane Austen's and a background very similar to hers. The difference is that Susanna Moodie came to Canada, extending thus the mental and physical dimensions of her life, and it is hard to imagine Jane Austen doing that. There is an essential stasis in the Austen viewpoint which was jolted loose by Moodie's experience, and this element of experience corresponds (in both the poetic and the common sense) with that process of dislocation and reassembling which characterizes modern life and, since the Cubists, has characterized more and more modern art and poetry. One senses it at the end of a poem like "The Immigrants" (from *The Journals*):

> my mind is a wide pink map
> across which move year after year
> arrows and dotted lines, further and further,
> people in railway cars

> their heads stuck out of the windows
> at stations, drinking milk or singing,
> their features hidden with beards or shawls
> day and night riding across an ocean of unknown
> land to an unknown land.

In such a poem one is aware of the strong historical sense that pervades the work of Margaret Atwood; the sense of a land and even a human culture that suddenly assumes the quality of vast age, even though its passage from the neolithic to the nuclear has taken little more than three centuries. But one is also aware of a kind of transference which gives much of the spiritual and compelling quality to Atwood's verse. In this case it is the attribution to a woman more than a century ago of a kind of knowledge which only the poet in the present can have; there is an inversion of the situation in one of the poems of *Power Politics*, where that painful perceiver, the experiencing woman of the cycle, sees almost as in a lurid film the progression of feminine experience and herself as the centre of it:

> At first I was given centuries
> to wait in caves, in leather
> tents, knowing you would never come back
>
> Then it speeded up: only
> several years between
> the day you jangled off
> into the mountains, and the day (it was
> spring again) I rose from the embroidery
> frame at the messenger's entrance. . . .
>
> But recently, the bad evenings
> there are only seconds
> between the warning on the radio and the
> explosion; my hands
> don't reach you
>
> and on quieter nights
> you jump up from
> your chair without even touching your dinner
> and I can scarcely kiss you goodbye
> before you run out into the street and they shoot

But there are different transferences in the other poems, extending links between what is perceived and the perceiver, noting that the perception which seems objective can be subjective, that what we see is in ourselves as well as or perhaps rather than outside, and that, in all this, incomprehensible patterns exist. The poet sees the people looking at totem poles as the "other wooden people," and finds life only in the decay of one pole that has fallen on the ground; people handle Eskimo carvings, and when they have finished, the tactile experience has transferred to their hands the shape of the stone. The mental landscapes and the real landscapes interpenetrate, and solid and tangible as objects seem in Atwood's poems, their very materiality can suddenly be seen as a quality of the immaterial, though not dissolving or insubstantial for all that; it remains solidly, visually and sometimes tangibly there, striking its resonances in the mind, which form themselves into the final reality. The reader becomes like the man in "Progressive Insanities of a Pioneer":

> By daylight he resisted.
> He said, disgusted
> with the swamp's clamourings and the outbursts
> of rocks,
> > This is not order
> > but the absence
> > of order.
>
> He was wrong, the unanswering
> forest implied:
>
> > It was
> > an ordered absence

What Margaret Atwood gives us, however, is not exactly an ordered absence; it is rather that ordering of apparent chaos through the search for analogies and correspondences which is the modern poet's historic task.

There is obviously much more to be said of Atwood as a subtle and complex poet, but perhaps the most important thing I have left unsaid she has implied herself in one of the poems of *Power Politics*:

> Beyond truth,
> tenacity: of those
> dwarf trees & mosses,
> hooked into straight rock
> believing the sun's lies & thus
> refuting/gravity
>
> & of this cactus, gathering
> itself together
> against the sand, yes tough
> rind & spikes but doing
> the best it can

Here is not merely an attitude to life that is evident in all Atwood's writings — an attitude appropriate to an age when survival has become the great achievement. Here is also the metaphor that expresses a personal poetic, even a personal ethic. To be (tenacity) is more certain than to know (truth); one does the best one can, shapes one's verses like one's life to the improbable realities of existence ("the sun's lies"), and in this age and place they are the realities that impose a defensive economy, poems close to the rock, poems spiny as cactuses or caltrops.

When I read Atwood's second novel, *Surfacing*, and her topography of the Canadian literary consciousness, *Survival*, (published almost simultaneously in the autumn of 1972), what impressed me was the extent to which these recent books developed in more discursive forms the personal ethic, linked to a personal poetic, which I had found emanating from the poems of her latest book of verse (though assuredly not her last, for so many of her poems have appeared recently in journals that one expects a new volume every season). I found the continuity, the sense of an extraordinarily self-possessed mind at work on an integrated structure of literary architecture, not only interesting and indeed exciting in so far as it concerned Margaret Atwood herself, but equally interesting and exciting as an index to the development of our literary tradition; a generation, even a decade ago, it would be impossible to think of the Canadian literary ambience fostering this kind of confident and sophisticated sensibility.

The titles of Atwood's most recent books are themselves of immense significance. *Surfacing: Survival*. In each case the soft French prefix in place of the hard and arrogant Latin *super*, and in each case a word that suggests coming out to the light with gasping relief. Margaret Atwood's confidence lies in continuation, not in triumph. She has not written — and is unlikely to do so — a book called *Surmounting* or *Surpassing*. "We shall overcome" is a hymn of the American resistance, an underdog's paean to Manifest Destiny; it has no place in the Canadian resistance.

Thus, while *Survival* is certainly a polemical work, it is concerned with elucidating and perhaps eventually changing states of mind rather than with directly provoking action. It is really an application to the whole field of Canadian writing of the ethic worked out in Atwood's poetry, though the ethic is modified: "Beyond truth, / tenacity," indeed, but tenacity becoming a kind of truth, since ultimately it teaches us the reality of our condition; by being resolutely what one is, one comes to know oneself.

This is not evident on first opening the book, for *Survival* is one of those mildly exasperating books in which a brilliant intelligence has been unable to put the brakes on its activity and has run far ahead of the task it has undertaken, so that all readers get more than they bargain for, and the disappointed are probably as numerous as the gratefully surprised. It was planned originally with utilitarian intent as "a teacher's guide for the many new courses in Canadian literature," and vestiges of that intent survive in the lists of recommended texts, "useful books" and research resources which in themselves form a kind of survival course for one's interest as they intrude on the ten essays on aspects of the Canadian literary personae which form the essential substance of the book.

Atwood presents, and supports with much shrewdly chosen evidence, the proposition that our literature is still scarred and misshapen by the state of mind that comes from a colonial relationship. All Canadian attitudes are — she suggests — related to the central fact of victimization imposed or at least attempted, and she lists and grades these attitudes, from *"Position One: To deny the fact that you are a victim"* (which objectively considered is the ultimate in victimization), to *Position Four: To be a creative non-victim,"* the position of those whom Atwood tells "you are able to accept your own experience for what it is, rather than having to distort it to make it correspond with others' versions of it (particularly those of your oppressors)."

Such numerological schemes, even when they are propounded by serious authors (e.g. Jung's Psychological Types and Toynbee's and Spengler's lists of cultures and civilizations) have always a flavour of perverse absurdity, as if the author were aspiring to Pythagorean guruhood, and Margaret Atwood's inclination to carry her propaganda for Canadian literature as a form of national salvation into the schools and lecture rooms suggests that the assumption might not be wholly unjust. But the absurdities of the intelligent are always worth observing for the serious things they reveal, and there is plenty of sound argument, together with a proportion of rather splendid nonsense, in *Survival*.

It is the colonial situation, Margaret Atwood suggests, that has made Canadian writing, whether it has sprung from an attitude of denial or a recognition of experience, a literature of failure; it reflects an attitude to life that aims no higher than survival. The French Canadians recognized this fact and turned it into a self-conscious way of life, with its doctrine of *La Survivance* as the national aim; the English Canadians recognized it explicitly in their pioneer literature and implicitly in their literary identification with animals, whom typically they see as victims, and whose triumph can never be other than survival, since they cannot surmount their natures to be other than animals who live on to face another danger and, if they are fortunate, another survival.

In her argument — which, of course, is much more intricate than this very brief paraphrase could suggest — Atwood has indeed isolated a familiar Christian syndrome. We have no heroes; only martyrs. (Any other people would have written an epic about Dollard at the Long Sault rather than Brébeuf; would have made a folk hero out of Gabriel Dumont, not Louis Riel.) We pride ourselves with puritan smugness on our ironic modesty. With an inverted Pharisaism, we stake what claim to moral superiority we may propose, not on our successes, but on our failures. All this, of course, has been recognized and commented on in a desultory and somewhat embarrassed way by other writers, but none of them, before Atwood, has stoically recognized and gathered these scattered insights, and, in a manner now becoming customary among Canadian critics, has built them into a scheme which provides an alternative, or perhaps a supplement, to those constructed by Northrop Frye and D. G. Jones. The main difference between her and Frye and Jones is that their maps are descriptive, charts for explorers; hers are tactical, tools in a campaign, charts to help us repel a cultural invasion.

In developing a thesis that fits so many facts in our life and literature, Atwood presents a salutory vision of a people who express their nature mainly in struggle against frustration of some kind or another. It is a vision that cannot be accepted in literal totality. There are Canadian writers who do not fit into the pattern in any real way, like Robertson Davies; others, like Purdy and Layton, only partly belong. And preoccupations—even obsessions—with survival and failure are not peculiar to Canadian literature. Survival is the core of a recurrent mythic pattern, exemplified in many literatures and a multitude of works from the *Odyssey* and the *Book of Job* down to such classics of a colonizing (not a colonized) culture as *Robinson Crusoe*, *The Coral Island* and *Kim*. Any number of modern writers in countries of all kinds display the survival-equals-failure syndrome. It dominates most of Orwell's novels, for example, and Orwell showed himself a model Canadian—according to Atwood's scheme—by remarking that every life, viewed from within, is a failure.

Margaret Atwood—I am sure—would answer that it is survival without triumph as the only way out of the failure that is the characteristic Canadian predicament and the characteristic theme of an astonishingly high proportion of Canadian writing. And, even if we must deny universal application to her thesis in Canada, it is impossible to dispute that the poets and novelists of failure and survival are too haunting and too numerous not to give a special flavour to our literature.

Yet criticism is such a Protean activity, so necessarily conditioned by the need for empathic understanding between the critic and every single author he discusses, that no critical map of the literary terrain of a country or a time can be accepted as more than a frame of reference, a usable hypothesis, at least in so far as we are seeking enlightenment in the books and authors which are its nominal subjects. Once we recognize that criticism is as much about the critic as it is about what he criticizes, we realize that even our best Canadian critic, when he is not directly reacting to a book or a poem, is merely offering an apparatus constructed so subtly that in itself it is a work of literary artifice, relevant mainly to the creativity of Northrop Frye. In the same way, the prime importance of *Survival* to the reader—if not necessarily to the writer—is perhaps not what it says about Canadian books, much of which we can learn in other places, but the fact that it develops in another form the themes and insights that have emerged from Atwood's practice of poetry.

For when we read *Survival*, when we seek to distil the spirit that inspires it, we go down below the polemics, and come to a mental toughness and resilience that resembles the dwarf trees of Atwood's poem in all their predictable tenacity; we come to a defensive strength very much like that of "this cactus, gathering / itself together / against the sand," and this tenacity, this defensive strength are, in Atwood's vision, the reality one begins by recognizing. But beyond this recognition of one's place, one's predicament, beyond the mere will to continue there exists the journey of self-discovery that begins at the basic levels. Recognition, self-exploration, growth. This is the pattern of hope that at the end of *Survival* Margaret Atwood presents for Canadian literature, and, through its literature, for the awareness and the life of the Canadian people. Let me quote two passages:

> I'm not saying that all writing should be "experimental," or that all writing should be "political." But the fact that English Canadian writers are beginning to voice their own predicament consciously, as French Canadian writers have been doing for a decade, is worth mentioning. For both groups, this "voicing" is both an exploratory plunge into their own tradition and a departure from it; and for both groups the voicing would have been unimaginable twenty years ago. . . .

> The tone of Canadian literature as a whole is, of course, the dark background: a reader must face the fact that Canadian literature is undeniably sombre and negative, and that this to a large extent is both a reflection and a chosen definition of the natural sensibility. . . . When I discovered the shape of the national tradition I was depressed, and it's obvious why: it's a fairly tough tradition to be saddled with, to have to come to terms with. But I was exhilarated too: having bleak ground under your feet is better than having no ground at all. Any map is better than no map as long as it is accurate, and knowing your starting points and your frame of reference is better than being suspended in the void.

And let me end with the two questions that Margaret Atwood leaves to her readers: Have we survived? If so, what happens *after* Survival?

One could dip through *Survival* picking many other passages that have roughly the same intent as these: what seems to me important about them is that they present the process of thought out of which *Survival* developed as a kind of journey of exploration and realization; an attempt to come to terms with the reality of the writer's environment, or rather the reality of her culture, which means also the reality of herself. And once that reality is established, once the darkness has been recognized and the eyes have become accustomed to it, then, as Margaret Atwood also says, you can see the "points of light — a red flower, or a small fire, or a human figure . . . in contrast to their surroundings: their dark background sets them off and gives them meaning in a way that the bright one would not."

Thus, in *Survival*, we meet, stated in expository terms (and with a personal narrative implied in the exposition) the ideas we have already absorbed osmotically from the reading of her verse, and we recognize that in part at least *Survival* is a work of self-examination, an attempt to reduce to rational terms — almost to homiletic terms — the emotions, the insights which Margaret Atwood had already expressed metaphorically in the poems and in *The Edible Woman.*

It is with this almost Buddhistically self-examinatory inclination of Atwood's in mind that we have to consider her second novel, *Survival* [*sic*]. In every way — complexity of action, range of characters, variety of themes, use of metaphor and fantasy — it is a much sparser and more concentrated book than her first novel, *The Edible Woman*; more than ever one is reminded of the "cactus, gathering / itself together / against the sand. . . ." The large screen of urban Canada, with its obvious possibilities of farce and caricature, is abandoned; so is the Gothic fantasy with which the theme of emotional cannibalism is enacted in the earlier novel. The social criticism is less diffuse, more pointed. And thematically, there is a surface resemblance between *Surfacing* and *Survival* at which the reader is tempted to grasp, perhaps at his peril.

Certainly *Surfacing* concerns survival, and like the book *Survival*, it is concerned with Canadian victims to such an extent that one can identify among its fauna a majority of the types of victim described therein. As major characters, or drifting but ominous shadows, there appear victim animals (a heron and some fish and frogs), victim Indians (it is too far south for victim Eskimos), victim sham pioneers (it is too late in history for real ones), victim children, victim artists (the chapter heading "The Paralyzed Artist" in *Survival* perfectly describes Joe the frustrated potter in *Surfacing*), victim women and victim French Canadians. That leaves out victim explorers, victim immigrants, victim heroes and victim jail-breakers, all featured in *Survival*, but it may be a point in the novel that the narrator contains all these missing roles, since she is an explorer of her own past, she is a migrant into a new self, she is as much a heroine — and a martyred one — as the novel admits, and she is breaking the jail of her imprisoned spirit.

A further link between *Survival* and *Surfacing* is, of course, the fact that in both books Canada is the victim of a sickness of colonialism, symbolized in the first paragraph of the novel by the white birches which are dying, as the elms have already died, by a disease that is "spreading from the south." That disease is personified by the Americans who are ravaging the Canadian wilderness, but its pervasiveness is only revealed to us completely when we realize that the heron whose death is central to the action has been wantonly killed, not by Americans, but by Canadians who have become indistinguishable from Americans.

One can overstress these didactic elements which *Surfacing* has obviously absorbed from the fact that, round about the same time, Atwood was developing the ideas she expounded in *Survival*. One might invert the comparison and suggest that certain personal elements in *Survival* are there because of the fictional preoccupations that carried over from the writing of *Surfacing*. For, like *The Edible Woman, Surfacing* is the account of a *rite de passage*; it is a novel of self-realization, hence of life-realization. Yet it also appears to possess what has so far missed the critics — at least those I have heard discussing the book with a solemnity I find it hard to associate with the Margaret Atwood I know — an element of self-criticism, almost of self-mockery. But let me leave that point while I sketch out the general scheme of *Surfacing*.

The narrator is a young woman who has heard of the disappearance of her botanist father from his cabin on a lake somewhere in the Shield country, and who goes there with three companions — her lover Joe and two self-styled *émancipés*, David and Anna. It is a journey into her past, for she has not been to the lake for nine years and has been estranged from her parents — except for visiting her dying mother in hospital — for that long; it is also a journey, though she does not realize this to begin with, into her real self. She is significantly nameless; she names the other characters, and they name each other, but all of them refer to her only as "you." She is a failed painter, as Joe is a failed potter, David a failed rebel and Anna a failed wife.

"I" is indeed in the state of inner atrophy which Marian reaches in *The Edible Woman* when she loses the power to eat; if Marian cannot assimilate physical food, "I" cannot absorb or generate feeling. She describes herself as being nothing but a head, untouched and untouching. And yet, through the events that explode out of her return to the scene of her childhood, she is able to recover herself as a whole being.

It is a process of surfacing, but before that of submersion. The metaphors of drowning and near-drowning recur constantly. Her brother is almost drowned as a child; her father, she finally discovers, had drowned accidentally in searching for Indian cliff paintings on the rock walls that fall sheer into the lake; her own point of crisis occurs when, diving in an attempt to locate the paintings, she encounters the floating corpse of her father, weighted down by his camera. The surfacing in this instance becomes almost literally a rising from death into life.

By this time other realizations have surfaced in the narrator's mind: about her childhood as she has relived it through returning to the lake island, reshaping it and re-ordering the characters nearer to true relationships as she calls it up into memory; about her companions whose pose of liberation is reduced to a cluster of behavioural clichés borrowed from the Americans they pretend to despise; about the pollution of every kind that man takes with himself into the wilderness; above all about that monstrous indifference to the suffering of other living beings which echoes through Atwood's poems as the greatest of human crimes. Faced with the dead heron:

> I felt a sickening complicity, sticky as glue, blood on my hands, as though I had been there and watched without saying No or doing anything to stop it: one of the silent guarded faces in the crowd. The

trouble some people have being German, I thought, I have being human. In a way it was stupid to be more disturbed by a dead bird than by those other things, the wars and riots and the massacres in the newspapers. But for the wars and riots there was always an explanation, people wrote books about them saying why they happened: the death of the heron was causeless, undiluted.

"I" must shed all she has acquired, must unlearn adulthood, must return through her childhood and beyond humanity, become like the victim animals, as she is in the crucial chapter of the book when, having fled from her companions and allowed them to depart, she lives naked on the island, surviving like a beast on wild roots and mushrooms, until the delirium that is panic in a dual sense passes away from her. Then she returns, like Marian after she has eaten the cake that is her surrogate self in *The Edible Woman*, to a consciousness beyond beasthood, beyond the animistic world of primitives and children. The gods have departed; she is alone, with the child she now wants growing in her womb. "The lake is quiet, the trees surround me, asking and giving nothing." One senses, as the novel ends, that benign indifference of the universe of which Camus speaks. There is not [sic] hope; the narrator has gone beyond that recourse of the weak. But there is sanity. Doug Fetherling has reproached me with not appreciating the mystical in Atwood. But I find no mysticism here, any more than I find it in the purest, most intellectual forms of Buddhism. What I do find, as I find in that true Buddhism, is a courageous coming into the light of reality.

So there is sanity in this ending, and there is no mockery in it, of self or of other. Yet at the same time there is mockery in all that part of *Surfacing* where "I" is still that detached observing head which feels nothing and has prejudices but no passions. "I," as head, detects with a bitter satiric eye the shams of her companions, the fact that under their anti-American skins they are Americans. But "I" as ultimate narrator, who we must assume to be "I" in the form she takes in the final sane pages of *Surfacing*, and who is perhaps nearer to the author than the unregenerate "I," implicitly mocks her own attempt to find a nationality that will fit a villainy which is universal where man survives. And in so doing she casts an ironically oblique light on *Survival* itself, which is indeed a work with a villain, colonialism.

So, if we consider Atwood's most recent books, *Survival* and *Surfacing*, and observe them in relation to her poems and especially to *Power Politics*, we see the versatility with which her intelligence plays over the horizons of her perceptions. In the poems these perceptions are expressed with metaphorical tightness and conciseness; they become sharp goads to the feelings. In the essays that form *Survival* they are transformed into discursive nets that entrap the reason. In *Surfacing*, the perceptions are projected in a strange winter light of feeling, until, passing through the destructive element of satire, they are etched with the lineaments of myth.

No other writer in Canada of Margaret Atwood's generation has so wide a command of the resources of literature, so telling a restraint in their use.

(1974)

Breaking the Circle [*The Circle Game, Survival, The Journals of Susanna Moodie, The Animals in That Country*, and *Surfacing*]   Rosemary Sullivan*

Poets and critics, in their search for a usable Canadian tradition, centre their discussions around two themes: history and geography. Their desire to define a distinctive Canadian tradition expresses itself as a nostalgia for history and for a unique sense of place, so that they often seem to be advocating a "village pump" school of literature. But one must distinguish between sociology and mythology. The creation of a usable past, as Eli Mandel has written, is really the creation of a mythology; geography becomes the core of a mythic, rather than an historical, reality and the poem's centre becomes a place remote from the poet's natural country.[1] This may be why, in many Canadian poems, the poet-geographer becomes archaeologist and the poet-historian becomes mythographer; the themes of place (and for that matter, displacement), lead by inevitable stages to timeless myths and to the possibility that all places are one place. At its most complex, the quest for myth becomes anti-historical — what Robert Kroetsch has called the impulse to decreation, breaking down the highly structured myths of history and breaking back into prehistorical realities.

Margaret Atwood is one of a young generation of poets in Canada who insist that a poet must be grounded in his or her own culture. Dennis Lee is most radical in insisting that poets write out of a civic space and Atwood clearly believes that the poet speaks simultaneously from a private and cultural or civic consciousness. It would seem that Canadian poetry has found its Whitman, not in any single poet but in a generation of writers who believe (as Van Wyck Brooks said of Whitman), that the function of the poet in "the most radical and primitive sense of the word . . . is to give a nation a certain focal center in the consciousness of its own character." The "focal center" of Atwood's work is complex. It functions as a psychological, cultural, and mythic symbol, and she develops it at some length in "The Circle Game," the title poem of her first book. Children are

*From *Malahat Review: Margaret Atwood: A Symposium*, edited by Linda Sandler, no. 41 (January 1977):30–41 [out of print]. Reprinted by permission of the author.

playing ring-around-the-rosie in what seems a whimsical game, but as the poetic image dissolves into symbol, the game becomes a tranced ritual of exclusion; the children are circumscribing reality, laying foundations for those garrisons of the mind that structure adult perceptions. The children are juxtaposed to lovers who are playing the circle game, withdrawing into a private fantasy or projecting a private reality. The circle game is a game involving barriers. The players set up artificial enclosures, fortresses, to guard a familiar world and exclude alien or inconvenient emissaries from other worlds. And since the circle game is a game of ritual exclusion, it can be played with psychological barriers, with language and with cultural myths. Atwood, of course, rejects the theory that language is the only key to the articulations and conduct of the mind, or the only instrument of knowledge. In cultural terms, the circle game defines the garrison mentality that preoccupies Atwood, and the modern concept for the natural world. The circle game sets up a counter-impulse throughout her work—an impulse to break out of the circle. This means unleashing the anarchic impulse to crack open all form, formula and language:

> I want to break
> these bones, your prisoning rhythms
> > > (winter,
> > > > summer)
> all the glass cases,
>
> erase all maps,
> crack the protecting
> eggshell of your turning
> singing children:
>
> I want the circle
> broken.

The circle game is a metaphor for the notion of order.[2] Atwood's variations on the theme of anarchy are hardly unique—they derive from a romantic tradition which places high value on psychic truth. Chaos, psychic chaos in particular, is highly esteemed because, once unleashed, it dissolves the profane self and alters the sensibility. What makes Atwood's response to this tradition interesting is her cultural context, her almost cynical honesty and her artistic solutions.

Atwood is often described as a writer with an acute historical sense, but, in fact, she is acutely anti-historical because she rejects the discriminations that an historical sense implies. *Survival*, her thematic guide to Canadian literature, is a travesty of history. Atwood is concerned with the relation between national consciousness and the literary imagination and *Survival* is a fascinating attempt to define cultural mythology. Her thesis—that every culture has a central symbol that functions like a code of beliefs—derives from a theory proposed by Northrop Frye. Frye suggests that "in every age there is a structure of ideas, images, beliefs, assumptions, anxieties, and hopes which express the view of man's situation and destiny generally held at that time. . . ."[3] Atwood contends rather audaciously that this syndrome can be evoked by a single symbol, which, in Canada, is the now infamous concept of *Survival*.

As cultural history *Survival* fails. But it does define a collective myth. Atwood seems to be working from George Steiner's premise that the past rules us by means of highly selective myths, which are imprinted, almost like genetic information, on our sensibilities. *Survival* is a cultural manifesto which exposes one of Canada's most self-destructive myths. The Survival mentality explored in the book is a colonial mentality—the nation cannot act because it sees itself as *acted upon*, it accepts a passive role and, with perverse narcissism, perpetuates it. Colonialism becomes a posture, a substitute for morality, a religion.

One of Atwood's most fascinating books of poems is *The Journals of Susanna Moodie*, based on the writings of that eminent pioneer. Moodie provides Atwood with a persona and a way of exploring the moral and psychological problems of the colonial situation. Atwood tends toward oversimplification, and there is often a quality of naive dogmatism in her writing, but *Journals* is a documentary narrative and its premise is that a personal confrontation with history provides insight into, perhaps even release from, historical process.

Moodie, as immigrant, serves Atwood as a Canadian archetype. As Atwood says in her "Afterword," "We are all immigrants to this place even if we were born here: the country is too big for anyone to inhabit completely, and in the parts unknown to us we move in fear, exiles and invaders." The immigrants demand that the place be responsive, have a human "face," and they try to exclude everything "outside the circle / they draw by their closed senses." This is the theme of "Disembarking at Quebec":

> Is it my clothes, my way of walking,
> the things I carry in my hand
> —a book, a bag with knitting—
> the incongruous pink of my shawl
>
> this space cannot hear
>
> or is it my own lack
> of conviction which makes
> these vistas of desolation, . . .
>
> The moving water will not show me
> my reflection.
>
> The rocks ignore.

I am a word
in a foreign language.

The wilderness refuses to comply with Moodie's expectations — this is the central paradox of settlement. North America began, as Leslie Fiedler once wrote, as an idea in the mind of Europe. But the process of accommodating that idea to reality was not the same in Canada as in the United States, because Canada's cultural inception rests on the premise that you cannot abdicate from history. Canada deliberately, selfconsciously, grafted two sensibilities together. In Atwood's reading of history, however, the graft never happened. The old world order could not accommodate the experience of Canada, and Moodie could not have discovered the code of a new reality without suffering a violent dislocation of her sensibility. This is what Moodie's confrontation with the wilderness is all about:

We left behind one by one
the cities rotting with cholera,
one by one our civilized
distinctions

and entered a large darkness.

It was our own
ignorance we entered.

I have not come out yet

My brain gropes nervous
tentacles in the night, sends out
fears hairy as bears, . . .
I need wolf's eyes to see
the truth.

I refuse to look in a mirror.

Whether the wilderness is
real or not
depends on who lives there.

To have wolf's eyes, is to penetrate the wilderness. Moodie fails. "There was something they almost taught me / I came away not having learned," she says. The penalty of failure is a garrison mentality. The operative myth of American literature is the frontier and its correlative, the open road, but in Canadian literature the frontier is all around us — we are encircled. And we respond to this "huge, unthinking, menacing, and formidable physical setting," as Northrop Frye calls it,[4] by retreating into the circle game. If the historical Moodie does not escape this failure, her literary archetype does. Moodie is resurrected as the spirit of the land, and according to Atwood, she embodies the violent duality of Canada's soul, where nature and culture "coexist" as hostile kingdoms, mutually subversive.

The nightmarish experience of being invaded by the wilderness is something that recurs in Atwood's work, in "Progressive Insanities of a Pioneer," in *Surfacing*, and here, in "The Planters":

> I see them; I know
> none of them believe they are here.
> They deny the ground they stand on,
>
> pretend this dirt is the future.
> And they are right. If they let go
> of that illusion solid to them as a shovel,
>
> open their eyes even for a moment
> to these trees, in this particular sun
> they would be surrounded, stormed, broken
>
> in upon by branches, roots, tendrils, the dark
> side of light
> as I am.

To know the wilderness is to be invaded by chaos. It is to understand, that the ordered social world coexists with an alien order. But Atwood's personae are always trying to impose order on nature. In "Progressive Insanities of a Pioneer," human conceit knows no bounds:

> He stood, a point
> on a sheet of green paper
> proclaiming himself the centre,
>
> with no walls, no borders
> anywhere; the sky no height
> above him, totally un-
> enclosed
> and shouted:
>
> Let me out!
> (*The Animals in That Country*)

This egocentrism will not do. There must be another order: "something not lost or hidden / but just not found yet." The desire to transcend the self sometimes leads to mysticism. In *Surfacing* it leads to a wilderness myth.

Where would one go to recover the wilderness now? Westward, of course, and Canadian writers are still going west. The journey westward is a fantasy of beginnings, it is the active expression of an impulse to get out of history. "Migration: C.P.R." records this journey:

> Escaping from allegories
> in the misty east, where inherited events
> barnacle on the mind; . . .
>
> and language is the law
>
> we ran west
>
> wanting
> a place of absolute
> unformed beginning.

The western myth does not work for Atwood's traveller — not just because the mounties got there first, but because the traveller cannot get outside the human world. Everything is stamped, named, imposed upon by metaphor: "and even the mountains / at the approach, were / conical, iconic." What Atwood is protesting is the humanization of the world — nature has become *sociable*, an aspect of culture. Her pilgrim, however, wants to see the world in its first, prehistoric, form. She wants to get back to the beginning, to "Mile Zero." She doesn't make it, but the persona of Atwood's novel, *Surfacing*, does.

In *Surfacing*, an unnamed narrator searches the wilderness of Northern Quebec for her father, a botanist, who has been reported missing. She is trying to re-establish contact with her past and to find a way of living in the present. This means that she must come to terms with a failed love affair and an abortion; she must revaluate all her cultural assumptions. In *Surfacing*, Atwood is challenging a whole way of seeing, a way of relating to nature. Charles Olson saw the issue with clarity: "It comes to this: the use of a man by himself and thus by others, lies in how he conceives his relation to nature, that force to which he owes his somewhat small existence." Atwood's subject is the polarization of man and nature that results from the modern compulsion to explain and to master nature. Language is one of the tools we use to achieve this mastery; we set ourselves, the perceiving subjects, apart from nature, the perceived object. The Cartesian logic of our language dictates, not only a split between subject and object, but the superior position of the subject — nature, in other words, is *acted upon*, it is our colony. Atwood's persona is intuitively seeking another code of language, another kind of vision. It is not surprising that she should explore North American Indian culture; that she should contrast technological man's alienation from nature with the primitive's mythical participation in nature.

We are close to the motivating impulses of the novel. The heroine rejects the husked and literal layers of contemporary consciousness, and tries to recover an earlier, more primitive mentality. In so doing she enacts a radical myth of renewal: she is plunged into total psychic chaos, which is a gateway to a sacred dimension, a primordial time of beginning. The implications of breaking the circle begin to emerge: anarchy leads us to the mythic theme of rebirth.

Atwood stages the return to "Mile Zero" with skill. Searching through her father's papers, the narrator finds some sketches of Indian rock paintings. Following her father's maps, she retraces his archaeological explorations. It is while she is diving in the lake, looking for underwater rock paintings, that she finds her father's bloated corpse:

> Pale green, then darkness, layer after layer, deeper than before, sea-bottom; the water seemed to have thickened, in it pinprick lights flicked and darted, red and blue, yellow and white. . . .
>
> It was there but it wasn't a painting, it wasn't on the rock. It was below me, drifting towards me from the furthest level where there was no life, a dark oval trailing limbs. It was blurred but it had eyes, they were open, it was something I knew about, a dead thing, it was dead. (p. 142)

Drifting in its watery element, the corpse reminds her of another dead thing, the foetus she aborted. Now, for the first time, she acknowledges that she was responsible for the death of something that was living. The lake is a fluid, silent world. Language sets up no barriers here, and it seems to her that this is her father's "message"; he has led her toward a vision bequeathed by gods "unacknowledged or forgotten," shown her a way of seeing the world "after the failure of logic."

Breaking with logic is breaking the circle game. It means being invaded by chaos and terror: "logic is a wall, I built it, on the other side is terror" (p. 174). But if you survive the experience of psychic chaos, the gods of the underworld may admit you to their sacred order. The narrator prepares herself by destroying the objects associated with her past by sacrificing human artifacts to the gods: "Everything from history must be eliminated." Burning a family album, she burns her identification with her dead parents in order to create herself. The ritual preparation, whether by coincidence or intent, corresponds with the stages of shamanic initiation outlined by Mircea Eliade in his study, *Shamanism: Archaic Techniques of Ecstasy.*[5] Shamanism, as described by Eliade, is a process of induction into the sacred. Whoever aspires to be shaman must go through a period of psychic isolation in which the mind swings between extremes of ecstasy and madness, and the aim of which is transformation from the human state. The prescribed rituals are outlined by Eliade and Atwood adapts these to her own end. They follow a precise psychological order: retreat to the bush—symbol of the beyond—to a kind of larval existence (the physical and psychic regression of Atwood's character); prohibitions as to foods, with certain objects and actions taboo (in her madness, the narrator intuits rules which dictate appropriate foods, permissible areas; the fasting induces hallucinatory states); hypnotic sleeping (the narrator builds a lair and sleeps in a position simulating a larval state); secret language (the narrator regresses to non-verbal communication); dismemberment or cleansing of the body in symbolic death (the narrator purges her "false body" in the lake water); spirit guides assist the aspirant in his quest for resurrection (the images of the miraculous double woman and the god with horns). This ritual accounts for the mythic quality of the latter part of the book. The reader has a double vision: here is both madness and a mystic's initiation rite, and the process simulates death and resurrection. The goal is perfect communion with nature in order to regain that lost innocence when man did not know death and understood the language of animals. After a period of fasting and waiting she has her vision, and the analogies with the under-water-world are obvious:

> Slowly I retrace the trail. Something has happened to my eyes, my feet are released, they alternate, several inches from the ground. I'm ice-clear, transparent, my bones and the child inside me showing through the green webs of my flesh, the ribs are shadows, the muscles jelly, the trees are like this too, they shimmer, their cores glow through the wood and bark.
>
> The forest leaps upward, enormous, the way it was before they cut it, columns of sunlight frozen; the boulders float, melt, everything is made of water, even the rocks. In one of the languages there are no nouns, only verbs held for a longer moment.
>
> The animals have no need for speech, why talk when you are a word
>
> I lean against a tree, I am a tree leaning
>
> I break out again into the bright sun and crumple, head against the ground
>
> I am not an animal or a tree, I am the thing in which the trees and animals move and grow, I am a place (p. 181)

In her experience of mystical translucency, the narrator sees herself as part of an evolving continuum, a world of verbs and chemical processes. The barriers between outer and inner worlds dissolve; the gulf between phenomenon and name, thing and thought is closed. This world, like the world of the lake, is silent. There are no nouns, no barriers between self and not-self.

The linguist Benjamin Whorf, in an essay called "Language and Logic," suggests that we tend to "cut up and organize the spread and flow of events . . . not because nature is segmented," but because our language prescribes it.[6] Our language "behaves" as if the universe were "a collection of rather distinct objects and events, corresponding to words." A language made up entirely of verbs (the language of the Nootka of Vancouver Island, for example) does not permit you to distinguish between yourself and your world; you and your world are part of a process, and anthropocentrism is out of the question. Atwood's narrator expresses something similar when she says, "I lean against a tree, I am a tree leaning," and this is presumably the kind of awareness Susanna Moodie saw in the eyes of the wolf.

When the wilderness at last reveals itself to Atwood's heroine, it has the shape of a wolf: "it gazes at me for a time with its yellow eyes, wolf's eyes, depthless but lambent as the eyes of animals seen at night in the car headlights." But now she is on the animals' home ground. She had expected a message, some revelation to take back with her, but the wolf's eyes are "reflectors," they reveal nothing: "It does not approve of me or disapprove of me, it tells me it has nothing to tell me, only the fact of itself."

The question is, can these insights be integrated with normal consciousness. The answer is no. There is no bridge from this experience into the narrative present, and in the penultimate chapter, the narrator abandons her "questionable" gods:

> No gods to help me now, they're questionable once more, theoretical as Jesus. They've receded, back to the past, inside the skull, is it the same place. They'll never appear to me again, I can't afford it; from now on I'll have to live in the usual way, defining them by their absence; and love by its failures, power by its loss, its renunciation. I regret them; but they give only one kind of truth, one hand.
>
> No total salvation, resurrection. . . . (p. 189)

The narrator has come a long way toward healing herself. She has come to terms with her past and with her posture of defencelessness: "This above all, to refuse to be a victim." She seems to have recognized that she cannot abdicate from history, or from society. But she has not broken the circle because she has not achieved spiritual regeneration.

What has gone wrong? In the first place, Atwood has settled for a ghost story:

> *Surfacing* is a ghost story which follows a certain formula. The heroine . . . is obsessed with finding the ghost, but once she's found it she's released from that obsession. The point is, my character can see the ghosts but they can't see her. This is important in ghostlore, because it means that she can't enter the world of the dead. She realizes, OK, I've learned something. Now I have to make my own life.[7]

What she has gained is expressed in negative terms: she has been released from an obsession. It is true that ghost stories, happy ones at least, end in exorcisms. But Atwood's decision to write a ghost story might have been a mistake. I feel that Atwood has not taken enough risk; she has not explored the potential of her own vision.

One problem is that Atwood's language fails her. Even in moments of intense mystical perception, her language is the language of logic. She does not experiment with language, she does not go far enough. This could be the problem of an analytic imagination seeking lyrical expression, or it could be that Atwood has chosen the stance of ironic deflation. We could read the novel as a contemporary satire on the fantasy of beginning again — the narrator ends by reaffirming history, collectivity, culture. But is this what actually happens? Or are we trapped at the end of the novel in the perfect circle of the self, caught in the heresy that "the mind is its own place"? Atwood leaves her character in the ironic world and even though her intent seems to have been to expose the perfect circle of the mind as demonic, we end in the tautology of self. At the novel's conclusion, the narrator is returned to the present, where regeneration seems possible. Yet there is a terrifying starkness to this present. The novel recovers no symbolism or new language informing and enriching the present, no sense of continuity with the mythological roots of the past, no lasting intuition from the momentary healing of the division between self and nature; the sacred and the profane, the narrator finds, are mutually exclusive. Nature and culture, she finds, are permanently opposed. There is an evasion implicit in the attempt to disengage oneself from history, from the inheritance of human culture, and while this seemed to be what Atwood was criticizing, the paradoxical result may in fact be that this is precisely what her narrator settles for. The quest for insight in the novel has been pursued by a process of decreation, a disengagement from time, from history, from language, but no bridge to re-engagement has been discovered. The myth of decreation, which seemed so rich in potential, has left us in ground zero, in a terrifying solitude in the absence of meaning. We have reverted to an absolute literalness where the individual must start again from nothing, essentially alone. Atwood has chosen to reflect one of the most evasive postures of our contemporary culture. The fear of the rigidifying implications of all circle games is so encompassing, that often commitment can be made only to the solitary occasion and the single self. The effect is a radical alienation from continuity, from tradition, from the inheritance of meaning stored in language, from the metaphor of immortality. Paradoxically, it may prove that this alienation is in fact the most entrapping of the circle games. Atwood's attempt to break out of the circle may end in a break from meaning.

Consequently this is an alienated book. There is no release here from the burden of the self, no commitment to a sustaining other that is meaningful, and the inability to postulate an acceptable definition of otherness, community, may even call into question the cultural affirmation of the novel. It could be argued that the heroine's personal limitations determine the outcome of the novel. Atwood has written with marvelous equivocation:

> The ending is ambiguous. People say to me, what is she going to do next? Will she marry Joe? I don't know what she's going to do next. I fill in what I know.
>
> Ideas in fiction are closer to algebra than you would think. What the heroine does at the end of *Surfacing* results from taking a hypothesis

and pushing it as far as it goes. What happens when you identify with animals?[8]

But a novel is not a formula. The heroine's visionary experience of nature *might* have proved the basis for a radical revision of her perception of the relation of self to other and to community as well. Perhaps the only way to break the circle game is through a true understanding of persons in relation. How to become human is an ethical question the novel sets itself, and Atwood's ironies are a form of artistic evasion of that question. The narcissism of the circle game claims the narrator, and confines Atwood herself in its prisoning rhythms. We have yet to see the circle effectively broken.

Notes

1. Eli Mandel, "Modern Canadian Poetry," *Twentieth Century Literature* Vol. 16 (1970), pp. 175–183.

2. For study of the historical precedents of this metaphor, see Marjorie Hope Nicolson, *The Breaking of the Circle: Studies of the Effect of the "New Science" on Seventeenth Century Poetry* (New York: Columbia University Press, 1960).

3. Northrop Frye, *The Modern Century* (Toronto: Oxford University Press), pp. 105–6.

4. Northrop Frye, *The Bush Garden* (Toronto: Anansi Press, 1971), p. 225.

5. Mircea Eliade, *Shamanism: Archaic Techniques of Ecstasy*, tr. William Trask (Princeton University Press, 1964), pp. 64, 288. In a discussion on Atwood at ACUTE, 1975, Germain[e] Warkentin was the first to point out the relevance of Eliade to *Surfacing* and suggested that the language metaphors be explored.

6. See *Selected Writings of Benjamin Lee Whorf*, ed. John B. Carroll (M.I.T. Press, 1956), pp. 240–44.

7. See the interview in this issue. [Linda Sandler, "Interview with Margaret Atwood," *Malahat: Atwood*, 7–27, quoted 11.]

8. Ibid. [Sandler, "Interview," quoted 12.]

Atwood Gothic [*You Are Happy, Surfacing, Survival, The Animals in That Country, The Circle Game*, and *Power Politics*]

Eli Mandel*

Margaret Atwood's *You Are Happy* offers not only her usual poetic transformations, identifications, witch-woman figures, animal-men, and photograph-poems but also an intriguing set of "Tricks with Mirrors." It is the mirror poems that suggest, more pointedly than usual in her work,

*From *Another Time* (Erin, Ontario: Press Porcepic Ltd., 1977), 137–45; in *Malahat Review: Margaret Atwood: A Symposium*, edited by Linda Sandler, no. 41 (January 1977): 165–74 [out of print]. Reprinted by permission of the author.

questions about duplicity and reflexiveness — concerns quite different from apparently clear and accessible social comment. She writes:

> Don't assume it is passive
> or easy, this clarity
>
> with which I give you yourself.
> Consider what restraint it
>
> takes. . . .
>
> It is not a trick either,
> it is a craft:
>
> mirrors are crafty.
>
> ....
>
> You don't like these metaphors.
> All right:
>
> Perhaps I am not a mirror.
> Perhaps I am a pool.
>
> Think about pools.
>
> (pp. 26–27)

Quite likely the speaker of the poem is meant to be taken as a lover; certainly she speaks to a Narcissus gazing at her as if she were a mirror; and to hear in the voice the artist's warning about craftiness may seem perverse, though the suggestion of allegory is so tempting in Atwood's works it is difficult to resist. In any event, the mirror voice does present ambiguous possibilities that call to mind apparently contradictory qualities in Atwood's writing: clarity and accessibility, certainly, combined with extraordinary deftness in manipulating contemporary modes of speech and image, and a compelling toughmindedness, a ruthless unsentimentality, which is somehow liberating rather than cynically enclosing. These modes and attitudes point to social concerns, but one senses that as surface qualities these may be concealing quite different interests. It is not my intention to deny the obvious, that she does handle with force and insight important contemporary social metaphors: the politics of love and self, the mystification of experience, woman as prisoner of the mind police, social institutions as models of the police state, the schizophrenic journey toward health, and so on. But the oracular qualities of her work, no doubt as attractive as social commentary to her readers, deserve more extended commentary than they have received. I am thinking of the gothic elements of her novels, her consistent and obsessive use of reduplicating images, and her totemic animal imagery.

Margaret Atwood's comment, in a conversation with Graeme Gibson, that *Surfacing* "is a ghost story" provides the point of departure for more than one commentary on her work. Less often noticed is the special form of ghost story Atwood employs, the story in *Journals of Susanna Moodie*, for example. Mrs. Moodie appears to Atwood, we are told, in a dream, later manifesting herself to the poet "as a mad-looking and very elderly lady"; the poems take her "through an estranged old age, into death and beyond" (p. 63). That makes her a ghost in the last poem, "A Bus Along St. Clair: December," where she tells us:

> I am the old woman
> sitting across from you on the bus,
> her shoulders drawn up like a shawl;
> out of her eyes come secret
> hatpins, destroying
> the walls, the ceiling
>
> (p. 61)

Her earthly life, portrayed in the earlier poems, involves a pattern not unlike the heroine's journey into the backwoods in *Surfacing*: a landing on a seashore apparently occupied by dancing sandflies, a pathway into a forest, confrontation with a wolfman and other animals, men in masks, deaths of children, including a drowning, sinister plants. Gothic tale is a better name than ghost story for this form, in which the chief element is the threat to a maiden, a young girl, a woman. In a well-known passage, Leslie Fiedler, (allegorizing like mad, incidentally), comments on the chief features of the form, its motifs:

> Chief of the gothic symbols is, of course, the Maiden in flight. . . . Not the violation or death which sets such a flight in motion, but the flight itself figures forth the essential meaning of the anti-bourgeois gothic, for which the girl on the run and her pursuer become only alternate versions of the same plight. Neither can come to rest before the other — for each is the projection of his opposite . . . actors in a drama which depends on both for its significance. Reinforcing the meaning . . . is the haunted countryside, and especially the haunted castle or abbey which rises in its midst, and in whose dark passages and cavernous apartments the chase reaches its climax.[1]

Substitute forest for haunted castle, and think of the ghosts of Mrs. Radcliffe's *The Italian*, and the ghost story or gothic form of an Atwood poem or novel begins to take shape. Obviously, it is richly suggestive of a variety of dark threats, either psychological or hidden in the social structure. Atwood's own political and social commentary on Canadian imagination employs, with superb wit and skill, a victor/victim pattern (the haunted victim, the haunted persecutor, perhaps?) to outline not only an endlessly repeated pattern, but a theory of colonialism, that is, victimization. We see the possibilities: if *Surfacing* presents itself as political and social criticism disguised as ghost story, could it be that *Survival* takes its unusual power precisely from the fact that it is a ghost story disguised as politics and criticism?

A further elaboration is suggested by Ellen Moers' comments in the chapter of *Literary Women* called "The Female Gothic": Gothic, says Moers, is writing that "has to do with fear," writing in which "fantasy predominates over reality, the strange over the commonplace, and the supernatural over the natural, with one definite auctorial intent: to scare. Not, that is, to reach down into the depths of the soul and purge it with pity and terror (as we say tragedy does), but to get to the body itself, its glands, muscles, epidermis, and circulatory system, quickly arousing and quickly allaying the physiological reactions to fear."[2] Moers' emphasis on physiological effect seems appropriate. It points to the kind of imagination found, say, in Michael Ondaatje's work as well as in Atwood's that might appropriately be called a physiological imagination, whose purpose is evident.[3]

Fear. But fear of what? Some say sexuality, especially taboo aspects of sexuality, incest for example: the gothic threat to a young woman carries implications of sado-masochistic fantasy, the victim/victor pattern of *Survival*. Ellen Moers suggests that in Mary Shelley's *Frankenstein*, the real taboo is birth itself: death and birth are hideously mixed in the creation of a monster out of pieces of the human body. (The image involves, as well, the hideousness of duplication and reduplication.) In Atwood's "Speeches for Dr. Frankenstein," her Dr. Frankenstein addresses his creation in unmistakable language about a botched creation, a birth/death confusion:

> I was insane with skill:
> I made you perfect.
>
> I should have chosen instead
> to curl you small as a seed,
>
> trusted beginnings. Now I wince
> before this plateful of results:
>
> core and rind, the flesh between
> already turning rotten.
>
> I stand in the presence
> of the destroyed god:
>
> a rubble of tendons,
> knuckles and raw sinews.
>
> Knowing that the work is mine
> How can I love you?
> (*The Animals in That Country*, p. 44)

If, as he says to his monster, Dr. Frankenstein might have trusted in beginnings, in seed, the narrator of *Surfacing*, it seems, distrusts virtually all births. How much of the haunting proceeds from an abortion? We discern a pattern of mixed birth/death in the book: the baby not born, the baby aborted, the baby about to be born as a furred monster, the drowned brother who didn't drown, the baby peering out of the mother's stomach, the embryo-like frogs, the frog-like embryo, the man-frog father in the waters, hanging from the camera with which he might have photographed the gods.

Who are the ghosts of *Surfacing* then? In *Survival*, which reads like a gloss on *Surfacing*, Atwood tells us that the ghost or death goddess of *The Double Hook* represents fear, but not fear of death, fear of life. And babies? Following a rather horrendous list of miscarriages, cancers, tumours, stillbirths and worse, which she finds in Canadian novels, Atwood remarks laconically, "The Great Canadian Baby is sometimes alarmingly close to the Great Canadian Coffin" (p. 208). Who are the ghosts of *Surfacing*? A mother, a father, a lost child, Indians, the animals: all symbols of vitality, life, our real humanity, that has disappeared and must be brought back. "It does not approve of me or disapprove of me," the narrator says of the creature who is elemental, as she thinks her father has become: "it tells me it has nothing to tell me, only the fact of itself" (p. 187). And she says of her parents after her paroxysm in the woods: "they dwindle, grow, become what they were, human. Something I never gave them credit for" (p. 189). Ghosts: only the human body, repressed, denied; only life denied. All proceeds from the ghosts: a derealized world: victimization, sexism, deformed sexuality, sado-masochism, tearing away at nature's body, at our own bodies.

But to say this is to accept the *allegory* of gothic that Atwood allows her narrator to spell out for us (it is worth noting that in the best gothic fashion, the daylight world after the horrors of the long night reveals that the ghosts are mechanical or waxwork figures). To say this is also to explain away not only the ghosts but one of the most disturbing and most characteristic of Atwood's qualities, her sense of doubleness, of reduplication, in word and image. Even the victor/victim pattern recurs and the tale told once in *Surfacing* will be told again. At the end, nothing is resolved.

The ghosts are sexual fears, repressed contents of the imagination, social rigidity. They are also literary images, book reflections, patterns from all those readings in gothic romance, perhaps even the unwritten thesis Atwood proposed for her Ph.D., on gothic romance. Reduplication. Margaret Atwood's first book of poetry bears the title *Double Persephone*. The first poem of *The Circle Game* is called "This is a Photograph of Me," and the speaker tells us that if you look closely at the lake, you will discern her image; in parenthesis we are told:

(The photograph was taken
the day after I drowned.

I am in the lake, in the center
of the picture, just under the surface.

It is difficult to say where
precisely, or to say
how large or small I am:
the effect of water
on light is a distortion

but if you look long enough,
eventually
you will be able to see me.)

(p. 11)

End of brackets. A kind of insane phenomenology takes over that precise meticulous speech; we enter a world of reflections within reflections, totemic duplication (consider the possibilities in the simple four-part structure: man masked; man unmasked; animal masked; animal un-masked) and de-realized experience. Mirror, water and reflection, games like cards and chess, maps or models, eyes and cameras make up the major duplications, though there are more subtle ones in births and ghosts, in movies, photographs, drownings, archeology, astral travel, revenants, echoes, icons, comic books and gardens. The list, I think, could be extended — or duplicated — but its obsessive nature should be clear. It should also be clear that the list points up the literary nature of Atwood's concerns, otherwise fairly successfully disguised by her field of reference, popular and contemporary imagery. In *You Are Happy*, a poem called "Gothic Letter on a Hot Night" gives, in a typically wry and throw-away manner, the reflexive pattern of story within story. Presumably this speaker faces a blank page and longs for stories again, but it is not clear whether that is bad (she ought not to live her life in stories) or good (she cannot write and therefore all the bad things the stories could do will remain undone). Either way, there is a sinister suggestion that the stories (like the poem one writes to drown one's sister, or the things that go on just outside the frame of the picture, the part you cannot see) will in fact, or could in fact, write the lives of the story-teller:

It was the addiction
to stories, every
story about herself or anyone
led to the sabotage of each address
and all those kidnappings

> Stories that could be told
> on nights like these to account for the losses,
> litanies of escapes, bad novels, thrillers
> deficient in villains;
> now there is nothing to write.
>
> She would give almost anything
> to have them back,
> those destroyed houses, smashed plates, calendars, . . .
>
> (p. 15)

An ambiguity, unresolved, is that the poem begins in first person but in the second stanza shifts to third person narrative. The three—the "I" speaking, the "you" addressed, and the "she" who tells stories—remain unidentified. Duplicity, in part, consists in trying to have it both ways. No doubt, Atwood would recoil from my reading backwards to the material from which she begins, and which often seems to form the object of her irony: don't live in stories, you are not literature, if you think you would like it when the gods do reveal themselves try it sometime. So *Surfacing* moves from the world of ghosts back to the place where the narrator can be seen for what she is, a poor naked shivering wretch, scarcely human. But the ambiguity is in the power of the material. *You Are Happy* ends with what looks like a dismissal of "the gods and their static demands," but leaves open the question—again—whether you can only do this if you have been there, have known them. Even in parody and irony (let alone social comments on literary forms) the problem, the puzzle about reduplication remains.

A similar question arises with Robertson Davies' *World of Wonders*; that is, should we read it psychologically, in Jungian terms, as Davies intends, or theatrically, as a series of beautifully structured and terribly inflated poses, or magically, as not only the charlatan's illusions but the magician's powers. This question is somewhere in the background of Michael Ondaatje's *The Collected Works of Billy the Kid* (all the deceit, the obvious lies, as Ondaatje says of another poem) and in Kroetsch's insistent attempt to uninvent the world he wants so desperately to be at home in. Perhaps the disclaimers are essential to the magic of repetition, a kind of Borgesian pretence that the story or poem is really an essay, or that the essay is a story. The problem is, whatever philosophic dilemmas duplication raises about time and cause, psychologically and poetically it seems far more sinister than the writer wishes to admit. Either a fraud or a magician, the crude choice would seem to be. To which we answer (and this involves the reduplication) neither: this is only a story about both.

Psychologically, as Borges points out in *Labyrinths*, the story of a world created by a written version of another world of endless reduplication, of halls of mirrors, is a horror. "Mirrors have something monstrous about them . . . because they increase the number of men."[4] In folklore, the doppelgänger motif, in which one meets oneself coming back as one goes forward, signifies either death or the onset of prophetic power. In Jung's commentary on the *I Ching*, synchronicity substitutes chance for cause, a randomness that plays havoc with notions of identity and opens the possibility of occult possession. The vegetable version of this pattern, in its benign form, is sacramental, and in its malign or demonic form, cannibalistic. Atwood's ironic awareness of such patterns pervades her humanized gardens and provides a structural principle for her novel, *The Edible Woman*. But whatever the psychological significance, the literary seems more difficult for her; for in literary terms, as Borges argues, the device of reduplication calls attention to the poem and hence to the fictional nature of the poem's reality. It de-realizes experience:

> Why does it disturb us that the map be included in the map and the thousand and one nights in the book of the *Thousand and One Nights?* Why does it disturb us that Don Quixote be a reader of the *Quixote* and Hamlet a spectator of *Hamlet?* . . . The inversions suggest that if the characters of a fictional work can be readers and spectators, we, its readers or spectators, can be fictitious. In 1833, Carlyle observed that the history of the universe is an infinite sacred book that all men write and read and try to understand, and in which they are also written.[5]

Borges remarks that tales of fantasy are not haphazard combinations: "They have a meaning, they make us feel that we are living in a strange world."[6] Focusing on the obvious, the map of Canada in a tourist agency, viewed by a window lady who sees her own reflection containing the mapped country, Atwood gives us a country stranger than we knew:

> look here, Saskatchewan
> is a flat lake, some convenient rocks
> where two children pose with a father
> and the mother is cooking something
> in immaculate slacks by a smokeless fire,
> her teeth white as detergent.
>
> Whose dream is this, I would like to know:
>
>   . . .   .
>
> Unsuspecting
> window lady, I ask you:
>
> Do you see nothing
> watching from under the water?
>
> Was the sky ever that blue?
>
> Who really lives there?
>   ("At the Tourist Centre in Boston")

Borges' temptation is solipsism (think of your life as a dream). But Atwood's poem characteristically questions the dream. No matter that this is the American dream of Canada, "a manufactured hallucination"; the Unsuspecting Reflection, water and sky in her own head, doesn't surface, lives with her unanswered questions.

It would be possible, I suppose, to read Atwood's career as a search for techniques to answer those questions honestly, resolve the reflecting/reflector dilemma by demystifying experience. Certainly by the time of *Power Politics* she attained an impressive command of deflating ironies; a poem like "They Eat Out" sets up opposing stereotypes of magical thinking in an atmosphere of fried rice and pop culture:

> I raise the magic fork
> over the plate of beef fried rice
>
> and plunge it into your heart.
> There is a faint pop, a sizzle
>
> and through your own split head
> you rise up glowing;
>
> the ceiling opens
> a voice sings Love is a Many
>
> Splendoured Thing
> you hang suspended above the city
>
> in blue tights and a red cape,
> your eyes flashing in unison.
>
>   . . .   .
>
> As for me, I continue eating;
> I liked you better the way you were,
> but you were always ambitious.

But writing has its own power, its metaphors, like mirrors in the language. No one knows what word the heroine of *Surfacing* will speak first. It is possible that she will say nothing. Silence can be the strategy of those who have endured. But if there is any sense to my argument that Atwood's obsessive concern with mirror and reflection is an attempt to resolve an impossible dilemma about writing and experience, or about fiction and wisdom; and at the same time, a sort of playing about with the fires of magical possession, then I would guess that tormented girl would turn towards us and say:

> You don't like these metaphors.
> All right: . . .
> Think about pools.

Notes

1. Leslie Fiedler, *Love and Death in The American Novel* (New York: Meridian Books, 1962), pp. 111–112.

2. Ellen Moers, *Literary Women* (New York: Doubleday and Company, 1976), p. 90.

3. Like Atwood, Ondaatje, especially in *The Collected Works of Billy the Kid*, and Robert Kroestsch in *The Studhorse Man* and *Badlands*, tend to bring together images of sexuality, dismemberment, and poetics, poetic and sexual obsessions leading to anatomies.

4. Jorge Luis Borges, "Tlon, Uqbar, Orbes Tertius," *Labyrinths* (New York: New Directions, 1962), p. 3.

5. Jorge Luis Borges, "Partial Magic in the Quixote," *Labyrinths*, p. 196.

6. Jorge Luis Borges, "Tales of the Fantastic," *Prism International*, Vol. 8, No. 1, (Summer, 1968), p. 15.

Circe's Emergence: Transforming Traditional Love in Margaret Atwood's *You Are Happy*   Jane Lilienfeld*

Margaret Atwood's earliest volumes through *Power Politics*[1] and the first part of *You Are Happy*, published in 1974,[2] question and anatomize the traditional nature of love between men and women. Atwood is searching for what Marge Piercy in another context calls "Doing it Differently."[3] Usually in Atwood's poetry and novels,[4] her lovers hack away at each other, clad in their social roles; interaction becomes a war, and sexual involvement causes pain to the women and shatters their selfhood. This warfare occurs because the restrictions on women in traditional sexual roles create the anger which infuses Atwood's women and causes them to resist what their lovers offer. The men seem to emerge unscathed, hardly aware that they gouge their lovers. Yet relations between men and women cause women pain by definition:

> You fit into me
> like a hook into an eye
>
> a fish hook
> an open eye
> *(Power Politics*, p. 1)

The men don't see the need for change — because they aren't hurt by being in power. But Atwood's women fight, their anger ferociously funny and defiant, to retain their individuality, their rage, and their special selfhood.

*From *Worcester Review* [Massachusetts] 5 (Spring 1977):29–31, 33–37. Reprinted by permission of the author and publisher.

Power Politics ends with the questions raised but still unanswered. The "Circe/Mud Poems" of *You Are Happy* represent a real advance, for in them Atwood uses women's anger to create new possibilities for love, for Circe is forced to imagine a new world in which love might consist of equality and compassion. Circe and Odysseus, divided at first, transcend harrassing anger. Their love flows into warmth and trust and becomes a union of equal adults. At the end of the cycle, the imagined island wherein a new kind of love is possible establishes the space in which occurs the final section of *You Are Happy*, "There is Only One of Everything." My discussion will trace the changes in Circe's and Odysseus' love, leaving the reader to discover for herself or himself how such love is granted to ordinary mortals in the final section of *You Are Happy*.

Homer tells us that Circe was a goddess, daughter of Helios and Perse "who in turn is daughter of Ocean."[5] Odysseus is made safe by Mercury from Circe's power, and is thus not transformed into a beast, even though he gets to enjoy often the warmth of Circe's bed. Homer indicates that Circe treated Odysseus and his men, whom she quickly transformed back from bestiality into their original selves, with lavish attention, feasting them sumptuously for many months. Circe helps Odysseus return home by way of Hades, "Persephone's home," there to consult Teiresias. Odysseus returns from Hades to Circe so that she may direct him past renewed dangers in his determined pursuit of Ithaca.

Traditionally this interlude in Homer is seen in allegorical terms as depicting the dangers inherent in women's sexuality. Supposedly the men do not have beast-like qualities until they accept Circe's invitation to enter her palace. But once inside her space they eat, that is, they unleash their appetites which she has enticed, and fall into bestiality. Odysseus is only saved from swinishness through the intervention of the gods.

Margaret Atwood's women are enormously powerful, but their power rarely destroys men. Circe points out that rather than having been transformed through her power, the men contained the bone and gristle for their own metamorphosis:

> It is not my fault . . .
>
> I did not add the shaggy
> rugs, the tusked masks,
> they happened . . .[6]

Bestiality is, in fact, inherent in all Atwood's men from the earliest poems. They do not hesitate to use that bestiality to transform women. In "Midwinter: Presolstice," in *Procedures for Underground*.

> All night my gentle husband
> sits alone in the corner of a
> grey arena, guarding a paper
> bag

> which holds
> turnips and apples and my
> head, the eyes closed
>   (p. 20)

In Circe's world, male animality does not result from Circe's magic, but grows directly out of the limited options for behavior perceived by the men who come to her.

Printed in italics, the first poem of "Circe/Mud Poems" lands Odysseus (never named, to make him generally representative) "within range of / my words" for this Circe's power lies in her language. She sets forth her needs in the next poem:

> Men with the heads of eagles
> no longer interest me
> or pig-men, or those who can fly
> with the aid of wax and feathers[7]
>
> or those who take off their clothes
> to reveal other clothes
> or those with skins of blue leather . . . .
>
> All these I could create, manufacture,
> or find easily . . . .
>
> I search instead for the others,
> the ones left over,
> the ones who have escaped from these
> mythologies with barely their lives;
> they have real faces and hands, they think
>   of themselves as
> wrong somehow, they would rather be trees.
>   (p. 47)

"These mythologies" occur in all cultures; they bind all to their patterns. One can only escape if one longs for definition from nature rather than from traditional masculinity. The men "who take off their clothes / to reveal other clothes," that is, whose inner life is defined by the strictures of the wraps provided by the culture, men "with skins of blue leather" like the ancient Celts' body painting for war, men who hunt other mammals, those "with the heads of eagles," have not escaped from the martial mythology that for Atwood is the basis of Patriarchal culture.[8]

But Circe does not live by male mythology. On her island "people come from all over to consult me" about their pain. She listens to the insides of the earth, "collecting the few muted syllables left over" and "dispenses" these "a letter at a time." Thus her power in this incarnation comes not from her ability to make bestial men appear as the animals they really are, but from the more positive sources of the earth itself. She can hear the inner language of the land, and can, like the old goddesses' servants at Delphi, make it available if not coherent. Circe's plight, however, is that she is alone, separated by cool disgust from the bestial men who want her (pp. 50–51). Her enormous power does not impede her wanting to love and to be loved.

Later in the narrative of this love affair, Circe relates in prose a story about a mud woman, a woman who could be said to represent Circe's earthly nature. Two young men, one identified as "another traveller" — another lover? — had constructed her: "[s]he began at the neck and ended at the knees and elbows: they stuck to the essentials" (p. 61). Her flesh "where small weeds had already rooted" was fertile, made so by her nature and their offerings of sperm. "She was swept away in a sudden flood. He said no woman since then has equalled her." Knowing how easy it would be for Odysseus should she become passive, muddy, and only a sexual cushion, Circe asks, "Is this what you would like me to be, this mud woman?" She finds the answer, not in muddy passivity, but in a suppleness of relationship that Circe and Odysseus briefly achieve.

Circe has no illusions about Odysseus. Ironically demystifying his heroic, epic exploits, she laughs at him;

> There must be more for you to do
> than permit yourself to be shoved
> by the wind from coast
> to coast to coast . . .

(p. 51)

Odysseus' pursuits seem to Circe nonsense. "Don't you get tired of saying Onward?" She reveals that the answer lies "at my temples / where the moon snakes . . . / Ask who keeps the wind / Ask what is sacred"

Circe is not offering Odysseus "mythologies" of war, rape, pillage, destruction; she is suggesting another mode of perception, an ability to see the moon as the uroborous, as the snake biting its tail, as that form which combines in it the mother's and the father's power, for the snake biting its tail is one of the oldest symbols of the androgynous force of life (p. 51).

Does Odysseus hear her? She sees that "You stand at the door / bright as an icon / dressed in your thorax. . . ." Odysseus' metal body recalls the men who wore the disguises of Patriarchal "mythologies." She recognizes the animosity inherent in his sexual assault on her, for his expectation "gleams / in your hands like axes." Aware how traditional love works, Circe asks, "[W]ill you hurt me?" Appearing as the only possible counterpart to Odysseus' traditional role, Circe dares him with taunts:

> If you do I will fear you,
> If you don't I will despise you
>
> To be feared, to be despised,
> these are your choices.

(p. 53)

As a ploy in their mutual seduction one of the other, Circe is offering Odysseus the age-old power politics between men and women: he will have to triumph over her or she will think him a worthless weakling. Is this the only mode? Will men and women be locked forever into traditional patterns of love and hate?

Searching for another mode, Circe turns to Odysseus in generosity. "There are so many things I want / you to have," Circe begins. But Odysseus appears to her to want only her power (p. 54), "you know how to take," she says, as the brutality of the next poem proves. Their love making is a battle. Odysseus holds Circe, "arms down," taking her head "by the hair"

> mouth gouging my face
> and neck, fingers groping into my flesh
> (p. 55)

Hardened by these circumstances, Circe adopts a "Face of steel," to reflect for Odysseus the meaning of his behavior. She says "Look at me and see your reflection" (p. 56).

Circe, forced by conflicting wants, enters an elemental battle between the forces of the moon and Odysseus' forces of might. She commands her amulet to transform Odysseus, asking help of "the worn moon rituals." But "the fist stutters, gives up." The moon is no match for Odysseus, perhaps because Circe has adopted male martial mythologies. Odysseus unbuckles "the fingers of the fist, / you order me to trust you" (p. 57).

Circle loses this battle. The fist "renounce[s]" her and "I open." But the metaphor of her baring herself to her lover is painful; Circe sees her open self as an amputated hand, the wrist in pain, the hand which opens and then closes on freedom (p. 58). Circe fears that heterosexuality demands that she relinquish her moon power. Yet in meeting Odysseus in sexual warfare, she has discovered a new source of strength.

> Last year I abstained
> this year I devour

One of the male mythologies about women is that their sexuality is rapacious, unassuageable, and dangerous. Here Circe celebrates her personal power; she enjoys her needs, her actions "without guilt / which is also an art" (p. 59).

Able to sustain the openness of that hand, Circe suddenly sees that Odysseus is, like her, similarly defenseless. She sees him without armour, in his own body, neither of them now hidden by "mythologies."

> Your flawed body, sickle
> scars on the chest, moonmarks, the botched knee
> that nevertheless bends when you will it to

Circe can now recognize Odysseus' relation to her through the very fact of his imperfections, for the marks of his warrior trade she finds are shaped like The Mother, "moonmarks."[9] His otherness, now revealed as like her own nature, becomes her resource. By his sickle scars he is a marked man; he is bound to and by battle, to Penelope, to a relentless future. But the way the mark is shaped, like the moon, like the sickle of the harvest, shows that Odysseus' being extends into the domain of women. At Circe's understanding of her lover's scars, the poem halts time. The future is written; they cannot escape it. But in the present Odysseus and Circe can reach and recognize one another. The hard polarities of traditional love blur as Odysseus, moon man, flows into Circe, knowing now his similarity to her. Both are equal human beings.

Because this is so, Circe remains rooted in herself and does not abandon her selfhood for Odysseus. She sees clearly "This is not what I want / but I want this also" (p. 60).

He is a part of her life, not its core.

Nor is the relationship eased into simplicity. Like any relationship, it ebbs and flows, now forming a strifeless union, now dashed into anger and hatred. But unlike the earlier relationships depicted by Atwood's previous poetry, that of Circe and Odysseus encircles a real if aching love. Thus the warfare between Odysseus' "mythologies" and Circe's reintegrated moon power continues, in the rest of the poem cycle, but its brief respites have allowed Circe to imagine an alternative in the last poem of the section.

"There are two islands / at least," she begins the final poem. On one island is the past, unfolding in relentless repetition, "the events run themselves through / almost without us." On that island, Odysseus' departure condemns Circe to a mindless reenactment of her old patterns. But she can imagine a place created out of "moonmarks," a place wholly other than painfully full of battle, a place, therefore, unlike traditional love. Here the lovers transcend the battles that she and Odysseus seemed bound to undergo.

> The second I know nothing about
> because it has never happened;
>
> this land is not finished,
> this body is not reversible.
>
> We walk through a field, it is November,
> the grass is yellow, tinged
> with grey, the apples
>
> are still on the trees,
> they are orange, astonishing, we are standing
>
> in a clump of weeds near the dead elms
> our faces upturned, the wet flakes
> falling onto our skin and melting

We lick the melted snow
from each other's mouths,
we see birds, four of them, they are gone, and

a stream, not frozen yet, in the mud
beside it the track of a deer

(pp. 69–70)

The flow of this poem, its clear, brilliant colors, its movement summarizes and transforms earlier moments of the love affair, and, back beyond them, poems in the first section of the volume, "November" and "You Are Happy." Now no longer a "Mournful November . . . the image / you invent for me," (p. 17) here the winter that was a "crystal / wall," a "puzzle" (p. 67) is fruitful for the lovers, bringing their lips together in kisses.

The best line in the poem, the apples "still on the trees, / . . . orange, astonishing" causes astonishment, the word is so perfectly chosen, so right for the moment of surprised pleasure at the blazing color. Are the apples dying? Are they mummified? How have they lasted past the harvest, the plundering of the birds? Like the lovers, they still exist, they demand a right to their lives; unusual and flaming, they assert their energies.

The birds, who earlier had been suicides, givers of "shit" and "blood" (p. 66), are here omens of the lovers' possible future. In the earliest poem of this sequence. Odysseus had tracked "antlers," in Homer, he had killed an enormous stag for his men. Here he does not need to hunt this death, either to feed his men or to assert his warrior capabilities. The deer and the lovers here return to the "mud," the transformative material of the poem, the source both of Odysseus, the flesh, and Circe, the granddaughter of Ocean. Hideous, hacked, and desecrated, in "You Are Happy," a deer had appeared

[i]n the ditch a deer
carcass, no head.

(p. 28)

But in this last poem of the series, the deer escapes with his life, after drinking fresh water. It seems that at this water the lovers, too, refresh themselves on the infinite possibilities of growth, implied by the coming seasonal change. Renewal after winter is always implicit in the icing over of the waters and the land.

The possibilities for Circe and Odysseus, fought through, transformed, have turned in the next sequence, "There is Only One of Everything," into the possibilities for mortals. The brutal words and cryptic phrase of "Circe/Mud Poems" are invented anew and transformed in the last section of poems in the volume. Words there blaze up in the absolute rightness of their choice, to singe the mind, and fade into other words, terse and perfect, which ricochet with reference back to the earlier poems of *Power Politics* and those occuring previously in *You Are Happy.*[10] The choice of Circe, to abandon her moon power and to seize love with a warring mortal whose scars are their meeting place, becomes the options for the woman in "There is Only One of Everything."[11] She is secure in a power she does not have to relinquish, in love with a man she does not threaten.[12] In "There is Only One of Everything," Circe has emerged as a powerful contemporary woman able to transform her lover and herself into new modes of being and giving.[13]

Notes

1. Margaret Atwood's early poetry includes: *The Circle Game* (Toronto: Anansi Press, Lt'd., 1966); *The Journals of Susanna Moodie* (Toronto: Oxford University Press, 1970); *The Animals in That Country* (Boston: Little, Brown & Co., 1968); *Procedures for Underground* (Boston: Little, Brown & Co., 1970).; *Power Politics* (New York: Harper & Row, 1971). See also her *Survival: A Thematic Guide to Canadian Literature* (Toronto: Anansi Press, Lt'd., 1972).

2. Margaret Atwood, *You Are Happy* (New York: Harper & Row, 1974).

3. Marge Piercy, *To Be of Use* (New York: Doubleday & Co., 1973), pp. 52–57.

4. Margaret Atwood's novels include: *The Edible Woman* (Toronto: McClelland and Stewart Ltd., 1969); *Surfacing* (New York: Simon & Schuster, 1972); *Lady Oracle* (New York: Simon & Schuster, 1976).

5. *The Odyssey of Homer*, trans. by Richmond Lattimore (New York: Harper & Row, 1967), p. 155.

6. Atwood, *You Are Happy*, p. 48. All future references to this volume will be incorporated into the body of the paper.

7. This phrase, which seems a direct reference to Stephen Daedelus and many of the ramifications of this Circe episode, seem to have reference to Joyce's own retelling of the myth in his *Ulysses*.

8. The title poem in *The Animals in That Country* deals very clearly with the animals in "this" country and "that." In "that country" the animals are men, and live according to patriarchal rules and rewards: their culture depends on killing other animals.

9. Odysseus' scar in Homer's *Odyssey* is the occasion of one of the most moving scenes in Western literature, as Odysseus is recognized by Eurkleia to be her master. Lattimore, p. 294.

10. See in *You Are Happy*, "There is Only One of Everything," p. 92, "Late August," p. 93, and "Book of Ancestors," pp. 94–6.

11. See "Head Against White," pp. 87–91; and "Eating Fire," pp. 79–83, particularly section v, p. 83.

12. See "Four Auguries," pp. 84–6, which recapitulates in similar imagery of trust in a winter landscape the last Circe poem, and foreshadows "There is Only One of Everything."

13. Mortal, ordinary love, a new place for Atwood's women, is celebrated as possible in "Is/Not," pp. 74–6.

Nature as the Nunnery
[*Surfacing*]
Francine du Plessix Gray*

In an early passage of Samuel Richardson's *Clarissa*, the heroine laments the fact that there are no more nunneries left where she can seek refuge from an obnoxious suitor. And her complaint offers an important insight into the ultrasecular nature of the literary form that Richardson was pioneering and into the consequences of this secular vision for women.

In the widest historical sense the 18th-century novel reconciled the values of medieval courtly love (and its complex romanticizing of female sexuality) with the Puritan idealization of marriage. Through this curious wedlock it participated in the demise of the monastic ideal that had prevailed in Europe until the Reformation and had suggested that women's first allegiance is to a divine order, rather than to any patriarchal rule. The novel, in George Lukacs's words, is "the epic of a world forsaken by God." It has described a society in which the theater of salvation — most particularly for women — is centered exclusively in the home, in *Kinder* and *Küche*.

One wonders whether the novel's origins in this supremely worldly ethic, and its courtly presentation of the female as sex object, have helped to make the novel impervious to the theme of women's spiritual quests. In what classical work does the heroine seek religious or mystical fulfillment with the intensity, for instance, of Dostoyevsky's Aloysha, Bernanos's country priest, or even the hero of Somerset Maugham's *The Razor's Edge*? The rarity of such a search is all the more striking because it flies directly against the reality of history. The experience of mystical vision is fully as frequent among women as among men. Catherine of Siena, Joan of Norwich, Theresa of Avila, Joan of Arc and, in our time, Simone Weil, are only a few of the names that come to mind in a long history of women mystics.

The nature of "female" mysticism and its barely explored literary possibilities have recently received increased scrutiny from a new generation of feminist theologians. Mary Daly and Rosemary Reuther, among many others, have attacked our Judeo-Christian tradition for its exclusively masculine imagery. And they have questioned the adequacy of such figures as Father and Son for a contemporary expression — either liturgical or literary — of women's spiritual quest. Since this new awareness, the woman novelist who also happens to be a feminist and who seeks to depict a religious vision uniquely "female" in character is not likely to have her heroine discover the predominantly male cast of the Judeo-Christian pantheon at the end of her spiritual pilgrimage. She would tend to seek

*From the *New York Times Book Review*, 17 July 1977, 3, 29. Copyright © 1977 by The New York Times Company and Francine du Plessix Gray. Reprinted by permission of Francine du Plessix Gray and The New York Times Company.

vision in other traditions more richly endowed with female symbols of ultimate reality. She could turn, for instance, to Eastern models such as the male-female pairing of Yin-Yang in Taoism, or the Shiva-Shakti of Tantric Buddhism; she could return to prehistoric images of the Great Mother cults; she could even resort to the heretic medieval tradition of Meister Eckhart, which refuses to attribute to the Godhead any human characteristics, sexual or other.

The interest in women's religious experience has become so intense that feminist historians are currently inclined to draw a distinction between what they call "the novel of social quest" and "the novel of spiritual quest." The theme of social quest, which has amply endowed literature from Charlotte Brontë and Colette to Lisa Alther and Marge Piercy, shows heroines acquiring a heightened sense of identity, purpose, vocation, power by risking a temporary alienation from society. In the novel of spiritual quest, however, which up to this decade had been tackled only by Doris Lessing, the protagonist undertakes a journey whose purpose is to attain a new relation to cosmic power, to some manifestation of transcendent deity.

The relentless centrality of a woman's search for religious vision in Margaret Atwood's *Surfacing* (published in 1972) makes it a novel unique in our time. And the singular prophetic power with which she depicts her heroine's quest makes it, for me, one of the most important novels of the 20th-century. Atwood is in her early 30's, Canadian, author of seven volumes of poetry and two other novels, *The Edible Woman* and *Lady Oracle*, and is generally hailed, a prophet in her own country, as the star of Canadian letters.

"Flow backwards to your sources, sacred rivers, and let the world's great rivers be reversed. . . ." The primeval, matriarchal direction of this women's chorus in Euripides is clearly the one Atwood has taken in her quest for religious symbols. The protagonist of *Surfacing* returns to the island in the Canadian wilderness where she had lived as a child to search for her father, a lone forest-dweller and student of American Indian lore who has been mysteriously missing for a month. The novel's pervasive religious imagery makes it clear that she has also returned to search for some power of communion with nature that her father failed to teach her fully, some way of contact with the primeval gods originally worshiped on her island. She is accompanied on this journey by three contemporaries, a woman and two men: decadent urban Bohemians, knee-jerk Canadian nationalists who deplore the "American capitalistic pig's" encroachment on their wilderness yet have themselves lost all sense of contact with nature.

Woman as visionary, protector and provider: Atwood reverses the Western stereotypes of male and female behavior more radically than any other novelist who comes to mind. Her nameless heroine is the one who teaches her male companions to fish, to hunt, to split logs, to build fires.

Her lover is totally dependent on her, domestically in need of sex and household. She, on the contrary, is only seeking vision. The annoying social task of choosing a male to live with is "like buying a goldfish or a potted cactus plant." Identifying her body with the virgin wilderness threatened by male technology, she sees sexual contact as "a sacrilege," a profane threat to her visionary powers.

The stages of the heroine's quest are starkly archetypal: Heroine of the thousand faces, she descends, like Persephone, into the world of the dead; she tests, like Perseus, the extreme limits of human endurance; she finds her ultimate vision in the self-enforced solitude. By plunging repeatedly into the glacial lake by the side of which she spent her childhood she reaches the first stage in her search and finds the body of her drowned father. Atoning for a previous abortion, she reaches the next stage of her quest through a reconciliation with nature: She decides to conceive, in accordance with primeval rites, "with the full moon over my left shoulder," a child whom she will bear by herself, "squatting on dry leaves," without the aid of male technology. "I'll lick it off and bite the cord, it will be covered with shining fur, a God, I will never teach it any words."

Surfacing is laced with religious allusions. And its Christian symbols, handled with the cool, offhand, ironic, collagist style that informs much of Atwood's fiction, are relegated to the dross of our technological civilization, to "the logic that failed." The handless arm of a woman shopkeeper is "miraculous like the toes of saints or the cut–off pieces of early martyrs." The Western ways of worship are "no more use now than silver bullets or the sign of the cross." "The animals die that we may live, hunters in the fall killing the deer, that is Christ also." Atwood substitutes naturalistic epiphanies of prehistoric character: "The Indians did not own salvation but they had once known where it lived. Their signs marked the sacred places, the places where you learned the truth."

In the terrifying last stages of her transformation, the protagonist dismisses her friends to remain alone in the sacred, tribal space of her father's house and loses much of her human identity. She enters a stage of savage hallucination, prowling through the island on all fours, feeding on roots and wild berries, sleeping in relays like a bobcat, kicking earth over her droppings so as not to show her traces, waiting to see "the fur growing" on her body. At the book's end, Atwood's metaphors blur all distinction between nature and humanity. The frog with gold-rimmed eyes is both her ancestor and her present self. "It includes me, it shines." "I lean against a tree, I am a tree leaning . . . I am not an animal or a tree, I am the thing in which the trees and animals move and grow." Finally, coming out of her trance, facing her matted hair in the mirror, returning to so-called civilization, opening a can of beans to nourish her starved body, she decides to take her transformed self, and her new knowledge, back to the city. And she marks her new selfhood with a message that must remain the common denominator of all profoundly feminist works: "This above all, to refuse to be a victim . . . give up the belief that I am powerless."

The debate that *Surfacing* has provoked among contemporary scholars is almost as fascinating as the novel itself. *Signs*, for instance, the superb journal of women's studies edited by Catharine Stimpson of Barnard College, has devoted part of a recent issue to an examination of Atwood's religious symbolism. In its Winter 1976 number two young theologians, Carol Christ and Judith Plaskow, raise the following questions: Are the overwhelmingly pantheistic symbols of Atwood's vision, and her archaic identification of woman's body with the forces of nature, a legacy of oppression or a potential source of wisdom and power? Might not her symbols of female naturism, with all the biological determinism they imply, reinforce the dangerous stereotypes that assign "earthiness" and "instinctualism" to females, and "transcendence" and "abstract thought" to the male?

But Atwood's genius rises above these debates. For her naturalistic epiphanies are of a strictly mythic nature and never tend to stereotyping or separatism. The female religious vision that she presents in her utterly remarkable book also marks the surfacing, I believe, of a future tradition of religious quest in women's novels. From Emily Brontë's moors to Doris Lessing's forbidden velds, women authors have turned to nature not only in search of heightened perception but also as a refuge from the patriarchal order. Atwood stands in that particular tradition. "For the woman who has not fully abdicated," Simone de Beauvoir wrote, "nature represents what woman herself represents for man . . . a kingdom and a place of exile." Until all forms of sexual dominance are abolished, nature may be the only form of nunnery left to us, the only sacred shelter remaining in that desacralized world which gave rise to Clarissa's sorrows and to the great power of the novel form.

Atwood's Gorgon Touch [Seven books of poetry, from *Double Persephone* to *You Are Happy*]   Frank Davey*

In the opening poem of Margaret Atwood's first book, *Double Persephone*, a "girl with the gorgon touch" walks through a formal garden searching for "a living wrist and arm."[1] But she finds only "a line of statues" with "marble flesh." This "gorgon" is apparently Medusa, whose

*From *Studies in Canadian Literature* 2, no. 2 (Summer 1977):146–63. Reprinted by permission of *Studies in Canadian Literature*.

glance turned men to stone. In the concluding poem of Atwood's most recent collection of new work, *You Are Happy*, another male figure appears with similarly sculptural qualities:

> On the floor your body curves
> like that: the ancient pose, neck slackened, arms
> thrown above the head, vital
> throat and belly lying
> undefended . light slides over you, ...
>
> (96)

But this statue comes to life, is willed by the voice of the poem out of the worlds of art and ritual and into that of flesh:

> this is not an altar, they are not
> acting or watching
>
> You are intact, you turn
> towards me, your eyes opening, the eyes
> intricate and easily bruised. . . .
>   ("Book of Ancestors," 96)

In the seven books of poems which lie between these passages, this opposition between the static, the mythological, or the sculptural and the kinetic, the actual, or the temporal has been a central concern. Atwood's consideration of this opposition has been simultaneously ethical and aesthetic; all attitudes toward form in her work have been subject to moral judgments. The sources of this antithesis lie in the earliest days of Anglo-American modernism. Its deepest roots are in T. E. Hulme's rejection of nineteenth-century empathetic realism for "some geometrical shape which lifts him [man] out of the transience of the organic" and in the searches of Proust for "the real without being of the present moment" and of Pound for "a fragment of time in its pure state." Throughout Margaret Atwood's poetry such goals are presented as attractive, attainable—in terms of both life and poetic form—but ultimately unsatisfying. The formal garden can be created and entered, but its marble flesh cannot be lifted from still dance into dancing life. Roles for lovers can be created and enacted in *Power Politics*, but the enactments cannot be relieved of a stylization which Atwood characterizes as both artistic and deadly. The lovers become lifeless statues:

> Your face is silver
> and flat, scaled like a fish
>
> The death you bring me
> is curved, it is the shape
> of doorknobs, moons
> glass paperweights

> Inside it, snow and lethal
> flakes of gold fall endlessly
> over an ornamental scene,
> a man and woman, hands joined and running
>
> (56)

In "Progressive Insanities of a Pioneer" (AC, 36–39) a farm can be created in formal images of fences and furrows, but it cannot be obliged to yield an ordered life. Here not only does art not bear life, but it loses even its own sterile order and predictability when shattered by "the unnamed whale" of temporality and process.

This kind of poem, which makes up the bulk of Atwood's work, is overtly and normatively concerned with aesthetics — the role of the artist, the nature of form, and the relationship of form to historical time. One can choose the aesthetics of space — style, sculpture, ritual, static beauty — or the aesthetics of time — flesh, earth, and process:

> Love, you must choose
> Between two immortalities:
> One of earth lake trees
> Feathers of a nameless bird
> The other of a world of glass,
> Hard marble, carven word.
>
> (DP, [13])

Many of Atwood's poems rest on this antithesis. "The animals in that country" — "ceremonial," "elegant," "heraldic," "fixed in their tapestry of manners" — are posed against the animals of "this country" that have "the faces of animals" and eyes that "flash once in car headlights / and are gone" (AC, 2–3). In "At the Tourist Center in Boston," a "white relief map" of Canada "with red dots for the cities" is posed against a reality of "slush, / machines and assorted garbage" (AC, 18–19). The imagery of alienation from process is even more overtly presented in "Totems" where the antithesis is between restored museum-display totempoles and an unrestored totempole fallen and neglected. The former are described as "static," "uprooted and transplanted," and as analogous to the tourists — "the other wooden people" — who pose nearby "for each others' cameras"; the latter is said to have "a / life in the progressing / of old wood back to / the earth, obliteration / / that the clear-hewn / standing figures lacked." The images are again the sculptural — "clear-hewn," "static," "pose" — versus the temporal — "decay," "progressing." The poles have been taken out of time (uprooted both from the earth and from the culture which created them) and inserted into space — into a "park," into "cameras," and into "replicas and souvenirs" (CG, 59–60).

The camera, as above, is a frequent symbol in Atwood for the conversion of time into space. The poem "Camera" (CG, 45–46) describes a "camera-man" who in his search for an "organized instant" asks all reality to "stop," to "hold still":

> you make me stop walking
> and compose me on the lawn;
>
> you insist
> that the clouds stop moving
> the wind stop swaying the church
> on its boggy foundations
> the sun hold still in the sky. . . . (45)

His subject, however, insists in turn that the spatial correlative which the camera creates is itself a participant in temporality:

> Wherever you partly are
> now, look again
> at your souvenir,
> your glossy square of paper
> before it dissolves completely. . . . (45)

Despite the time-fixing and light-fixing act of photography, historical time moves at nearly "the speed of light" to ravage both the photograph and the objects the camera-man hoped to save from time; ultimately the church is reduced to "a pile of muddy rubble / in the foreground" and the woman to a "small black speck / travelling towards the horizon / at almost the speed of light" (*CG*, 45–46). Two other poems that use photographs with disappearing subjects to argue the incompatibility of the art-object with temporality are "This Is a Photograph of Me" and "Girl and House, 1928." In the first the "drowned" narrator claims to be "in the lake, in the center / of the picture, just under the surface" — presumably under the surfaces of both the lake and the photo. Her appearance in the photograph is not a spatial phenomenon; it takes place in time — "if you look long enough eventually / you will be able to see me" (*CG*, 11). Temporality lurks, we may conclude, under the deceptively solid surfaces of appearance. In "Girl and Horse, 1928," the voice of the poem speaks from outside the photo to its girl-subject, insisting that her smile and her peaceful surroundings are illusory:

> Why do you smile? Can't you
> see the apple blossoms falling around
> you, snow, sun, snow, listen, the tree
> dries and is being burnt. . . .

Like the formal garden of *Double Persephone*, this illusion is an attractive one. In actuality, the "instant" of the photo ceases immediately:

> (On the other side
> of the picture, the instant
> is over, the shadow
> of the tree has moved. You wave,

> then turn and ride
> out of sight through the vanished
> orchard, . . .

But its illusion of permanence can bewitch the human mind, can became a "secret / place where we live, where we believe / nothing can change, grow older." The girl rides from the orchard "still smiling," in apparently happy ignorance of the effects of time (*PU*, 10).

As one reads through Margaret Atwood's body of poems, one finds her constructing a catalogue of evasions, evasions that are all extensions of this human need to "believe nothing can change." All represent an aesthetics of space and a denial of time. One is classical mythology — the formal gardens of Medusa in *Double Persephone* and of Circe in "Circe/ Mud Poems" of *You Are Happy*. Another is popular mythology — the Superman figure of "They Eat Out" in *Power Politics*, the comic book heroes wearing "rubber suits" of "Comic Books vs. History" in *Procedures for Underground*, or the "starspangled cowboy" with "porcelain grin" of "Backdrop Addresses Cowboy" in *The Animals in That Country*. Closely related is popular art — formulaic, "endless," and "stale":

> You take my hand and
> I'm suddenly in a bad movie,
> it goes on and on and
> why am I fascinated
>
> We waltz in slow motion
> through an air stale with aphorisms
> we meet behind endless potted palms
> you climb through the wrong windows.
> (*PP*, 3)

Technology provides various ways of evading time: the camera, the blueprint ("The City Planners," *CG*, 27), or the museum ("The Circle Game," *CG*, 41; "A Night in the Royal Ontario Museum," *AC* 20–21). A part of all of these is the philosophic evasion of humanism, the evasion of Atwood's pioneer who asserts man's timeless centrality in a processual nature palpably without centres. This poem, "Progressive Insanities of a Pioneer," contains Atwood's most vigorous portrait of the humanist:

> He stood, a point
> on a sheet of green paper
> proclaiming himself the centre,
>
> with no walls, no borders
> anywhere; the sky no height
> above him, totally un-
> enclosed
> and shouted:

> Let me out!
>
> *(AC, 36)*

The pioneer's sensibilities are spatially oriented throughout the poem; he is appalled by the absence of walls and borders: he constructs a house, fences, furrows, in stubborn resistance to the fact that "unstructured / space is a deluge." He attempts to name the objects in his environment — to use language's abstracting power to lift them out of time and into the spatial categories of generic reasoning. However,

> Things
> refused to name themselves; refused
> to let him name them.
>
> (39)

Ultimately, time triumphs over space. The "unnamed whale" of process, Atwood tells us, bursts through his fences, his fields, his clearings, and his subject-object categorizing mind. By implication, the aesthetics of space and of the humanist ordering of space are also discredited. The land here is metaphorically the raw material of any art — of love, husbandry, architecture, poetry; the farmer is the artist-lover of *Double Persephone* with his choice between "earth lake trees" and "a world of glass, / Hard marble, carven wood."

The Journals of Susanna Moodie narrates a similar struggle between time and space. This theme is signalled in the opening poem in which Mrs. Moodie laments that "the moving water will not show me / my reflection." She sees her adversaries as the sun ("The Planters," 16–17), change ("The Wereman," 19), unpredictability ("First Neighbours," 14–15), and "fire" — both literal fire and the "fire" of seasonal process ("The Two Fires," 22–23). She attempts to defend herself through time-denying form:

> . . . concentrate on
> form, geometry, the human
> architecture of the house, square
> closed doors, proved roofbeams,
> the logic of windows
>
> (22)

But the "white chaos" (23) of her environment continually insists itself upon her as the only reality. Whiteness and light, frequent images in Atwood for camera-defying cosmic energy, surround and absorb her. A photograph taken in her old age documents her temporality rather than arresting it:

> I orbit
> the apple trees
> white white spinning
> stars around me

> I am being
> eaten away by light
>   ("Daguerreotype Taken in Old Age," 48)

Susanna Moodie's death removes her from all possibility of spatial illusion — from walls, manners, categorizations, and clichés "set up . . . at intervals" (55); it confronts her with raw process — here, as elsewhere in Atwood, metaphorically termed "underground." "Underground" for Mrs. Moodie is a "blizzard," a "whirlwind," a "holy fire" ("Resurrection," 58–59). It moves her in the last lines of the book to declare war on spatial structure and location:

> I am the old woman
> sitting across from you on the bus,
> . . . .
> out of her eyes come secret
> hatpins, destroying
> the walls, the ceiling
>
> Turn, look down:
> there is no city;
> this is the centre of a forest
>
> your place is empty
>   ("A Bus Along St Clair: December," 61)

Such imagery of "underground" is one of Atwood's most important devices throughout her poetry for asserting the dominance of time over space. Time and process are subversive: they lurk under the surfaces of lakes, of photographs, under the ostensibly solid veneers of field and street. Process is liquid; substantiality — the basis of sculptural form — is an illusion man invents with his camera-eyes. Mrs. Moodie calls Canada a "land I floated on / but could not touch to claim" (30). The pioneer declares,

> The land is solid
> and stamped,
>
> watching his foot sink
> down through stone
> up to the knee.
>   (AC, 38)

Appearances are thus duplicitous: the appearance of stasis conceals process; the appearance of order conceals chaos; the appearance of solidity conceals liquidity; the appearance of predictability presages surprise. The double condition of "double" Persephone, desiring process but receiving stone, is reversed for many of Atwood's later protagonists. The doubleness of reality for them lies in the invisible underpinning of temporality in ostensibly spatial objects. This doubleness requires a "double voice," one with "manners" and one with "knowledge" ("The Double Voice," *JSM*, 42), and a possession of "procedures for underground." Time-transcending devices — mythology, art, imagination, stylization — must be recognized as either weapons or crutches used by the weak in the face of mutability.

Many Atwood poems imply, like "Girl and Horse, 1928," that the need to deny temporality is understandably human; many others present a persona who gives herself with zestful ironic self-awareness to games, poses, mythologies, and sculptural perceptions:

> We sit at a clean table
> eating thoughts from clean plates
>
> and see, there is my heart
> germfree, and transparent as glass
>
> and there is my brain, pure
> as cold water in the china
> bowl of my skull
>   ("A Meal," *CG* 33)

The persona of *Power Politics* has this kind of ironic awareness of her addiction to the aesthetics of the "circle game." Her lover is another of the men of stone Atwood's "gorgon" personae seem inevitably to encounter:

> You stay closed, your skin
> is buttoned firmly around you,
> your mouth is a tin decoration,
> you are in the worst possible taste.
>
> You are as fake as the marble trim
> around the fireplace, ...
>   (44)

His determined attempts to transcend time sometimes involve commercial mythology — "suspended above the city / in blue tights and a red cape / eyes flashing in unison" — and at other times political mythology:

> in a year there will be nothing left
> of you but a megaphone
>
> or you will descend through the roof
> with the spurious authority of a
> government official,
> blue as a policeman, grey as a used angel. . . .
>   (30)

His beloved, however, enters wholeheartedly into his spatial assumptions about the world:

> Put down the target of me
> you guard inside your binoculars,
> in turn I will surrender
>
> this aerial photograph
> (your vulnerable
> sections marked in red)
> I have found so useful
>
> (37)

Much of the charm of this book resides in the woman's mocking use of the man's spatial aesthetics and in the frankness of her entry into a mutually exploitive relationship. He wishes to be a statue; she treats him like one. He acts insensitively, selfishly; she decides she can be equally happy with a useful corpse as with a sensitive lover:

> I approach this love
> like a biologist
> pulling on my rubber
> gloves & white labcoat
>
> . . . .
>
> Please die I said
> so I can write about it
>
> (10)

Here again a doubleness asserts itself. Games are sterile but fascinating; statues are cold but beautiful; illusory order is false but addictive; the game of "love" is exhilarating, although not in any sense "loving." Beneath these various paradoxes lurks the central one of space subverted by time. "Power politics" for the persona is a children's game of pretense and fantasy. The verbal wit of the book suggests the exhilaration of gamesmanship rather than the pangs of conscience. The self-irony suggests both the double vision of Susanna Moodie and a duplicitous "procedure" for fantasizing away the processual underground.

The evidence of Atwood's first two books indicates that these considerations of the ethical dimensions of aesthetic systems have some bearing on Atwood's own aesthetics as a literary artist. In *Double Persephone* a direct link is visible between the formal garden inhabited by her personae and the formalism of the writing. Atwood exercises her own "gorgon touch" here—substituting formal rhythms and language for the colloquial language of historical time and replacing temporal characters with pastoral and mythological ones.

> The shepherdess with giddy glance
> Makes the amorous shepherd dance,
> While sheep hurtle the stiles for love
> And clouds pile featherbeds above; . . . .
>
> ("Pastoral," *DP*, [5])

In *The Circle Game*, a book with the thematic intention of discrediting the "games" by which mankind converts time into space, the language is more casual; and the surfaces of event, image, and characterization appear realistic.

> Love is an awkward word
>
> Not what I mean and
> too much like magazine stories
> in stilted dentists'
> waiting rooms.
> How can anyone use it?
>
> I'd rather say
> I like your
> lean spine
> or your eyebrows
> or your shoes. . . . (70)

However, the "underground" of the writing of *The Circle Game* is not the processual underground of the pioneer's farm — it is impersonal, mythological, and spatial. One notices this undercurrent in the first poem, "This is a Photograph of Me." The protagonist speaks as a dispassionate observer of herself. Presumably she speaks from the temporal world beneath the surface of the photo, and her detachment is only from the spatial world of the photographic image. But the aesthetic effect of the writing communicates detachment from both worlds: the language is factual, unemotional; the verbs are mostly ones of static condition; the concerns are spatial — where this persona is and of what size:

> I am in the lake, in the center
> of the picture, just under the surface.
>
> It is difficult to say where
> precisely, or to say
> how large or small I am. . . .
>
> (11)

At times in *The Circle Game*, the detachment from the self and from the human world in general is so complete that people are present only by synecdoche:

> The small carved
> animal is passed from
> hand to hand
> around the circle
> until the stone grows warm
>
> touching, the hands do not know
> the form of animal

>   which was made or
>   the true form of stone
>   uncovered
>   ("Carved Animals," 62)

Here, through both the synecdoche of "hands" and the passive voice of the
opening verb, the sculptural reality of the carved animal is made dominant. The syntax of the poem, which alternates "hands" and terms for the
"carved animal" ("stone," "animal") in the subject position, further
dehumanizes the "hands" by making them appear parallel if not equivalent to the carved stone. The language also has a strong sculptural quality:
the diction is factual, and the rhythm dispassionate. By creating linguisti-
cally unlikely junctures counter to the natural speech-pauses in the
language, the line breaks enforce an unmodulated and noncolloquial tone.
The temporal dimension of language as an emotional and personal
response to experience is thus largely eliminated.

   This tendency to embody a spatial aesthetic permeates all of Atwood's
poetry. At the most elementary level, many of the central statements of her
poems are assignations of relative spatial position: "I walk across the
bridge . . . You saunter beside me, . . ." (CG, 12). "In the background
there is a lake, / and beyond that, some low hills . . . / I am in the
lake, . . ." (CG, 11). "There is my country under glass, . . . and beside it
10 blownup snapshots . . ." (AC, 18). "When we were in it . . . now / we
are out of it . . ." (PU, 18). Adverbial phrases of location play key roles in
many of the poems: "kneeling on rock . . . above me . . . under my
shadow" (PU, 8–9); "under a tree . . . around you . . . on the other side
. . . out of sight" (PU, 10); "in this garden . . . outside the string borders
. . . in the evening forest . . . in the bay . . . in another land" (PU,
16–17); "Upon the wall . . . around it . . . on the upper lip . . . on the
skin" (PU, 46). Some poems combine such phrases with statements of
spatial location to become entirely about relative spatial placement:

>   Beside this lake
>   . . . .
>   my sister in bathing suit continues
>   her short desolate
>   parade to the end of the dock;
>   against the boards
>   her feet make sad statements
>   . . . .
>
>
>   (I sit in a deckchair
>   . . . .)
>
>   She moves the raft out
>   . . . .

. . . .
                The sun encloses
rocks, trees, her feet in the water, the circling
bays and hills . . . .
. . . .

(Under my hand the paper
closes over these
marks . . . .

The words ripple . . .
. . . towards the shore.)
    ("Younger Sister, Going Swimming," *PU*, 66–67)

Somewhat more revealing is the repeated concern of many of the poems with making statements of condition. The underlying implication of such statements is the existence of static qualities — identity, colour, shape: "This is before electricity . . . The porch is wooden, / the house is wooden and grey . . ." (*PU*, 7); "She is / a raw voice . . . She is everywhere, intrusive as the smells . . . She is a bulk, a knot / swollen in space . . . a raucus fact . . . immutable" (*AC*, 14–15). This concern with establishing the essence of things is further indicated by the large number of copula verbs in Atwood, especially in opening lines: "Here there are no armies" (*PP*, 38); "You are / the lines I draw around you" (*AC*, 60); "The streets are new" (*JSM*, 50); "Marriage is not / a house" (*PU*, 60); "There are two of them" (*CG*, 68); "There are similarities" (*CG*, 57). In *Procedures for Underground* and the later collections, most of the verbs are in the simple present tense and appear to indicate temporally uncircumscribed acton.

               The sun shines down

           on two cars which have collided
           at a turn-off, and rest
           quietly on their sides

           and on some cows which have come over,
           nudge each other aside
           at the fence, and stare; . . .
               ("The End of the World," *PU*, 32)

The static effect is amplified here and elsewhere by the selection of verbs denoting condition or minimal action — "shines," "rest," "stare," "refuse," "permit," "become":

           You refuse to own
           yourself, you permit
           others to do it for you:

           you become slowly more public, . . . (*PP*, 30)

The temporal indeterminacy of such verbs can contribute to the creation of mythological or surrealistic effects:

> I keep my parents in a garden
> among lumpy trees, green sponges
> on popsicle sticks. I give them a lopsided
> sun which drops its heat
> in spokes the colour of yellow crayon.
>
> They have thick elephant legs, ...
> ("Eden Is a Zoo," *PU*, 6)

On other occasions this indeterminacy suggests habitual on-going action and psychological estrangement from historical time:

> I walk the cell, open the window,
> shut the window, the little
> motors click
> and whir, I turn on all the
> taps and switches
>
> I take pills, I drink water, I kneel
> (*PP*, 19)

The result of such techniques is the removal of time as an operative dimension from much of the poetry. The speaker appears to be a spectator to her own life, standing outside both this life and its temporal context. The principle of cause and effect tends to disappear under such circumstances; events become juxtaposed in space rather than processually related. Such a condition prevails in "Progressive Insanities of a Pioneer" where the natural "oceanic" action of the land is in no sense caused or precipitated by the pioneer who has juxtaposed himself to it. It prevails in "After the Flood, We" in which the two lovers are introduced syntactically as parallel subjects—"I walk across the bridge . . . you saunter beside me"—inhabiting parallel but self-contained experiences:

> I walk across the bridge
> towards the safety of high ground
> . . . .
>
>
> gathering the sunken
> bones of the drowned mothers
> . . . .
>
>
> You saunter beside me, talking
> of the beauty of the morning,
> not even knowing
> that there has been a flood, ... (*CG*, 12)

The syntactic parallelism is both ironic, in implying the existence of a relationship that is etiologically nonexistent, and real, in specifying juxtaposition in space as the only operative link between its terms. A similar lack of cause and effect prevails between the lovers of *Power Politics* whose relationship, despite their physical interaction, also appears to be one of spatial juxtaposition rather than of mutual causation:

> You are the sun
> in reverse, all energy
> flows into you and is
> abolished; you refuse
> houses, . . .
>
> I lie mutilated beside
> you; beneath us there are
> sirens, fires, ... (*PP*, 47)

Here "you" and "I" are assigned parallel syntactic positions by the parallel syntax of "You are the sun" and "I lie . . . beside you." The spatial quality of the relationship is underlined by "beside" and "beneath"; the latter preposition joins the lovers to a list ("sirens," "fires") of spatially related objects. This use of parallel syntax to indicate parallel but noninterlocking relationship is one of the principal technical resources of *Power Politics*.

> You say: my other wives
> are in there, they are all
> beautiful and happy, . . .
>
> . . . .
>
> I say: it is only
> a cupboard, my collection
> of envelopes, . . .
>
> . . . .
>
> In your pockets the thin women
> hang on their hooks, . . .
>
> Around my neck I wear
> the head of the beloved, ...
> (*PP*, 50)

In this instance the distinctness of the lovers is emphasized by the ironic contrast between the parallel syntax and nonparallel content. The woman's dialogue is a non sequitur to the man's; the items "around my neck" are similarly irrelevant to the items "in your pockets." No temporal or causal relationship exists within either pair of items. The links are spatial: the juxtaposed lovers, their syntactically juxtaposed pronouns, their syntactically juxtaposed "pockets" and "neck," and the general juxtaposition created by the stanza arrangement. The over-all effect is one of collage — collaged lovers, objects, and stanzas.

Atwood's most recent work in *You Are Happy* shows little alteration in this manner of writing. A great number of poems are concerned with the making of statements of condition, in which verbs of action become indicators of states of being detached from temporal context.

> It is spring, my decision, the earth
> ferments like rising bread
> or refuse, we are burning
> last year's weeds, the smoke
> flares from the road, the clumped stalks
> glow like sluggish phoenixes . . .
>
> ("Spring Poem," 22)

When a first-person pronoun becomes a subject of these verbs, a self-detachment occurs in which the speaker seems to stand outside the atemporal frame in which the self exists and to view this self as an object outside of process.

> History
> is over, we take place
> in a season, an undivided
> space, no necessities
>
> hold us closed, distort
> us. I lean behind you, mouth touching
> your spine, ...
>
> ("Book of Ancestors," 95)

The very structure of many of the poems is spatial. Both sections and many stanzas in the multi-section poems ("Chaos Poem," "Tricks with Mirrors," "Four Auguries," "Head against White") appear to be in arbitrary sequence; no temporal logic would be offended by their rearrangement. Concluding lines gain their effect by the surprise of spatial juxtaposition rather than by temporal logic:

> . . . . overhead the weak voices
>
> flutter, words we never said,
>
> our unborn children
>
> ("Useless," 10)

> imprint of you
> glowing against me,
> burnt-out match in a dark room.
>
> ("Memory," 11)

> . . . I could wear them
> around my neck and pray to them
>
> like the relics of a saint,
> if you had been a saint.
>
> ("Repent," 18)

This structural technique resembles both that of modernist collage and that of the transcendence-seeking poetry of the early Imagist movement. The link between the juxtaposed elements is conceptual rather than temporal; their juxtaposition introduces juxtaposed contexts which propose an heuristic rather than a causal relation.

> . . . he slopes down,
> . . . .
>
> . . . roped muscles leaping, mouth open
> as though snoring, the photography
> isn't good either.
>
> ("Newsreel: Man and Firing Squad," 8)

Atwood's use of personae in this book seems entirely designed to objectify conditions of being, to create a verbal sculpture of an abstract proposition. Such are the ten "Songs of the Transformed." The "singers" all speak from outside themselves and regard their actions as repetitious, if not eternal.

> I crackle through your pastures,
> I make no profit / like the sun
> I burn and burn, this tongue
> Licks through your body also
>
> ("Song of the Fox," 40)

All have been, in fact, removed or "transformed" from time by human acts of mythology and stereotype. The Circe persona in the long poem "Circe/Mud Poems" appears designed to stand in place of Atwood's own life on an Ontario farm and to "transform" this life (much as the lives of the speakers in "Songs of the Transformed" have been transformed) out of its temporal context. The actual lovers become the mythological Circe and Odysseus; their farm becomes Circe's timeless island; their actual histories in time become the archetypal "story" of immortal woman and mortal man. Circe here is another Medusa-Susanna Moodie figure who dislikes the timeless world in which she has lived. Her island seems to her a place of "ennuie." Mythological men have become tiresome:

> Men with the heads of eagles
> no longer interest me
> or pig-men, or those who can fly
> with the aid of wax and feathers

> or those who take off their clothes
> to reveal other clothes
> or those with skins of blue leather

She seeks relief both from the unreality of such men and from the atemporality of her island:

> I search instead for the others,
> the ones left over,
> the ones who have escaped from these
> mythologies with barely their lives;
> they have real faces and hands, ...
>
> (47)

Odysseus, on the other hand, despite his knowledge that it would be death to submit to transformation out of time, is still tempted by the timeless qualities Circe possesses. He becomes passive and quiescent.

> The trees bend in the wind, you eat, you rest,
> you think of nothing,
> your mind, you say,
> is like your hands, vacant: . . . . (50)

He relaxes into the deathly unrealities of mythological story.

> Don't you get tired of killing
> those whose deaths have been predicted
> and are therefore dead already?
>
> Don't you get tired of wanting
> to live forever?
>
> (51)

At times, he seems to wish that Circe were not becoming alive, but would continue as a statue, a "woman constructed out of mud," one who "began at the neck and ended at the knees and elbows." Unlike a woman alive in historical time, such a statue would be "simple": "Is this what you would like me to be, this mud woman? Is this what I would like to be? It would be so simple" (61).

On the thematic level, Circe succeeds in escaping into time. Odysseus' fear of transformation releases the talismanic fist from her neck (57), and she becomes aware of two possible "islands," one repetitive and timeless —

> . . . the arrivals,
>
> the bodies, words, it goes and goes,
> I could recite it backwards
>
> (69)

— and the other in history, embodying events that have "never happened":

> The second I know nothing about
> because it has never happened;
>
> this land is not finished,
> this body is not reversible.
>
> (69)

At the conclusion of this section, she and Odysseus appear to walk on this second "island." Technically, however, the poem throughout is detached, sculptural, and spatial. Circe's consciousness is deliberate, self-detached, depersonalizing, and objectifying.

> We too eat
> and grow fat, you aren't content
> with that, you want more,
> you want me to tell you
> the future. That's my job,
> one of them, ...
>
> (66)

Even at the end of the poem, where one is to assume she has returned to history, she speaks with a self-detachment that places her consciousness outside the temporal frame in which her body exists and which presents this body as principally an object in a spatial design:

> We lick the melted snow
> from each other's mouths,
> we see birds, four of them, they are gone, and
>
> a stream, not frozen yet, in the mud
> beside it the track of a deer
>
> (70)

The theme of escape from space into time recurs in Atwood's work as frequently as events circle back on themselves in Circe's mythological home. From the Medusa of *Double Persephone* who yearns for a man who will resist her transforming gaze to the woman of the final poem of *You Are Happy* who sees her lover awaken from a sculptural pose, Atwood concerns herself with the tyranny of atemporal modes — mythology, stylization, ritual, cultural stereotype, commercial image, social manners — and with the contrasting richness of kinetic reality. Yet for Atwood art itself seems inevitably to possess the "gorgon" touch and to work to transform life into death, flesh into stone. Almost all of her major personae are the artist-as-transformer: Medusa the statue-maker, the Power Politician who transforms her lover into a comic-book hero, Susanna Moodie who can remake her husband into her "idea of him" (*JSM*, 19), Circe who can make men into animals or "create, manufacture" hierarchic lovers (*YAH*, 47). The struggle of these figures to abandon art and enter historical time is enlarged, by the extra-temporal aesthetic implicit in Atwood's use of language and form, into Atwood's personal struggle. In its own doubleness this struggle is impossible to resolve without her abandoning the practice of writing; it is therefore repeated in differing dramatic contexts from book to book. In each book, the language she employs communicates to the reader the presence of a consciousness divorced from the very temporal universe it argues he should enter. The reader thus experiences vicariously the dissociations from time and the detachment from being which the Circle Game or the game of Power Politics creates. The power of the poems is amplified by the implicit information in their language and form that the consciousness behind them suffers victimhood from the forces that the poems decry. Like Circe and Medusa, this consciousness has pathological power which it does not want, has insight into process and foreknowledge of event which only its alienation from process allows. Like a mirror, it creates art at the expense of its own participation in reality:

> Don't assume it is passive
> or easy, this clarity
>
> with which I give you yourself.
> Consider what restraint it
>
> takes: breath withheld, no anger
> or joy disturbing the surface
>
> of the ice.
> You are suspended in me
>
> beautiful and frozen, I
> preserve you, in me you are safe.
>
> It is not a trick either,
> it is a craft:
>
> mirrors are crafty.
> ("Tricks with Mirrors," YAH, 26)

Throughout Atwood's work the operative irony is that a voice, excluded from time but wanting in, owes its very ability to speak to the static forms made possible by its exclusion. Art, speech, and writing are "crafty"; they separate one from process and from one's kinetic self. Her personae, as above, and elsewhere in "The Circle Game," Power Politics, and "Circe/Mud Poems," taunt their lovers with this knowledge. If these men wish to make use of the transforming power of the lady-artist, they must forego the temporal woman they may also desire. Atwood's poems circle back on themselves, recreating one central drama of artist-woman engaged in an unsuccessful struggle to escape art for mortality. Essential to this drama is the implicit impossibility of resolution—an impossibility embodied in "the gorgon touch" with which Atwood's language, form, structure, and characterization are directed. Order here may conceal chaos, but only an embracing of order enables a speaking of either.

Note

1. References are to the following editions of Atwood's poems: *Double Persephone* (Toronto: Hawkshead Press, 1961) [*DP*]; *The Circle Game* (Toronto: House of Anansi, 1966) [*CG*]; *The Animals in That Country* (Toronto: Oxford University Press, 1968) [*AC*]; *The Journals of Susanna Moodie* (Toronto: Oxford University Press, 1970) [*JSM*]; *Procedures for Underground* (Toronto: Oxford University Press, 1970) [*PU*]; *Power Politics* (Toronto: House of Anansi, 1972) [*PP*]; *You Are Happy* (Toronto: Oxford University Press, 1974) [*YAH*].

The Poetry of Margaret Atwood [Six books of poetry, from *The Circle Game* to *You Are Happy*]   John Wilson Foster*

Margaret Atwood's current popularity stems in part from the fact that her poetry explores certain fashionable minority psychologies. With its cultivation of barely controlled hysteria, for instance, her verse is that of a psychic individual at sea in a materialist society. This hysteria, however, assumes specifically feminine forms and lends Atwood's work certain affinities (of which current popularity is the least important) with that of Virginia Woolf and Sylvia Plath. For like these two predecessors, Atwood confronts her own sexuality and the contemporary roles laid down by men for her to play. A minority psychology similar to that which informs her identity as a woman informs her national identity, for Atwood is a contemporary Canadian aware of belonging to a minority culture on the North American continent and in reaction recollecting and re-enacting her pioneer ancestors' encounter with the wilderness and with the native people. Appropriately, the Canadian ancestral experience—repository of the spiritual identity of a people—happens to be best commemorated in the journals and memoirs of some remarkable women, including Catharine Parr Traill, Susanna Moodie and Anna Jameson.

Charges of opportunism could easily be levelled against a poet so deeply involved with the minority psyche. But they are answerable by our exhibiting, as I hope to do here, the essential coherence of Atwood's poetic themes. Her poetry succeeds not by masterly technique or style but by a peculiar force of content, by exciting transformations of experience that

*From *Canadian Literature*, no. 74 (Autumn 1977):5–20. Reprinted by permission of the author.

appear only to the superficial reader as mere opportunities. Among the experiences of being an individual, a woman and a Canadian, Atwood intuits an underlying connection deeper than minority membership. These experiences flesh out in multiple guise the root formula of her poetry. Like a mathematical expression, that formula sustains a wealth of individual existences — of image, motif, subject and dramatic situation. Stated briefly, Atwood's poetry in the six volumes to date[1] concerns itself with the self's inhabitation of spaces and forms and the metamorphoses entailed therein. All that is thematically important derives from this: invasion, displacement, evolution and reversion, as well as those notions significant enough to warrant book titles — survival, ingestion (cf. *The Edible Woman*, a novel), and surfacing. The message of Atwood's poetry is that extinction and obsolescene are illusory, that life is a constant process of re-formation. The self is eternally divided in its attitude to the forms and spaces it inhabits, simultaneously needing, fearing, desiring and despising them.

Because the scenario of inhabitation takes place through space and time (spaces in time become forms and forms become spaces), we can see its pertinence to the contemporary Canadian's encounter not only with the landscape and its inhabitants but also with the past preserved in part by that landscape — that is, with his pioneer ancestors (whose journey itself enacted the scenario), with the native people and with his own primordiality. Also, since roles are spaces and forms, we can see its pertinence to the current re-definition of femininity. And behind the feminine and Canadian, the individual. If the self's identity as woman and as Canadian is threatened by the variety of the Canadian past and present, its identity as human being is threatened by the fact that self apparently cannot exist *outside* forms and spaces. At best, self is merely reflected off the surfaces of others' forms of self. This is the frightening phenomenology of Atwood's world superimposed, skin-like, upon the illusory solidity of its rocks, animals, artifacts and people.

Atwood's spaces are rooms, houses and even the human body, but in the beginning they are the spaces fashioned by her pioneer ancestors — the cabin and the clearing. How these spaces were created, inhabited, defended and sometimes abandoned is recorded in the journals and letters of the pioneers and early visitors themselves, which thus provide an illuminating background to the poetry. Always they concern a journey: the journal and guide are the archetypal Canadian literary forms which function in the Canadian literary imagination as does the novel in the English, something Atwood has recognized in subtitling her critical work *A Thematic* Guide *to Canadian Literature* and in "re-writing" the *journals* of Susanna Moodie. There was to begin with the ocean voyage and after, more important, the journey across the land. Ireland, Seamus Heaney has noted, has "no prairies / To slice a big sun at evening," and he adds: "Our pioneers keep striking / Inwards and downwards." New world pioneers on the other hand encountered such prairies and much else that Ireland lacks: towering mountains and awesome gorges, deserts, icefields and inland seas. The long journey from landfall to backwoods is an overland movement ("surfacing," one might call it) that even today the Canadian can re-enact, as Atwood does in "Migration: C.P.R." which chronicles a journey from "the misty east" through "the inner lakes," prairies, mountains and "faulted gorges" to the forest by the western ocean.

The pioneer's "long day's journey in the woods," as Mrs. Traill describes it in *The Backwoods of Canada* (1836), ended not with welcome but with the hostility of wilderness, wild animal and settler. In "Paths and Thingscape," Atwood's Mrs. Moodie complains: "I am watched like an invader / who knows hostility but / not where." All are begrudging and "unforgivingly previous" to her. Rarely in *The Journals of Susanna Moodie* or in *Roughing It in the Bush* (1852), or in the journals of Mrs. Jameson and Mrs. Traill is the red man anything but benign towards the white man, but behind the annoyance of the Indian asked in "First Neighbours" about the toad-like object on the stick lies the real hostility between the races.[2] In fact, the white man desired the removal of the red man "back from the extending limits of civilisation," as Mrs. Jameson noted, "even like these forests, which fall before us, and vanish from the earth, leaving for a while some decaying stumps and roots over which the plough goes in time, and no vestige remains to say that here they *have been*."[3] It is upon the "malignant face" of the forest, that most formidable prior occupant of the clearing, that Atwood's Mrs. Moodie, like all pioneers, vents her greatest wrath. "A Canadian settler *hates* a tree," adds Mrs. Jameson, "regards it as his natural enemy, as something to be destroyed, eradicated, annihilated by all and any means" (I, p. 96). Settlement could not take place but by the penetration and destruction of the forest. The old was obliterated by the new.

But the new is at first mere negation. Disembarking at Quebec, Atwood's Mrs. Moodie is "a word / in a foreign language," but later in the bush her husband is not even that, but is merely "an X, a concept / defined against a blank" ("The Wereman"). The clearing represents the settler's negative and unintelligible signature upon the wilderness, the displacement of its prior occupants. But soon it signifies a new phase in the scenario of inhabitation: the *immigrant* upon landing who became a *pioneer* upon striking for the backwoods has upon clearing become a *settler*. The pioneer has become a new person as the clearing is a new feature of the landscape. A new flora appears which the settler begins to name as though it had just been created.[4] The landscape is culturally virgin with no associations.[5] It is also, and in this notably different from Mrs. Jameson's native Ireland, too new for ghosts.[6] For forest and pioneer, settlement is obliteration and a fresh beginning.

The cabin, erected immediately after the first minimally necessary felling, is a space within a space. Like the clearing it is at first blank, a mere negation of the bush. Soon both cabin and clearing are havens (concentric areas of withdrawal) against the forces of the old that return to deny the new. In "Dream 3: Night Bear Which Frightened Cattle," the "lighted cabin" is the last refuge from the bear which invades the clearing like "an echo" of the previous inhabitants. The settler's life is a nightly siege, terrified as he is of being ambushed outside by nightfall. Indeed, cabin and clearing create for the first time in the wilderness the vital dialectic of inside and outside.[7] "Survival" means the successful mainte-nance of the inside against the outside constituted by annoying settlers, "trespassing" Indians, wolves and bears, the oppressive summer and "relentless iron winter" (Jameson), the bush and the darkness. The clearing, inside relative to the bush, is outside relative to the cabin, a dialectic Atwood exploits in "Two Fires" when the clearing is mercifully inside the burning forest, but mercifully outside the burning Moodie cabin.

> (each refuge fails
> us; each danger
> becomes a haven)

Here, as in other poems, Atwood represents the enclosed spaces of her locales by parentheses.

Even when positive, the cabin and clearing remain precarious. Mrs. Jameson sees the clearing as a man-made island resisting "a boundless sea of forest." In *The Circle Game*, in such poems as "After the Flood, We," "Descent Through the Carpet" and "Winter Sleepers," Atwood also sees the landscape paradoxically as aquatic. The image of a re-forming sea conveys the idea that the forces displaced by the cabin and the clearing are not really obliterated after all but are, by an Archimedean principle, merely re-located. Nothing is destroyed in Atwood's universe: it simply assumes another space, another form. The forces of the wilderness, *outside* the clearing, shift, when the clearings link up to create villages, towns and finally the suburbs of "The City Planners," *downwards*. The suburban homes, Atwood prophesies,

> capsized, will slide
> obliquely into the clay seas, gradual as glaciers
> that right now nobody notices.

The clearing reverts; the wilderness resumes. Because in "Progressive Insanities of a Pioneer," from *The Animals in That Country*, she sees the wilderness, by being an "unstructured space," as "a deluge," Atwood likens the cabin to an ark, a motif recurring in her poetry and suggesting that the settler and his descendants at best merely float on top of the unseen forces of the wilderness.

"In exile," writes Atwood, "survival / is the first necessity." The physical toll in survival is obvious, but in *The Journals of Susanna Moodie* Atwood has, as it were, read between the lines of *Roughing It in the Bush* in order to re-create the assault upon the pioneer psyche. The scenarios of journey and settlement are scenarios of profound personality change. European civilized self-assurance quickly gives way, as it does in the first poems in *The Journals of Susanna Moodie*, to feelings of worthlessness and self-negation when the settler is confronted by the unstructured space of the bush. In consequence, the clearing is as much psychic as physical, head-space for the embattled personality. But it is also by virtue of precisely that a prison which excludes the distant civilized world as well as giving the illusion of preserving it.[8] When Atwood's pioneer stands, the centre of a space unenclosed by any walls or buildings, paradoxically he cries "Let me out!" ("Progressive Insanities of a Pioneer"). Comparably, one old woman in *Roughing It in the Bush* speaks of the settler as "a bird in a cage," a view Susanna Moodie came to share when she described the purpose of her book as "revealing the secrets of the prison-house." Climate did not help: Anna Jameson writes of being "imprisoned by this relentless climate" and of being "completely blockaded by ice and mud."

The feeling of imprisonment frequently led to lethargy and to "inaction, apathy, and, at last, despondency. . . ."[9] That it is a short step from this to the feelings of persecution suffered by Atwood's Mrs. Moodie is evidenced by Mrs. Jameson's fearful resolve to "try all mechanical means to maintain the balance of my mind, and the unimpaired use of my faculties, for they will be needed" (I, p. 172). Though Atwood's Mrs. Moodie imagines persecution, her fears are grounded in the reality of frequent deaths at the hands of fire, fever, drowning and wild animals. But paranoid delusions are the outgrowth of a schizophrenia rooted in exile itself. In "Thoughts from Underground," Mrs. Moodie posthumously recalls the agonizing dilemma of wanting to love Canada and actually hating it:

> I said I loved it
> and my mind saw double.

At first it is a case of the settler physically inhabiting Canada and psychically inhabiting the homeland (a body-mind dislocation common in Atwood's poetry), but later it is a case of the self torn between occupying the present inside the clearing and the displaced past outside the clearing. The latter wins. *The Journals of Susanna Moodie*, like Atwood's other volumes, records how the settlers who dared invade the primal and aboriginal wilderness are in turn invaded and repossessed. John Howison wrote of how the settlers' "habits of thought at length become assimilated to those of the Indians, and they conceive that they have wandered out of their sphere, whenever they mentally or sensibly lose sight of the wilderness" (p. 165). Atwood's Susanna Moodie reverts not only to Indian but also to animal form, reflecting the role animals played in the physical and psychical world of the Canadian settlers. In "The Wereman," Mrs. Moodie is a fox, an owl and a spider, for it is as if there is one continuous spirit of the wilderness that assimilates the settler's European self and that merely incarnates itself in various forms. His wife is not even sure she herself has not been transformed: "I can't think / what he will see / when he opens the door." This wilderness spirit is indestructible, which is why Atwood's Mrs. Moodie can speak posthumously and why Atwood, as a poet and as the writer of *The Journals*, is Mrs. Moodie "re-incarnated."

Mrs. Moodie is not merely native and animal, but in the end she is the landscape itself. Ironically, she who inhabited the clearing, displacing prior occupants, is in psychic reality inhabited like the land by the animals. Only when she rounds the first hill when leaving ("Departure from the Bush") is she "unlived in." This total loss of the old self is indistinguishable from acute schizophrenia (it is as though the posthumous poems are not just Atwood's fancy but also the living Mrs. Moodie's fantasies) when at the end of the volume she becomes one with the landscape: "at the last / judgement we will all be trees."[10] She lies beneath Toronto, herself one of the displaced wilderness forces driven beneath the settlers' brittle surface arrogance.

The pioneer's physical journey was also a psychic journey during which the haughty Old World assumption that the self—humane, civilized, superior to the rest of Creation—existed splendidly independent of its chosen habitats was gradually broken down. For Atwood, the pioneer journey is in addition an extended metaphor for her own journey through the emotional landscape of everyday life. Indeed, the journey can no longer be literal because although Canadians still traverse a vast terrain, they cannot recapture the settlers' imperious feeling that they had discovered the land. That Indians had pre-empted the settlers did not diminish that feeling (the Indians were not really people and when deceased could not qualify even as ghosts), whereas in "Migration: C.P.R." Atwood's characters feel themselves everywhere pre-empted, if not by pioneer ancestors, then by the natives; prairie objects, for example, are

> (like an inscribed shard, broken bowl
> dug at a desert level
> where they thought
> no man had been,
> or a burned bone)

The pioneer journey in the metaphoric sense is most graphically presented in "Journey to the Interior" from *The Circle Game.* The similarities Atwood notices at the opening of the poem are not between coastal and interior topography but between the real Canadian landscape and that psychic landscape Atwood inhabits. The coast and interior are in fact radically different (a luxury of Canada's vast landmass) and offer a variation on the distinction between outside and inside we have already noted. But there is an inversion. The wilderness outside the clearing represented danger and unfamiliarity and the clearing safety, whereas the coast in "Journey to the Interior" represents the security of everyday life and the interior the unknown where there is a "lack of reliable charts." The interior is the metaphoric wilderness, that Atwoodesque landscape of lines broken by a curious metrical whim, familiar objects ("lucent / white mushrooms and a paring knife / on the kitchen table") suddenly highlighted and menacing, odd repetitions that are evidence not so much of a poet's laziness as of a journey become a circling in an undecipherable forest.

Atwood's poetry is a journey into this interior landscape between insight and hysteria. Her poetic voice, slightly paranoid—it is difficult to know whether the "we" of so many of her poems actually signifies another person, or whether the poet is using a schizophrenic version of the royal "we"—suits her theme of the metamorphosing and divided self. Like the historical Susanna Moodie, she is a civilized city dweller confronted by what is primitive and irrational in the land around her. And like her, too, she is conscious of being inadequately equipped for the journey. "Provisions" is the contemporary and psychic equivalent of "Looking in a Mirror" from *The Journals of Susanna Moodie* in which Mrs. Moodie's china plate and shawl from India become casualties of the forest. "Provisions" has us confronting the wilderness

> in thin
> raincoats and rubber boots
> on the disastrous ice, the wind rising,

with the environmental and intellectual paraphernalia of the irrelevant city, and is placed appropriately at the beginning of *The Animals in That Country* as though to warn us of the dangers ahead. But the journey is completed, for many of Atwood's poems concern the psychic hazards of "settlement"; that is, of making sense of our lives and the world around us, and of creating fulfilling relationships.

In "The Planters," Mrs. Moodie's husband is seen moving "between the jagged edge / of the forest and the jagged river." Edges—transitional slivers of doubt between hazard and security, the known and the unknown—were naturally important to settlers. Atwood is preoccupied by edges ("There is no center," she proclaims in "A Place: Fragments"), and in "Evening Trainstation Before Departure" asserts: "I live / on all the edges there are." And there are many: mountain road-sides (in "Highest Altitude"), ends of forests, deserts and glaciers ("Habitation"), beaches ("Notes from Various Pasts"), a roof's edge and the edge of a mirror (both "Head Against White"). Even Atwood's poetic lines, broken off at conjunctions, prepositions and other weak joints, have jagged edges. All of these are metaphors for mind and emotion pressing against the outer limits of those forms they are forced to inhabit, and simultaneously hugging those boundaries in exquisite fear of the chaos beyond them. The choice is between safe imprisonment and dreadful freedom.

Images and situations of entrapment abound. The city is a prison in "The End of the World: Weekend, Near Toronto" from which the drivers are "intent on getting out." Rooms are recurring and menacing enclosures in Atwood's poetry: in "Frame," she occupies a room whose window she fashioned herself (and showing everyday but typically distorted Atwood images) and from which "I dream / always of getting outside." These spaces become forms containing the self which in turn expands to fill and threaten them. In corollary, the body is a space to be worn, explored or even abandoned. In "Fortification" it is "a metal spacesuit"; in "First Prayer," the speaker thinks of her body as a chrysalis-cast or a flayed skin. This notion is taken even farther in "Astral Traveller" when the speaker leaves her body but finds it difficult, no doubt because of her ambivalence, to return.

It is skin, that membraneous edge between inside and outside, by which Atwood is especially fascinated, though it sometimes takes the forms of outlines, margins or surfaces. The fighting bull in "Bull Song" thinks it a mistake "to have shut myself / in this cask skin," and in "Corpse Song" the decomposed body, addressing the living, exclaims: "I resent your skin, I resent / your lungs, your glib assumptions." There is a sexual aspect of Atwood's dermophobia (or is it dermophilia?); it is as though a diffuse, vaginal sexual urge resents the forms nature has decreed for sexual expression and gratification. In "More and More" the speaker wishes to assimilate the world and, apparently, sexually absorb her partner, "if possible through the skin," but unfortunately instead of leaves she has "eyes / and teeth and other non-green / things which rule out osmosis."

In the light of this, it is small wonder that Atwood is drawn to all the orifices leading from the inside to the outside — highways, doorways, eye-sockets, gills and mouths. Of these, the mouth is the most important. The pioneer's concern with provisioning is transformed by Atwood into a sexual preoccupation. Her belief is that eating is a brute fact opposed to love which, the speaker in "Is/Not" reminds her lover, is not a case of merely filling cavities. It is difficult not to see Atwood's ambivalence towards mouths and eating as a metaphor for her ambivalence towards the phagic receptivity of the female form, with its vaginal mouth, and the male's active delivery of the seminal "food." Not surprisingly, the killers of the hen in "Song of the Hen's Head" who desire its edible treasures are "scavengers / intent on rape."

Like Susanna Moodie, then, Atwood both desires and fears escape from the imprisonment of form. Tantalizing images of unstructured space attend her poetry. In "Migration: C.P.R." the travellers after jettisoning on their way west their "eastern suitcases" emerge with faces scraped blank; however, the rider is attached:

> (but needing new
> houses, new
> dishes, new
> husks)

The pioneers were compelled to provide themselves with these new husks, but the husks these contemporary travellers assume are new only in the sense of being novel; actually they are secondhand: primordial, aboriginal, ancestral. Yet if on this level we can no longer find unstructured space, we can still dream of doing so, still entertain the Canadian fantasy of trail-blazing, as Atwood does when she resurrects Captain Cook and has him ill at ease in a fully-mapped world and at length re-entering "a new land cleaned of geographies" ("The Reincarnation of Captain Cook").

On other levels, the uncharted is a genuine threat and seduction. In commending the unstructured space of the wilderness to her lover in "Attitudes Towards the Mainland," the speaker tries to convince him of its solidity. But he will not believe in its solidity; for him it is a place in which one can drown. Both are right, but the solidity of the speaker's wilderness is not the solidity of depth but the solidity of brittle surface off which the self is merely reflected. Atwood's poetry is filled with reflective surfaces — mirrors, eyes, glass, photographs. They suggest how we merely "surface" — float, skate or cast reflections — through life, rarely penetrating behind or below. In "Tricks with Mirrors," for example, the loved one is forever trapped behind the narcissistic reflection of the lover. Fancifully, the subjects in "This Is a Photograph of Me" and "Girl and Horse, 1928" are similarly trapped behind the photograph which is in each case a mere surface representation of an instant. They are part of a solid world only in the sense of being dead and no longer selves. The solidity of unstructured space, which is fatally incompatible with self, is usually represented in Atwood's poetry, befitting the Canadian landscape, as green. Susanna Moodie is "crept in / upon by green" in "Departure from the Bush"; water is a "green violence" in "River"; a "green vision" invades the progressively insane pioneer; (the Boston strangler is the subject of "The Green Man"); and those charting the land in "The Surveyors" find themselves "changed / by the gradual pressures of endless / green on the eyes." We cannot inhabit this green unstructured space even if we discover it; the most we can do, and the most Atwood and other pioneers do, is to wrest a living-space *from* the wilderness. Otherwise we become an indistinguishable part of the landscape, retreat to the animal and primitive recesses of our being. What this means emotionally and sexually is that we cannot gratify our desires fully, truly inhabit the other person, this side of *becoming* that person. Atwood in "A Pursuit" follows the other "Through the wilderness of the flesh / across the mind's ice," wanting the other to be a place she can inhabit. Success would be a kind of death. Self and the spaces and forms it occupies are synonymous.

In the matter of confronting his primordial and aboriginal past, the contemporary Canadian can be more truly a pioneer than the early settlers. The latter, pre-Darwinian, would not have acknowledged their own animal origins, neither did they acknowledge that the native people were their ancestors in Canada. Atwood on the other hand realizes that mutual inhabitation of the land binds native and settler as surely as racial genetics. These acknowledgements entail their own kind of journey. Archetypally, it is a Heaneyesque journey "inwards and downwards" rather than outwards and across as was the pioneer journey, a journey "underland," as Atwood describes it in "Procedures for Underground," rather than overland. For evidence of the predecessors lies beneath us and, in one more sense of the word, the poet "surfaces" with this evidence after her subterranean exploration. It is also a journey *back* instead of forward ("We must move back," writes Atwood in "A Place: Fragments," "there are too many foregrounds"), in recognition of the fact that metamorphosis is not just spatial — that inhabitation of successive forms and spaces we have already noted — but temporal, that is to say, evolutionary. But because these metamorphoses can be replayed — by vestigiality, by re-enactment, by dream, by the racial memory that is imagination — we can't be one with the past. The traumatic feeling of being cut off from the past is assuaged by this but above all by the life-forms and culture-forms that have been long since vacated by their temporal substance but can be inhabited once more by a protean poetic imagination.

Because the Canadian landscape is so various and primitive, and not cultivated to a European degree, it facilitates man's awareness of the primordial. Vast and depthless lakes seem to commemorate the aquatic origin of life. Atwood exposes the nerve of our fascination with and fear of making the descent. For it is a kind of drowning, daydreams and nightmares of which haunt her poetry. "Descent through the Carpet" begins with a real sea outside a window, but it is a mere surface that reflects the mountains and sailboats. Paradoxically it is inside, through a carpet depicting plants, that the poet begins her descent, drifting down to a darkness populated by "the voracious eater" and "the voracious eaten." When her daydream is shattered, she ascends, breaking the skin of the water; her own skin "holds / remnants of ancestors / fossil bones and fangs." Here and elsewhere, "surfacing," in yet another sense of the word, refers to this decisive evolutionary breakthrough: the appearance of the terrestrial air-breathers.

Human embryonic gills testify to our aquatic origins. In "For Archeologists," Atwood asserts that our terrestrial progenitors too — in this case early cave-painters — "survive" in us not as vestige but as an imprinted and as yet undecoded part of our structure. Less dubitably, the blue jay's reptilian ancestor survives in the bird's "lizard eye." The entire panorama of our evolution is attempted in "A Night in the Royal Ontario Museum" in which the museum becomes a labyrinth down which the poet is forced to view the increasingly ancient relics and remnants of our ancestors. Past Greek and Roman marble, past Chinese bronze and Amerindian wood, the poet reaches—as though at the labyrinth's centre—mastodons, fossil shells and finally "thundering / tusks dwindling to pin- / points in the stellar / fluorescent-lighted / wastes of geology."

If fossils are casts, hollow forms which life has vacated, so too are the skins of animals preserved in museums. In "Elegy for the Giant Tortoises," Atwood imagines the huge reptiles, outdated in their ill-fitting and useless armour, ascending the steps of a museum towards "the square glass altars"

> where the brittle gods are kept,
> the relics of what we have destroyed,
> our holy and obsolete symbols.

Gods in animal forms are represented by the Indian masks Atwood sees in the Royal Ontario Museum. These too are casts, of a cultural rather than animal kind. Even when no longer worn they remain for the poet potent and menacing, as do totem-poles no longer in use.

> Why then is my mind
> crowded with hollow totems?
> Why do I see in darkness
> the cast skins, poised
> faces without motion?

she asks in "The Totems." The totem-animals once inhabited her but one night crept out through her eyes, leaving their totems behind. This explanation identifies the poet with Susanna Moodie (cf. "Departure from the Bush") but also with the native people whose totems are the preserved records of the people's having been inhabited by the animal spirits. But in fact the animal gods "with metal feathers and hooked / oracular beaks and human bodies" still exist but merely, in the titular line of another poem, "avoid revealing themselves." There are still ways of reaching them. In "Fishing for Eel Totems," Atwood turns her preoccupation with eating to magical effect, catching a tongue-shaped eel, eating it, thereby ingesting knowledge of the earlier language: "After that I could see / for a time in the green country." The oral origins of myth are suggested too in "A Messenger."

It is clear that Atwood has been profoundly influenced by Indian mythology, especially from British Columbia where she lived for a time. Many of the poems in *You Are Happy*, and certain poems elsewhere (for example, "The Totems"), resemble Indian tales of origination. Moreover, Atwood's animal imagery is not naturalistic but heraldic and emblematic, and this heraldic stylism she shares with totem-carvers. Consider, for instance, the animals in "Buffalo in Compound: Alberta" which walk in profile "one by one, their / firelit outlines fixed as carvings" and enter "the shade of the gold-edged trees." Even more telling are the metamorphoses which operate within Atwood's sexual and pioneer contexts but which are also the transformations that inspire totemism and involve, as they do in Atwood, men, animals and the landscape. "A carver," wrote Viola E. Garfield, "may include a figure representing the dwelling place of a story character, a camp site or place of refuge, or any phenomenon he desires. He always depicts it as animate. Features of the landscape are usually illustrated as land animals, while those of the sea are given the anatomical characteristics of ocean dwelling creatures. Sometimes they are carved with human, rather than animal, attributes."[11] The relationship between man and animal is paramount. "In the beginning people and animals were not distinct and separate, but animals were people, and many retain the ability to think and act as people in the present world . . . Down through the generations men have been known who assumed animal form. . . ."[12] Anthropomorphism and zoomorphism animate *The Journals of Susanna Moodie* and indeed much of Atwood's poetry, and are aspects of the primordial unity to which her characters and personae revert. The section of poems in *You Are Happy* entitled "Songs of the Transformed" seems especially indebted to Indian cosmology, concerning as they do human spirits in animal shapes. It is no coincidence that "Owl Song," in which the owl is the heart of a murdered woman, bears a resemblance to the Tlingit and Haida tale of the unkind woman turned to an owl and depicted on totem poles (Garfield, pp. 26–27). We could even argue that the stylistic metamorphoses with which we are familiar in poetry — metaphor, simile and personification — are in Atwood's poetry derived as much from a totemic awareness as from poetic convention.

As much as the journey overland, the journey underland is a journey inwards, an exploration of the self and its relationships. Atwood has discovered on this journey that one price of evolution has been our loss of an ancient language of signal and skin. The words we use are really vestiges of more potent words that now, as the poet tells us in "Notes from Various Pasts,"

> lie washed ashore
> on the margins, mangled
> by the journey upwards to the bluegrey
> surface, the transition

The act of love is one way back to that submarine reality. In "Pre-Amphibian" the lovers are released from the lucid solidity of day into an aquatic primordial night where their ancestors, in a suggestively sexual image, are "warm fish moving." When the act is completed, the lovers are "stranded, astounded / in a drying world" with the air "ungainly" in their new lungs. In such a poem as this, Atwood betrays a horror of fixed form, which is associated with daylight, solidity, dry land, coldness, mind and racial orphanhood. The lover in "Eventual Proteus" has, as the relationship developed, re-enacted the evolutionary scenario—he has been rock, fish, mammal and bird—but now that he has reached the condition of man (that is, the relationship has peaked) and evolutionary forms have given way to dull social spaces ("vacant spaces / of peeling rooms / and rented minutes"), love is no longer possible. The lover cannot resume the legends of his disguises: his emotional shape is brittle and final.

Yet the alternative to fixed forms and spaces is the emptiness they enclose, and of hollowness and vacuity Atwood has a morbid dread. Equally feared is the water from which ancestral forms must be dredged. Her pervasive fear of drowning seems to be a fear of the poetic imagination, and her relative indifference to poetic form I read as a studied and negative concern with it, a determination not to succumb to its hollow and dermal illusions of solidity. Fear of drowning and the recurring images of surfacing seem in addition to indicate a thinly-veiled queasiness about birth: the phylogenetic ocean might equally be the amniotic fluid and her references to skin references to the amnion. But it is hard, too, not to read fear of drowning, after Virginia Woolf, as a disguised repudiation of a sexuality that leads to merely banal coupling. Better, it would seem, to return directly, at least in imagination, to the presexual unity of being to which coupling seems a clumsy attempt to revert. Either way, the price paid is the unique integrity of the self, and this Atwood is loath to surrender. Drowning images the loss of self; "going under," which is a necessary operation to recover the past, is also the process of succumbing to anonymizing forces hostile to the self; "surfacing" is to come through with both a knowledge of the past and an intact self.

Not that old forms are acceptable simply because they represent a kind of dry land. Feelings of being marooned, beached and stranded pervade Atwood's poetry; wreckage and relics of relationships are strewn on her shores. Often these feelings derive from Atwood's sense of being a woman in a man's world. It is as if women have suddenly surfaced, been cast precipitately among the air-breathers and are uncertain what roles to inhabit. The poems in *Power Politics* and the "Circe/Mud Poems" sequence in *You Are Happy* are re-examinations of women's inherited roles, the former psychological and the latter mythological.

The Circe episode in *The Odyssey* is, like other myths Atwood has borrowed (of Proteus, the phoenix, Frankenstein and Amerindian totemism), a myth of metamorphosis, pressed by Atwood into curious service of her two overriding themes. First of all, Circe is contemporary woman addressing contemporary man. When Circe disclaims all responsibility for her actions in *The Odyssey* (itself a male fantasy), she is contemporary woman renouncing the roles men have created for her. It was not she who turned the men into swine, she asserts, but their own masculine nature no longer at one with the female sea on whose rim they have been spilled. She did not desire Ulysses, either his presence ("One day you simply appeared in your stupid boat") or his putative charms. Indeed, she is tired of masculine mythic heroes, of male heraldry and hollow heroics: "Men with the heads of eagles / no longer interest me." She searches instead for those who have escaped mythologies (as she wants to escape *The Odyssey*) and if they desire a metamorphosis, "they would rather be trees."

This echo of Susanna Moodie ("at the last / judgement we will all be trees") connects these Circe poems with Atwood's pioneer theme. Homer's sea, in the two italicized poems framing the Circe sequence, is transformed into a forest: his epic has become a Canadian odyssey. Circe is the voice and spirit of the wilderness — now female — resenting the penetrations of the male pioneers. As though addressing a pioneer, Circe asks petulantly of Ulysses: "Don't you get tired of saying Onward?" Yet Atwood is not being anti-pioneer. Circe at length comes to accept Ulysses, and is even apprehensive about his departure which is inevitable because "you leave in the story and the story is ruthless." Beginning in rebellion against her role in the epic, she at last defers to its narrative ineluctability. Likewise, the woman must accept the man, and the bush the pioneer.

Forms, spaces and roles are inescapable. Besides, "form," as Gaston Bachelard tells us, "is the habitat of life." And also, we might add, of identity. In reflecting this, Atwood's poetry is emphatically prepositional, even though the poet identifies prepositions, because they "pre-position" substance, with the enemy. The inescapable must constantly be resisted. In her first volume of poems, Atwood repudiates all prepositions except one: "with." The closing lines of "A Place: Fragments" express the enigma and dilemma of Margaret Atwood's highly personal relationship to the confusion that is womanhood and Canada:

> not above or behind
> or within it, but one
> with it: an
>
> identity:
> something too huge and simple
> for us to see.

Notes

1. *The Circle Game* (Toronto: Anansi, 1967; first published by Contact Press, 1966), *The Animals in That Country* (Toronto: Oxford, 1968), *The Journals of Susanna Moodie* (Toronto: Oxford, 1970), *Procedures for Underground* (Toronto: Oxford, 1970), *Power Politics* (Toronto: Anansi, 1972), and *You Are Happy* (Toronto: Oxford, 1974).

2. "First Neighbours" is a good example of how Atwood adapts incidents from Mrs. Moodie's book: it was not Mrs. Moodie who asked the Indian about the deer liver, but a young

friend, and the Indian laughed when replying. *Roughing It in the Bush* (Toronto: McClelland and Stewart, 1923), p. 483.

3. *Winter Studies and Summer Rambles in Canada*, II (London: Saunders and Otley, 1838), pp. 249–50.

4. "It is a remarkable fact . . . that when one growth of timber is cleared from the land, another of quite a different species springs up spontaneously in its place," observes Mrs. Jameson, I, p. 95; see also Mrs. Traill, *The Backwoods of Canada* (Toronto: McClelland and Stewart, 1966), p. 78. Of her habit of naming whichever plant was new to her, Mrs. Traill allowed: "I suppose our scientific botanists in Britain would consider me very impertinent in bestowing names on the flowers and plants I meet with in these wild woods," p. 61. We might call this an Adamic motif in pioneer literature. Compare Mrs. Moodie: "Every object was new to us. We felt as if we were the first discoverers of every beautiful flower and stately tree that attracted our attention, and we gave names to fantastic rocks and fairy isles, and raised imaginary houses and bridges on every picturesque spot which we floated past during our aquatic excursions," p. 263. If the pioneer's self-comparison with Adam was not conscious, comparison with Robinson Crusoe was: see Traill, p. 53, Moodie, p. 342, and *Early Days in Upper Canada: The Letters of John Langton* (Toronto: Macmillan, 1926), p. 113.

5. "In Canada the traveller can enjoy little of the interest derived from association, either historical or poetical," Jameson, II, p. 104.

6. Mrs. Moodie records a conversation she had on this topic with a friend, and adds: "The unpeopled wastes of Canada must present the same aspect to the new settler that the world did to our first parents after their expulsion from the Garden of Eden; all the sin which could defile the spot, or haunt it with the association of departed evil, is concentrated in their own persons," Moodie, p. 251.

7. This phrase I borrow from Gaston Bachelard's *The Poetics of Space*, trans. Maria Jolas (Boston: Beacon Press, 1969).

8. "The sympathies which once bound the settlers to the world, and made them feel a common interest with the rest of mankind, are in the course of time broken and annihilated, and they listen to details of recent battles, murders, earthquakes, and conflagrations, with as much *nonchalance* as if the events had happened in a planet that had long since ceased to exist." John Howison, *Sketches of Upper Canada* (Edinburgh: Oliver and Boyd, 1821), p. 164.

9. Moodie, p. 448. Both Howison, p. 164, and Jameson, I, p. 171 speak of lethargy as a hazard of settler life.

10. This notion of Mrs. Moodie's is not very different from the notions of the paranoid schizophrenic Septimus Smith in Virginia Woolf's *Mrs. Dalloway*.

11. *Meet the Totem* (Sitka: Sitka Printing Company, 1951), pp. 43–44. For a further account of Northwest totems, see Viola E. Garfield and Linn A. Forrest, *The Wolf and the Raven* (Seattle: University of Washington Press, 1948).

12. Garfield, p. 7. The important role of animal and bird skins in Indian tales of transformation (see Garfield and Forrest) might illuminate Atwood's pre-occupation with skin.

The Woman as Hero in
Margaret Atwood's *Surfacing*   Josie P. Campbell*

Margaret Atwood's *Surfacing* has been called "a remarkable, and remarkably misunderstandable book."[1] It has been read as a book about death, mortality,[2] and as an illustration of Atwood's critical stance in *Survival*.[3] It has also been read as a ghost story,[4] a particularly intriguing point of view, since Atwood herself, in an interview, said: "For me, the interesting thing in that book is the ghost in it, and that's what I like. And the other stuff is there, it's quite true, but it is a condition; it isn't, to me, what the book is about."[5] She goes on to say about ghost stories: "You can have the Henry James kind, in which the ghost that one sees is in fact a fragment of one's own self which has split off and that to me is the most interesting kind and that is obviously the tradition I'm working in."

Taking Atwood at her word, for the moment, what we have is a sort of psychological thriller, where the protagonist searches for or comes in conflict with that fragmented self, which appears as a ghost. And on one level, *Surfacing* is a ghost story, although whether or not this knowledge opens up the meaning of the novel for us remains to be seen. In fact, *Surfacing* has several ghosts (although Atwood does not mention this in the interview), both father and mother of the narrator-protagonist. Hamlet, by comparison, may have had it easy, with only his father/ghost to worry about.

The "other stuff" as a "condition" of *Surfacing* is given shape, in part, by the father/ghost, just as in *Hamlet*. In both the novel and the drama, the protagonists come to terms with the self, the narrator of *Surfacing* in the lake, but ultimately in the garden, and Hamlet, in the graveyard, and perhaps more fully in the final duel. Of course both works are quite different, not merely on the obvious level, as novel and drama, but because in one the quest is for the lost father, while in the other the search is not for the father as object, but to revenge his loss.

I would not wish to push a comparison between *Hamlet* and Atwood's *Surfacing* any further; what is most illuminating in even a casually tentative comparison, however, is the shape given to the "stuff" by the father/ghost hovering around the edges and occasionally passing through the form itself. The heroes of both works learn to accept loss and to confront their own mortality as conditions of life. What may seem surprising is that the hero of *Surfacing* is a woman, who, not unlike *Hamlet*, pushes to the outer limits of her existence in order to discover the self.

Marge Piercy has noted in an essay on Atwood that although her books are varied, "yet through every one of them run victor/victim- and

*From *Mosaic*, Special Issue on "Post-War Canadian Fiction," 11, no. 3 (Spring 1978):17–28. Reprinted by permission of the publisher.

quest for self-themes, a set of symbols, and a developing underlay of theory."[6] George Woodcock suggests that theory is directly related to Atwood's critical book, *Survival*, in which the novelist is concerned to reach beyond "a recognition of one's place, one's predicament, beyond the mere will to continue," to the "journey of self-discovery that begins at the basic levels. Recognition, self-exploration, growth."[7] In *Surfacing*, this "pattern of hope," as Woodcock continues, is "etched with the lineaments of myth."

On reading Atwood's novel, one discovers that it involves more than the mere "lineaments" of myth; its total structure and meaning are informed by the mythic heroic quest, demonstrated in Joseph Campbell's *The Hero with a Thousand Faces*. Thus the "etching" goes quite beyond the borders of Canada, except in details of place; despite her polemics in *Survival*, Atwood has written very little about any geography except that vast and fascinating country of the mind.[8] In this sense, she is akin to Campbell, who would, I think, agree that consciousness is the central task of humankind everywhere.

It seems extraordinary to me that in so much of the commentary on *Surfacing*, whether it deals with religious allusions and symbols or with Laingian psychological interpretations, critics mention only briefly Atwood's indebtedness to Campbell, viewing the mythic pattern as merely a minor element of the novel, almost as if they fear to unravel the sometimes knotty mythic figures and patterns to be found in the work. As a result, much that is crucial to the novel's meaning remains unexplored. Only Francine du Plessix Gray, in her essay "Nature as the Nunnery" (*The New York Times Book Review*, July 17, 1977), has looked at the novel's mythic patterns and understood them as radical precisely because the protagonist, a woman, *is* the hero in the archetypal sense of the term: "Heroine of the thousand faces, she descends, like Persephone, into the world of the dead; she tests, like Perseus, the extreme limits of human endurance. . ." (p. 29).

One of the problems of so-called myth criticism is that it tends often to be too schematic, a danger that appears all too possible when one is working with what seems such an all-inclusive myth as that in *The Hero with a Thousand Faces*. The problem is not, however, so much with the myth itself, as with the interpretation of it, for the myth of the hero, as Campbell views it, is not formula (as it is frequently mistaken) but metaphor for a process which in turn dynamically and reflexively generates the myth itself. Paradoxically the mythic process remains the same, yet is continually created anew for the hero. As Campbell pointed out in his *Primitive Mythology*, myth always has a dual function: (1) as "ethnic idea," the mythic image binds the individual to his family's society: (2) as "process" or "way" mythic ritual can lead to the transformation of the individual, which dissociates him from his historical situation and takes him into some sort of "ineffable experience." One can immediately see the tension or possibility for dramatic interplay between these two functions. The first serves as a "magical device" to ensure security for the individual and his society. The second is the "process" of the hero, who, like the shaman, is released, in part, from the societal system into the psyche, where he is put in touch with both the soul and its world. In this sense, the hero amplifies his perceptions of experience and deepens his realizations of that experience. The tension between the dual functions of myth may be resolved if the hero returns to his society, for his process toward self-awareness suggests metaphorically the potential movement of society itself from stability (with its attendant self-satisfaction and ultimate sterility) towards "new depths of realization." Even if the hero does not return, his process of self-realization may still suggest the possibility of heightened awareness for his society. Of course, it is also possible for the society to turn its back on the hero and remain locked in its historical condition.

If one reads in Campbell a method of exploration (and certainly his very use of language suggests this) rather than a collection of cultural artifacts, then the myth of the hero is not reductive but expansive. Atwood's novel (as well as nearly all of her poetry and her critical work) seems to me to be a creative or poetic "meta-criticism" of Campbell's theories; the process of the protagonist of *Surfacing* not only informs her of new depths of realization but illuminates the idea of the "way" of the hero as Campbell perceived it.

According to Campbell, the hero is

> the one who, while still alive, knows and represents the claims of the superconscious which throughout creation is more or less unconscious. The adventure of the hero represents that passage to the moment in his life when he achieves the illumination of self-awareness. In participating in this adventure, the hero must leave the every-day world and move into a region of supernatural wonder, where he encounters extraordinary forces. The hero then returns from this mysterious adventure to his fellow men. Frequently the hero's quest involves atonement in some form with his father, and ultimately with his mother, for they are finally the same. Through them, the hero discovers the self and is twice born through that moment of illumination. Although the shape-shifting form of the heroic myth may show numerous variations, its deep structure always reveals three major components, and as we can see, the components clearly indicate myth as process: *Separation, Initiation,* and *Return.*[9]

Both structurally and thematically, this mythic heroic process provides Atwood's *Surfacing,* with its meaning and its richness.

The novel itself is divided into three parts, with each division focusing on a major stage of the heroic monomyth. A first reading of *Surfacing* may give the impression that the narrator is disjointed, chaotic, as restive as the narrator's own mind. In large measure, this is due to the numerous flashbacks that suggest by their form the twists and turns of the protagonist's memories. Nevertheless, the narrator's quest for her missing father, which contains the central action of the novel, moves in straightforward fashion, leading her not only to her father, but to her mother, and finally to herself.

Part I of *Surfacing* begins with the narrator, who remains unnamed throughout the novel, "venturing forth" to seek her father, a retired botanist, who is missing, perhaps dead, on an isolated island in the Canadian wilderness. She seems an unlikely hero, or at best reluctant, almost preferring not to find him, having dissociated herself from her family because of an event in her life which she cannot share with them, indeed cannot face herself. Her separation from her family is further emphasized by her guilt over her mother, who had died earlier of a brain tumor. The narrator could not bear to attend the funeral, perhaps her way of not accepting her mother's death and her guilt for not allowing her mother to die in nature, to decompose naturally, rather than be kept alive by artificial means, to end up anyway in a narrow coffin. Despite her long separation from her family and her ambivalence toward seeing her father again, she does return to the island wilderness to search for him, even though his neighbors have not been able to find him: "But they must have missed something, I feel it will be different if I look myself."[10]

The protagonist's dissociation from her parents (through death, and her own willfulness) mirrors her separation from her own past, her historical condition, as she reconstructs it out of "memories fraudulent as passports" in order to repress one moment of her life she cannot bear to remember: "A section of my own life sliced off from me like a Siamese twin, my own flesh cancelled. Lapse, relapse, I have to forget" (p. 56). Nine years ago she had been involved in a disastrous affair with her art teacher, a married man. The affair led to pregnancy and an abortion, disguised in her own mind as a wedding. This wedding, one of the "fraudulent" memories constructed by the narrator, who has in fact never been married, is a point misunderstood by at least one reviewer of *Surfacing*, with the result that the entire meaning of the novel is somewhat distorted.[11] It is not until rather late in the novel that the wedding is revealed as fictive and that the narrator acknowledges the abortion: "It wasn't a wedding . . . I was emptied, amputated; I stank of salt and antiseptic, they had planted death in me like a seed" (p. 169).

Because of this one traumatic moment in her life, she is unable to face her own guilt in the "murder," and she separates herself not only from her private past, but from her parents, and more crucially, from all emotion: "The other half, the one locked away, was the only one that could live; I was the wrong half, detached, terminal" (p. 129). She is "nothing but a head," she says. As a result, she is alienated from her historical present as well as her past. She travels to the island with her friends, Anna and David, and her current lover, Joe, but she only uses them for transportation. She does not share her past with them, and she remains detached from theirs, projecting on them her own repression of memory: "My friends' pasts are vague to me . . . any one of us could have amnesia for years and the other wouldn't notice." (p. 35). The alienation from her friends becomes more pronounced throughout the novel, until finally she views them as "A ring of eyes, tribunal; in a minute they would join hands and dance around me, and after that the rope and the pyre, cure for heresy" (p. 180).

The dislocation of the narrator from her own personal history, past and present, is reinforced symbolically by the strangeness of the terrain she moves through. She can no longer find her way through a landscape once familiar to her and now as alien as the detached halves of her self are to each other. The opening line of the novel: "I can't believe I'm on this road again" suggests the narrator's anxiety over the geography of her past: "Now we are on my home ground, foreign territory." She knows that if her father is alive, she will leave without seeing him: "If he's safe, I don't want to see him" (p. 33). How can she face him when she believes that neither parent would have been able to forgive her: "They never forgave me, they didn't understand the divorce; I don't think they even understood the marriage which wasn't surprising since I didn't understand it myself" (pp. 33–34). The realization that the marriage and divorce are fictional constructions of the narrator becomes clear to her and the reader alike as the novel unfolds, with the result that the reader's perceptions are engaged, with the narrator's, in a continual process of amplification and readjustment.

Part I of *Surfacing* ends with the narrator pushing herself "reluctantly into the lake," an image that serves as a metaphor to reveal the protagonist's incipient descent into the self to discover within her psyche the split between the head and feeling. As she says: "I'm not against the body or the head either: only the neck, which creates the illusion that they are separate" (p. 91).

Part II of the novel initiates the protagonist into the mysterious realm of the self where the possibilities of reintegration of the two halves can be seen. If she can find her father, she believes, he may have the answer to dispel the "illusion" that body and head are separate. She views her father as a rationalist (he taught her and her brother arithmetic, their mother taught them to read and write), although she is somewhat discomforted by her father's reasonableness: "He said Jesus was a historical figure and God was a superstition, and a superstition was a thing that didn't exist. If you tell your children God doesn't exist they will be forced to believe you are the god, but what happens when they find out you are human after all, you have to grow old and die?" (p. 124). Nonetheless, she searches for some talisman or message he might have left her and discovers "strange drawings of a stiff childish figure, faceless and minus the hands and feet, and on the next page a similar creature with two things like tree branches or antlers protruding from its head" (p. 69). At first she does not understand these pictures, thinking her father "crazy, loony," until she finds an explanatory letter describing the sites of ancient rock drawings. With the acknowledgement that the drawings are not hallucinatory, but tracings of pictographs, the narrator must also acknowledge her father's sanity and the possibility of his death. She can confirm this possibility only by visiting the site of the rock drawings.

The heart of the initiation the protagonist undergoes centers on the "nuclear moment" of "illumination" through her father's death and her own spiritual death of self by her complicity in the abortion of her child. As is often the case with mythic and legendary heroes, there is something special about the time, place, and person that meet for a crucial instant: she looks for the best place to dive: "It faced east, the sun was on it, it was the right time of day . . ." (p. 165). As she dives, she observes: "My other shape was in the water, not my reflection but my shadow, foreshortened, outline blurred, rays streaming out from around the head" (p. 165). The rays are, of course, literally the ripples of water as she breaks its surface, but they are also suggestive of rays emanating around the head of one with godlike powers. There is no mistaking the superhuman effort it takes for her to dive deeper and deeper.

> My spine whipped. I hit the water and kicked myself down, sliding through the lake strata, gray to darker gray, cool to cold.

> Pale green, then darkness, layer after layer, deeper than before, seabottom. . . .

> The green canoe was far above me, sunlight radiating around it, a beacon, safety.
>
> (pp. 165–167)

As Marge Piercy has rightly pointed out, "In *Surfacing* . . . the primary metaphors are of a descent through space, time and water and then a hazardous return to the surface."[12] There is little doubt that the narrator is moving deeper into her psyche. The images she sees are carefully linked: "a dead thing," the corpse of her drowned father, is at first believed to be her "drowned brother before she was born" (who was "miraculously" saved by her mother), then her dead child (who was not saved by the protagonist) and finally, her own life.

The imagery surrounding the dive itself is remarkably like that surrounding the abortion: "They slipped the needle into the vein and I was falling down, it was like diving, sinking from one layer of darkness to a deeper, deepest: when I rose up through the anaesthetic, pale green and then daylight, I could remember nothing" (p. 133). But this time there is no anaesthetic, no escape into repressed memory. Rather, memory is turned into a creative force.

Under the water is her drowned father, but it is also her "drowned" past, the "break" in the self (in the very beginning of the novel Anna read her hands and discovered this "funny break in the palm line," her own lost child: ". . . it was in a bottle curled up, staring at me. . . . It was there when I woke up, suspended in the air above me like a chalice, an evil grail. . . . That was wrong, I never saw it" (p. 168). To realize her guilt ("I could have said No but I didn't") is to destroy the "faked album" of her past and the "paper house" she had tried to live in. If she cannot totally eradicate the "evil grail," at least she does not have to continue to drink from it. She can at last be honest with Joe and Anna and David, and more importantly with herself.

Her initiation into the depths of the self has allowed her to recognize the split within her, but now she must find some way to heal that wound. To see is not necessarily to act. The narrator realizes that "the power from my father's intercession wasn't enough to protect me, it gave only knowledge and there were more gods than his, his were the gods of the head, antlers rooted in the brain. Not only how to see but to act" (p. 179).[13] What she requires is the "thing her mother had hidden," and she finds it in the scrapbooks her mother had saved, a pictograph the narrator herself had drawn: "On the left was a woman with a round moon stomach: the baby was sitting up inside her gazing out. Opposite her was a man with horns on his head like cow horns and a barbed tail" (p. 185). This drawing is one of the most important and one of the most ambiguous images in the novel. Whatever meaning the picture had for the narrator as a child, "its first meaning was lost now like the meanings of the rock paintings"; she has to read "[its] new meaning with the help of the power" (p. 185), that is, the transformative power she has attained through her discovery of her dead father. The narrator never explicitly states the meaning of the pictograph, but rather enacts its meaning. The drawing suggests a way for her of closing "the break" in her psyche:

> I unclose my fist, releasing, it becomes a hand again, palm a network of trails, lifeline, past present and future, the break in it closing together as I purse my fingers. When the heartline and the headline are one, Anna told us, you are either a criminal, an idiot or a saint. How to act.
>
> (p. 186)[14]

The second part of *Surfacing* ends on a note of hope which looks toward the last part of the novel: "But nothing has died, everything is waiting to become alive" (p. 186).

Part III of the novel focuses on the preparation of the hero for her return to community, her "surfacing." The impregnation of the narrator by Joe in the last part of the novel has been viewed by Rosemary Sweetapple as reinforcement of a stereotypical relationship between men and women: man is "divine and infernal"; woman is a "potentially creative victim." Moreover, as far as Sweetapple is concerned, the meaning of the moon-mother (which the narrator acts out) and the horned man (Joe) "turn out to be no different from the original meaning of the picture she made as a child."[15] But the narrator does not believe the meaning is the same.

Admittedly, the picture of the moon-mother is rather puzzling. Based on evidence from the text itself, however — particularly from the subsequent actions of the narrator — it seems that Atwood may be making use of the Demeter-Korê myth, where the finding of Korê by Demeter expresses the experience of a *rite de passage*, from girlhood to womanhood. In this myth, rape, victimization, downfall as a girl, death, and sacrifice are central experiences, whether they occur through an impersonal god or in relation to a male who remains essentially alien. But it must be remembered that Korê is not overcome by the male, although this may seem paradoxical, since the "being-given-to-womanhood," is to the female self, in the myth, the moon-goddess. Atwood seems to underscore this aspect of the myth in her novel, for if anything, it is Joe who is overcome by the protagonist.

In addition, one of the most important aspects of the myth, without going into its complex variants, is that the resurrected Korê is a Korê who can no longer be abducted (victimized). There are also strong androgynous overtones to the myth: the *processes* of spiritual growth become the "knowledge" of woman, and she experiences the male ultimately as "a mere variant of her own self."[16] Also, what is crucial to the myth, and I think to Atwood's novel, is the resurrection motif. Korê is "resurrected" by her mother, and in turn, Korê will eventually "resurrect" her own child.

The male, in the myth, and Joe, in the novel, are necessary only in a functionary way. In *Surfacing*, the narrator makes it clear that she has no emotional feeling for Joe, at least at the moment:

> . . . I'm impatient, pleasure is redundant, the animals don't have pleasure, I guide him into me, it's the right season, I hurry.
>
> He trembles and then I can feel my lost child surfacing within me, forgiving me, rising from the lake where it has been prisoned for so long . . . the two halves clasp, interlocking like fingers, it buds, it sends out fronds. This time I will do it by myself, squatting, on old newspapers in a corner alone. . . .   (pp. 190–191)

Not only does the narrator initiate the encounter, she directs it from start to finish to restore those "two halves." Of Joe she remarks: "he thinks he has won, act of his flesh a rope noosed round my neck, leash, he will lead me back to the city and tie me to fences, doorknobs" (p. 192). In one sense, stereotypical sexual roles have been reversed; the protagonist uses the male for her own purposes.

The above scene, which seems so disconcerting to feminists, is necessary within the form of the novel. I agree with Susan Schaeffer, who states in her very excellent article on *Surfacing*, " 'It is Time that Separates Us,' " that victimization as a subject central to liberationism is not the main theme of the novel.[17] The impregnation of the narrator (if indeed she is impregnated—we are never sure of this, of course, and neither is the narrator, as she later admits—although the fact itself is unimportant) works out neatly, perhaps too neatly, given the events of the novel. The past is linked to the present and to the future: as the "lost" child is to be born again, so too is the narrator. She does not go back to the city—yet— with her friends, but stays on the isolated island alone: "From any rational point of view I am absurd; but there are no longer any rational points of view" (p. 199). She has moved into the very process of myth itself.

By remaining on the island, she hopes for some message from her parents to compensate for the anger she feels at their desertion of her through death. Although she finds herself "crying finally, it's the first time," she is not "mourning" but "accusing" them: "Why did you? They chose it, they had control over their death, they decided to leave and they left, they set up this barrier, They didn't consider how I would feel, who would take care of me. I'm furious because they let it happen" (p. 202). She is not ready to release her parents to themselves, into their death, for she has yet to achieve an integrated awareness of self which will allow her to *become* and to act out of that sense of becoming.

The search for her parents involves a highly complex set of rules, as in a serious game.[18] A significant step in this game is to reverse the mirror in the cabin so that it faces the wall and no longer "traps" her (as she saw Anna trapped in her gold compact). As she steps "out of the self" and her world envisioned in the mirror, so she steps out of her own time and into that of her parents, running the double risk of madness and death. Atwood reveals the protagonist's passage from one time into another through a symbolic ritual bathing in the lake: "My false body floated on the surface." When the narrator does see her mother, feeding the jays, an image associated with her throughout the novel, she has no words for her daughter: "She looks at me, past me; as though she knows something is there but she can't quite see it" (p. 213). Finally, her mother can be released to death, not in a coffin, but into nature itself, as one of the jays, the narrator thinks.

Her encounter with her father is similar to that with her mother. He has no message except to liberate the protagonist unto herself: ". . . It does not approve of me or disapprove of me, it tells me it has nothing to tell me, only the fact of itself" (p. 218). As with her mother, he returns into nature: "A fish . . . no, antlered flesh . . . flesh turned to icon, he has changed again, returned to water" (p. 219). As she releases her parents to their death, she acknowledges that they are not "gods"; they dwindle, grow, become what they were, "human" (p. 221). To accept their humanness is to accept her own with all her frailties and subsequent guilt.

Although the central action in the novel focuses on the search for the lost father and the narrator clearly seems to identify with him throughout much of the novel (he is the analytical scientist, she is nothing but a "head"), Atwood seems to suggest that both parents are external representations of the two halves of the protagonist. She has already admitted that to be a "head" is to be the wrong half, "detached, terminal." Her father's gods are not enough; her mother's power is also essential.[19] But there is no salvation in either, she discovers. She can only accept her father ("the effort it must have taken to sustain his illusions of reason and benevolent order, and perhaps he didn't" [p. 221]) and her mother ("collecting the seasons and the weather and her children's faces, the meticulous records that allowed her to omit the other things, the pain and isolation and whatever it was she was fighting against . . ." [pp. 221–222]). Her acceptance of both "halves" — head and feeling — is evidenced in the act of turning the mirror around and viewing herself ironically in a stage most people would assume mad, "a natural woman . . . A new kind of centerfold." The image is not her final one, however.

The end of *Surfacing* appears somewhat, if not completely, positive, as the narrator re-enters her own time, affirming: "This above all, to refuse to be a victim . . . withdrawing is no longer possible and the alternative is death" (pp. 222–223.)[20] She "tense[s] forward, toward the demands and questions" of Joe, who has returned to the island for her. Even though her "feet do not move *yet* [my italics]," the word "yet" suggests that she will move. The final line of the novel, "The lake is quiet, the trees surround me, asking and giving nothing" is played off against the protagonist's possible return to community inherent with its probability of failure. But solitude would be withdrawal, which the narrator has already rejected, as if realizing that if nature demands "nothing" of her, it also gives her "nothing." The ambivalence expressed at the end of *Surfacing* suggests the conflict of the problematic hero of the novel after he has attained self-recognition: "The ideal thus formed irradiates the individual's life as its imminent meaning; but the conflict between what is and what should be has not been abolished and cannot be abolished in the sphere wherein these events take place — the life sphere of the novel; only a maximum conciliation . . . is attainable."[21] The protagonist is only aware of her becoming, which alone allows her to choose her future.

Obviously numerous interesting aspects of *Surfacing* have been omitted from this discussion: the use of Americans as equivalent to killers, the conflicts between civilization and nature, the relationships among David, Anna, Joe, and the narrator, and the use of animal victims as objective correlatives for the narrator as victim to name only a few, but they have been treated elsewhere.[22] Instead I have concentrated on the "adventure of interiority," that content of the novel which is "the story of the soul that goes to find itself, that seeks adventures in order to be proved and tested by them, and by proving itself, to find its own essence,"[23] because I believe this to be the center of the novel and to contain its meaning. Atwood brilliantly reveals through the structure of *Surfacing* how the process of myth, used in spinning out this remarkable "ghost story," becomes a critical tool toward self-awareness, while at the same time the form of the novel also acts as poetic meta-criticism of the mythic process itself. Atwood's use of novelistic form lends richness and complexity to *Surfacing* as it draws the reader along with the protagonist into new and deeper perceptions of her journey towards a consciousness of the self as it moves towards its own becoming.

Finally, we recognize that what stirs and excites us about Atwood's novel is its human centrality, with its rare view of a woman's enormous capacity to confront heroically the ghosts of her psyche and — if only momentarily — to conquer them.

Notes

1. Susan Fromberg Schaeffer, " 'It is Time that Separates Us': Margaret Atwood's *Surfacing*," *Centennial Review*, 18 (Fall 1974), 319.

2. Schaeffer, p. 319.

3. Rosemary Sweetapple, "Margaret Atwood: Victims and Survivors," *Southern Review*, 9, (1976), 50.

4. Keith Garebian, "*Surfacing*: Apocalyptic Ghost Story," *Mosaic*, 3 (Spring 1976), 1–9, *passim*. Garebian calls *Surfacing* a "special kind of ghost story"; I agree, but not for the reasons he gives.

5. Quoted in Graeme Gibson, *Eleven Canadian Novelists* (Toronto, 1973), p. 29.

6. "Margaret Atwood: Beyond Victimhood," *American Poetry Review* (November/December, 1973), p. 41.

7. "*Surfacing* to Survive: Notes on the recent Atwood," *Ariel*, 4 (July, 1973), 22, 28.

8. See Nancy Regan's very provocative, but unpublished, study, "The Geography and History of the Mind: An analysis of the Works of Margaret Atwood," M.A. Thesis, University of Rhode Island, 1975, *passim*.

9. *The Hero with a Thousand Faces*, Bollingen Series 17 (Princeton, 1973), *passim*; see especially, however, 30, 126–149.

10. Margaret Atwood, *Surfacing* (New York: Popular Library, 1972), p. 29. Future references to Atwood's novel are from this edition and will be cited in the text.

11. Rosemary Sweetapple, pp. 50–69. This essay, despite some perceptive comments, should be read with caution because so much of the text of Atwood's novel is simply misread.

12. "Beyond Victimhood," p. 43.

13. To *see* is "the stage of Narcissus looking into the pool, of the Buddha sitting contemplative under the tree, but it is not the ultimate goal of the hero; it is a requisite step, but not the end. The aim is not to *see*, but to realize that one *is*. . . ." (Campbell, p. 386) Implicit in the verb *to be*, as Campbell makes clear later, is to act in the world, for in recognizing the essence of the self, "separateness, withdrawal, is no longer necessary."

14. The hero of myth and legend is frequently one or, perhaps, all three of these figures; one need only think for a moment of Antigone, Perceval of the Grail legends, and of course, Hamlet. See the numerous examples given in Campbell, *Hero, passim*. In *Surfacing*, the narrator may be seen in at least two of these roles: she sees herself as a criminal for "murdering" her child; her friends view her as an idiot. The question of the saint is left open, but she certainly suffers (she says in Ch. 1: "I can't really get here unless I've suffered.")

15. ". . . Victims and Survivors," (p. 59).

16. Erich Neumann, *The Great Mother: An Analysis of the Archetype*, trans. Ralph Manheim, Bollingen Series 47 (Princeton, 1972), 314–21.

17. p. 319. Schaeffer discusses the resurrection motif in *Surfacing* in a perceptive and intelligent way, although she is not concerned generally with many of the aspects I find important to the form and meaning of Atwood's novel.

18. There are numerous games — victim/victor, pain and loss, and sexual games — played out in Atwood's poetic works, *The Circle Game* and *Power Politics*. An interesting essay on the games heroes play is "The Game and Play of Hero," by John Leyerle in *Concepts of the Hero in the Middle Ages and the Renaissance*, ed. Norman T. Burns and Christopher J. Reagan (Albany, 1975,) pp. 49–82. Leyerle's essay, even though it concerns middle-English literature, is valuable for its provocative exploration of heroic action as literary form, which has implications beyond medieval literature.

19. See, for example, the narrator's recognition of her mother's power in the scene where she frightens away an intruding bear from the camp: "My mother stood up and walked toward it. . . . She yelled a word at it that sounded like 'Scat!' and waved her arms, and it turned around and thudded off into the forest." (p. 95) Although her mother tells her she was "scared to death," the narrator does not believe her: "She had been so positive, assured, as if she knew a foolproof magic formula: gesture and word." The mother has also "resurrected" the narrator's brother from death by drowning.

20. Piercy points out that in both *The Edible Woman* and *Surfacing* "the protagonist is a woman who becomes aware she has lost her identity — her self — who comes to experience herself as victim, and finally to reject that state" ("Beyond Victimhood," p. 41.) But Piercy also finds the ending of *Surfacing* to be unsatisfying, asking how the narrator can simply "stop being a loser after deciding to?" (p. 44). Piercy's reading of the novel does not take into account its formal structure, which in a sense not only accommodates Atwood's ending but would make a "more positive" resolution (that is, socio-politically positive) ring false.

21. George Lukacs, *The Theory of the Novel*, trans. Anna Bostock, (Cambridge, Mass., 1975), p. 80.

22. In addition to those essays cited above, see Joan Harcourt, "Atwood Country," *Queen's Quarterly*, 80, No. 2 (Summer 1973), 278–81 and Linda Rogers, "Margaret the Magician," *Canadian Literature*, 60 (Spring 1974), 83–85; also Roberta Rubenstein's excellent essay, "*Surfacing*: Margaret Atwood's Journey to the Interior," *Modern Fiction Studies*, 22 (Autumn 1976), 387–99 for a somewhat different view of Atwood's use of the mythological quest.

23. Lukacs, p. 89. The form of the adventures, or more specifically the space in which adventures take place, is explained rather clearly in Atwood's *Survival: A Thematic Guide to Canadian Literature* (Toronto, 1972); so, too, is the whole idea of victim/victor quest for self (*passim*).

Atwood's Adult Fairy Tale: Lévi-Strauss, Bettelheim, and *The Edible Woman*   T. D. MacLulich*

The Edible Woman is a perplexing book. Or so I find it. And it can be an exasperating book to present to students. All the obvious "interpretations" seem either forced or shallow. Yet the book does need interpreting. Why, exactly, does Marian stop eating? What is the meaning of the cake in the form of a woman which figures so conspicuously in the final scenes of

*© Canadian Literary Research Foundation. From *Essays on Canadian Writing*, no. 11 (Summer 1978):111–29. Reprinted by permission of Robert Lecker.

the book? *The Edible Woman* exists primarily as a series of haunting images, a sequence of dream-like hallucinations which flicker through the mind of the protagonist, Marian MacAlpin. Where, in this stream of subjective images, can the reader find a firm point of reference? Is there any way of seeing past the obviously distorted perceptions of the central character? Even after repeated readings the book resists any tidy formulation of its meaning; nonetheless, it retains an ambiguous power to fascinate. This paper, then, is an attempt to explore the sources of the book's uneasy appeal.

My reaction to *The Edible Woman* does not seem to match the prevalent opinion. Atwood's two subsequent novels, her poetry, and her book of criticism have all received more acclaim or have generated more controversy. Most critics writing on Atwood appear satisfied with only a facile passing tribute to the deft satire contained in *The Edible Woman.* One of the few extended comments on the book is Alan Dawe's introduction to the New Canadian Library edition. Dawe writes: "The book is about what anyone — male or female, with or without a college degree — can do to maintain his sanity and humanity in the plastic and over-packaged world that exists in the second half of this century."[1] Here Marian is seen as a victim of society; her erratic conduct is understood as a search for sanity in an insane world. The book's kaleidescopic images, its manic characters and their improbable actions, are taken as exaggerations for comic effect of tendencies actually present in the external world. Dawe's analysis is typical. Most critics describe the book as primarily a novel of social commentary, an up-to-date comedy of manners. If we add the notion that *The Edible Woman* may be seen as a feminist polemic, depicting the narrow range of opportunities society offers to women, we have summarized the usual range of viewpoints.

This interpretation probably explains the critical disinterest in *The Edible Woman*. Today a novel about events in the external world is thought of as somehow more superficial than a novel which seeks to portray inner psychological events. Catherine McLay, for example, despite remarking that Atwood's first two novels are "not as dissimilar" as might be thought, seems to justify her decision to write on *Surfacing* rather than *The Edible Woman* by arguing that "*Surfacing* probes more deeply into the mind of the heroine" than does *The Edible Woman.*[2] Frank Davey makes a rather similar comparison. Davey writes that Marian's story "is a discovery of the predatory and enslaving nature of a world outside herself." On the other hand, he says of the narrator of *Surfacing*: "Her story is the discovery of the predatory and mechanical within herself."[3] *Surfacing* is the more fashionable book, an obviously "mythic" narrative, in which the author engages — to use Robert Kroetsch's phrase — in "unhiding the hidden."[4] However, to contrast the two books in this way may be an error. In *The Edible Woman*, no less than in *Surfacing*, the actions and images are an index of the central character's state of mind. Properly understood, I shall argue, *The Edible Woman* is also an "inner" or "mythic" narrative.

Alan Dawe's introduction draws attention to non-realistic aspects of Atwood's novel. He writes that "even the most comic — the most slapstick — scenes of *The Edible Woman* have an element of terror in them" (p. 5). Dawe is responding to the irrational elements in the book: the incongruity between the normality of Marian's surroundings and the extremity of her behaviour; the illogicality of much of Marian's thinking; the compulsion which returns Marian's mind to certain grotesque ideas. These aspects of the novel raise a question: Are the characters Marian meets deformed because the world is in fact misshapen or because Marian's vision is highly coloured by her inner disturbances? I suggest that the book's imagery and incidents offer considerable evidence for seeing the story as a working-out of Marian's problems, not of society's madness. Graeme Gibson seems mistaken when he remarks that "the protagonist in the second book has a much more fundamental need to survive" than Marian MacAlpin.[5] Why should life-and-death inner conflicts be more momentous when conducted in wilderness settings than in urban surroundings? The narrator of *Surfacing* faces death by exposure and incompetence in woodcraft; Marian faces death by self-starvation. The two dilemmas seem equally serious — and are equally of inner or psychological origin.

A logical place to begin an inquiry into the meaning of *The Edible Woman* is with the title metaphor. I propose that the structural methods of the anthropologist Claude Lévi-Strauss offer a useful point of departure. When Lévi-Strauss investigates myths he is not interested in uncovering the meaning of any one story or myth but rather in demonstrating that myths as a whole have structure — that mythology is used by tribal peoples as a way of thinking about the world around them. Lévi-Strauss argues that mythology is a form of reasoning, with its own logical principles. The same can be said of literature; moreover, the underlying structures of mythological and literary narratives are similar, if not identical. Although Lévi-Strauss does not emphasize the content of individual myths, he does propose that one of the central topics — perhaps *the* central topic — of mythic thought is the dichotomy between culture and nature. In *The Raw and the Cooked* Lévi-Strauss explores a vast cycle of tales in which the cooking of food is the motif which signifies an attempt to bridge the gap between artificial human society and the natural world. I would contend that the desire to mediate between culture and nature is also a central theme in Atwood's book.

Another important feature of Lévi-Strauss's method is the analysis of the "structure" of mythical narratives by breaking them down into simple units or motifs. The pattern in which these motifs are joined is then shown to be recurrent, so that whole large families of myths may be viewed as transformed versions of the same basic story — in other words, as attempts to deal with the same underlying contradiction. I intend to undertake a much less ambitious analysis, simply comparing certain features of *The Edible Woman* to features found in the popular children's story "The Gingerbread Man." First, I will summarize a simple version of "The Gingerbread Man." The story begins when the gingerbread man which the old woman is baking is magically animated while cooking in her oven. When she opens the oven door, the gingerbread man runs away, pursued by the old man and the old lady and their domestic animals, and boasting all the while of his fleetness of foot. When he reaches a river, the gingerbread man is temporarily halted until a fox offers to transport him across the river. The gingerbread man embarks on the fox's back, but in order to remain dry he is soon forced to climb onto the fox's head. The fox then tosses his head, catches the gingerbread man in his mouth, and eats him. The story concludes with the fox's remark that "gingerbread men are made to be eaten."[6] Clearly, this story involves the motif of eating, and the fear of being eaten. Almost as clearly, the story concerns the split between nature and culture. The gingerbread man is meant to be food for representatives of society, but by running away seeks to align himself with wild creatures such as the fox.

Using Lévi-Strauss's method of showing the parallel structure of two myths, we may demonstrate a close correspondence between events in "The Gingerbread Man" and *The Edible Woman.*

	Gingerbread Man is mixed and baked	Gingerbread Man is animated	Gingerbread Man runs away	Gingerbread Man meets the fox	Gingerbread Man is eaten by the fox	The fox is satisfied
common motif	preparation	unexpected rebellion	escape and flight	meeting with false friend	exploitation	natural role fulfilled
	Marian is shaped by society	Marian behaves irrationally	Marian runs away from Peter	Marian meets Duncan	Marian tricked by Duncan	Duncan is satisfied

If, as this table suggests, *The Edible Woman* is viewed as a transformation of "The Gingerbread Man," the following "rules" of transformation are revealed: food preparation is changed into the process of socialization, and eating is changed into sexual relations. Nonetheless, the transformation preserves the opposition between culture and nature. Plainly it makes sense to equate Marian's family and Peter with society. And Duncan is Peter's opposite in many ways. Duncan's behaviour is spontaneous and introspective in contrast to Peter's calculated and socially conditioned behaviour. Duncan is outside the normal power-structure of society, whereas Peter is on his way to a prosperous career. Moreover, Duncan is explicitly linked with nature by the book's imagery. When Marian meets Duncan near the Museum, he is described as an animal: "He was wearing a shaggy sweater. She stroked it with one of her hands as though it was a furry skin. Beneath it she could feel his spare body, the gaunt shape of a starved animal in time of famine. He nuzzled his wet face under her scarf and hair and coat collar, against her neck" (p. 171). Later, just before they make love in the hotel room, Marian "could feel his breath against the side of her neck, sharp and cool, and then his face pressing against her, nudging into her flesh, cool; like the muzzle of an animal, curious, and only slightly friendly" (p. 254). Equating Duncan with the fox also draws attention to another of Duncan's traits, his deceptiveness. Like the fox, Duncan is an incarnation of the trickster figure, a character type found throughout the folk-tales of many peoples.

The next thing to notice about "The Gingerbread Man" is that the central character is a kind of food. That is, the gingerbread man occupies a category intermediate between nature and culture, but a category which exists only for the benefit of culture. Thus, the action of the story can be summarized in this way: "food-for-culture" (the gingerbread man) rebels against its normal role (being eaten) and tries to assert its right to an autonomous existence (by running away); however, instead of achieving an independent life as a wild animal "food-for-culture" is simply transformed into "food-for-nature" (by being eaten by the fox). The point at issue can be clarified if we notice that it is only *domestic* animals who pursue the gingerbread man. These animals are also part of culture. The flight of the gingerbread man threatens the continued existence of society, for he is (in terms of the story) all the food in the world. The whole story can be seen as a parable suggesting that since it is the nature of food to be eaten, food might as well be eaten by members of society rather than by wild animals. Thus, the story can be viewed as an apology for mankind's custom of killing animals and harvesting plants in order to sustain human life. This might well be the primary meaning of an earlier myth from which the modern children's story is descended.

In *The Edible Woman* the parallel to being eaten by the fox is being seduced by Duncan on the pretense that he is sexually innocent and needs a helping hand to develop his unpractised masculinity. Just as the fox tricks the gingerbread man, Marian is tricked by Duncan. On the morning after their love-making, Marian asks the hackneyed question: "How was it for you last night?" Duncan's reply is devastating to Marian's conception of herself as a nurse-like, motherly figure:

> "You want me to say it was stupendous, don't you? . . . That it got me out of my shell. Hatched me into manhood. Solved all my problems."
>
> "Well. . . ."
>
> "Sure you do, and I could always tell you would. I like people participating in my fantasy life and I'm usually willing to participate in theirs, up to a point. It was fine; just as good as usual."
>
> (p. 264)

Marian has been deceived. However, unlike the gingerbread man Marian has not been destroyed by her encounter. Surely this difference is significant. The gingerbread man is eaten because it is natural for food to be consumed. Marian survives because — to be very literal-minded — sex is not fatal. In fact, sex is a natural part of living. Marian has performed a grown woman's sexual function, albeit inadvertently.

In "The Gingerbread Man" the eating is literal. In *The Edible Woman* it is the sexual activity which is literal. The images of eating are metaphoric, an instance of what George Woodcock terms the "emotional cannibalism"[7] Marian projects into her experience of the world around her. Marian's metaphors impose a ruthless dualism on the world; all activities are understood as transactions between two parties, who are respectively the aggressor and the victim, the exploiter and the exploited. Moreover, these transactions are only of two kinds, resulting in either deception or destruction.

Deception			Destruction		
"vehicle" of metaphor	breaks down into deceiver	deceived	"vehicle" of metaphor	breaks down into aggressor	victim
advertising	advertiser	consumer	hunting	hunter	animal
role-playing	actor	audience	eating	person	animal or plant
			technology	techni-cian	ordinary person

This dualistic way of thinking presents Marian with a dilemma. She does not want to become a victim, but she has a repugnance towards the deceivers and aggressors. She flees, without knowing where she is going. She goes to Duncan because, until she learns better, she thinks his way of life is an alternative, neither exploiting nor exploited. Duncan appears at first to have successfully opted out of society. Marian eventually learns that Duncan's non-conformity is not a new and non-exploitive method of meeting the world, but is merely the obverse side of Peter's conformity. The unknown alternative, the middle way between aggression and submission, still eludes her at the novel's end; but she does seem to have renewed her commitment to the search for such a way of life.

Understood in this way, *The Edible Woman* becomes a parable illustrating the complex nature of society. In social communities no one can be wholly independent of other people; the community is maintained only through a process of cooperation and at times of self-sacrifice. Life can only exist at the expense of other life. Everyone in society is "food" for his fellow man; everyone is both eater and eaten.

However appealing this interpretation of *The Edible Woman* may be, it cannot be final. Marian's mind obsessively returns to images which portray social processes as deceptive or destructive; she does not see "eating" as a benign activity. Clearly, any interpretation of the novel must accommodate the violence of Marian's responses to the world around her. For another way of seeing Atwood's novel, we can again exploit the comparison with "The Gingerbread Man." Hearing this story read, children will not understand the central character as symbolic food. Rather, they will identify with the rebellious little man, and experience the story as one of a large group of children's books in which a child or a child-like character tries to run away from parental figures. From this viewpoint, the story is a cautionary tale warning young children of the dangerous consequences of seeking to assert one's independence at too early an age. In this reading, the baking of the gingerbread man and his subsequent animation become metaphoric. The preparation and the cooking in the oven become symbolic of the child's education and possibly even of the mother's pregnancy. The flight of the gingerbread man symbolizes the child's growing urge to assert his separateness from his parents, and his taunting suggests that he is resentful of the punitive treatment he has received or fears he may receive from his parents.

This interpretation is corroborated by two other versions of the gingerbread man's story. In one version, the old couple are explicitly described as childless, and the gingerbread man is presented as a substitute for their missing child.[8] In another version, the couple's own child is set to watch the oven in which the gingerbread man is baking, but is warned under no circumstances to open the oven door—a prohibition which he immediately violates.[9] In these versions, the correspondence between gingerbread man and child is clear, as is the analogy between baking and pregnancy. Experienced in this manner, the story of the gingerbread man tells how a precocious child-hero flees from threatening parental figures, boasts about his self-sufficiency, and meets a disguised parental adviser who turns out to be even more threatening than the original parents. The message which the story embodies is clearly that the child should submit to his parents and remain dependent; specifically, he should not become prematurely curious over sexual matters (where do babies come from?). He should give up egocentric self-assertion in favour of submitting to the discipline of family and society.

At this point it is useful to re-write the comparison between *The Edible Woman* and "The Gingerbread Man" in a way that emphasizes the differences between the two stories:

"birth" of Gingerbread Man	protagonist is small and young	boasting while seeking autonomy	advisor bigger and older	eating	death of Gingerbread Man
Marian conditioned by society	protagonist is an adult	uncertainty while seeking autonomy	advisor seems young	sexual encounter	Marian survives

The gingerbread man is a child, whereas Marian is an adult; the gingerbread man is over-confident, whereas Marian is increasingly unsure of herself; the gingerbread man meets a more experienced adviser, whereas Marian meets an immature, child-like figure; and the gingerbread man is destroyed, whereas Marian survives. All these changes (except the last) result from two consistently applied rules of transformation. Marian's story has been displaced towards maturity, and the gender of the central character has been changed. "The Gingerbread Man" is told from a child's viewpoint—the gingerbread man should have been content to remain a dependent child. *The Edible Woman* adopts an adult viewpoint—Marian should learn to grow up, and accept the responsibilities that go with maturity. The gender change means that the typically masculine assertiveness of the central character is replaced by the passivity which is conventionally thought of as feminine.

The reader familiar with Lévi-Strauss's thought will recognize that the foregoing analysis pushes well beyond the boundaries Lévi-Strauss sets for himself. In particular, I have begun to talk about the "meaning" of events or characters, not merely about the abstract "structure" of the stories under consideration. The departure from Lévi-Strauss's methods arises because my intention goes beyond arguing that Atwood's novel is one of a large family of stories in which the motif of eating plays a prominent part. In addition, I wish to penetrate beneath the surface of this particular story, and bring its less explicitly stated themes to light.

Further analysis of *The Edible Woman* can be facilitated by introducing a new comparison. This time Atwood's novel will be paired with the classic fairy tale called by the Brothers Grimm "Little Red Cap" and known widely in English-speaking countries as "Little Red Riding Hood." Like *The Edible Woman* the story of Little Red Cap contains a constellation of images which link eating with sexuality. Bruno Bettelheim writes in *The Uses of Enchantment:*

> All through "Little Red Cap," in the title as in the girl's name, the emphasis is on the colour red, which she openly wears. Red is the colour symbolizing violent emotions, very much including sexual ones. . . .
> Little Red Cap's danger is her budding sexuality, for which she is not yet emotionally mature enough. The person who is psychologically ready to have sexual experiences can master them, and grow because of it. But a premature sexuality is a regressive experience, arousing all that is still primitive within us and that threatens to swallow us up.[10]

Little Red Cap has strongly ambivalent feelings about the sexuality symbolized by her costume. On the one hand, as Bettelheim writes: "In directing the wolf to Grandmother, she acts as if she were telling the wolf, 'Leave me alone; go to Grandmother, who is a mature woman; she should be able to cope with what you represent; I am not.' "[11] On the other hand, by directing the wolf to Grandmother Little Red Cap succeeds in eliminating a more experienced sexual rival. Thus, the story's view of sexuality is divided. To be eaten by the wolf, as are Grandmother, and Little Red Cap, is to experience sex as a destructive and violent act; however, the fairy tale comes to a happy conclusion. The woodcutter frees both Grandmother and Little Red Cap, still alive, from the wolf's belly. Then the wolf is executed, in a manner befitting his crime, by having heavy stones sewn into his belly. The entire story holds out the promise of a successful development towards maturity, but admonishes the child about the consequences of a precocious sexuality. As Bettelheim observes: " 'Little Red Cap' in symbolic form projects the girl into the dangers of her oedipal conflicts during puberty, and then saves her from them, so that she will be able to mature conflict-free."[12] The gingerbread man was irreversibly consumed by the fox; but Little Red Cap is redeemed from her error, reborn from the wolf's belly as a more obedient and dutiful child. The happy ending distinguishes the fairy tale from the cautionary tale. And it is the fairy tale ending which Atwood has assimilated into her novel.

The story "Little Red Cap" joins several motifs which also figure prominently in *The Edible Woman*. Redness, sexuality, and fear of being eaten are vividly brought together in Atwood's novel at the party in Peter's apartment. Marian's dress acts as an advertisement of her sexuality, announcing her surrender to Peter. Throughout the party Peter stalks her with his camera, trying to capture the new Marian on film. But throughout the party Marian experiences Peter's behaviour as something more sinister:

> He had a camera in his hand; but now she saw what it really was.
>
> (p. 243)

> Once he pulled the trigger she would be stopped, fixed indissolubly in that gesture, that single stance, unable to move or change.
>
> (p. 245)

> That dark intent marksman with his aiming eye had been there all the time, hidden by the other layers, waiting for her at the dead centre: a homicidal maniac with a lethal weapon in his hands.
>
> (p. 246)

Marian's mind here links Peter's sexuality with his use of mechanical objects to destroy things. Camera is seen as gun, a valid equation insofar as both are impersonal, technological devices by which Peter masters objects and beings at a distance from himself. In other words, Marian runs from Peter when she realizes he is a modern technological version of the wolf. However, in *The Edible Woman* the wolf figure turns out to be double. Duncan, the erstwhile rescuer, turns out to be a wolf in sheep's clothing. Duncan is not mechanical, but he is self-centred and exploitive, just as Peter is. Atwood has adopted the fairy tale plot structure—her heroine survives—but has transposed the tone of the story towards uncertainty.

The result is not the wish-fulfillment Bettelheim describes as so beneficial to children, but a problematic story, challenging to grown-up intellects — a sort of adult fairy tale.

Marian's reasons for fearing Peter can be clarified by examining an earlier scene which also unites redness, cameras, and guns. This is the scene in the bar of the Park Plaza Hotel, during which Peter tells his story about rabbit-hunting. As this story is being told, Marian grows disoriented:

> Peter's voice seemed to be getting louder and faster — the stream of words was impossible to follow, and my mind withdrew, concentrating instead on the picture of the scene in the forest. I saw it as though it was a slide projected on a screen in a dark room, the colours luminous, green, brown, blue for the sky, and Peter stood with his back to me in a plaid shirt, his rifle slung on his shoulder. A group of friends, those friends whom I had never met, were gathered around him, their faces clearly visible in the sunlight that fell in shafts down through the anonymous trees, splashed with blood, the mouths wrenched with laughter. I couldn't see the rabbit.
>
> (p. 69)

Marian imagines Peter as vicious, and sees him wielding weapons of mechanical destruction. The reason Marian can't see the rabbit is because she unconsciously feels she is the rabbit. Peter is Marian's lover; yet Peter is seen as threatening to tear her apart, wishing to gut her as bloodily and casually as he gutted the rabbit.

Peter's hunting story and Marian's reaction to it constitute a displaced primal scene, evoking the child's tendency to see sexual intercourse as a violent physical struggle. As Bettelheim remarks in discussing "Little Red Cap": "While most children do not know about those animals of which one dies during the sex act, these destructive connotations are quite vivid in the child's conscious and unconscious mind — so much so that most children view the sexual act primarily as an act of violence which one partner commits on the other."[13] Moreover, a woman's monthly menstrual cycle provides evidence which can be interpreted — however illogically — as indicating that sexual activity may result in a form of dangerous injury. Already, when Peter stalks Marian with his camera, she is wearing a red dress. She is symbolically covered with menstrual blood, advertising her sexual maturity. She fears that the symbolic turning inside-out represented by the dress only foreshadows a literal enactment of Peter's wish to spread her insides all over the landscape as he splashed the rabbit's guts over the trees. In short, Marian fears destruction by sex.

Why does Marian view sex in such an abnormal way? We cannot investigate Marian's childhood traumas, for we know virtually nothing of her earlier life. But we do know something of how Marian views parental figures. Marian's landlady, the fearsome "lady down below," has an adolescent daughter and is old enough to be Marian's mother. The lady down below is carefully dressed, her house is meticulously clean and fussily decorated — clearly, she has an anal character. Moreover, she disapproves of overt sexuality, and seeks to protect her daughter from corrupting experiences. Marian tells us: ". . . when we first considered renting the apartment she made it clear to us, by discreet allusions to previous tenants, that whatever happened the child's innocence must not be corrupted, and that two young ladies were surely more to be depended upon than two young men" (pp. 14–15). The lady down below is not a comforting mother-figure. Quite the reverse — she is a witch-figure. Similarly forbidding are the older ladies who work in Marian's layer at Seymour Surveys. They make it clear to her that sexuality as signalled by impending marriage, is incompatible with further work for the company. Like the little boy in one version of "The Gingerbread Man," Marian is not supposed to manifest her sexual curiosity openly. Her punishment is dismissal from her job.

Marian's uneasiness over sex is linked with a quite prominent, though little-discussed, complex of images in the book. These are the repeated images relating to pregnancy, childbirth, and children. *The Edible Woman* contains two pregnancies (Clara's and Ainsley's), a baby (Clara's third child), and Clara's two pre-school age children. Discussions on the theme of feminine reproductive powers figure largely in Marian's conversations with Ainsley, and the same topic is considered by Clara's husband Joe at Peter's party. However, throughout the novel the presentation of pregnancy and childbirth is distinctly negative. The pregnant Clara is described as looking "like a boa-constrictor that has swallowed a watermelon" (p. 31). Her children's most apparent trait is their ability to produce large quantities of excrement at inconvenient times. At Marian's dinner party, Clara's children contribute a pungent tang to the atmopshere:

> Marian hovered about, handing diaper pins and pretending to be helpful, but secretly wondering whether it would be bad taste to go down and get one of the many odour-killing devices from the lady down below's bathroom. Joe bustled about, whistling and bringing fresh supplies; Clara made apologetic remarks in Peter's direction. "Small children are like this, it's only shit. Perfectly natural, we all do it. Only," she said, joggling the youngest on her knee, "some of us have a sense of timing. Don't we, you little turd?"
>
> (p. 179)

Marian reflects: "Clara didn't deny that her children stank, but neither did she take any pains to conceal it. She admitted it, she almost affirmed it; it was as though she wanted it to be appreciated" (p. 179). No wonder, in a previous scene, when Clara phones Marian and Marian asks "How are you?" Clara replies succinctly, "Shitty, thanks" (p. 28).

Marian fears sex and finds children disgusting. Her attitudes are not those of a reasonable and mature adult. In fact, Marian is best understood as someone overcome by regressive anxieties. Her emphatic linking of children and excrement is very close to an equation psychoanalytic thought suggests is often made by young children: column of feces equals child. Marian seems to find all natural processes repellent; she views them as forms of excreting. Her attitude resembles Len Slank's horror when told by Ainsley that he is to become a father: "Now I'm going to be all mentally tangled up in Birth. Fecundity. Gestation. Don't you realize what that will do to me? It's obscene, that horrible oozy . . ." (p. 159). Marian too seems repelled by the fluid, untidy processes of nature.

Marian's peculiar attitudes can be better understood if we observe the close link between Marian and the equally neurotic Len Shank, who on several occasions is pointedly described as Marian's particular friend. There is a very marked degree of similarity between Len's fate and Marian's fate, for both fall victim to calculating members of the opposite sex. Peter is an "other-directed" individual, who derives his life-style from external sources such as *Playboy* magazine. In planning marriage with Marian, he is merely proposing to exchange one pre-existing life-style for another. Like Peter, Ainsley is "well-packaged," and her conduct — particularly her pregnancy — is derived from the notions of fashionable psychological gurus. Len is emasculated by Ainsley (think of the tie hanging on the doorknob) just as Marian fears she will be eviscerated by Peter. The agent of violence in Len's case is a baby; even a vicariously experienced pregnancy seems to threaten his physical integrity. Marian fears that continued relations with Peter may literally lead to the creation of a destructive new growth within her body.

Marian's rejection of her own body explains why she stops eating. If nothing goes in, nothing will come out: she will cease being "dirty." Actually, Marian does not immediately reject all food. First, she stops eating most forms of meat. Then, as she realizes that vegetables were once alive, these too gradually become forbidden to her. Most of the shrinking list of foods left Marian are manufactured or processed foods such as noodles or canned rice pudding. These are artificial foods, whose appearance is as unlike the organic substance as possible. In addition, Marian begins to consume vitamin pills, another manufactured alternative to organic food. We have a paradox here. Marian is using the products of the consumer society to sustain a rebellion which is ostensibly directed against that very society. Either Atwood's novel is confused on this point, or Marian's real rebellion is not against Peter and the society he represents. In fact, I suggest that Marian's real rebellion is against herself. She is, to use a phrase that Ainsley reiterates in the book, rejecting her femininity.

Marian's rejection of femininity is clearly visible in her reaction to the ladies at the office Christmas party:

> She examined the women's bodies with interest, critically, as
> though she had never seen them before. And in a way she hadn't, they

had just been there like everything else, desks, telephones, chairs, in the space of the office: objects viewed as outline and surface only. But now she could see the roll of fat pushed up across Mrs. Gun[d]ridge's back by the top of her corset, the ham-like bulge of thigh, the creases round the neck, the large porous cheeks; the blotch of varicose veins glimpsed at the back of one plump crossed leg, the way her jowls jellied when she chewed, her sweater a woolly teacosy over those rounded shoulders; and the others too, similar in structure but with varying proportions and textures of bumpy permanents and dune-like contours of breast and waist and hip; their fluidity sustained somewhere within by bones, without by a carapace of clothing and makeup. What peculiar creatures they were; and the continual flux between the outside and the inside, taking things in, giving them out, chewing, words, potato-chips, burps, grease, hair, babies, milk, excrement, cookies, vomit, coffee, tomato-juice, blood, tea, sweat, liquor, tears, and garbage. . . .

(p. 167)

Marian is horrified to realize that such processes are going on inside her own body: "At some time she would be — or no, already she was like that too; she was one of them, her body the same, identical, merged with that other flesh that choked the air in the flowered room with its sweet organic scent; she felt suffocated by this sargasso-sea of femininity" (p. 167). Such organic processes functioning within oneself seem to threaten decay and dissolution. And Marian, at several points in the novel, does fear that she is dissolving. Moreover, Marian has come to equate femininity with liquid, indefinite, and "dirty" internal processes. Her reaction is ultimately a form of self-loathing; she sees herself, as well as all other women, as refuse or excrement. Earlier, when Peter made love to her in the bathtub, Marian had fleetingly wondered whether he didn't think of her as a "lavatory fixture" (p. 62). Now she is very close to taking her figure of speech literally.

As Marian continues to look at the office ladies, she comes near to panic. Her reaction at this point is revealing: ". . . she wanted something solid, clear: a man; she wanted Peter in the room so that she could put her hand out and hold on to him to keep from being sucked down. Lucy had a gold bangle on one arm. Marian focussed her eyes on it, concentrating on it as though she was drawing its hard gold circle around herself, a fixed barrier between herself and that liquid amorphous other" (p. 167). This is only one of many defensive reactions Marian displays throughout the book. Marian consistently sees the world around her as composed of hard, threatening objects. In response, she tries in many ways to erect a protective or "masculine" shell around her vulnerable or "feminine" inner self. Marian's detached attitude to life, her state of apparent emotional anesthesia, is another means of protecting herself. And Marian's precise and analytical language is also defensive. Marian uses words the way Peter uses mechanical objects — as a means of mastering the external world, and of keeping experience at arm's length.

The dualities Marian imposes on the world can now be re-stated as a dichotomy between masculinity and femininity. Deception and destruction are seen by Marian as masculine; to be deceived and destroyed are seen as feminine. More generally, Marian sees change, with its threat of dissolution, as feminine; she sees permanence as masculine. Moreover, Marian's distinction between masculinity and femininity can be aligned with the dichotomy between culture and nature discussed by Lévi-Strauss:

masculine	feminine
aggressor	victim
deceiver	deceived
permanence	change
culture	nature

Marian's rebellion, which at first sight appears to be simply a flight away from culture, is really more complicated. By refusing to eat, she is fleeing from her own feminine or natural self; she is trying to opt out of the distressingly messy cycle of natural processes. But Marian's conduct leads to a new dilemma. Marian faces starvation.

I have argued that when Marian stops eating she is not simply enacting in her own life a more humane and compassionate ethic than that practised by the society around her — though, at one level of meaning, she is doing that. Fundamentally, Marian is regressing to childish behaviour and childish modes of thought. Marian's behavior combines two immature reactions to sexuality and pregnancy. As children often do, Marian sees sex as a violent and destructive activity; and Marian's repugnance towards pregnancy originates in a childish fear that the swollen body of a pregnant woman may at any moment burst apart. In addition, we might argue that Marian, like a child, is striking back at parental figures by refusing to eat. Refusing food is one of the child's strongest weapons for arousing expressions of parental concern; the child is asserting his or her autonomous existence by prompting a response in the parents. Thus, Marian's behaviour is partly a "look at me!" gesture, a cry for attention.

Despite her aversion to sex, when Marian flees from Peter's party she ends up in bed with Duncan. This apparently inconsistent turn of events can take place because in this encounter Marian views herself not as a sex-object, but as a combination of nursemaid and mother to the overly "latent" Duncan. In short, she regards Duncan as a child. Duncan has earlier expressed his life's ambition as becoming an amoeba. A trickster, he is evasive and formless. A grown man, he behaves like a child. Running away from an over-rigid society, Marian nonetheless needs some means of assuring herself of her continuing identity. She turns to the immature-seeming Duncan as a safe source of human contact. Thus, she is close to panic when it seems Duncan is not responding to her attempt at acting out an oedipal mothering wish:

> She clenched her hands on the sheet. She was tense with impatience and with another emotion that she recognized as the cold energy of terror. At this moment to evoke something, some response, even though she could not predict the thing that might emerge from beneath that seemingly-passive surface, the blank white formless thing lying insubstantial in the darkness before her, shifting as her eyes shifted trying to see, that appeared to have no temperature, no odour, no thickness and no sound, was the most important thing she could ever have done, could ever do, and she couldn't do it. The knowledge was an icy desolation worse than fear.
>
> (p. 254)

Fortunately for Marian, Duncan soon takes the initiative:

> "Lie down," he said.
> She sank back, still with the sheet clutched around her and her knees drawn up.
> He put his arm around her. "No," he said, "you have to unbend. Assuming the foetal position won't be any help at all, god knows I've tried it long enough." He stroked her with his hand, gently, straightening her out, almost as though he was ironing her.
>
> (p. 254)

But Duncan is a false refuge for Marian. Marian must strike out on her own, and throughout the latter stages of the book, this realization slowly makes its way up from the depths of Marian's mind to full consciousness.

I began this paper by quarrelling with the interpretation which sees *The Edible Woman* as primarily a satire on society. Yet the psychological scrutiny to which I have subjected Atwood's novel does not, in the end, preclude understanding the novel as a feminist comment on the status of women. Feminine identity, which figures so largely as a theme in the novel, is not viewed by contemporary Freudian thought as a matter of simple biological determinism. Rather, a girl's sense of identity is seen as being socialized into a different mold than that prepared for a male child. Thus, the classical Freudian formulas which feminists find so offensive — "penis envy," "castration complex" — have been reinterpreted as reflections of the oppressed status of women in a patriarchal society. Women are in no way inferior because they do not possess penises. They are viewed as weaker because they lack masculine sex characteristics, and they have too often internalized this unfair judgment of inferiority.[14]

Therefore, I wish to explicitly repudiate the notion that Marian could solve all her problems by marrying Peter and settling down like a broodhen on a nest. The point is that Marian must accept herself *as she is*. When Len Slank objects to becoming a father, Ainsley accuses him of "uterus envy" (p. 159). Actually, Len feels degraded by being implicated in so gross a biological process as birth. Marian too feels inferior and unclean because of her reproductive potential. Marian must first accept herself as a woman—and this includes accepting the biological *potential* for giving birth. What Marian does with her biological nature is another matter; but first the simple fact of feminine anatomy must be acknowledged. Marian is unconsciously rebelling against society's implicit labelling of women as degraded by virtue of their biology. Her first step in making a new life for herself must be to accept her biology as a share in the common lot of all human beings, not as a stigma of second-rate status.

We come at last to the most puzzling image in Atwood's novel: the "edible woman" herself, the cake-doll which Marian bakes and offers in turn to Peter and to Duncan. Marian ices the cake-woman in red, repeating the red of her own party dress. So it seems the edible woman must be Marian herself. But the cake-woman is also a *small* woman: therefore a child. The cake reminds us of the two dolls Marian has unexplainedly preserved from her childhood. These two dolls may be one of the few hints we have concerning Marian's earlier existence. Playing with dolls enacts a young girl's identification with her mother, and expresses a wish to have a child of one's own just as Mummy does. However, even the best-loved doll may be subjected to sudden acts of violence, which result from the child's need to express hostilities towards the parents (especially towards the mother) which cannot safely be acted out overtly. The mental process is simple enough: parent disciplines child; child cannot fight back directly, so child disciplines doll. Hence, Marian lectures her cake-woman shortly before Peter arrives: " 'You look delicious,' she told her. 'Very appetizing. And that's what will happen to you; that's what you get for being food' " (p. 270). Marian may be reenacting the chastisement which she herself has received from society.

Marian explains the cake to Peter as being a substitute for herself. Peter is invited to act out his supposed violent desires on the cake instead of on Marian. Peter rejects the cake, and leaves. The relationship is clearly over. What has happened? Has Peter refused to acknowledge the truth about himself? We have Marian's assertion that Peter is out to destroy her, but surely this is dubious evidence. The other derogatory judgments of Peter, offered by Ainsley and Duncan, come from equally untrustworthy sources. The book actually offers us no valid reason for thinking of Peter as anything other than a relatively normal, though admittedly conservative and conventional, rising young professional man. In fact, before she confronts Peter with the cake Marian herself has a glimpse of this viewpoint: "Peter was not the enemy after all, he was just a normal human being like most other people" (p. 271). Marian quickly rejects her insight, but if we condemn Peter too quickly we may be using a knee-jerk reflex, an intellectual's automatic assumption of superiority over the advocates of pragmatic methods. Peter should be given the benefit of the doubt. He refuses the cake and leaves Marian because he does not recognize himself

in Marian's irrational accusation. He feels no desire to destroy Marian—
just a conventional desire for a secure home and a comforting mother-wife
of his own. If anyone is vicious in this scene it is Marian, who offers Peter
her symbolic child as a substitute for herself. Unconsciously, Marian is
seeking to punish Peter for his imagined attack on her. Of course Peter
rejects the cake. To eat it would be to perform symbolic cannibalism not
only on Marian but on his own child.

After Peter has gone, Marian confronts the cake herself. She thinks:
"As a symbol it had definitely failed" (p. 271). However, she begins to see
the cake in another light. Marian has thought of the cake as symbolizing
femininity. But she now begins to look at it as what it most certainly is:
food.

> Suddenly she was hungry. Extremely hungry. That cake after all was
> only a cake. She picked up the platter, carried it to the kitchen table and
> located a fork. "I'll start with the feet," she decided.
>
> (pp. 271–72)

When Ainsley comes upon Marian eating the cake, she exclaims: "You're
rejecting your femininity" (p. 272). Ainsley is quite wrong. Marian is
primarily eating a cake. Insofar as she is performing a symbolic action, she
is accepting her femininity by incorporating the feminine cake-woman or
cake-child into herself. It could even be argued that Marian is symbolically
impregnating herself, or at least accepting the possibility of pregnancy.

Duncan is the final character to confront the cake. Skilled in the
analysis of symbols, he also knows when not to carry out an over-elaborate
analysis of hidden meanings. He sees a cake rather than a woman's head;
he eats it without compunctions. When Marian asserts that Peter has been
trying to destroy her, Duncan disagrees. Yet his response is ultimately
ambiguous:

> "That's ridiculous," he said gravely. "Peter wasn't trying to destroy
> you. That's something you made up. Actually you were trying to destroy
> him."
> I had a sinking feeling. "Is that true?" I asked.
> "Search your soul," he said, gazing hypnotically at me from behind
> his hair. He drank some coffee and paused to give me time, then added,
> "But the real truth is that it wasn't Peter at all. It was me. I was trying to
> destroy you."
>
> (pp. 280–81)

Duncan sheds more darkness than light on the symbolic significance of the
cake, and on the meaning of the novel as a whole. We do not know how to
take his final comment, after he finishes eating the cake: "He scraped the
last chocolate curl up with his fork and pushed away the plate. 'Thank
you,' he said, licking his lips. 'It was delicious' " (p. 281). Is Duncan
merely referring to the cake, or is he speaking metaphorically of Marian?
Perhaps, as Duncan himself has pointed out, these symbolic considerations

are no longer relevant: "What does it matter, you're back to so-called reality, you're a consumer" (p. 281). Marian must now carry on her life in the real world, accepting full responsibility for her actions. If she has learned anything, it is that all life is lived at the expense of other creatures, and that she cannot rely on anyone outside herself to supply the answers to important questions or to validate her actions.

Lest the end of this paper seem to forget the beginning, let me return once more to the story of the gingerbread man. There is an obvious parallel between the gingerbread man and Marian's miniature cake-woman. In fact, a correspondence can be established between the story of the gingerbread man and the events of the novel's final pages:

Gingerbread Man baked	Gingerbread Man comes alive	Gingerbread Man runs away	Gingerbread Man meets fox	Gingerbread Man eaten by fox	Fox is no longer hungry
Marian bakes the cake	Marian sees the cake as symbolic	Peter goes away and Ainsley disapproves	Duncan talks with Marian concerning deception	Duncan eats the cake	Marian and Duncan go their own ways

By baking the cake, Marian is splitting herself into two parts. The cake represents her feminine self, the vulnerable and inferior person society would like her to be. Marian is trying to protect what she sees as the real Marian, the autonomous human being endowed with independent desires and needs. Yet Marian finally eats some of the cake. That is, she reverses the mental separation symbolized by the creation of the cake-woman. At the novel's end she is a whole person again. Her fate is uncertain, but she will face it squarely instead of trying to escape.

Surfacing has often been viewed as providing a more complete treatment of the issues raised in Atwood's first novel. *Surfacing* presents a possible solution to Marian's dilemma at the end of *The Edible Woman*, namely pregnancy and a more enduring liaison with a man. But what *Surfacing* gains in completeness, it may lose in evocative power. The rootless condition of Marian MacAlpin echoes the plight of many people today; the difficulty of imagining a more satisfactory ending to Marian's story seems an appropriate reflection of the way many people today see their lives. The events in *The Edible Woman* enact a psychodrama, but do not anatomize it as *Surfacing* does. The unresolved ending of *The Edible Woman* forces the reader to attempt his own interpretation of the novel's meaning. Atwood does not serve her message up on a platter, but lets the symbols and incidents reverberate within the reader's mind, in the manner in which Bettelheim describes fairy tales working in the minds of chil-dren — and in the manner art has always worked within the human mind.

Notes

1. Margaret Atwood, *The Edible Woman*, introduction by Alan Dawe (Toronto: McClelland & Stewart, 1973), p. 2. All subsequent quotations are from this edition.

2. Catherine McLay, "The Divided Self: Theme and Pattern in Margaret Atwood's *Surfacing*," *Journal of Canadian Fiction*, 13 (1975), 82.

3. Frank Davey, "Atwood Walking Backwards," *Open Letter*, 2nd ser., no. 5 (Summer, 1973), 77.

4. Robert Kroetsch, "Unhiding the Hidden: Recent Canadian Fiction," *Journal of Canadian Fiction*, III, 3 (1974), 43–45.

5. Graeme Gibson, *Eleven Canadian Novelists* (Toronto: Anansi, 1973), p. 20.

6. *The Gingerbread Man*, illustrated by Carl and Mary Hauge (Racine: Golden Press, 1973).

7. George Woodcock, "Margaret Atwood: Poet as Novelist," *The Canadian Novel in the Twentieth Century*, edited by George Woodcock (Toronto: McClelland & Stewart, 1975), p. 315.

8. Paul Galdone, *The Gingerbread Boy* (New York: Seabury Press, 1975).

9. *The Gingerbread Man*, pictures by Ed Arno (New York/London/Richmond Hill: Scholastic Book Services, 1967).

10. Bruno Bettelheim, *The Uses of Enchantment: The Meaning and Importance of Fairy Tales* (New York: Vintage, 1977), p. 173.

11. *The Uses of Enchantment*, pp., 173–74.

12. *The Uses of Enchantment*, p. 172.

13. *The Uses of Enchantment*, pp. 175–76.

14. A range of contemporary comment on the psychoanalytic view of women can be found in Jean Strouse, ed., *Women and Analysis: Dialogues on Psychoanalytic Views of Femininity* (New York: Grossman, 1974).

Margaret Atwood's *Lady Oracle*: Fantasy and the Modern Gothic Novel

Susan J. Rosowski*

During an interview, Margaret Atwood observed, "we've been so cut off from our social mythology that we hardly know what it is; that's one thing that has to be discovered."[1] Her novel *Lady Oracle* is such a discovery; it is a journey through myths. But it is also a Gothic novel, historically a form that "open[s] horizons beyond social patterns, rational decisions, and institutionally approved emotions. . . ."[2] In *Lady Oracle*, Atwood turns this tradition back upon itself, confronting the Gothic dimensions that exist *within* our social mythology. To do so, she uses

*From a paper delivered at the Midwest Modern Language Association Convention, Minneapolis, 3 November 1978, and a slightly altered version, published earlier in *Research Studies*, Washington State University Press, 49, no. 2 (June 1981):87–98. Reprinted by permission of the journal and the author.

fantasy to extend thematic and technical possibilities of the modern Gothic novel.

Lady Oracle begins with a jarring mixture of Gothic horror and comic familiarity. After having simulated her own death, the narrator is in Terremoto (Earthquake), where she must identify the real and valuable elements in herself with which to construct a new life. Her search, a psychic journey through myths, begins with a loose, cultural sense of myth, "any real or fictional story, recurring theme, or character type that appeals to the consciousness of a people by embodying its cultural ideals or by giving expression to deep, commonly felt emotions."[3] Clearly, the narrator has incorporated the advertising myth of ideal beauty: sunbathing, she has fantasies of herself "as a Mediterranean splendor, golden-brown, striding with laughing teeth into an aqua sea, carefree at last, the past discarded."[4] But the cultural ideal is contradicted by her recalling "I had no suntan lotion (Maximum Protection: without it I'd burn and freckle), so I'd covered my shoulders and thighs with several of the landlord's skimpy bath towels" (p. 7). The rest of the novel explores this contrast between mythic ideal and human reality as the narrator moves from temporal, cultural myths to archetypal myths, "patterns of imagery" that "are oracular in origin, and derive from the epiphanic moment, the flash of instantaneous comprehension with no direct reference to time."[5]

The narrator begins her psychic journey by recalling her historical past, represented primarily by her mother. But in this return she reaches only roles others expected her to play in their personal fantasies. Her relationship with her mother "was professionalized early. She was to be the manager, the creator, the agent; I was to be the product" (p. 67), the thin, accomplished daughter of the fashionable wife of a successful doctor. Remembering that "my mother named me after Joan Crawford," the narrator senses the negation behind the act, wondering "did she give me someone else's name because she wanted me never to have a name of my own?" (p. 42). The question leads ultimately to the negation underlying modern social mythology: the social rituals enacted by our cultural agents—the family, school, literature, film, advertising—transmit conceptualizations that are inadequate for human existence.[6]

Attempting to play the role imposed upon her, the child encounters the disparities between human reality and fantasy character that will permeate the rest of her life. Most basically, the character she is expected to play is thin; she is fat, a physical incongruity that will prevent her from being accepted in any of the adult world's conceptualizations. But this physical incongruity only announces other incongruities: the child named Joan is uncertain which of Joan Crawford's sides she is expected to emulate—whether the beautiful, ambitious, ruthless screen characters or the serious, unhappy, tragic woman who played those characters. And she reacts to her mother with similar confusion, for her mother, too, is a composite of disparate creations, existing in mirrored reflections with "three actual heads, which rose from her toweled shoulders on three separate necks" (pp. 66–7). Human reality shows only dimly through the created appearance: "her lips were thin but she made a larger mouth with a lipstick over and around them, like Bette Davis, which gave her a curious double mouth, the real one showing through the false one like a shadow" (p. 68).

The narrator's mother functions as a cultural agent who transmits social mythology—fictional constructs into which the child is expected to fit. The implications of this mythology, initially comic, become increasingly menacing, for by it human reality appears monstrous. To explore these implications, Atwood uses the structural and thematic form of a journey into the Gothic. As an adult, the narrator creates her own fictional construct: she earns her living by writing Costume Gothic novels. Through them, she confronts similarity between ordinary human existence and the Gothic and, finally, enters mythic dimensions of her imaginary world.

Initially, the two worlds appear safely separate—one fantasy and the other real. The fantasy Costume Gothic represents life reduced to situation: it works on the premise that faceless characters placed within certain forms, represented by clothes and settings, automatically adopt the roles defined by their situations. The procedure seems reassuringly simple: when she began to write novels, the narrator "thought if I could only get the clothes right, everything else would fall into line. And it did: the hero, a handsome, well-bred, slightly balding man, dressed in an immaculately tailored tweed cloak, like Sherlock Holmes's, pursued the heroine, crushing his lips to hers in a hansom cab and rumpling her *pelisse*" (p. 156). Behind the Costume Gothic, as behind other fictional constructs, is the similarly reassuring and simple appeal of escape—escape from the demands for individual responsibility in a complex world. Thus "the heroines of my books were mere stand-ins: their features were never clearly defined, their faces were putty which each reader could reshape into her own, adding a little beauty" (pp. 34–5). But increasingly it becomes clear that beneath the apparent separation of fantasy from reality is connection, a connection that Atwood presents by reversing the usual technique of the Gothic. The Gothic novel characteristically evokes rising horror over the disjuncture between the Gothic world created by the novel and the ordinary world, usually represented by the narrator; *Lady Oracle* evokes rising horror over the similarity between the two worlds.

Gradually we realize that in her own life, the adult narrator perceives the world in myths as limited as those of her childhood or of the Costume Gothics she writes. Her self image as a Fellini heroine is countered by an equally one-dimensional construct: "in fact it was less like a Fellini movie than . . . [a] Walt Disney film" (p. 9). And, like a character in one of her Gothic novels, she automatically and passively adopts the roles suggested by her situation. While a girl, this role is defined by her obesity: she "played kindly aunt and wisewoman" to other girls in her class (p. 93). When she loses weight and, by doing so, destroys the basis for her role as confidante, she assumes that "this was the formal beginning of my second self" (p. 137). But her perception of her new self is simplistic. Because she looks different, she assumes she *is* "a different person"; and she willingly sacrifices her own past to the demands suggested by her new appearance: "I was the right shape, but I had the wrong past. I'd have to get rid of it entirely and construct a different one for myself, a more agreeable one" (p. 141). The past she constructs, however, is not for herself, but for the roles imposed on her by others. Rescued by a Polish Count after she fell from a bus, she meets his expectations by acting the part first of an "easygoing art student manquée" (p. 150) and then of mistress, following a principle of passive adaptation to a given situation: "if you find yourself trapped in a situation you can't get out of gracefully, you might as well pretend you chose it. Otherwise you will look ridiculous" (p. 149). As she says quite simply, "I'd always found other people's versions of reality very influential" (p. 160).

Similarly, she can interact with others only in the terms of such constructs. She meets, for example, Arthur, the man she will marry, while "pacing out the route which was about to be taken" by one of her characters, "Samantha Deane, the heroine of *Escape from Love*, as she fled from the illicit attentions of Sir Edmund DeVere" (p. 162). Her first perception of Arthur is of "a skinny, confused-looking young man" (p. 164), perhaps the most human description of him in the novel. But this reality is almost immediately transformed into a fictional hero: "He was wearing a black crew-neck sweater, which I found quite dashing. A melancholy fighter for almost-lost causes, idealistic and doomed, sort of like Lord Byron, whose biography I had just been skimming" (p. 165). The role recognized—that of a Byronic freedom fighter—the narrator next goes "to the public library—the same one where I got my costume books—and took out all the Bertrand Russell's books I could find" (pp. 165–6), researching the role she herself must assume to enter Arthur's fictional world.

Once established, fictional constructs become impervious to human reality. This central truth underlies ordinary human behavior. The disparity between myth and reality is so great that eventually individuals resist and, finally, reject their simplistic roles. After her marriage, for example, Arthur stops appearing to the narrator as "a cloaked, sinuous and faintly menacing stranger." She realizes that "he couldn't be that: I lived with him, and cloaked strangers didn't leave their socks on the floor. . . . I kept Arthur in our apartment and the strangers in their castles and mansions, where they belonged" (p. 216). But the fictional model itself—the myth of the Byronic hero—remains unaltered: the narrator continues to dream of "a tall man in evening dress, with an opera cloak and smoldering eyes" who whispers, " 'Let me take you away. We will dance together, always.' It was a great temptation, despite the fact that he wasn't real" (p. 23).

The temptation, of course, lies precisely in the fact that he wasn't real. In their everyday lives, individuals go to great lengths to protect their escape fantasies, incorporating new actors into fantasy roles as others slip out of those roles. An artist who calls himself the Royal Porcupine and who works in " 'Con-create poetry' " (p. 241), displaying frozen bodies of dead animals that had been run over by cars, succeeds Arthur as the narrator's Byronic hero. Meeting the Royal Porcupine, the narrator believes "finally I had met somene who would waltz with me," again ignoring discrepancies with reality so she can preserve the dream. When they meet in Simpson's at the Red Hot Stand, the narrator admits "I found his cape a little incongruous in Simpson's Basement, and the sexual fantasies I'd been having about him drooped slightly. Still, there was something Byronic about him" (p. 254).

Changes are inevitable, however, when complex human beings are forced into limited fictional constructs. Tension between fantasy and reality builds until the fictional construct, embraced originally as an escape from human reality, demands finally its sacrifice. Human existence takes the form of a sequence of discarded selves: the narrator's mother discarded her daughter; the daughter in turn discarded her mother; the husband discarded the wife; the daughter discarded the father; and so on. Self sacrifices extend the sequence. Throughout the novel, cloak imagery represents the camouflage of a role, donned to meet others' versions of reality. The narrator's childhood obesity was such a protection, a "magic cloak of blubber and invisibility" (p. 141); Arthur's "aloofness was . . . like a figurative cloak" (p. 197); and the Royal Porcupine actually wears "a long black cloak" (p. 239).

But as the narrator discovers, each fantasy role, assumed as protection against the threatening demands of human reality, "turn[s] into a trap" (334), in which the fiction threatens to consume the real. Without a sense of personal identity on which to base wholeness, there is no means by which one might integrate separate roles, and the demands of each role, "complete in itself but rendering the others worthless" (211), are that other roles be discarded. Myth is perceived as normal and real; everything not in it becomes ghostlike: "the difficulty was that I found each of my lives perfectly normal and appropriate, but only at the time. When I was with Arthur, the Royal Porcupine seemed like a daydream from one of my less credible romances, with an absurdity about him that I tried to exclude from my fictions. But when I was with the Royal Porcupine, he seemed plausible and solid. Everything he did and said made sense in his own terms, whereas it was Arthur who became unreal" (p. 259). Finally, the narrator, wondering "was I hurting [Arthur], was I being unfaithful?" is unable to respond, for when she is outside Arthur's version of reality, he "faded to an unsubstantial ghost, a washed-out photo on some mantel-piece I'd long ago abandoned," and "how could you hurt a photograph?" (p. 259).

In asking the question, the narrator evokes a moral norm from the reader who, applying "a standard . . . close to his everyday outlook,"[7] must answer that people are not photographs, that one does hurt others, and that the most monstrous sacrifice of all is the sacrifice of human morality. By moving outside the novel for this norm, thereby departing from the traditional Gothic pattern in which "there is a moral norm present in the story,"[8] Atwood underscores the sacrifice to which the similarity between ordinary human existence and the Gothic myth leads. It is a sacrifice of complexity and, with it, morality.

The process is circular. To maintain one's fantasy, one must refuse to admit human complexities, for they will destroy fictional simplicity. Yet human beings are complex; even the Royal Porcupine gradually becomes "gray and multi-dimensional and complicated like everyone else" (p. 269). Refusing to be fitted into simplistic roles, human beings instead go through menacing metamorphoses. A birth-death struggle results. The Royal Porcupine, confronted with the narrator's discarding the fantasy shared with him, shaves his beard, removes his cloak, and becomes Chuck Brewer, commenting of his former self, "I killed him. . . . He's over with, he's finished" (p. 270). The irony is that without the fantasy, there is no basis for the relationship. For the narrator, "it was horrible. He'd thought that by transforming himself into something more like Arthur he could have Arthur's place; but by doing this he'd murdered the part of him that I loved" (p. 271). Eventually the relationship is ended, and the self each created for the other is sacrificed.

As the narrator moves through her own past, then, she meets discarded selves that return to haunt her. She is pursued by her former self as the Fat Lady; by the "astral body" of her mother (p. 173), and by "the wraith of Arthur" (p. 11). In this respect, *Lady Oracle* is like other Gothic novels in which "the center of the fiction" is "the experience of the enlightened person feeling haunted by some demonic self."[9] But in *Lady Oracle*, Atwood turns the Gothic tradition back upon itself, for the ghosts result from the mythic mode of which they are a part: demonic selves or ghosts result from the attempt to model ordinary human existence upon a social mythology that is Gothic.

Structurally, as well as thematically, Atwood in *Lady Oracle* goes beyond simply incorporating elements of the Gothic: she layers historical developments of the Gothic novel to trace the narrator's journey into the mythic dimensions of her own existence. At the first, simplest level, the narrator composes novels in the Radcliffe mode of "a novel in which the central figure is a young woman who is simultaneously persecuted victim and courageous heroine."[10] On the next level, the assumptions behind the narrator's Costume Gothics are those by which she lives her own life. Exploring the consequences of ordinary human existence modeled after this mode, the narrator presents the birth myth in the Shelleyan mode of Gothic, in which "emphasis is not upon what precedes birth, not upon birth itself, but upon what follows birth: the trauma of the afterbirth."[11] And, finally, Atwood takes the Gothic myth into a modern context with her thematic focus on the self.

The birth-death struggles in *Lady Oracle* are, ultimately, the narrator's. As she did in *Surfacing*, so in *Lady Oracle* Atwood works in the Henry James tradition of the ghost tale, in which ghosts are "a fragment of one's own self which has split off."[12] By using an author of Gothic novels as her persona, Atwood extends the tradition of the Gothic novel as in the "literature of process" which "reflects its creator's mind."[13] Attempting to actualize herself in terms dictated by a Gothic world masquerading as ordinary, the narrator creates characters to meet demands which seem innocuous, even reasonable. Her role as Lady Oracle, the poet, is such a creation. But distance exists between the self and the created character. As Lady Oracle gains strength, the narrator perceives this distance: "I felt very visible. But it was as if someone with my name were out there in the real world, impersonating me, saying things I'd never said but which appeared in the newspapers, doing things for which I had to take the consequences: my dark twin, my funhouse-mirror reflection" (pp. 250–1). Separation between self and created character widens, and Gothic dimensions of the character's role emerge: the character grows to monstrous proportions. The narrator begins to perceive her own creation, Lady Oracle, as "taller than I was, more beautiful, more threatening. She wanted to kill me and take my place, and by the time she did this no one would notice the difference because the media were in on the plot, they were helping her" (p. 251). Finally, the self must destroy its own creation to save itself from being consumed. But in destroying its creation, the self must return to its own lack of identity and, finally, to the knowledge that the created character is a desperate attempt of the self to affirm its own reality.

And this insight is what Atwood adds to the Gothic mode. In such novels as *Frankenstein* and *Caleb Williams*, each character "has his autonomous and explicable nature; each becomes a demonic spectre or projection *only* as a result of the perversion of social love; each has a nature distinct from that demonic role."[14] This distinct nature is denied characters in *Lady Oracle*. Instead, Atwood focuses on the birth-death throes of the self; the motivating fear is that the self will be annihilated. On one level, this fear concerns possible rejection by another: the narrator never told Arthur she wrote Costume Gothics because of "fear, mostly. When I first met him he talked a lot about wanting a woman whose mind he could respect, and I knew that if he found out I'd written *The Secret of Morgrave Manor* he wouldn't respect mine" (pp. 33–4). But the more basic fear concerns the absence of self. If human existence consists of autonomous fantasies which exclude people and negate human contact, then love is "merely a tool, smiles were another tool, they were both just tools for accomplishing certain ends." From such a realization, the narrator feels "I'd never really loved anyone, not Paul, not Chuck the Royal Porcupine, not even Arthur. I'd polished them with my love and expected them to shine, brightly enough to return my own reflection, enhanced and sparkling." And, finally, "it seemed to me impossible that anyone could ever really love anyone, or if they could, that anything lasting or fine would come of it" (p. 282–3). From her realization of her failure to love, she moves to the failure of others to love her — or even to perceive her as a separate person. Instead, each insists she conform to his or her fictional construct: to her mother, she must be the thin, beautiful, accomplished daughter; to Paul, the heroine in distress; to Fraser Buchanan, the rich, seductive author; to the Royal Porcupine the poetic muse; and to Arthur the compassionate political sympathizer. Each, like Paul, "wouldn't know at all what to do with me" if she or he had her, for "I was not the same as my phantom" (p. 283).

In a world in which reality has been sacrificed to fantasy, one has no basis for a belief in one's own reality without the fantasy. The horror of possible annihilation is, then, ultimately a psychological fear over absence or lack of personal identity. The narrator's early obesity represented such an attempt to assert her indisputable reality: "I ate to defy [my mother], but I also ate from panic. Sometimes I was afraid I wasn't really there. I was an accident; I'd heard [my mother] call me an accident. Did I want to become solid, solid as stone so she wouldn't be able to get rid of me?" (p. 78). Determined that "I wouldn't ever let her make me over in her image, thin and beautiful" (p. 88), she eats "steadily, doggedly, stubbornly, anything I could get. The war between myself and my mother was on in earnest; the disputed territory was my body" (p. 69). Gradually, she creates in herself an irrefutable defiance of her mother's image, swelling "visibly, relentlessly before her very eyes. I rose like dough, my body advanced inch by inch towards her across the dining-room table, in this at least I was undefeated" (p. 70), finally reaching five feet eight and weighing two hundred forty-five pounds (p. 74). But, just as Lady Oracle does later, so now the narrator's own creation becomes monstrous to its creator: "One day . . . I happened to glance down at my body. . . . There, staring me in the face, was my thigh. It was enormous, it was gross, it was like a diseased limb . . ." (p. 121).

These birth-death struggles of the self that run throughout *Lady Oracle* represent the relationship between the individual and her social mythology: the individual creates and destroys characters in response to that mythology. To find her personal identity beneath those creations, she must seek, therefore, in myth, for the two are inextricably fused. In her journeys into her mirrored reflections through self hypnosis, the narrator frees herself from the temporal-spatial framework of her historical past.

She finds the elements that characterize cultural myth, but in a purified form:

> She sits on the iron throne
> She is one and three
> The dark lady   the redgold lady
> the blank lady   oracle
> of blood, she who must be
> obeyed   forever
> Her glass wings are gone
> She floats down the river
> singing her last song

In these journeys into herself, the narrator confronts an absence of personal identity similar to that she reached through her journeys into her historical past: she moves beyond "the dark lady" and "the redgold lady," stereotypic characters of the Costume Gothic created to meet plot requirements, to "the blank lady" who is "oracle / of blood, she who must be / obeyed forever." Here again, the narrator reaches the modern horror — a blank self without actuality who becomes, therefore, an "oracle / of blood," for to survive she must destroy her own creations that, in growing, threaten to consume her.

As the distinction between reality and fantasy, between ordinary and Gothic existences, breaks down, previously sacrificed selves seek recognition, each a former creation become monstrous. In her own life, the narrator imagines that "below me, in the foundations of the house, I could hear the clothes I'd buried there growing themselves a body. It was almost completed; it was digging itself out, like a huge blind mole, slowly and painfully shambling up the hill to the balcony . . . a creature composed of all the flesh that used to be mine and which must have gone somewhere" (pp. 320–1). The resurrected creature embodies the most terrifying physical characteristics of previous selves, a combination of blankness and obesity, for "it would have no features, it would be smooth as a potato, pale as starch, it would look like a big thigh, it would have a face like a breast minus the nipple. It was the Fat Lady" (p. 321). More important, she embodies the relationship between self and creation that runs throughout the novel, offering first an illusion of escape, as "she rose into the air and descended on me as I lay stretched out in the chair. For a moment she hovered around me like ectoplasm, like a gelatin shell, my ghost, my angel; then she settled and I was absorbed into her" (p. 321); but, once embraced, threatening to consume her creator: "within my former body, I gasped for air. Disguised, concealed, white fur choking my nose and my mouth. Obliterated" (p. 321).

Attempting to escape into her fictional world, the narrator finds "it was no good; I couldn't stop time, I could shut nothing out" (p. 277). Fictional characters, like created selves, begin to assume a threatening life of their own, seeming "more real than usual, nearer to me, charged with an energy greater than I gave them" (p. 277). Confusion and fear result; with them comes the potential for morality. Requirements of her Gothic novel dictate that "sympathy for Felicia was out of the question, it was against all the rules, it would foul up the plot completely. . . . she had to die" (p. 319); the narrator, no longer able to escape into a simplistic fictional construct, questions the sacrifice, for "what had [Felicia] ever done to deserve it? How could I sacrifice her for the sake of Charlotte?" (p. 319).

But a world in which social mythology follows Gothic premises requires the sacrifice of self to the fictional construct, a sacrifice the narrator confronts when she allows herself to enter the fantasy world of the Costume Gothic in terms of human complexity. Previously discarded characters return: Felicia, entering the forbidden maze characteristic of the Gothic setting, finds four women in its central plot: all, like herself, cast in the role of Lady Redmond. When she opens a door that stands on one side of the plot, Felicia sees her husband, Redmond, on the other side: "Then she knew. Redmond was the killer," for Redmond "wanted to replace her with the other one, the next one, thin and flawless" (p. 342). Increasingly fused with the fictional Felicia, the narrator recognizes the birth-death struggle of self in another's fictional construct. Remaining on her side of the door, she feels safe, refusing to be drawn into his fantasy role. But "cunningly, he began his transformations, trying to lure her into his reach" by representing each of the myths the narrator had perceived in others — her father's "white gauze mask"; the Royal Porcupine's "red beard and moustache"; Lady Oracle's lover's "burning eyes and icicle teeth"; and, finally, Arthur's "turtle-neck sweater." It is only to Arthur that she responds, but as she does so, she perceives not Arthur but her transformation of him into a Byronic hero who promises he'll rescue her and they'll dance forever. Refusing the fantasy, she confronts the death of self behind the fictional construct as *"the flesh fell away from his face, revealing the skull behind it; he stepped towards her, reaching for her throat"* (p. 343). At the mythic center of the novel, the center of the maze, the narrator reaches the modern Gothic horror: just as she has murdered others (or the characters they play), so others are prepared to murder her (or her created characters) if she refuses to conform.

But it is not enough to resist others' versions of reality; one must have her own version of reality to oppose to others' mythologies. And it is precisely that core of personal identity that the narrator lacks. Thus in the narrator's mythic return — in her attempt to restructure herself so that she can move forward in the real world — she is pursued by demons of her old selves and threatened by potential monsters of new ones. Images of past selves sacrificed by herself or by others sweep around her, and "panic . . . rolled in an ice-gray wave back over my head, carrying with it the shapes of my fear. . . . Faces formed and disintegrated in my head" (p. 15).

Finally she realizes "there was no sense trying to get away, I'd brought them all with me, I could still hear their voices, murmuring like a faraway but angry mob. . . . I couldn't keep them out" (p. 310).

Her intention had been to free herself from old creations which had become monstrous, so that "I could start being another person, a different person entirely" (p. 20). To do so, she has simulated her death by drowning, dismembered her former physical self by sawing her hair off, "strand by strand" (p. 14), and buried "my funerary costume, my former self" (p. 19). But having long confused reality and fantasy, she is threatened by the fiction of death, for it reproduces too closely her actual lack of personal identity. The two roles she plays simultaneously — murderer and victim — turn against each other; and the distinction between self and creation, never clear, threatens to break down completely. Though she reassures herself that "the clothes were my own, I hadn't done anything wrong," she still feels guilt, "as though I was getting rid of a body, the corpse of someone I'd killed" (p. 20). And, having confronted the complexity of real life, she finds that she can no longer easily assume the simplistic roles of her Costume Gothics, fearing "maybe they were right, you could stay in the tower for years, weaving away, looking in the mirror, but one glance out the window at real life and that was that. The curse, the doom" (p. 313). She is "the blank lady" of the poem, suspended, waiting passively for a new role suggested by her situation. Unable to act, she can only ask, "where was the new life I'd intended to step into, as easily as crossing a river? It hadn't materialized, and the old life went on without me. I was caged on my balcony waiting to change. . . . I was waiting for something to happen, the next turn of events (a circle? a spiral?). All my life I'd been hooked on plots" (p. 310).

In the end, *Lady Oracle* returns to its beginning — to the present in which the narrator has destroyed her old self and must, inevitably, create a new one. But her exploration of her self, while resulting in confrontation and at least limited, momentary understanding, does not result in a personal mythology adequate to oppose the prevailing social mythology. The narrator thus returns to the initial myth of social human existence as normal and moral, but with a difference, for the reader now realizes with horror the Gothic dimensions of this myth. We watch in helpless recognition as the narrator, having been provided with the fantasy construct of the book, *Nurse of the High Arctic*, assumes the role of the nurse in yet another thinly veiled Gothic myth. In doing so, she creates a new character that is, if anything, potentially more monstrous than her previous ones. With this circular movement, Atwood suggests possibilities for the modern Gothic novel by fusing elements traditionally kept separate — social mythology and Gothic horror. For in *Lady Oracle*, Gothic horror exists not "beyond social patterns, rational decisions, and institutionally approved emotions," but within them.

Notes

1. *Eleven Canadian Novelists*, interviewed by Graeme Gibson (Toronto: Anansi, 1973), pp. 14–15.

2. Robert B. Heilman, "Charlotte Brontë's 'New Gothic'" in Austin Wright, ed., *Victorian Literature: Modern Essays in Criticism* (New York: Oxford University Press, 1961), p. 84. My emphasis.

3. *American Heritage Dictionary of the English Language*, ed. William Morris (Boston: Houghton Mifflin, 1976).

4. (New York: Simon and Schuster, 1976), p. 7. Subsequent references to this edition will be included in the text.

5. Northrop Frye, *Fables of Identity: Studies in Poetic Mythology* (New York: Harcourt Brace and World, 1963), p. 15.

6. Donna Gerstenberger discusses Atwood's *Surfacing* in terms of literature's "exploration of conceptual limits and modes," in "Conceptions Literary and Otherwise: Women Writers and the Modern Imagination," NOVEL, 9 (Winter 1976), 141–150.

7. Robert D. Hume, "Gothic Versus Romantic: A Reevaluation of the Gothic Novel," *PMLA* 84 (March 1969), 287.

8. Hume, p. 287.

9. Francis Russell Hart, "The Experience of Character in the English Gothic Novel," in *Experience of Character in the Novel*, ed. Roy Harvey Pearce (New York: Columbia University Press, 1968), p. 95.

10. Ellen Moers, "Female Gothic," in *Literary Women* (Garden City, N.Y.: Doubleday and Company, 1976), p. 91.

11. Moers, p. 93.

12. *Eleven Canadian Novelists*, p. 30.

13. Hume, p. 282. The term "literature of process" is, of course, Northrop Frye's, "Towards Defining an Age of Sensibility," *ELH*, 23 (June 1956), 144–152.

14. Hart, p. 97.

[Review of *Two-Headed Poems*]   Douglas Barbour*

"Travel is dangerous; nevertheless, we travel," says Margaret Atwood, her speaker, in "The Bus to Alliston, Ontario"—signalling, perhaps, in her very speech, a new expansion of her field of vision. The landscape, dense with snow & desperate with the accompanying dead, is familiar Atwood country, gothic & ambiguous, but the tone here, & in many other poems in *Two-Headed Poems*, betrays a kind of stark hope found all too seldom in the earlier poems. Or do we simply remember only the bleakest versions of her vision? After all, *The Journals of Susanna Moodie* also moved to a final, possible acceptance of the world. Still, Susanna Moodie only fully adapted to this dangerous & treacherous country *after* her death; she could be one of the dead who "ride with us on this bus, / whether we like

*From *Fiddlehead*, no. 121 (Spring 1979):139–42. Reprinted by permission of the author.

it or not," an example of those "cramped histories, violent / or sad, earthstained, defeated, proud, / the path in small print, like almanacs, / mundane as knitting." But the persona of many of these new poems has made her awkward peace with nature in *this* life, & because she has done so the poems speak of broader vistas, greater hope than Margaret Atwood has previously dared to offer us:

> Every summer the apples
> condense out of nothing
> on their stems in the wet air
> like sluggish dewdrops
> or the tree bleeding.
>
> Every fall they fall
> and are eaten,
> by us or something else,
> wasps or snails, beetles,
> the sandpaper mouths of the earth.
>
> Every winter a few remain
> on the branches, pulpy & brown,
> wrinkled as kidneys or midget brains,
> the only flesh in sight.
>
> In spring we say the word *apple*
> but it means nothing;
> we can't remember those flavours,
> we are blunt & thankless
>
> But the apples condense again
> out of nothing on their stems
> like the tree bleeding; something
> has this compassion.
>
> ("Daybooks II")

I agree. Something here does have this compassion, but Atwood has seldom, if ever, said so before.

All of which is not to say she's singing sweet silly songs of superficial happiness. The world still menaces; sometimes as it approaches her daughter, slyly, like the wolf in the tale, it terrifies her even more than before, because she has more to lose. Yet the fact of her daughter appears to have opened up new spaces for poetic exploration. Some of the most interesting poems in *Two-Headed Poems* are those which speak of & to her daughter, or, equally important, of & to her forbears. Atwood, especially in the moving "Five Poems for Grandmothers," explores with compassion & complex clarity the flow of blood down the generations of mothers/daughters, the women's line of connection to the past & the future. Admitting "How little I know / about you finally," the poet nevertheless performs her subtle excavations of the past that lives in this still living presence of that past, her grandmother. And she admits the human futility of her act while simultaneously implying its necessity & value beyond what she actually says:

> Against the disappearance
> of outlines, against
> the disappearance of sounds,
> against the blurring of the ears
> and eyes, against the small fears
> of the very old, the fear
> of mumbling, the fear of dying,
> the fear of falling downstairs,
> I make this charm
> from nothing but paper; which is good
> for exactly nothing.

The important connection is made in the fifth poem:

> Goodbye, mother
> of my mother, old bone
> tunnel through which I came.
>
> You are sinking down into
> your own veins, fingers
> folding back into the hand,
>
> day by day a slow retreat
> behind the disk of your face
> which is hard and netted like an ancient plate.
>
> You will flicker in these words
> and in the words of others
> for a while and then go out.
>
> Even if I send them,
> you will never get these letters.
> Even if I see you again,
>
> I will never see you again.

The whole poem delicately & precariously balances the loss it registers — that communication gap the final lines insist upon — against the positive recognitions of the deeper connections the sequence as a whole has discovered. It wins our emotional assent precisely to the degree that it refuses to falsify the small but real affirmations it can finally reach.

If poems such as this sequence, the various poems on family & especially her daughter, & the 13 "Daybooks" (whose very title insists upon attending to *this* world as it is *now*) seem to say the world is acceptable in ways the earlier poems seldom tried to articulate, other poems remind us that Atwood's earlier landscape paranoia was (& is) based on recognitions which the news & history continue to force upon us. The prose-poem "Marrying the Hangman," with its garish tales of women trapped then & now, insists that this story & the stories of her friends, "which cannot be believed and which are true," must be faced, & perhaps faced out. "Four Small Elegies" rubs our noses in the violence men will do to each other— "Those whose houses were burned / burned houses. What else ever happens / once you start?" And "Footnote to the Amnesty Report on Torture" says all this horror goes on, goes on; it may just be a part of bureaucracy now, a job like any other job, but it does go on. Yet even this poem seems to me to enter areas Atwood has previously not touched. It concentrates on "the man who works here" ("He isn't a torturer, he only / cleans the floor: / every morning the same vomit"), a man glad to have a job so he can feed his family & growing more frightened every day as even the smallest cogs in such a machine must:

> As he sweeps, he tries
> not to listen; he tries
> to make himself into a wall,
> a thick wall, a wall
> soft and without echoes. He thinks
> of nothing but the walk back
> to his hot shed of a house,
> of the door
> opening and his children
> with their unmarked skin and flawless eyes
> running to meet him.
>
> He is afraid of
> what he might do
> if he were told to,
> he is afraid of the door,
>
> he is afraid, not
> of the door but of the door
> opening; sometimes, no matter
> how hard he tries,
> his children are not there.

The poem is all the more frightening for its calm understatement. In expressing compassion for both the obvious victims & this less obvious one, it achieves a large, complex, & genuinely moving humanitarian gesture, & it does so because it refuses the easy dogmatic assertions of "good" & "evil," acknowledging instead the forces which push us individually into the gray areas where judgement is so difficult. And yet so necessary, for the poem does judge, bringing home the genuine political terror of the situation. Politics plays a large role in many other poems, most powerfully when apprehended obliquely, as in parts of "Solstice Poem" & of the "Day-books." Other reviewers have pointed out how the two heads of the title poem represent English Canada & Quebec. That's one application, & in so far as it's easily seen it makes their speeches sound too obvious. I prefer the oblique approach, though "Two-Headed Poems" has many fine satiric jabs.

Still, what makes *Two-Headed Poems* so successful a collection for me are the affirmations, so difficultly won, which it articulates. In "A Red Shirt," the poet argues against a man's insistence that "Young girls should not wear red" both by making the shirt for her daughter & by insisting on

> the procession
> of old leathery mothers,
>
> the moon's last quarter
> before the blank night,
>
> mothers like worn gloves
> wrinkled to the shapes of their lives,
>
> passing the work from hand to hand,
> mother to daughter,
>
> a long thread of red blood, not yet broken

as well as the primal delight her daughter expresses wearing the red shirt. The expansiveness of Atwood's humane vision is most fully felt in "All Bread," a richly complex acceptance of the deaths which naturally serve life & one of her finest poems:

> Good bread has the salt taste
> of your hands after nine
> strokes of the axe, the salt
> taste of your mouth, it smells
> of its own small death, of the deaths
> before and after.
>
> Lift these ashes
> into your mouth, your blood;
> to know what you devour
> is to consecrate it,
> almost. All bread must be broken
> so it can be shared. Together
> we eat this earth.

What more need be said.

Atwood's Sacred Wells [*Dancing Girls*, poetry, and *Surfacing*]

Russell Brown*

"Think about pools."

There is a Margaret Atwood story—"The Resplendent Quetzal"— which opens with a young Canadian woman in Mexico, sitting at the edge of a sacrificial well. The well is an unprepossessing relic of an ancient civilization, now reduced to an object at which tourists come to gaze, their attention superficial and brief. Sarah, the woman at this well, is herself a tourist, but unlike the ones she watches hurrying by, she has some time to spend and feels at least some sense of the symbolism of this once-sacred site. Still Sarah is also disappointed in the well, almost as much so as other tourists: it is less interesting to look at than she had imagined, and shallower than her guidebook had promised. A guide who has finished lecturing his tour group flirts with her briefly, but it is not romance that Sarah longs for. Rebuffed, the guide flicks his cigarette into the well and departs.

This brief scene is an extremely significant one in Atwood's canon. Some of her most important images are clustered together here, images which reappear in her work to the point of obsessive concern. Frequently drawn together in this way, they become structural elements; they form a constellation which does not readily yield single or easy meaning. Their reappearance is a sign of an ongoing investigation, of a continued pursuit of the meaning and inter-relationships of certain themes and of the metaphors which convey them. The result is that when we read widely in Atwood's work the images in any single story or poem take on enriched significance; they trigger previously established associations. We experience a sense of déjà vu: not unpleasant, it is the feeling of drifting back into a familiar dream.

I

"You from around here?" she asked.
"No," Morrison said.[1]

The tourists at the beginning of "The Resplendent Quetzal" stand out because the figure of the tourist is so often present in Atwood's world. The person not "from around here," embodies a general sense of dislocation, a feeling of not being at home: these are so much a part of the fiction and poetry that they become more atmosphere and mood than content.

More than half the stories collected in *Dancing Girls* revolve around tourists and other individuals estranged from the culture in which they

*From *Essays on Canadian Writing*, no. 17 (Spring 1980):5–43. Condensed for length by permission of the author and reprinted by permission of *Essays on Canadian Writing*.

find themselves. Sometimes these are people with whom the protagonist must enact transactions which are invariably uncomfortable — as in "The Man from Mars," where a strange foreign man pursues and dismays the central character. When we encounter such outsiders, the stories suggest, our problems arise from our inability to understand or interpret unfamiliar patterns of behaviour: "Her mother volunteered that the thing about people from another culture was that you could never tell whether they were insane or not because their ways were so different" ("The Man from Mars," *DG*, p. 32).

In other stories, it is the protagonist who is the outsider, the traveller into foreign lands. "Lives of the Poets" begins with a woman "lying on the bathroom floor of this anonymous hotel room"; "The Grave of the Famous Poet" opens with a pair of young vacationers riding a bus into a Welsh town. In "A Travel Piece" the central character's job is that of travel writer: "a professional tourist, she works at being pleased and not participating; at sitting and watching" (*DG*, p. 152).

Elsewhere in "A Travel Piece," the authorial voice defines "tourists" as "those who are not responsible . . . those who make the lives of others their transient spectacle and pleasure" (*DG*, p. 152). In such poems as "At the Tourist Centre in Boston" and "Interview with a Tourist," these people are treated more negatively still: they are those who always see things superficially, who perpetually condescend to unfamiliar cultures, and who impose what they desire on what they find.

This sense of the tourist accounts for some of the attraction the historic figure of Susanna Moodie holds: for Atwood, Moodie becomes an embodiment of these failures. . . .

All of the characters of *Life Before Man*, Atwood's most recent novel, are, in fact, "refugees" in some way or another, with the defence mechanisms and sense of alienation which that condition entails. Tourists, immigrants, refugees, "exiles and invaders" — there is a pervasive failure to claim one's own territory, a failure which inevitably also shows up as a failure to assert identity.

The way the alienation felt by the tourist severs him from the place where he finds himself, allowing him to treat it as "spectacle," is nowhere more clear than in *Surfacing*, with its depiction of what it is like to be on "home ground, foreign territory." In that novel David exhibits the attitude of the tourist at its most frightening, and it is that attitude which permits him to reduce the world — and with it his companions — to an emotionally distant environment, one suitable as raw material for his film *Random Samples*, most valued when most bizarre.

But there is no easy escape from the sense of displacement that may lead one to become a David. Even those who are not tourists, even those who do not travel to unfamiliar places, are not found comfortably at home. The image of the boarding house appears in Atwood's landscapes almost as often as that of the tourist, and for the same reason — to suggest that there is never any "home ground," that all occupy turf which is not theirs.

Atwood conveys the sense of a lost home ground most clearly in an early poem about the state of mind produced by living in a boarding house (*ATC*, p. 28–29). . . . Throughout *Dancing Girls*, boardinghouses, rented rooms, and hotels are almost the only accommodations mentioned, and all exude a sense of residents who "never lived here"; nowhere is there stability; nowhere does a genuine "home" exist. Within these temporary shelters, the inhabitants are driven to compensate for their rootlessness by engaging in petty struggles, symbolic but intense, that mark off territory as their own. Like the psychological warfare over a bathroom that opens *Dancing Girls*, battles over borders are being covertly fought by many of Atwood's characters. Others simply redecorate, or rearrange furniture, as they attempt to turn rented rooms into their own.

The inhabitants who share these roominghouses are always the same rootless immigrants, the same aliens and tourists that turn up elsewhere. In "Polarities," Morrison — a man marked by "his own search for place" — notices that his landlady "seemed to prefer foreign students, probably because they were afraid to complain." In the title story, Ann — a Canadian in America who finds it confusing to be a foreigner and not be seen as one — has a landlady who plays stationary tourist by requesting that each new boarder wear his "native costume" for her children.

There are few permanent residences in the novels either. . . .

The danger suggested . . . is always that of xenophobia: at some point one identifies the "other" as being not merely foreign but as truly "alien": the stranger comes to be seen as "a man from Mars." In the conclusion to "A Travel Piece," the protagonist, horrified by the actions of those with whom she is sharing a lifeboat, feels as if she is confronted with "four Martians and one madman waiting for her to say something" (*DG*, p. 153). But the strength of Atwood's version of this is that she never lets us escape so easily: she always eventually forces us to confront the question with which "A Travel Piece" concludes: "Am I one of them or not?"

II

. . . . The well, even more than the tourists, is what commands our attention in that opening scene of "The Resplendent Quetzal." Like the totem poles in "Some Objects of Wood and Stone," it is a remnant of a lost religion, an object which serves to remind us that lives were once lived on a more mythic plane. The condition of tourism is that of a fallen state. The tourist passes among the relics of a visionary people without even seeing that there has been a loss: he prefers replicas and photographs to the thing itself.

Still, if the well no longer has the meaning it once did, if "There are few totems that remain / living for us," that does not mean that the world does not contain objects which can function for us as these did for their time and people. "Some Objects of Wood and Stone" continues:

> There are few totems that remain
> living for us.
> Though in passing,
> through glass we notice
>
> dead trees in the seared meadows
> dead roots bleaching in the swamps.
> (CG, p. 60)

"Dead trees" and "dead roots" are not much to cling to perhaps, and we notice them only "in passing," but there is still a sense here that something remains to stir deep, instinctual responses.

So it is elsewhere in Atwood's world: certain things take on unexpected import, become keys to hidden meaning, gateways to visionary insight. We may not understand what we have encountered but if we are sensitive we may at least catch glimpses that tell us there is something there:

> . . . each of the
> few solid objects took some great
> implication, hidden but
> more sudden than a signpost
> ("Migration: C.P.R." CG, p. 53)

Atwood repeatedly depicts totems and totem-like objects that still exist in our world and that can convey the numinous world to us; they are the *sacramenta* that we may stumble across in our daily lives. Since the world of myth is linked for Atwood, as for most modern writers, with the world of the unconscious self, this phenomenon is like that described by Joseph Campbell:

> The unconscious sends all sorts of vapors, odd beings, terrors and deluding images up into the mind—whether in dream, broad daylight, or insanity. . . . And they may remain unsuspected, or, on the other hand, some chance word, the smell of a landscape, the taste of a cup of tea, or the glance of an eye may touch a magic spring, and then dangerous messengers begin to appear in the brain. These are dangerous because they threaten the fabric of the security into which we have built ourselves and our family. But they are fiendishly fascinating too, for they carry keys that open the whole realm of the desired and feared adventure of the discovery of the self.[2]

These objects with "great implication hidden" are ontophanous, able to serve as reminders of what Mircea Eliade calls "the plenary manifestation of Being." Moving through Atwood's landscapes, we find ourselves among objects that have meaning packed into them like so many Jacks-in-the-box. Her fiction and poetry so often contain descriptions of such things that the work itself becomes one of the signposts, pointing out the "underground" realms. Along with the sacrificial well, and the "wooden people" of "Some Objects of Wood and Stone," there is "a talisman" carried by the protagonist of the story "Giving Birth": "It's a rounded oblong of opaque blue glass, with four yellow and white shapes on it . . . it makes her feel safer to have it in the room with her" (DG, p. 238). Perhaps not always so explicitly "magical," a host of other significant objects manifest themselves. There are, for example, Marian's famous cake at the conclusion of The Edible Woman, and the petroglyphs in Surfacing: "a talisman, my father has left me the guides, the man-animals and the maze of numbers" (S, p. 149). The very titles of poems and stories name more: "Playing Cards" (CG), "This is a Photograph of Me" (CG), "Three Desk Objects" (PU), "Weed Seeds Near a Beaver Pond" (PU), "Buffalo in Compound, Alberta" ("the god / of this place" [PU]), "Hair Jewelry" (DG), "The Grave of the Famous Poet" (DG), and the subtitle "Carved Animals" (CG). There is the fabulous bird which gives its name to "The Resplendent Quetzal" (DG), and the "Dancing Girls" who are said to have appeared in one final splendid party given by that foreign student in the room next door before he was evicted.

That both the Quetzal and the Dancing Girls are rumoured only and remain unseen, that the sacrificial well is disappointing and the famous grave proves dull, does not deny their significance, for we are, as we have seen already, living in a time and a place where, like tourists, we may get only unsatisfactory glimpses of these mana-endowed things. They are too often like the tortoises depicted in "Elegy for the Giant Tortoises," "the relics of what we have destroyed, / our holy and obsolete symbols" (ATC, p. 23). . . .

In the poetry Atwood's two ways of seeing become a common structural device: a visionary mode of perception is balanced against a quotidian one.[3] . . .

Still, even if we fail to perceive the hidden nature of the things around us, that richer world is not entirely lost to us nor does it cease to make demands on us. As "Two Gardens" in Procedures for Underground reminds us, the "underground" meaning remains even though we may deny it, the numinous impinges though we may think we can hold it apart. . . .

III

Now this country is underwater;
we can love only the drowned
("Interview with a Tourist," PU, p. 23)

As Joseph Campbell has pointed out, one of the tasks of the individual in search of enlightenment is to find the centre of things, the omphalos, which is the point of contact between time and eternity, the "place of breakthrough into abundance."[4] Every important religious site (the Bo tree, Calvary) has been thought of as such a centre, and all shrines and sacred places participate, at least symbolically, in centredness and thus serve as portals to the numinous realm.

Discovery of the centre means renewal: ". . . the World Navel is the symbol of the continuous creation; the mystery of the maintenance of the world through that continuous miracle of vivification which wells within all things."[5] Of course one of the greatest discoveries that the individual makes is that the centre is everywhere, that the other world is always available, and hence anything, properly understood, may serve to convey us there. Still the experiences of certain objects fill our needs better than others; some things seem natural gateways. The sacred well in "The Resplendent Quetzal" is one such object. Wells and other bodies of water have always provided symbolic representations of entrances to an unseen, mysterious world beneath the surface of our own. The presence of lakes and pools, coupled with larger patterns of descent, of "journeys to the interior," and of submerging, is ubiquitous in Atwood's writing; and, in *Survival*, Atwood alludes to drowning as a convenient "metaphor for the descent into the unconscious" (*Surv.*, p. 55). Several critics have provided discussions of the metaphoric structures of Atwood's quests for depths; the best of these is an essay by Roberta Rubenstein entitled "*Surfacing*: Margaret Atwood's Journey to the Interior." Rubenstein describes the action of *Surfacing* — with its heroine's climactic plunge into a lake that contains a primitive rock painting, her father's drowned body, and a vision of her own repressed guilt — as an "archetypal journey into the self" which is also a "symbolic journey into both the private and collective heart of darkness."[6]

Although the personal material of the subconscious self is part of what is discovered in those underwater explorations, the primitive and powerful imagery of universal myth also lies there and it is that which has the greater power to transform:

> . . .
> in the water
> under my shadow
> there was an outline, man
> surfacing, his body sheathed
> in feathers, his teeth
> glinting like nails, fierce god
> head crested with blue flame
> ("Dream: Bluejay or Archeopteryx," *PU*, p. 9)

In "The Resplendent Quetzal," Sarah never makes the plunge we have come to expect, but she does something in the conclusion of the story that may be even better. Grasping the nature of symbolic and ritual action in an intuitive moment, she throws a surrogate self into the well. This final act, we sense, moves her back into participation with her mythic unconscious and gives her fragmented psyche a new potential for wholeness.

"The Resplendent Quetzal" thus contains the repeated pattern of Atwood's narratives — a submerging, whether symbolic or actual, in search of vision that may permit a final surfacing of the restored or renewed individual. . . .

In Atwood's version of our history, we live not only after a fall but after the deluge — and the waters have not receded. We move on the surface of that great flood, while a rich and valuable world lies beneath our feet, a world that is lost to us because it is "far undersea."

Even to recognize our inundated condition, as in "After the Flood," is a small victory (*CG*, p. 12). . . .

The cause of the catastrophe that has come to pass is suggested in several places, among them this passage from *Surfacing*: "In the bay the felled trees and numbered posts showed where the surveyors had been, power company. My country, sold or drowned, a reservoir; the people were sold along with the land and the animals, a bargain, sale, *solde*. Les soldes they called them, sellouts, the flood would depend on who got elected, not here but somewhere else" (*S*, p. 132). The world in *Surfacing* is being covered over because of a desire for "power," because of greed and political venality, but the pattern that Atwood wants us to recognize is larger than this. Recall the opening of "The Resplendent Quetzal" once more: there is a third element there, besides those of tourist and well, one which seemed less important but which is also the most disturbing feature of the scene: the cigarette butt which the guide discards. Even without being told, the reader knows it is probably an American cigarette that falls upon those once-sacred waters. A Canadian tourist has travelled to Mexico to see a Mexican guide throw a bit of American refuse into one of the few remaining sites of a once-vital indigenous culture.

The throwing of the cigarette into the well may be viewed as an act rich in meaning. In Freudian terms, for example, it could be read as a displacement of the sexual violation that the guide longs for, since it follows his brief flirtation with Sarah. Though such a reading is reductive by itself, it is worth holding in mind for the sets of paired oppositions which it evokes: guide and tourist, male and female, the modern society of cigarette butts, the lost world of sacred wells. Indeed — as the production of such parallels begins to suggest — the cigarette is not so much symbolic as synedochic, a very small part directing our attention to the much larger whole which has produced it.

The cigarette is one result of a system of values to which Atwood frequently calls our attention, against which she is labouring to warn us. The discarded cigarette floating on the water suggests the pervasive presence of the products of commerce, especially American commerce, and of the technology that furnishes them — the same technology that has literally flooded the landscape in *Surfacing*. The fact that it is a cigarette further reminds us of the unhealthful byproducts of many of those products, as well as of the fact that they fulfill needs which they also create.

The pollution of the sacred well is not merely attributed to "commercialism" or to "technology" however. The cigarette represents something still larger as well: the omnipresent mass culture of modern society. This meaning of the cigarette becomes clear in reading the whole of "The Resplendent Quetzal," because it is one of a series of objects that belongs to the mass, and mass-produced, culture and that overwhelms what remains of an older, more personal order of things.

The restaurant at which Sarah and her husband dine, and which she thinks about as she sits beside the well, is the chief embodiment of this pattern. We first recognize this when we see the Mexican children who come not to meet for play but to watch TV, for they find there "a re-run of *The Cisco Kid*, with dubbed voices" (*DG*, p. 162). This moment is perhaps the most devastating in our entire experience of the story: we see that Hollywood fantasies not only sanitize those social orders not yet fully assimilated to the mass culture, but that these sanitized versions of the past are eventually retranslated and returned back to the youngest members of that society, providing them with a false tradition and a history that never existed.

The restaurant is more, however, than the focus of a vanishing social order. As Sarah sits thinking about it, a nearby tourist says of her recent sight-seeing, "What beats me is why they built all those things in the first place," and another answers, "It was their religion, that's what he said" (*DC*, p. 163). We are not merely reminded that the ancient religions are being forgotten: the juxtaposition of these remarks with description of the restaurant's interior makes it plain that the process is continuing, that Christianity is now likewise being secularized:

> On the bar beside the television set there was a crêche, with three painted plaster Wise Men, one on an elephant, the others on camels. The first Wise Man was missing his hand. Inside the stable a stunted Joseph and Mary adored an enormous Christ Child which was more than half as big as the elephant. . . . Beside the crêche was a Santa Claus haloed with flashing lights, and beside that a radio in the shape of Fred Flintstone, which was playing American popular songs, all of them ancient.
>
> (*DG*, pp. 162–63)

The crêche, which should be a repository for the symbolism of the central Christian mystery — God become man — has, like the well, become seedy and neglected, allowed to lose its significance. The adjacent Santa Claus, the saint become completely desacralized by his adoption into the culture of commerce, signals the reason for the decay within the manger, his flashing-light halo an indication of how far the miraculous has been displaced by the technological.

The figure of Fred Flintstone completes the progression away from the crèche: he stands both as ultimate devaluation of the primitive and as an example of the only mythic figure that modern society possesses — the cartoon character. His function as a radio shows how quickly even modern myths are harnessed by technology, but at the same time this technology has been hopelessly trivialized, the real potential of the electronic age reduced to a radio in the shape of a banal cartoon character playing superficial and outworn music.

The obvious source of the disruption depicted here is the exportation of American culture — *The Cisco Kid*, Fred Flintstone, popular song — but Atwood will not let Canadian readers escape their share of responsibility. As in *Surfacing*, where the "Americans" who killed the heron turn out to be Canadians after all, there is a shock of recognition when we listen to the only song that we actually hear.

> "*Oh someone help me, help me, plee-ee-ee-eeze . . .*"
> "Isn't that Paul Anka?" Sarah asked.
>
> (*DG*, 163)

Nor is Canada the only country that has willingly become part of the modern mass culture. After all, in the opening scene those were "Mexican tourists," and "Sarah found it reassuring that other people besides Canadians and Americans wore big hats and sunglasses and took pictures of everything" (*DG*, p. 154).

It is mass culture that has "drowned" the world. Realizing that fact means that the question of myth and of sacred object is not as simple as it first seemed. It is not that we have no myths and no totems: *The Cisco Kid* and Fred Flintstone-as-a-radio are proof that we do. It is rather that the mythic narratives and the totemic objects that we now possess are false or dangerous. They have been corrupted by their sources and degraded by their ends. Their unfortunate omnipresence has formed an overlay — or to borrow a term from geology, an overburden — obscuring the more meaningful world in which we once lived. The modern deluge of these offspring of the marriage of commercial technology with popular consciousness creates an obscuring surface over the more essential world in which we once dwelt.

For this reason Atwood regularly shows us that there are bad totems as well as good, objects of dangerous power as well as benign. . . .

It is not only the flood of consumer goods that has drowned the world, it is also the mythos that has been created for consumers, the myths that these objects, their producers, and possessers have brought into being, often just to explain and justify the new technological era. Like the Mexican boys watching *Cisco Kid* re-runs, we see the image of ourselves given back, however distortedly, in these myths, expressed in the omnipresent forms of popular entertainment, conveyed by the engulfing media.

We can no longer see the truth of our world because a new one has risen up around it like

> . . . the mist that has risen
> everywhere as well
> as in these woods
> ("After the Flood, We," *CG*, p. 12)

Atwood returns to this problem often [in "Backdrop addresses cowboy" (*ATC*, p. 50), *Surfacing, Lady Oracle*, and *The Edible Woman*]. . . .

Ours is a fallen world drowned in advertising and escape literature; man is damned to live out inauthentic lives in it, lives lived "by quotation."

Atwood's version of the Fall is not, however, simply historical. In the present age each individual recapitulates that lapse, because the child is born without imposed culture. An important scene in *Surfacing*, when the protagonist finds childhood notebooks, demonstrates this—and helps explain why Atwood's characters generally seek anamnesis. There is an Atwood poem that proposes to look at a soul "geologically"; elsewhere the word "archeological" repeatedly occurs to describe the investigations that compel us inward. The scrapbooks extend that metaphor: there is a geology of character offered in them; a stratum at a time, we see the archeology of the psyche recorded. The passages describing these books, pp. 90–91, 158, are worth our attention . . . .

By reversing the surfacer's process of discovery, we can reconstruct the history of development presented here. At the core of being lies primaeval, mythic material, and an intuitive religious vision that unites God with man, man with animal, Christ with Satan.[7] The most important single act in *Surfacing* is probably this rediscovery of the primitive stuff of which visions are made and the assertion of rights to this lost "first meaning" ("mine, I had made it"), but as the subsequent contents of the scrapbooks show, this state of innocence does not last. The child's primal vision is displaced; we feel the "shades of the prison-house" beginning to close in.

At first, the loss is not so great. The singleness of the loose page gives way to more generalized, but still powerful mythic content: "early people" with rays coming out of their heads—an anticipation of that important moment when the surfacer looks into the lake and sees "My other shape . . . , not my reflection but my shadow, . . . rays streaming out from around the head" (*S*, p. 141). As the child gets older, the record of the myths which she intuitively glimpsed in the depths of her mind is replaced by a collection of less vital and less meaningful mythologies given her by her culture and her society. Semi-divine beings give way to Easter eggs and rabbits. Just as the crèche in "The Resplendent Quetzal" calls our attention to the modern failure to understand one of the central events in Christianity, so these childish pictures indicate that another crucial event—the death and resurrection of God—has also suffered a devaluation: like a

Christmas reduced to Santa Claus, Easter seems to have become puerile fantasies of bunnies and eggs.

The "translation" (to use a word that is generally important in *Surfacing*) of the narrative of Golgotha and Resurrection into a story about a rabbit that brings eggs to children marks a transitional phase in the development of individual consciousness. After all, this juvenile story of Easter does show the child's continuing responsiveness to essential myth ("perhaps it was a vision of Heaven"), partly because the tale of the Easter bunny points, however distantly, to the pagan fertility rituals that form a tradition older than Christianity, underlying and giving force to its later customs. At the same time we recognize these Easter fantasies as part of a general modern abandonment of religious stories for secular fables that will turn sacred holidays into occasions for commerce.

As the surfacer's most recent scrapbook shows, the modern mythos of the consumer society has completed the covering over of her earliest picture and its first meaning. The magazines and mail-order catalogues of her childhood, like the comic books of her brother's, provide a new, impersonal set of images that replace her earlier, personal ones ("no drawings at all, just illustrations cut . . . and pasted in" [S, p. 91]). There is a very real fall recorded here, since the pastoral order that prevailed in the world of rabbits gives way to the hostile warring world depicted by her brother.

The existence of *two* scrapbooks at this stage of childhood may indicate that it is also the point at which socially-defined sex roles are furnished for the child, with the boy offered various heroic models (soldier-spaceman-superhero) and the girl given two "safe" domestic ones: "lady" and "mother." The extent to which these female roles are arbitrarily limited, superficial, and depersonalized is shown by the way the childhood scissors have trimmed the figures: to "dresses . . . no bodies in them" (S, p. 91).

It is striking that two separate books exist *only* at this final and most fallen stage of the child's development. It may suggest that both brother and sister previously shared in the acts of creation recorded here — operating together in a kind of undivided androgynous consciousness. Or it may call our attention to the uncertainty that runs throughout the novel about the actual status of this brother. He seems to have existed, but much of what we are told about him turns out to be untrue; he most often serves as a way for the protagonist to talk about her own repressed memories: ". . . it wasn't ever my brother I'd been remembering, that had been a disguise" (S, p. 143). Perhaps, then, the appearance of a "male" scrapbook is a similar disguise, a response by the surfacer to the necessity of segregating and suppressing the maleness of her own nature. Such an understanding of things would help explain a passage in the opening chapter, Anna's reading of her friend's palm: " 'Do you have a twin?' I said

No. 'Are you positive,' she said, 'because some of your lines are double. . . . You had a good childhood but then there's this funny break' " (S, p. 8).

The process by which primal myths, essential narratives, and undivided images of self are covered over with new ones that serve modern society by suppressing individuality and encouraging materialism, is one in which Marian McAlpin, Joan Foster, and the protagonist of *Surfacing* are sometimes victims, but they are also implicated as collaborators: in their complicity we read Atwood's own anxieties about the place of artist and writer in the consumer society. Does the work of the creative artist help us regain the world of lost meaning — or does it become another obscuring layer on the surface? By allowing her work to be published and circulated through the channels of commerce, will the artist inevitably become corrupted, become part of the ineluctable process she protests?

Surfacing deals most directly with those questions. . . .

IV

. . . . The mirror as an image and a metaphor is perhaps the most ubiquitous of all of the elements repeated in Atwood's poetry and fiction, but it is missing from "The Resplendent Quetzal." At best we are aware of the lack of reflections in that story, when Sarah looks into the well and finds the water muddy-brown, the bottom murky. Still, as "Tricks with Mirrors" reveals, mirror and pool are actually the same, though we often make the mistake of not recognizing their identity.

Mirrors are dangerous. . . . .

It is our awareness that every mirror may really be a pool and that every photograph has a world behind it which gives richness to Atwood's work. The mythic patterns of action that we internalize, our understanding of our roles in life, and our images of our self: all are derived from what we see around us, from the "mirror" that our environment — whether social, cultural, or psychic — holds up to us. The danger is that by attending to these reflections we may not see the depths that lie behind or beneath them. The true beginning of vision for the surfacer comes when she looks into the lake and sees "not my reflection but my shadow" (S, p. 141). It is why the poet protests when her companion cannot see the drowned world at their feet and why — in "A Dialogue" — she can speak of her sister's perception of a lake as a dark swamp while for the poet it is like "clear day."

It is the fear of what that unseen world may hold that is much of the source of terror for the "professional tourist" of "A Travel Piece." Her awareness of a world under the surface makes her usual world of "spectacle" ". . . come to seem like a giant screen, flat and with pictures painted on it to create the illusion of solidity. If you walked up to it and kicked it, it would tear and your foot would go right through, into another space which Annette could only visualize as darkness, a night in which something she did not want to look at was hiding" (*DG*, p. 140). On the other hand, this world beneath the surface is the source of vision, of all visions — as it is of that longed-for one which concludes "Giving Birth," the last story in *Dancing Girls*. Jeannie, the fictional projection of the I-narrator, discovers that it is partly to herself that she has given birth, and that in consequence she can see the world with new perception:

> All she can see from the window is a building. It's an old stone building, heavy and Victorian with a copper roof oxidized to green. It's solid, hard, darkened by soot, dour, leaden. But as she looks at this building, so old and seemingly immutable, she sees it's made of water. Water, and some tenuous jellylike substance. Light flows through it from behind (the sun is coming up), the building is so thin, so fragile, that it quivers in the slight dawn wind. Jeannie sees that if the building is this way . . . then the rest of the world must be like this too, the entire earth, the rocks, people, trees. . . .
>
> (DG, p. 244)

We must "look long enough" to rid ourselves of the distortion of light on surface, and move through the mirror, or the lake, or the picture. To do so would be like "Seeing the ice / as what it is, water" ("Woman Skating," *PU*, p. 65). As happens so often in Atwood's landscapes, the apparently solid world will turn out to be a permeable one once the initial surface is broken through. Mirrors become pools; earth, water; substance, mist [, as in the "Progressive insanities of a pioneer," *ATC*, p. 38]. . . . In such a world the best strategy may be to become one with the watery realm[, as in "Hypotheses: City," *PU*, p. 37]. . . .

The quest from the earliest of Atwood's writing to the most recent work has been for a sacred space — which is why all maps are found inadequate. The space may be sought in the external world — in Canada, Mexico, Italy — but that world can at best offer entrances to the true locus, which is an interior one: "there are no destinations / apart from this."

The discovery of the gateways to that internal world [may] become the final goal to which all other efforts are directed. Often — like Sarah sitting beside her sacred well — Atwood's characters discover that they are at the entrance already, and need only to recognize it and to find how to pass through. It is no accident that Sarah's is a sacrificial well: the act needed to open these portals usually is a sacrificial one. The need "to clear a space" in *Surfacing* demands the immolation of history; compulsive fasting, in *The Edible Woman*, brings Marian's loss of ego; Joan Foster enacts an almost ritualistic death of identity in *Lady Oracle*.

As "The Resplendent Quetzal" makes clear, the *symbolism* of sacrifice may be enough, the mythic pattern of the scapegoat that releases us from the sin of selfhood may still hold if intuitively understood. Sarah grasps that when, without knowing why, she steals the plaster Christ child from the crèche ("Separated from the dwarfish Virgin and Joseph, it didn't look quite so absurd" [*DG*, p. 168]) and throws it into the well. The moment of ritual sacrifice is re-enacted once more: the most primal of human urges is paid homage to. In this sacramental act, Sarah overcomes her deadening reserve and breaks through — we hope — into a new kind of existence.

The plaster Christ penetrates the depths for Sarah. The pool is breached once more. As always, it is not *surfacing* but *submerging* which is the crucial action, an action which often depends on *subverting*, even if it means the subversion of the whole of modern culture.

If one reaches the underwater world the future remains a secret of the deep: perhaps it goes beyond telling. The poem "Pre-Amphibian" suggests one possibility, however. It may be that the drowned world can be redeemed, the inundating waves pushed back. If that is so, then "when / these tides recede," we will have made our next evolutionary step (recall that the surfacer is left pregnant with "the first true human; it must be born, allowed"); we will awaken and find ourselves

> stranded, astounded
> in a drying world
>
> we flounder, the air
> ungainly in our new lungs
> with sunlight steaming merciless on the shores of morning
> ("Pre-Amphibian," *CG*, p. 64)

V

> There may be a Position Five, for mystics; I postulate it but will not explore it here, since mystics do not as a rule write books. (*Surv.*, p. 39)

Ultimately the hidden world that Atwood seeks has been covered over by more surfaces than just the one provided by our modern condition. It has been obscured by something more pervasive, more inevitable, and more inescapable — language itself. The narrator of "Giving Birth" makes a story of her experience, creating a new character — Jeannie — in order to tell that story, but as she does this she cannot help but reflect upon the layers with which she covers over the events as she speaks of them. "The point . . ." she begins, about to explain how she has named her fictional counterpart after Stephen Foster's Jeannie, and then interrupts herself to say,

> (for in language there are always these "points," these reflections; this is what makes it so rich and sticky, this is why so many have disappeared beneath its dark and shining surface, why you should never try to see your own reflection in it; you will lean over too far, a strand of your hair will fall in and come out gold, and thinking it is gold all the way down, you yourself will follow, sliding into those outstretched arms, toward the mouth you think is opening to pronounce your name but instead, just

before your eyes fill with pure sound will form a word you never heard
before . . .)

(*DG*, p. 231)

Language itself, the medium in which we are doomed to attempt our
accounts of reality, as well as the fictions we create from it when normal
language does not represent our realities satisfactorily, and what the
surfacer calls the "pure logic . . . secreted by my head" that produces
language in the first place — all of these turn out to be both dangerous
mirror and beckoning pool. Julia, the poet of "Lives of the Poets" realizes
this: "But what was her mistake? Thinking she could save her soul, no
doubt. By the word alone" (*DG*, p. 207). Still if Julia despairs, she also
articulates most clearly Atwood's hopes for redemption: "Things would
get better, time would reverse itself . . . silence would open, language
would flow again" (*DG*, p. 206).

"Giving Birth" stands out among the short stories as the one which
most shows a character achieving such a redeemed state. The protagonist
longs for a vision, thinks it has not come, and then abruptly experiences it
after all. She feels trapped by words in the story, but as she gives birth she
experiences "finally . . . the disappearance of language" (*DG*, p. 241). As
nowhere else in Atwood's writing, the sacred and the profane worlds seem
able to coexist with one another, albeit briefly. And, at the same time,
fiction and reality converge within the very fabric of the story itself.

"Giving Birth" is Atwood's only real venture into what is sometimes
called metafiction — that self-reflexive mode that calls attention to its own
fictive nature and thus to its own surfaces. Such fiction always offers its
readers the fascinating paradox of the mirror/pool. It becomes more
opaque since we begin to see the surfaces again that we have learned to
ignore (language, structure, the narrator — all the inventions of story-
telling and the processes involved in making a story coalesce — are brought
to the foreground where we become aware of them). At the same time,
such a story becomes unexpectedly transparent as well. Rather than simply
seeing through the patterns of words on the page to the characters and the
plot, we find ourselves seeing through those as well — to an author
managing and manipulating those events, a living human being struggling
to find and convey the meaning of her own human existence. As we
progress through "Giving Birth," we are aware not only of the narrative
voice bringing Jeannie into being but of Atwood standing just behind that
voice and creating *it*; not only of a narrator using Jeannie to talk about the
birth of her child, but of Atwood using both narrator and Jeannie to talk
about her own recent experiences of actually having given birth. This story
completes the project of the first three novels: the subversion of conventional narrative. It shows the surfaces and it invites us to consider the
unspoken words and the unarticulated reality that lie beneath.

Along with some of her contemporaries, Atwood sees every act of intellection as distancing from a more primary world. Looking back at the whole of her work, we can now recognize in Atwood's writing a persistently mystical vein — for she would have us not only be more aware of the primary reality we inhabit but of the primal material of the universe itself. She, like many mystics, does not want to renounce the world but rather to draw us more deeply into it, to pull us through its surfaces and into the true and essential dimensions which have been waiting for us all this time.

We see now why the well itself is such a powerful symbol for Atwood. It emerges into our daily world but its existence begins in another, underground, realm. It is a source of the water that we must have to survive and that lies everywhere around us — hidden, yet at our feet. We can drink from such wells and we can drown in them, but we must learn to see them as the portals they are. And as the portals they may be.

Notes [revised by author]

1. Margaret Atwood, "Polarities," *Dancing Girls* (1977; rpt. Toronto: Bantam-Seal, 1978), p. 64. All further references to this work (*DG*) appear in the text.

————, *The Circle Game* (1966; rpt. Toronto: House of Anansi, 1967). All references to this work (*CG*) appear in the text.

————, *The Animals in That Country* (Toronto: Oxford Univ. Press, 1968). All references to this work (*ATC*) appear in the text.

————, *The Edible Woman*, (Toronto: McClelland and Stewart, 1969). All references to this work (*EW*) appear in the text.

————, *The Journals of Susanna Moodie* (Toronto: Oxford Univ. Press, 1970). All references to this work (*JSM*) appear in the text.

————, *Procedures for Underground* (Toronto: Oxford Univ. Press, 1970). All references to this work (*PU*) appear in the text.

————, *Surfacing* (1972; rpt. Don Mills: PaperJacks, 1973). All references to this work (*S*) appear in the text.

————, *Survival* (Toronto: House of Anansi, 1972). All references to this work (*Surv.*) appear in the text.

————, *Lady Oracle* (Toronto: McClelland and Stewart, 1976). All references to this work (*LO*) appear in the text.

————, *Life Before Man* (Toronto: McClelland and Stewart, 1979). All references to this work (*LBM*) appear in the text.

2. Joseph Campbell, *The Hero with a Thousand Faces* (1949; rpt. Cleveland: World, 1956), p. 8. The relevance of the mythography of post-Jungians such as Campbell and Robert Graves for Atwood is evident. See especially, Josie P. Campbell, "The Woman as Hero in Margaret Atwood's *Surfacing* (*Mosaic*, 11, No. 3 [Spring 1978], 17–28) for connections between *Surfacing* and *The Hero with a Thousand Faces*. In many ways my essay and hers are complementary.

3. Frank Davey, in "Atwood's Gorgon Touch" (*Studies in Canadian Literature*, 2 [1977], 146–63), makes a similar observation. Davey, however, sees the continued antitheses in Atwood's poetry as being between time, process, and decay on the one hand, and space, stasis, and the attempt to control on the other — a reworking of the Dionysiac/Apollonian dualism (Heraclitean and Platonic are the terms Davey prefers in *From There to Here: A Guide to English-Canadian Literature since 1960* [1974]) within which he often locates authors for discussion.

4. Campbell, p. 43. See pp. 40–46 et passim.

5. Campbell, p. 41.

6. Roberta Rubenstein, "*Surfacing*: Margaret Atwood's Journey to the Interior," *Modern Fiction Studies*, 22, No. 3 (Autumn 1976), 398, 397.

7. Compare Rubenstein, p. 396.

Demons, Doubles, and Dinosaurs: *Life Before Man*, *The Origin of Consciousness*, and "The Icicle"   Ildikó de Papp Carrington*

Margaret Atwood's fourth novel, *Life Before Man*, is introduced by two epigraphs, one from Björn Kurtén's *The Age of the Dinosaurs*, and the other from Andrei Sinyavsky's fantastic short story "The Icicle." In her review of this novel, Sherrill E. Grace has emphasized the differences between Sinyavsky's fantasies and Atwood's domestic realism.[1] But Atwood's use of "The Icicle" epigraph is her announcement that under the novel's realistic surface lies a non-realistic structure. Like her first three novels, like three of her short stories ("Giving Birth" and "The Resplendent Quetzal" in *Dancing Girls* and "Scarlet Ibis" in *Bluebeard's Egg*), and like *Bodily Harm*, *Life Before Man* is a romance. "The Icicle" contributes a thematic pattern of fantasy to the novel's romance structure. But *Life Before Man* should also have a third epigraph from *The Origin of Consciousness in the Breakdown of the Bicameral Mind* by Julian Jaynes. Jerome H. Rosenberg and Lorraine Weir have both called attention to Jaynes's influence on Atwood's traditional themes in *Two-Headed Poems*.[2] *Life Before Man* also acquires structural and thematic clarity if the symbolic experiences of its three protagonists are laid on the grid of Jaynes's thesis about bicameral, pre-conscious man's relationship with his gods and conscious man's persistent longing for the departed deities.

The connection between the two epigraphs and the purpose of "The Icicle" epigraph emerge by relating the epigraphs to *The Origin of Consciousness*. The epigraph from *The Age of the Dinosaurs* describes fossils not only as "a part of the organism itself," but as "some kind of record of its presence, such as a fossilized track or burrow."[3] The epigraph from "The Icicle" describes another kind of record, the presence of the dead within the living. "The Icicle's" first-person narrator, Andrey, who can see both the past and the future, addresses a man of the future who will contain all of Andrey's past incarnations, transformed but still living within him:

*From *Essays on Canadian Writing*, no. 33 (Fall 1986):68–88. Reprinted by permission of *Essays on Canadian Writing*.

Hey! You there, man of the future! Listen to what I say! . . . Look, I'm smiling at you, I'm smiling in you, I'm smiling through you. How can I be dead if I breathe in every quiver of your hand?

Here I am! You think I don't exist? You think I've disappeared forever? Wait! The dead are singing in your body; dead souls are droning in your nerves. Just listen! It's like . . . the hum of telegraph wires. . . . We were people too; we also laughed and cried. So look back at us.[4]

This epigraph is a clue to the novel's non-realistic structure. Although Atwood quotes neither the beginning of the first paragraph nor any of the second paragraph, the second paragraph is important. It not only shows that the fossils and the singing dead are at least partially analogous vestiges of the past, but also explains the mysterious auditory hallucinations of Elizabeth Schoenhof, one of the novel's three protagonists. "Dead souls" sing in her nerves: "in her right ear," she hears a "humming" like "a power line in winter" — Sinyavsky's humming "telegraph wires" — and "Angel voices" like "someone . . . singing" (pp. 61, 60, 60, 88). But Sinyavsky's dead are "people," not angels. The idea that hallucinated voices are divine is a direct allusion to Jaynes's thesis in *The Origin of Consciousness*. According to Jaynes, in the right hemisphere of the bicameral brain of pre-conscious man, the voices of the dead were hallucinated as the voices of the gods. Heard and obeyed as deities by the living, the ancestral dead lived on and sometimes spoke not only in the minds but also through the voices of the living. But as bicamerality disappeared, these hallucinated voices gradually faded, and man became what he is today: conscious of himself and cut off from his pre-conscious certainty of continuous and intimate divine guidance in all his affairs.[5]

Thus, through the link between the epigraphs and *The Origin of Consciousness*, the double meaning of the novel's title also emerges. *Life Before Man* not only refers to the paleontological fantasies of Lesje Green about the dinosaurs who lived before man, but also alludes to the pre-conscious men who lived before us. Just as Elizabeth's hallucinations link her with this pre-conscious past, so do Lesje's symbolic fantasies. These tenuous links, however, are ironic.

Jaynes argues that as the deities of pre-conscious men "recede[d]" or were "reduced to darkly communicating with men in angels," the resulting "power vacuum" was filled by "a belief in demons" and demonic possession (*OC*, p. 232). Demons haunt the living in *Life Before Man*. This haunting motif connects *Life Before Man* to both *Surfacing* and *Lady Oracle*, although the gods and goddesses of these two earlier novels have disappeared. Instead of dead ancestors as helpful spirit-guides or as comic muse, here there are demons whom the characters try either to deny or to convert into spirit guides. But for personal and social reasons they fail in both attempts. They can internalize them only as destructive doubles.

Although this fusion of the protagonists and the demons creates a dark difference, the underlying narrative structure in *Life Before Man* is basically the same as it is in all of Atwood's novels and in the three short stories already mentioned. This structure follows the first half of the romance pattern anatomized by Northrop Frye in *The Secular Scripture*. In a romance the questing protagonist is searching for a unifying vision of identity. On his search he is accompanied by characters who function as ghostly guides or demonic doubles. The climax of the search is the protagonist's descent into a submarine or subterranean oracular place.[6] This descent occurs in the climax of *Life Before Man*, but the results are darkly ironic. When Atwood announces "I'm writing in the ironic mode,"[7] she is explicitly acknowledging that her work is included in Frye's observation that "In our day ironic modes are the preferred ones for serious fiction."[8] The irony in *Life Before Man* is complicated by the fact that this novel, with its three protagonists instead of one, is not primarily about a young woman's struggle to discover and define her identity. It asks a much more complex question: If the living are not only inescapably connected to the dead but also, like the dinosaurs, inexorably moving towards their own death, what *is* identity, and how can it be maintained? A Jaynesian reading of the novel offers an answer to this question, for his concepts illuminate the novel's structure and themes as these emerge through the symbols — the demons, doubles, and dinosaurs — that Atwood uses to develop her three point-of-view characters.

Life Before Man uses a triple point of view to tell the story of a triangle. Instead of her usual female first-person narrator, Atwood uses the third-person limited point of view and makes one of her central characters a man, Nate Schoenhof, split between two women, his wife, Elizabeth, and his lover, Lesje. By cutting back and forth between the three, Atwood reaps one of the advantages of using a multiple point of view, which she defines as follows: "Now I can have Characters B and C think for themselves, and what they think won't always be what Character A thinks of *them*."[9] Thus she can reveal the distorted perceptions of her three characters and let the reader in on subtle sexual ironies that they fail to recognize. These ironies coalesce into thematic significance.

But Elizabeth is much more important than Nate or Lesje. The five-part novel begins and ends with a chapter narrated from Elizabeth's point of view; part 1, part 3, and part 4 end the same way. Thus Elizabeth's experiences structure the novel. In addition, she is the only character with first-person interior monologues. These have two paradoxical functions. Although fragmentary, they bring the reader inside her mind as she debates with herself, sometimes audibly addressing Jaynesian voices or holding imaginary conversations with her dead lover, with a psychiatrist, with her husband, and with the hated aunt who raised her. Thus the reader knows Elizabeth better than he or she knows the other two characters presented only from the outside. But this split point of view also divides her identity and prepares for its blurring and erosion.

The split voice is reminiscent of the split point of view in *The Edible Woman*. So is Elizabeth's stasis. Like Marian at the end of part 1 of *The Edible Woman*, Elizabeth in the first chapter is lying on the bed, staring at the ceiling. Fifteen of her chapters open with similar stasis. "I don't know how I should live," she begins (p. 11). Chris Beecham, her lover, has committed suicide. Her reaction to this event is what Frye defines as the "logical" beginning of a romance, "some kind of break in consciousness."[10] And starting with this prescribed initial crisis, Elizabeth repeatedly manifests behaviour described by Jaynes. He maintains that bicamerality has not disappeared completely; one of its vestiges in conscious man is schizoid behaviour. Schizophrenics and even normal people under great emotional stress relapse to the bicameral mind. They may then hear voices, speak in other people's voices, feel split in two, experience an erosion of the ego and a loss of body image boundaries, fall through space or time, and even lose consciousness (*OC*, pp. 404–32). Elizabeth eventually experiences all these forms of behaviour. In this opening chapter she sees on the ceiling a crack symbolizing not only the split in herself but also the instability of her world. After three paragraphs in the first person, the point of view suddenly switches to the third:

> She is not in. She's somewhere between her body, . . . lying sedately on the bed, . . . and the ceiling with its hairline cracks. She can see herself there, a thickening of the air, like albumin. . . . She knows about the vacuum on the other side of the ceiling. . . . Into the black vacuum the air is being sucked with a soft . . . whistle. She could be pulled up and into it like smoke.
>
> She can't move her fingers. She thinks about her hands, lying at her sides, rubber gloves: she thinks about forcing the bones and flesh down into those shapes of hands, one finger at a time, like dough.
>
> (p. 12)

Although the pre-Jaynesian narrator of *Surfacing* has often been described as schizophrenic, Elizabeth's fantasies here of leaving her body, melting on the ceiling, being "pulled up," and losing her hands seem to echo the self-description of schizophrenic patients quoted by Jaynes: "When I am melting I have no hands. . . . Why do I divide myself in different pieces? I feel . . . that my personality is melting and that my ego disappears and that I do not exist anymore. Everything pulls me apart."[11] Another patient complained that "the feeling that should dwell within a person is outside longing to come back and yet having taken with it the power to return."[12] Atwood's switch from the first-person to the third-person point of view also emphasizes Elizabeth's introduction at a moment of great emotional stress, for this switch makes Elizabeth's "ego" or "I" disappear, both metaphorically and syntactically.

Although the other two point-of-view characters, Nate and Lesje, are presented only in the third-person, they are also split characters in many other ways. In the first chapter written from his point of view, Nate, sent by his wife to identify Chris's body, symbolically identifies his double. Looking at Chris's nearly headless corpse, he thinks, "Nate's other body" (p. 16). Nate's own head is divided against itself. A lawyer temporarily turned trendy toymaker, Nate is split professionally because he sees himself as "a lump of putty, helplessly molded by the relentless demands and flinty disapprovals" of the two Mrs. Schoenhofs, his mother and his wife. His mother wants him "to be a radical lawyer." His wife's "desires are hopelessly divided." "Half of her wants a sensitive, impoverished artist, the other half demands a forceful, aggressive lawyer" (p. 41). As if two women weren't enough, he is also split between his wife and Lesje, his newest lover. He recalls a wooden man he had made out of rings and compares his body's "stiff fragments" to that "segmented man." "Dismembered" and "separated," he laments the lack of a literal double. "He should have two sets of clothes, two identities, one for each house; it's the lack of this extra costume or body that is cracking him apart. He knew in advance . . . that separation is painful; he did not know it would also be literal" (p. 244). In "Writing the Male Character," Atwood has indirectly explained why she created Nate's pain: "The confusion and desperation and anger and conflicts that we find in male characters in novels" are also "out there in the real world," for things are changing, "new attitudes overlapping with old ones, no simple rules any more."[13]

Also confused and also split, Lesje, half-Ukrainian and half-Jewish, is cracked apart by her "hybrid" background. She has no sense of belonging to either half of her family, but both her Ukrainian and her Jewish grandmothers "thought she should scrap half her chromosomes, repair herself, by some miracle" (p. 65). She cannot speak either grandmother's language, but that deficiency does not guarantee her acceptance as a Canadian. William, her lover before Nate, "finds her impossibly exotic" and therefore "a trophy and . . . testimony to his own wide-mindedness," but he won't marry her or give her a child because she is not "a woman of . . . his own kind" (p. 29). People "mispronounce her name, giving her the look that says, we thought you were one of us but now we can tell you aren't" (p. 112). Elizabeth condescends to her as *"outlandish,"* as if she expected her to "play the violin and do charming ethnic dances, like something from *Fiddler on the Roof"* (p. 211). Lesje's situation, like the narrator's in *Surfacing*, is paradigmatic of Canada's national situation; Lesje's thoughts on her split background occur on 15 November 1976, the day the Parti Québécois was elected in Quebec.

These similarities between the three split characters blur the separate and sharply defined identities expected from the triple point of view, but, as will be shown, the blurring extends much farther. Lesje gradually changes places with Elizabeth and becomes her double. The differences between the living and the demonic dead characters also begin to disappear. Elizabeth gradually becomes like Chris, her dead aunt, and the other ghosts. At the end of the novel, the similarity between Elizabeth and Lesje is deepened by their joint resemblance to Lesje's demonic dead grandmothers. But these parallels between the dead and the living are ironic. The living are demonic and destined to die, but split within themselves and blurring and dissolving into each other, they are also split off from the past. To stress the meaninglessness of a present divorced from any significant link with the past as it erodes into a formless future, *Life Before Man* is narrated primarily in the present tense, sometimes even the flashbacks. Although Lesje, Elizabeth, and Chris all work in the Royal Ontario Museum, classifying and preserving fragments of the dead past, none of these characters is part of a continuous living tradition.

This meaninglessness is mirrored, first of all, in the plot: a dreary game of musical beds. In addition to the main triangle of the Schoenhofs and Lesje, there are others: the Schoenhofs and Chris, the Schoenhofs and Martha, who precedes Lesje, who in turn has had an affair with William before her affair with Nate. When Elizabeth discovers Nate's attraction to Lesje, she beds William, in another example of what the narrator in *Surfacing* calls "geometrical sex" to "complete an equation."[14] Thinking of all these relationships, Lesje feels that she has "blundered into something tangled and complex, tenuous, hopelessly snarled" (p. 208). With the exceptions of births and deaths, there are no real divisions in time within the characters' experience of a formlessly continuous present.

One reason for this amorphousness is that the structuring social formalities have disappeared. Lesje cannot tell her mother that she has stopped living with William and started living with Nate.

> Marriage is an event, a fact. . . . So is divorce. They create a frame-work, a beginning, an ending. Without them, everything is amorphous, an endless middle ground, stretching like a prairie on either side of each day.
>
> (p. 192)

A second, more important reason, closely connected to the first, is the weakening of religion, a phenomenon that Atwood considers one of the primary shapers of the novelist's purpose in creating fiction. A year after publishing *Life Before Man*, she defined her credo: "I believe that fiction writing is the guardian of the moral and ethical sense of the community. Especially now that organized religion is scattered and in dis-array, . . . fiction is one of the few forms left through which we may examine our society . . . in its typical aspects; through which we can see ourselves and the ways in which we behave towards each other, through which we can see others and judge them and ourselves."[15] To dramatize her examination of a society in which "organized religion is scattered and in disarray," Atwood creates Lesje's symbolic obsession with dinosaurs. Her recurrent fantasies about wandering in a prehistoric past repeatedly interrupt the flow of narrative realism. Critics scolding Lesje for this "regressive need to escape . . . from the boring or threatening present to a prehistorical world of her own making" fail to recognize the religious purpose of her need.[16] The paleontologist longs to be a prophet. Using the Old Testament prophets as illustrations, Jaynes defines religion as "the nostalgic anguish for the lost bicamerality of a subjectively conscious people," a desperate longing to hear the divine voices of the *"elohim,"* "the mighty ones," again (*OC*, p. 297). As a child Lesje was taught neither the Jewish nor the Ukrainian Orthodox ritual, but, because her Jewish grandmother took her to the museum on the Sabbath, the museum became Lesje's church: "It was quiet and smelled mysterious, and was full of sacred objects" (p. 95). These "sacred objects" include the dinosaur bones that the adult Lesje passionately longs to resurrect into living animals. *"Live again!* she . . . wanted to cry, like some Old Testament prophet, like God, throwing up her arms, willing thunderbolts" (p. 80). Jaynes quotes the Psalmist's thirsty longing "for living gods! / When shall I come face to face with gods?"[17] Lesje can come face to face with her living gods only in her fantasies about a paradisiacal lost world of luxuriant vegetation in which she blissfully watches dinosaurs re-imagined in gorgeous colours.

The dinosaurs' symbolic function is, therefore, both satiric and elegiac, for *they* are her gods, her "mighty ones," her escape not only from the dreary reality of her affairs but also from the heavy burden of her scientific knowledge of man's insignificance in geological time. She once hoped to ascend the shrine-like steps of the museum holding the hands of both grandmothers, thus symbolically healing the split not only between the right and left halves of her multicultural self but also between her desire for a living faith and the dead weight of her scientific education. As Atwood asks in "The Right Hand Fights the Left," "Why should there be a war? / Once there was none. / The left hand sang the rituals, / the right hand answered."[18] But now Lesje has learned that this hope for healing rituals, which is a hope for the restoration of bicamerality, was in vain. Like the narrator in *Surfacing*, she longs for something after logic, but her gods are only fossils.

The theme of meaninglessness is also developed through the novel's method of narration. First, the shapelessness of the characters' experience of time — of past, present, and future — is ironically emphasized by the novel's division into fifty-nine short chapters, all dated like entries in a journal. That only birth and death can alter this meaningless march of time is shown by the point of view from which birth and death are narrated and by the non-chronological order of the key chapters about the most important death, Chris's suicide. The one birth is deliberately diminished in significance by its narration from Nate's point of view. "Shut out from" the delivery of his first child, he feels "cheated" because, as his wife repeatedly tells him, "he had no idea of what it was like, and she was right, he hadn't" (pp. 164–65). He also has very little memory of the past, but, like Lesje, he escapes into fantasies about an adolescent movie-paradise, a flowery subtropical island where he will be happy with her in the future. However, all he knows about the future "with certainty" is "that someday he will die" (p. 276).

The certainty of death encases the novel like a shroud: crammed with past, present, and future deaths, it begins with Chris's suicide and ends with Auntie Muriel's funeral. The importance of Chris's suicide in shaping time is shown through symbolic structure: the two key chapters about the events causing it are flashbacks that interrupt the chronological order of the narration. Both of these chapters are also narrated from Nate's point of view. But this time he is not shut out. He is forced to recognize Chris's triumphant possession of Elizabeth, but he also witnesses her humiliating dismissal of Chris, sent "slinking across the street like a straggler from a defeated army" (p. 236). Two weeks later, when Nate recognizes Chris's headless corpse as his own double, Atwood's choice once again of Nate's point of view suggests that as a male Nate cannot experience birth; he can experience only death, and only as a passive, helpless spectator. In contrast, in chapters narrated from Elizabeth's point of view, she sits by the bedside of both her dying mother and her dying aunt and holds their hands. She gives maternal comfort, a comfort which Nate consciously seeks from a series of women. Thus Chris's suicide precipitates the novel's main action, Nate's gradual estrangement from the controlling but no longer comforting Elizabeth and his increasing involvement with Lesje.

But "action" is precisely the wrong word for what happens, for Nate's exchange of comforting women is riddled with ironies. Lesje believes that he makes "a gift of himself, handing himself over to her. . . . to do something with" him and his life (p. 116). This "gift," however, is an ironic pun on Nate's name, "Nathanael: Gift of God" (p. 50). Like Elizabeth when she was a bride, Lesje "feels very lucky" to get this gift, but she fails to understand Nate's remark as he hands himself over: "It isn't fair" (p. 116). The reader, however, realizes what Nate means: he wants to be rescued. But the problem is that so does Lesje. Through him she wants to live in "an adult world where choices had consequences, significant, irreversible" (p. 221). Instead of acquiring her own unique significance, however, she finds herself becoming Elizabeth's double. The process begins as an aftermath of Nate's initial impotence with Lesje: in a hotel bedroom he can do nothing, but later in his wife's bed his desire for revenge becomes an aphrodisiac. Unaware of the reason for Nate's sexual success, Lesje is horrified by the "almost" incestuous "violation" of intercourse in "Elizabeth's bed" (p. 169). Lesje begins to think "that she and Elizabeth are interchangeable" (p. 169), and listening to her "inner" voice, which whines and criticizes and begrudges, she fears that "If she isn't careful, she'll turn into Elizabeth" (p. 267).

The crucial difference between Lesje and Elizabeth, however, is the ever-present and constantly reiterated fact of Elizabeth's children. The phrase "the children" is repeated like a litany by all the characters. Lesje's furious resentment of Nate's love for his two daughters finally drives her to the edge of suicide. In the beginning of the novel, baffled by Chris's suicide, she considers herself incapable of imitation. But at the end, full of "the fear of being nothing," she understands why he killed himself: "He'd wanted to be an event, and he'd been one" (p. 293). As a non-event, she longs for the traditional structure of her dead grandmothers' lives. She wants ancestors, roots, and rituals. Once she had scorned her grandmothers' emphasis on the importance of *"a mother's blessing,"* but now, in an italicized paragraph of direct quotation, she remembers hearing one of the grandmother's stories. "Now she wants" their dead "voices back . . . she wants to be endorsed, sanctified" (pp. 268–69). This reference to hearing "voices" identifies her longing as what Jaynes, discussing the "vestiges of the bicameral mind in the modern world," labels "the quest for authorization" (*OC*, pp. 315, 317). When her Jewish grandmother died, Lesje, like the hallucinating ancestor-worshippers described by Jaynes, wanted to preserve her grandmother's body with "her . . . gold jewelry and . . . amber beads spread out beside her" (p. 95).[19] But just as her gods are only fossils, there is no apotheosis here, either. Her ancestors are only dead old women whose voices, very much *unlike* the grandmothers' voices recalled in "Five Poems for Grandmothers," were both literally and culturally "foreign" to Lesje even when her grandmothers were alive (p. 269).[20]

Thus the only way for Lesje to authorize her position is to throw away her birth control pills and trick Nate, reluctant to father another child, into impregnating her. As in *Surfacing*, the woman uses the man, but not for expiation this time. Lesje is seething with jealousy and the desire for revenge: "If children were the key, if having them was the only way she could stop being invisible, then she would goddamn well have some herself" (p. 293). This self-serving trick is *not*, as one critic defines it, a "truly creative act, . . . an act of moral responsibility for the creation of life,"[21] but merely a very bitchy act of survival, not very different in either method or motive from Arabella's crude trick in *Jude the Obscure*. Lesje needs to be pregnant to stay alive and to secure her primary significance in Nate's life. Although the chart in her museum office continues to show her the "hundred and twenty million years" of dinosaurs and the "mere dot" of man, her pregnancy nevertheless enables her to "hold on somehow to her own importance" (pp. 210, 308). She has defined her identity by controlling Nate, by using him to move into the identity that Elizabeth has begun to vacate.

Elizabeth's struggle to maintain her sense of identity and reality structures the novel's five parts. Her self-image is shaped by four relationships: her marriage with Nate and her affair with Chris, in both of which she is the powerfully dominant partner; her maternal role; and her hatred for Auntie Muriel. Her refusal to leave her children, as Chris wants her to, is evidence of the most positive and permanent trait in her character, a strong sense of parental responsibility. But, as the novel unfolds, she loses all her defining roles except the maternal one. At the climax of her aunt's funeral, when she recalls Coleridge's "Kubla Khan" and completes the romance protagonist's underground descent, her identity dissolves into the black vacuum she feared in the first chapter.

The novel begins just before Hallowe'en, reduced from its original significance as the eve of (what Elizabeth calls) All Souls' to a time when witches and demons haunt the living.[22] This introductory emphasis on the supernatural, like Lesje's recurrent fantasies about dinosaurs, develops into a constant pattern in which Elizabeth's realistically described domestic routine is displaced by the darker elements of romance. After Chris has blown his head off, Elizabeth personifies Hallowe'en jack o'lanterns as "disembodied heads" (p. 51). In this description we recognize her as she later recognizes herself: obsessed by masturbatory fantasies of an "Armored dildo," she is Coleridge's woman wailing for her "demon lover" (pp. 11, 213). She is full of erotic memories of Chris's "hot" eyes, his "smoky" sheets, and his resemblance to "Dracula" (pp. 24, 159). But this vampire analogy is misleading: unlike Atwood's other drained women in "The Grave of the Famous Poet," "Under Glass," and "Lives of the Poets," here the woman also drains the man of blood and energy.[23] At first Elizabeth refuses to face her responsibility for Chris's suicide, but later she admits her guilty use of him: "What if she'd left him alone. Foregone that jag, energy flowing into her" (p. 161). So her difficulty in living without him also makes *her* Dracula or the demon, an exultantly powerful female demon or witch. "I treated him the way men treat women. . . . but never me, not on your goddamned life. He couldn't take it." She wonders if she feels "pity for him at last, or . . . contempt" (p. 161). This cannibalistic symbiosis clarifies Atwood's purpose in using Elizabeth's point of view to narrate the parallel chapters at the ends of part 1, part 3, and part 4, the climactic funeral chapter in part 5, and the conclusion.

At the end of part 1, when the children come to the door on Hallowe'en, Elizabeth recalls Chris coming to the door and pulling her out on the dark porch for a secret embrace. She sent him away, but now she sees the children as "souls, come back, crying at the door, hungry, mourning their lost lives. You give them food, money, anything to substitute for your love and blood, hoping it will be enough, waiting for them to go away" (p. 53).[24] At the end of part 3, the lost souls clamouring at the door return. In a flashback significantly in the present tense, Elizabeth relives the symbolically suicidal deaths of her deserted mother and catatonic sister, both of whom she had protected maternally. Then she dreams that her children are lost. In this recurrent nightmare she recognizes her two daughters as doubles of her mother and sister, whom "She's shut . . . out, . . . but they come back anyway" (p. 187). Although time goes on, "Nothing ever finishes" (p. 188).

At the end of part 4 it is Elizabeth who has become the lost soul, locked out of the lives of the living and loving. Nate has moved into Lesje's house. Depressed by her husband's departure, on her thirty-ninth birthday Elizabeth confronts herself in the mirror and glimpses a fantastic image of her own metamorphosis in the future: "In the glass oval, behind her own face, rigid and . . . puffy in the muted light, she can trace the shadow of her face as it will be in twenty years" (p. 247). Not only do the melting candles of her birthday cake make her see her aging self as a "melting woman," but one of her children asks, "Mummy, . . . are you going to die?" (pp. 252, 250). The symbolism of the candle episode is defined by Frye's observation that "entering a world of . . . *reduced* dimensions is a central symbol of descent."[25] The reduced Elizabeth considers suicide, but it is hardly necessary, for when she goes to Lesje's house and stands outside on the dark porch, she is already "discarded, invisible" (p. 251). She wants to scream her protest: "Look at me, I'm here, you can't get rid of me that easily," but she is voiceless (p. 252). Then, terrified that her dreams about her children foretold their future, the wandering ghost rushes home.

The fourth relationship feeding Elizabeth's identity is the violent energy of her lifelong rebellion against everything her aunt represents. In an interview Atwood has described Elizabeth's relationship with her aunt: "She absolutely hates, loves, and detests her Aunt — which gives her a lot of energy. Her hatred drives her on."[26] Convinced that her childless, repressed aunt has crippled her, Elizabeth insists, "I live my life despite you" (p. 123). Although she takes her daughters to visit her aunt in a consciously ambivalent attempt to give them a sense of their ancestry, these visits also give Elizabeth an opportunity to gloat. Flaunting both her motherhood and her sexual promiscuity, she repeatedly compares her aunt to a witch. But gradually, like Lesje listening to herself, Elizabeth hears her own voice "using Auntie Muriel's phrases" (p. 262). When the aunt is dying of cancer and Elizabeth visits her in the hospital, she sees, "She's . . . melting, like the witch in *The Wizard of Oz*," and instead of being "jubilant," Elizabeth is "terrified," too, has already begun to melt, and not just by aging (p. 279).

Her terror is exhibited ever more dramatically in the stress-induced behaviour that Jaynes classifies as a relapse to the bicameral mind. The voices she hears and the vacuum she fears have escalated: she feels herself falling forever into space. During a planetarium lecture on black holes, she associates Chris with the "man in a silver suit" that the lecturer uses to illustrate disappearance into a black hole. "He's an optical illusion" (p. 77). Later, in another episode that emphasizes Lesje's role as Elizabeth's double, Elizabeth looks at her child's drawing of the sun in the sky. When Lesje looked at this drawing, immediately after intercourse in Elizabeth's bed, she saw the sun as "a bursting lemon" and thought that someday she, too, would "dissolve." At that moment, considering this future only as an illustration of the scientific law that nothing in nature is "immutable," she was able to consider her eventual dissolution "soothing" (p. 169). But

Elizabeth, deprived of both lover and husband, now sees the sky as "an illusion" concealing "the dark of outer space," and is once again terrified. Her fantasy makes her faint. "Somewhere out there the collapsed body floats, . . . tugging at her with immense gravity. Irresistible. She falls towards it, space filling her ears" (p. 205).

At the climax of this tightly organized pattern, the aunt's funeral in part 5, Atwood again alludes to Jaynes's discussion of pre-conscious man's hallucination of ancestral voices, often projected through the mouths of corpses or idols (OC, pp. 149–75). Since her aunt chose her own funeral hymns, Elizabeth feels that she is "hearing Auntie Muriel's own voice, . . . projecting itself through the mouths of the . . . mourners" (p. 297). At the grave Elizabeth fears that she, too, is possessed by another voice: "If she opened her mouth, . . . something disreputable would come out" (p. 300). Jaynes defines such a fear in a conscious mind as one of the effects of "demonization" or demonic possession (OC, pp. 348–52). Suddenly, without her volition, Elizabeth "hears herself murmuring" a line from "Kubla Khan": "Ancestral voices prophesying war" (p. 300). "Poetry," which Jaynes says began as "the divine speech of the bicameral mind," is one of the contemporary vestiges of bicamerality still within the conscious mind. As evidence, Jaynes cites the "actual auditory hallucinations" of Milton, Blake, and Rilke (OC, pp. 375–76). Coleridge's introduction to "Kubla Khan" puts him in this company. Subtitled "A Vision in a Dream," "Kubla Khan" describes an auditory and visual hallucination.[27] Thus, Elizabeth's repetition of Coleridge's line is an example of what Jaynes labels as "hallucinatory echolalia" (p. 424).

As the grave reminds Elizabeth of the poem's "caverns" and "*caves of ice*," she feels the "black vacuum" sucking "at her" and "falls through space" (p. 300). Her loss of consciousness is also characteristic of demonization (OC, p. 348). Recovering from her symbolic descent into this "Coleridgean chasm,"[28] she thinks of Chris, her demon lover, and of "his power over her," which originated in his pretense of being "Métis, that mythical hybrid; archaic, indigenous, authentic as she was not" (pp. 301, 160). But this imaginary background is fake, just as the third eye he jokingly stuck on his forehead was only a cheap plastic Christmas toy, completely divorced from the meaning of Christmas, and just as his only link with nature was with stuffed animals; he was "a taxidermist, . . . a glorified custodian of dead owls" (p. 172).[29] So the oracular voices that Elizabeth hears "summoning" her "from underground" and warning her that "She's built a dwelling over the abyss," are *not* authentic, divine voices but demonic ones, the voices of her demon lover and her witch aunt, both of them internalized doubles. Frye stresses that an important stage of the ascent from the lower world is "recognizing the demonic as demonic."[30] But without the vitalizing energy of demonic love and hate, Elizabeth's identity and the world itself have become "transparent" and unreal (pp. 301, 302).

Although Atwood's novel fictionalizes Jaynes's theories, her use of Sinyavsky's story "The Icicle," as already indicated, also helps to make it a romance. "The Icicle" is a fantastic story, while *Life Before Man* is full of the daily, gritty, surface detail of domestic realism; but, as has been shown, this realistic surface is constantly displaced by the elements of romance: the nightmares, fantastic images, and full-blown fantasies of Elizabeth and Lesje. Some of these clearly seem to be derived from Sinyavsky's story.

Atwood assigns her two female characters experiences that are all given to Andrey, the first-person narrator in "The Icicle." For a short time he possesses the ability to see both the past and the future. In the beginning of the story, he suddenly finds himself plunging back into a forest of the prehistoric past. "I hurtled headlong into an abyss with an almost physical — and unpleasant sensation of falling. I fell down and down and down, . . . and when I came to, all my surroundings were different and I was not quite the same ("I," p. 41). Later, he is "Frightened of falling into an abyss five hundred, a thousand, or ten thousand years deep" because these terrifying descents, like Elizabeth's fainting fits, have shown him that "there was nothing that seemed stable . . . or could be taken at its face value" ("I," p. 59). The first thing no longer stable is his own life. Staring at the candles at a New Year's Eve party, which, like Elizabeth's birthday party, marks the passage of time, he associates the candles with the burning-out of the guests' lives. Like Elizabeth, he identifies with one of the melting candles; the other guests have already burned out, but he is "still . . . smouldering" ("I," p. 151). After this fantasy about death in the future, the guests lose their individual identities: "The outlines of their bodies and faces began to waver. . . . Each line broke up and became blurred, giving birth to dozens of breathing shapes." As a result, "everything was mixed up and in flux and I had no means of knowing where one person ended and another began" ("I," p. 155). This confusion includes a confusion about his own identity. Like Elizabeth, he looks at himself in the mirror and sees his many past and future selves: "Is *that* what I shall be like?" he asks ("I," p. 169). On the basis of these experiences, he concludes that "there is no such thing as 'I' and 'he,' " neither in the present nor in the past or future, for " 'nobody knows who was who or who will be who. Perhaps you —yes, you— are me' " ("I," pp. 58, 115–16). This confusion defines both Elizabeth's and Lesje's merging of identities. And like Elizabeth on Lesje's porch, Andrey stands in the dark, a voiceless ghost, locked out of the house where his beloved lives. This image of exclusion is a recurrent nightmare of his future death ("I," pp. 102–03, 121).

Although the ghostlike Elizabeth still fulfills the responsibilities of her maternal role, the pregnant Lesje — probably the third Mrs. Schoenhof — has usurped the maternal identity. Looking at Elizabeth at the end of the novel, Lesje, like Andrey, sees the future: she sees a woman "on the last day of her life," like the dying aunt, then imagines Elizabeth and herself also fusing into witchlike old women, cancerous with hate (p. 309). This is Lesje's recognition of the demonic as demonic. Like her two witchlike grandmothers, who could not function as her helpful spirit-guides, and whose obsessive hatred of each other united them in "an odd parody of marriage," Lesje and Elizabeth have melted into one woman, future grandmothers, "each keeping the other locked in her head, a secret area of darkness like a tumor or the black vortex at the center of a target" (pp. 93, 309).[31] In their jealous war over Nate, the prophecy of the ancestral voices has been fulfilled.

The conclusion of the novel, narrated from Elizabeth's point of view, equates the Xanadu of "Kubla Khan" with the paradisiacal Chinese Communist posters that Elizabeth looks at in the museum. Jaynes includes Marxism in his list of the many "substitutes" invented by "the contemporary world" to replace the system of divine authority that disappeared with bicamerality (*OC*, pp. 440, 442). He emphasizes Marx's belief that there is "a paradise to be regained," the "lost 'social childhood of mankind where mankind unfolds in complete beauty' " (*OC*, p. 444). The posters' lush crops and happy collective heroes picture a future Communist utopia just as unattainable as the forever-lost dream world of Xanadu: "they paint not what they see but what they want," Elizabeth thinks (p. 316). Similarly, the last lines of "Kubla Khan" describe what Coleridge wanted: "For he on honey-dew hath fed, / And drunk the milk of Paradise." But he could never re-enter his "vision" or hear the "song" of his divine voice again.[32] Elizabeth echoes these lines: "China is not paradise; paradise does not exist. . . . Nevertheless she longs to be there" (pp. 316, 317). Yearning for the poster-paradise, symbolically behind glass, she is once again the lonely ghost excluded from life.

Elizabeth's longing echoes Lesje's acknowledgement of the futility of her fantasies about the lost paradise of the Mesozoic: "*The Mesozoic isn't real. It's only a word for a place you can't go to any more because it isn't there*" (p. 290). Jaynes insists, "You cannot, absolutely cannot think of time except by spatializing it" (*OC*, p. 60). There is always only the present, in which time is conceptualized as space, but there is no future or past place. Thus Lesje's obsession with geological time and Elizabeth's fear of falling into space are symbolically the same experience, as they are in "The Icicle," and the final step in their merging into doubles. As Atwood remarks of another writer's poetic vision, both characters see "the human figure like a tiny dot at the intersection of geological time and astronomical space."[33]

Therefore, a Jaynesian reading of *Life Before Man* shows that it is not about the discovery of identity as a permanently defined construct, but about the characters' daily, existential experiencing of identity as a constantly shifting pattern of alteration, attrition, and inevitable loss. Frightened by the spiritual emptiness of their experience, Lesje and

Elizabeth hunger for some significance, but in the ironically meaningless process of being exchanged by Nate, they become each other's and their ancestors' doubles, neither unique, nor significant, only persistently demonic. Thus, like Nate's first name, the two women's surnames, Schoenhof and Green, are also ironic, for there is neither a "beautiful court" nor a green place for either of them. The Chinese posters, Elizabeth knows, conceal "malice, greed, despair, hatred, death" (p. 316). Similarly, Lesje's own "vengeful act" forces her recognition that "Man is a danger to the universe, a mischievous ape, spiteful, destructive, malevolent" (p. 293). Before her pregnancy she thinks, "All she wants is a miracle, because everything else is hopeless" (p. 270). Once she is pregnant, however, she cannot imagine her baby as a "shining . . . god" or as "the first true human," like the miraculous baby in *Surfacing*.[34] Instead, she foresees that a "child conceived in such rage" will be a cross between a demon and a dinosaur, "a reptile, a mutant . . . with scales and a little horn on the snout" (p. 293). Atwood's Jaynesian comments on the characters of another novelist are also applicable to her own three characters here: "The only answer for these . . . spiritually famished people would be God."[35] But her novel shows that no matter how deeply her characters long for them, deities, like dinosaurs, are extinct. Thus, the only "miracle" is Elizabeth's survival. "She has no difficulty seeing the world as a transparent veil or a whirlwind. The miracle is to make it solid" (p. 302). Diminished as she is, she struggles on to do that; in the last scene she plans to return to her symbolic porch to feed her living children.[36]

Notes

1. Sherrill E. Grace, " 'Time Present and Time Past': *Life Before Man*," *Essays on Canadian Writing*, No. 20 (Winter 1980–81), pp. 165–70.

2. Jerome H. Rosenberg, " 'For of Such is the Kingdom . . .': Margaret Atwood's *Two-Headed Poems*," *Essays on Canadian Writing*, No. 16 (Fall–Winter 1979–80), pp. 130–39; Lorraine Weir, "Atwood in a Landscape," in *Margaret Atwood: Language, Text, [and] System*, ed. Sherrill E. Grace and Lorraine Weir (Vancouver: Univ. of British Columbia Press, 1983), pp. 143–53.

3. Margaret Atwood, *Life Before Man* (New York: Simon and Schuster, 1979), n. pag. All further references to this work appear in the text.

4. Abram Tertz (Andrei Sinyavsky), "The Icicle," in *Fantastic Stories* (New York: Pantheon, 1963), p. 83. All further references to this work ("I") appear in the text.

5. Julian Jaynes, *The Origin of Consciousness in the Breakdown of the Bicameral Mind* (Boston: Houghton Mifflin, 1977), pp. 201–03. All further references to this work (*OC*) appear in the text.

6. Northrop Frye, *The Secular Scripture: A Study of the Structure of Romance* (Cambridge, Mass.: Harvard Univ. Press, 1976), pp. 97–126, 129. Compare the circular ravine in *The Edible Woman*, the deep lake in *Surfacing*, the double maze in *Lady Oracle*, the damp underground prison in *Bodily Harm*, the Aztec sacrificial well in "The Resplendent Quetzal," the dark place into which Jeannie descends in "Giving Birth," and the deep, dark river in "Scarlet Ibis." See Russell M. Brown, "Atwood's Sacred Wells," *Essays on Canadian Writing*, No. 17 (Spring 1980), pp. 5–43; Catherine McLay, "The Dark Voyage: *The Edible*

Woman as Romance," in *The Art of Margaret Atwood*, ed. Arnold E. and Cathy N. Davidson (Toronto: House of Anansi, 1981), pp. 123–38; Robert Lecker, "Janus through the Looking Glass: Atwood's First Three Novels," in *The Art of Margaret Atwood*, pp. 177–203; Ildikó de Papp Carrington, " 'I'm Stuck': The Secret Sharers in *The Edible Woman*," *Essays on Canadian Writing*, No. 23 (Spring 1982), pp. 68–87, and "Another Symbolic Descent" *Essays on Canadian Writing*, No. 26 (Summer 1983), pp. 45–63.

7. Margaret Atwood, "Northrop Frye Observed," in *Second Words: Selected Critical Prose* (Toronto: House of Anansi, 1982), p. 406.

8. Frye, p. 134.

9. Margaret Atwood, "Writing the Male Character," in *Second Words*, p. 426. Rpt. from *This Magazine*, 16, No. 4 (Sept. 1982), 4–10. Originally delivered in a somewhat different version as a Hagey Lecture at Waterloo University, February 1982.

10. Frye, p. 102.

11. Janes, p. 425. Quoted from P. S. Schilder, *The Image and Appearance of the Human Body* (London: Kegan Paul, French, Trubner, 1935), p. 159.

12. Jaynes, p. 418. Quoted from E. Meyer and L. Covi, "The Experience of Depersonalization: A Written Report by a Patient," *Psychiatry*, 23, No. 2 (May 1960), 215–17.

13. Atwood, "Writing the Male Character," p. 428.

14. Margaret Atwood, *Surfacing* (Toronto: McClelland and Stewart, 1972), p. 152.

15. Margaret Atwood, "An End to Audience?" in *Second Words*, p. 346. This address was delivered in the Dorothy J. Killam Lecture Series, Dalhousie University, 8 Oct. 1980. Rpt. from *Dalhousie Review*, 60, No. 3 (Autumn 1980), 415–33. For another definition of the writer's moral responsibility to society, see Margaret Atwood, "A Disneyland of the Soul," in *The Writer and Human Rights*, ed. Toronto Arts Group for Human Rights (Garden City, N.Y.: Anchor-Doubleday, 1983), pp. 129–32.

16. Linda Hutcheon, "From Poetic to Narrative Structures: The Novels of Margaret Atwood," in *Margaret Atwood: Language, Text, [and] System*, p. 28.

17. Jaynes, p. 313. The quotation is from Psalm 42.

18. Margaret Atwood, "The Right Hand Fights the Left," in *Two-Headed Poems* (New York: Simon and Schuster, 1978), p. 57.

19. See Jaynes, pp. 161–65, 188–89, *et passim*.

20. See Margaret Atwood, "Five Poems for Grandmothers," in *Two-Headed Poems*, pp. 34–41.

21. Hutcheon, p. 29.

22. Atwood seems to have confused November 1st and November 2nd, or at least her character has. On Hallowe'en Elizabeth refers to "All Souls" (p. 53), but November 1st is All Saints' Day (or Allhallows, from which the word "Hallowe'en" is derived, since the night before Allhallows is Allhallows Eve[n]). November 2nd is All Souls' Day. Elizabeth's confusion might be Atwood's way of showing that her character no longer knows the religious significance of the two days.

23. Margaret Atwood, *Dancing Girls* (Toronto: McClelland and Stewart, 1977), pp. 91, 96, 82. The woman poet who supports her voracious lover in "Lives of the Poets" begins by having a symbolic nosebleed, but when she suspects his infidelity, she is energized by jealous rage.

24. See *Surfacing*, p. 155, where the narrator is unsure whether feeding the dead will bring them "back" or make them "stay away." See also Jaynes, pp. 161–65, where he discusses feeding the dead.

25. Frye, p. 108, emphasis added.

26. "An Interview with Margaret Atwood," in *Interviews with Contemporary Writers*,

Second Series, 1972–1982, ed. L. S. Dembo (Madison: Univ. of Wisconsin Press, 1983), p. 377.

27. Samuel Taylor Coleridge, "Kubla Khan," in *The Portable Coleridge*, ed. I. A. Richards (New York: Viking, 1950), p. 156.

28. Margaret Atwood, "Superwoman Drawn and Quartered: The Early Forms of *She*," in *Second Words*, p. 50. Rpt. from *Alphabet*, No. 10 (July 1965), p. 78. The actual grave, Coleridge's "caverns" and "caves," and the "black vacuum" that Elizabeth imagines are all analogous to the underground places listed in note 6 above. See also Frye, p. 111: "On the lower reaches of descent we find the night world, often a dark and labyrinthine world of caves and shadows."

29. Perhaps even the "eyeless" owl that Chris keeps in his room — to suggest an Indian totem or idol? — is a clue to his lack of authenticity (p. 24). The jewels stuck into the eye-sockets of "speaking" idols were, according to Jaynes, "hypnotic gems" that contributed to bicameral worshippers' hallucination that the idols were speaking gods (p. 170). The emptiness of the eye-sockets of still extant idols is a visual reminder of the gods' muteness. See also Jaynes, pp. 165–75.

30. Frye, p. 137.

31. Compare Joan Foster's recognition of her dead mother as "a vortex, a dark vacuum" in *Lady Oracle* (New York: Simon and Schuster, 1976), p. 330.

32. Coleridge, p. 158.

33. Margaret Atwood, "Introduction," in *The New Oxford Book of Canadian Verse in English* (Toronto: Oxford Univ. Press, 1982), p. xxxvii. The comment is about Al Purdy.

34. *Surfacing*, pp. 162, 191.

35. Margaret Atwood, "Ann Beattie: *Falling in Place*," in *Second Words*, p. 367. Rpt. from *The Washington Post Book World*, 25 May 1980, pp. 1, 9.

36. Compare these themes of change and survival to the conclusion of George Woodcock's "Metamorphosis and Survival: Notes on the Recent Poetry of Margaret Atwood," in *Margaret Atwood: Language, Text, [and] System*, p. 141: "Seen from this point in her life, her work — in prose and verse alike — presents a unity that reflects her dominant themes, tenacious survival and constant metamorphosis." Woodcock does not discuss *Life Before Man*.

[Review of *True Stories*]   Ann Mandel*

Alain Resnais' recent film *Mon Oncle d'Amerique* opens with a shot of a beating valentine-shaped heart very like the heart on the cover of Margaret Atwood's latest collection of poems, *True Stories*. Next we see shots of the sea, hear discussions of crab behavior, and the film then proceeds to follow the lives of three individuals, rather as Atwood does in *Life Before Man*, in specific environments and milieus in order to observe their behavior given certain situations. Resnais is interested in a behavioral theory which posits that origins and events which happen to us very early

*From review of *True Stories*, by Margaret Atwood, and *Wilson's Bowl*, by Phyllis Webb, *Fiddlehead*, no. 131 (January 1982):63–70. Reprinted, Atwood portions only, by permission of the author.

in childhood determine how we will subsequently act, that we have a unique death rooted in us from the beginning—that we are true to our original story. Atwood's book, too, begins with the sea, poems on crabs and questions of origin, but the first, title, poem flatly denies there is *a* true story, even one's own:

> The true story is vicious
> and multiple and untrue
>
> after all. Why do you
> need it? Don't ever
>
> ask for the true story.

The difference comes from the difference in hearts. Though neither looks like a real heart, Atwood's is also a vagina and glows with light, like a sun, like a nuclear explosion. This heart is source, energy, entrance, exit; opening and conclusion. Her crab, too, hermit and predator, is ancestor and double, timid vagina dentata and reminder of old nightmares. *True Stories* is very much concerned with first and last things, but Atwood knows that origins and endings are much more complex than words and lives can explain, and her knowledge is born from her recognition of the corporeality of existence: of love and of power, of torture and of daily life. The heart is a body among a jumble of particular physical things and feelings. Knowing any thing, any one, is not simple, is not true. . . .

Both books [*True Stories*, and *Wilson's Bowl*, by Phyllis Webb] are elemental, seasonal. . . . The sea, its creatures and garbage, wash through the lines of many poems in *True Stories*. Tidal love pounds against an ear; the water waves vague fears towards the poet's body: "Tattered brown fronds / (shredded nylon stockings, / feathers, the remnants of hands) / wash against my skin." The earth and its new growth are for both poets reminders of death:

> It isn't winter that brings it
> out, my cowardice,
> but the thickening summer I wallow in
> right now, stinking of lilacs, green
> with worms & stamens duplicating themselves
> each one the same
>
> I squat among rows of seeds & imposters
> and snout my hand into the juicy dirt:
> charred chicken bones, rusted nails,
> dogbones, stones, stove ashes.
> Down there is another hand, yours, hopeless,
> down there is a future

. . . . Like *Wilson's Bowl*, *True Stories* begins on an island, a tropical landscape of sea, heat, rain, and stone, with poems which fuse the closeness of nature with the distance of a loved person. This first section closes in a colder climate with fourteen "Small Poems for the Winter Solstice." The dark middle section, "Notes Towards a Poem That Can Never Be Written," contains poems on torture, carols of death and of poetry's dilemma. The final section, poems on death, love, and nature, grows towards the summer solstice and a departure.

Similarly, throughout these books both poets struggle with the inadequacy of language to deal with the material world, insist on the necessity of that struggle. In Webb, poems are trapped in the body, cross-hatched on bones. In Atwood, people are tortured for speaking, their bodies insisting that poems be written. Poetry escapes the body; it nevertheless has its own power: "A word after a word / after a word is power."

Both poets reject received truths: the stories handed down by the powerful to the weak, governments to citizens, technologies to societies; the visions passed on by saints and poets to the rest of us in our partial banal worlds. Michel Foucault suggests that in the present we see truth as a form of scientific discourse, transmitted under the control of political and economic apparatuses and subject to ideological debate. We also, he says, have a myth which believes that truth is accessible to certain free spirits, the result of protracted solitude, the privilege of "those who have succeeded in liberating themselves." Hence there is powerful truth (accepted by the majority) and powerless truth (individual). Foucault argues that, instead, truth is neither outside power nor lacking in power; nor is it impossible. The problem is not error, lie, illusion, or ideology; it is changing the means by which truth is produced. Truth is a political question — hence, he writes, "the importance of Nietzsche," who argued for the necessity of lies to vanquish the "one true world," a world "false, cruel, contradictory, misleading, senseless." Both Atwood and Webb refuse the idea that truth is ideologically arguable or the preserve of, say, poets. Furthermore, as Foucault too insists, they know that individuals and relationships are not simply acted upon by *a* power controlling truth; rather all relationships — between men and women, among families, within groups — are the "changing soil" (Foucault) in which sovereign power is grounded and which allows power to function. Acts between people are incorporations of power, as Atwood has shown in many poems and in her novels. Power is not abstract any more than truth is; it is not a repressive negation of the body but an assertion of control on bodies, a notion central to Atwood's book and implicit in Webb's quarrels with visionaries and philosophers.

"The political significance of the problem of sex is due to the fact that sex is located at the point of intersection of the discipline of the body and the control of the population," Foucault writes in *Power/Knowledge*. The heart of that heart of Atwood's, the vagina, she repeatedly shows being attacked. Chastity devices, abortions, rapes, a woman "caught in the war / & in labor, her thighs tied / together by the enemy / so she could not give birth," mutilations, prostitution: tortures perpetrated against the source of life, against women's power, against "Enemy territory," in the name of love, religion, marriage, ideology — these tortures and others depicted in the middle section of *True Stories* "did not happen last year . . . but last week. / This has been happening, this happens." They are true stories, and Atwood is not quick to supply them with meanings or morals. Some familiar figures and emotions appear: the detached maker of torture machines, the self tortured by fears of "what you might do / yourself, or fail to," the sense that one's own bones are latent weapons, the hope, rejected, that there's a reason for, a shape and plot to, the atrocities one reads of. It *can* happen to blameless you. These are old-but-true stories, but in the face of them "the word *why* shrivels and empties / itself." "Witness is what you must bear," all the more so because if in "safe" countries the most honest poems will be ignored, there are places where the most courageous act, the only possible act, is the truthful poem.

The power of these political poems of Atwood's comes from their insistence that torture is not abstract but physical, that *bodies* are flayed, beaten, burnt, sliced, torn. "Such things are done as soon / as there are sides," but whatever the reason, the will to power has more to do with bodily knowledge, desire, and control than with abstract justification. Atwood takes recourse neither to the idea of universal guilt in which we are all accomplices to injustice nor to placing blame on capitalism, socialism, narcissism or any other "ism." There are those tortured bodies. They defy explanation. . . .

On the back jacket of *Wilson's Bowl* . . . there's a quotation from Atwood: "Phyllis Webb moves outwards from the personal centre, through the persona/l, to a view of tragic humanity in the world at large, and back again." The movement she traces is similar to the movement of *True Stories*, as I've tried to suggest, but the main difference between the two books I feel lies precisely in Atwood's use of "tragic," appropriate for Webb but not I think for her own work or view. . . . For Atwood, I think, the physical world is something different. Though she has broadened the political range of her poems, she never leaves the particularity of image, of *things*, which are certainly reminders to her and to us of mortality, but are also weapons against dehumanizing abstractions. There is no justice in destruction, and it's how we deal with that that counts. In the more personal first and last sections of *True Stories*, the physical world is full of possible metaphors and messages for the poet, but she sees it finally as indifferent to our lives, whatever pretensions to shared meaning we may have.

Goodbye, we credit

> the apple trees, dead
> and alive, with saying.

> They say no such thing.

Landscapes, lush or stark, polluted or pastoral, offer various temptations, illusions, reminders of loss, and paradoxical comfort. On the boundaries between stony beach and moving sea, desert and marsh, polluted ocean and lush garden, one can be seduced to merge simply with an endless natural cycle, or be reduced to a safe absence of human needs and longings. It's tempting to reject the polluted and cheapened worlds of chemical clutter and commercial sentiment for some clean abstract place over *there*, untouched and untouchable. What mediates between a bleached-bone life and unthinking sentience is love, not Platonic but present and wanted, even in absence. Love humanizes even poetry: "Nothing like love to put blood / back in the language." It brings the world up close, it touches us, and "What touches / you is what you touch."

After a series of tropical poems, time and light thin down and the poems move, as we all do, towards a dark solstice. It's an apparently clear and undistracted motion — though eclipse is at any time possible — with a chilly conclusion. We start with a clean sheet and end up under one; it all ought to be simple. "Small Poems for the Winter Solstice" mediates on conflicting desires for clarity and confusion, knowledge and trust, on the paradoxes of intangible presence and tangible absence, as they are involved in and affect love for another person. As we wish lives were guiltless, lucid, comprehensible, as we wish events and moments were as readily dealt with as carving a turkey, so love we fondly imagine can be neat and poetic. But love is for some body which we didn't invent, and takes place along with Christmas dinners, starvation, famine, feeding the dogs, amid a "waste of particulars, / truth, facts. Teeth, gloves & socks." It is part of the tangible world; it needs the intangible, unknowable presence of another being, who is also a creature of ungovernable flesh, hair, and blood:

> There's no choice, I have to take you
> with all the clutter,
> the fears, justified
> or not, the smoky furniture,
> dubious flesh, fatigue, the nagging
> of daily voices, your obscure heart
> neither of us can see, which beats
> softly under my hand. . . .

Not a romantic heart, a real one. Its presence marks humanity, as do certain absences:

> if there were nothing
> but killing or being killed then why not

kill? I know you by your
opposites. I know your absence.

Atwood has always spoken from an unromantic position despite her
use of Gothic devices. She has consistently used a technique in which the
inner mind, and the irrational or unconscious mind, becomes material,
visible, imagined, either as recognizable landscape or surreal terrain — a
romantic technique which produces anti-romantic results. In *True Stories*
the natural physical world is more present and less the result of projection
or paranoia, at the same time that love seems more possible and less a
tricky conceit. As death fills *Wilson's Bowl*, so an awareness of physical
death is in every poem in *True Stories* and especially in its concluding
section. Every moment, every poem, is the poet's last, as every second may
be the last for those she loves. Death is rooted in earth and grows up as
mushrooms, to be eaten at every meal, which is also the last. It floods the
air, falls as fruit in orchards, intensifies the taste of that fruit, intensifies
especially care for others. The love lyrics here are the stronger for the
poet's acute sense of the mortality of love. "Love":

> This word
> is far too short for us, it has only
> four letters, too sparse
> to fill those deep bare
> vacuums between the stars
> that press on us with their deafness.
> It's not love we don't wish
> to fall into, but that fear.
> This word is not enough but it will
> have to do.

Love is fragile and necessary as air: "I would like to be the air / that
inhabits you for a moment / only. I would like to be that unnoticed / &
that necessary." Everything moves to conclusion. In high summer, one is
already approaching the winter solstice, at high noon wading into a
sunset:

> We wade
> through moist sun–
> light towards nothing, which is oval
>
> and full. This egg
> in my hand is our last meal,
> you break it open and the sky
> turns orange again and the sun rises
> again and this is the last day again.

This shining egg is the upturned "white zero" of a lover's face, the O
in love, a hen's daily miracle, a gift, the tides' moon, the endlessly final
sun. It's a story among all the other stories which blur the air, thicken and

plump it till the skin feels its touching. Like the mushrooms which "smell of death and the waxy / skins of the newborn," these poems contain decay and hope, the vulture's clean work and the messy detritus of living. The origins of behavior — to love or not to love, to torture or not to torture — lie in more than one story, one's story. Atwood's insistence on the welter and spawn of existence is part of her denial of the "true story," her emphasis on the intricate entanglements of language and power, political and private acts, poetry and the body.

In "Poems of Failure," Webb writes of nights spent piecing together diamonds of red and purple velvet, "Mapping it into some kind of crazy / poncho. I am absorbed in the fitting together of pieces," though larger maps of countries and stars elude her. Atwood too takes pieces from places, moments, and things and offers them as what fragmentary gifts are possible in a multiple and unperfectable world. The whole story can only be made up of whole cloth. We don't need it.

[Review of *Second Words*]   Margarets Atwood*

It has long been our opinion that "Margaret Atwood" ("Peggy" to her friends), purported author of some 20 odd books, does not really exist. It's true that there is an individual by that name who goes shopping, appears on the CBC and performs other mundane chores of this nature, but objective evidence supports the conclusion that this person is merely a front for a committee.

To begin with, we have conflicting media sightings: can the motherly, cookie-baking, pussycat-loving comedienne described by Greta Warmo-dota in her May profile in *The Griswold Examiner* possibly be the same as the threatening succubus and man-devouring squid depicted by Alan Peevish and Frank Slug, among others? How to reconcile the author of *Power Politics* with the woman who was runner-up in the 1965 Conser-mers' Gas Miss Homemaker Contest? As the Celtic-Bilgarian ethnologist Gwaemot R. Dratora notes in his recent *National Geographic* piece, "In Search Of The Elusive Atwood," "Pinning down the real Atwood has a lot in common with Pooh trying to catch the woozle: each time round the bushes, there's a whole new set of tracks." Wode M. Gratataro, noted Transylvanian architect, has commented less kindly, "Atwood is to litera-ture what urban sprawl is to town planning," a sentiment echoed more elegantly by the Estonian-Italian postmodernist linguist and expert on metafiction, Trogwate d'Amorda: "Confronted by this gargantuan excres-cence, one can only creep about, like Gulliver among the Brobdingnag-

*Copyright Margaret Atwood. First appeared in the *Globe and Mail*, 20 November 1982, L2. Reprinted by permission of the author.

ians, recognizing a fingernail here, a nostril there, but at a loss to grasp the over-all form."

With the current book we find ourselves in the vicinity of what a nineteenth-century phrenologist would have called the Bump of Criticism. *Second Words* is a gathering of fugitive and occasional pieces pertaining more or less to literature and churned out by the Atwood committee over a period of 22 years. Lest the unwary fork out hoping to get a how-to manual, we hasten to add that this is the Atwoods writing primarily about other people's work rather than their own. Some of the 50 articles included are book reviews of such writers as Adrienne Rich, Audrey Thomas, W. D. Valgardson, Al Purdy, James Reaney, E. L. Doctorow, Marge Piercy and Ann Beattie, which originally appeared not only in Canadian organs such as *The Globe and Mail* but also in inferior publications, such as *The Washington Post* and *The New York Times*. (How Atwoods can reconcile this fact with their alleged nationalism we'll never know. Maybe they have some wishy-washy liberal theory about dialogue creating understanding, though as Yggep Doowta, financial columnist for *MacLoon's*, would say, it's gotta be for the money.)

What's wrong with these reviews, we feel, is that they are soft in the underbelly. Reading them, you'd think that all these writers are Shakespeare. Where is the celebrated Atwood viciousness? Could those fangs have been wax all along? Atwood makes a shift at explaining this phenomenon by saying she won't review a book she hates, and she probably has some twisted notion about the task of the reviewer being to explain and qualify rather than to mince and shred. But as newspaper readers, let's be honest, we want blood, and there's not enough of it in these pages.

But not all of *Second Words* is recycled newsprint. Though in one place Atwood looks down her extensive nose at what she calls "the footnote crowd," she's quite capable of exuding a footnote or two herself, as the extensively annotated articles on Rider Haggard, Gwen MacEwen, John Newlove and Canadian supernaturalism indicate.

As a book reviewer and critic, Atwood is definitely on the conservative side. Postmodernism seems to have wafted right by her, and she's not at all up to in-depth analyses of metonymy and synecdoche, although she does throw out these terms in passing. She still seems to believe that creation is primary and that criticism of a work should bear some relation to what is actually on the page, a point of view which the inner circle will spot immediately as hopelessly old-fashioned. But then, as a critic she is — as she's the first to point out — not a pro.

In "Canadian Monsters" (which is not about politicians), she compares herself to an amateur Victorian fern collector, which we find suggestive: indeed she appears to have a mind that's a cross between Leopold Bloom and a caddis-fly larva. Anything that comes along gets stuck onto whatever structure she's currently hammering together, which makes for a texture which is eclectic, to say the least.

Perhaps it's her lack of professional status that accounts for a certain frivolity and even audacity in these pieces; one-liners abound, as do jokes in questionable taste and word-play which some may admire but we regard as jejune. When we find her, in "Writing The Male Character," comparing men to dung beetles (although, admittedly, she expresses a curious delight in the latter), we feel she has gone too far. Some things are sacred, and we, unlike Atwood and Henri Fabre, do not include beetles.

What emerges from a swift perusal of this volume is that Atwood is to words as a pig is to mud. She's probably one of those people for whom oral sex means the invention of a new metaphor. But is there anything of value under the fancy footwork? Can she be taken, uh, *seriously?*

Well, it depends who by. Certainly not by the male members of the University of Victoria English Department, but then they didn't take her seriously anyway. To her credit, we have to admit that some of her positions — on the human-being status of women, not to mention men, on Canadian autonomy, on torture and repression — platitudinous though they may be, are not ones we can argue with, although she does vacillate about the extent to which writers should involve themselves politically.

Apart from these considerations, literary historians will use this tome to trace Atwood's progress from retiring graduate student through firebrand and target to retiring non-graduate-student; and Atwood cultists will want to add this volume to their T-shirt collection. The cover painting of "Atwood" by Charles Pachter is noteworthy. And *Second Words* is a perfectly safe Christmas gift, as there are no words in it which might bring a blush to the cheek of your Aunt Agatha, though we won't vouch for "opinions" and "Uncle Bill."

Those who wish to make Atwood gnash her tusks will say *Second Words* is her most accomplished work to date, but our own view is that the Atwoods would be much better off spending their time on poetry and fiction. We trust that in the future they will see their way clear to doing so.

Margarets Atwood write travel pieces for The New York Times.

In Darkest Atwood
[*Murder in the Dark*]

Elspeth Cameron*

Murder in the Dark is a parlour game in which a detective and a murderer are secretly designated by lot. The lights go out and everyone mills around until a scream announces that a victim has been chosen. When the lights go on, everyone must answer the detective truthfully except the murderer: he must lie. Margaret Atwood's new work of fiction, *Murder in the Dark,* uses this game to provide a metaphor for the writer. Like the murderer, the writer must lie. If the lies are convincing enough, they will fool the reader into thinking this version of reality is the real one.

The association of fiction with the dark arts is not new in Atwood, or in literature generally. What is dramatically new about this book is its form, for Atwood dispenses with the plot line that usually provides the skeleton for her fiction. She offers instead thirty-one set pieces varying in tone, content, perspective, and style. It is as if — in keeping with her sinister title — she has shifted the word "plot" from its literary sense to its more macabre meaning as a conspiracy, or even to its simple application as a burial space in a cemetery. Plots, she writes in a piece ironically called "Happy Endings," are "just one thing after another, a what and a what and a what. Now try How and Why."

Atwood's exploration of the "How" and "Why" of fiction defies conventional arrangement. Her discomfort with traditional plot (perhaps her suspicion of the ease with which she can imitate it) can sometimes be felt in her earlier fiction: in the mechanical set-up of *The Edible Woman,* the hyperthyroid parody of narrative in *Lady Oracle,* the slow oozing of story line in *Life Before Man,* or the experiments with different "shapes" of short story in *Dancing Girls.* Her disdain for neat plans emerges in this collection in a piece called "Iconography":

> He wants her arranged just so. He wants her, arranged. He arranges to want her.
> This is the arrangement they have made. With strings attached, or ropes, stockings, leather straps. What else is arranged? Furniture, flowers. For contemplation and graceful disposition of parts to compose a unified and aesthetic whole.

What Atwood strives for in place of this cluttered and claustrophobic interior décor — which is reminiscent of funeral parlours and tombs — is an arrangement like that in nature: one in which function defines space, line, and colour with ruthless economy. Such arrangements are cleanly pleasing and frequently geometric — like strawberries, "each white five petalled yellow centred flower and conical fine-haired dark red multi-seeded dwarf

*From *Saturday Night* 98, no. 3 (March 1983):70–72. Reprinted by permission of the author.

berry rendering itself in dry flat two dimensional detail" or like the remote but vivid memory of "a blue line. This was on the left, where the lake disappeared into the sky."

Atwood groups the pieces into four loose categories. The structure draws the reader into a pilgrimage that begins conventionally enough but moves outward through experience toward philosophical abstraction. The first section, which opens with a piece called "Autobiography," traces the development of a persona through a series of illuminating experiences — making poison, reading *Boy's Own Annual* in the attic, stealing horror comics, going to the Victory Burlesk — spanning the time from earliest memory to adolescence. On its own, this section resembles W. O. Mitchell's *Who Has Seen the Wind* or Alice Munro's *Lives of Girls and Women*. It is the world of touch, taste, and smell by which we all approach life's absurdity and mystery.

But the perspective changes abruptly in the second section. As in some of Atwood's most striking short stories, such as "The Resplendent Quetzal," the next five pieces take place in Mexico, where people are "drawn to dark places." The persona — now a young woman travelling with a man — is looking for "the real experience." "Why do we travel? In other words, what are we doing here?" Since Mexico provides a landscape and a set of experiences markedly unlike those the woman has known as a child in Canada, the relationship between the surface world of the senses and some inner reality can be more clearly detected.

But can it? Crawling through clammy tunnels or scaling dizzying pyramids to glimpse the gods of this alien country ironically confirms the similarities between other and self: the same faith in the darker powers, the same hatreds and delight in destruction, the same craving for benevolent deities.

The third section begins with "Murder in the Dark" and moves through the particular and the universal to the aesthetic. In six experimental pieces that read at times like an LSAT test for advanced aesthetes, Atwood dramatizes writerly problems: the "crime" of verisimilitude, the responsibility (or irresponsibility) of subversive literature, the difference between men's and women's novels, the grip of allegory, the topsy-turvy power of humour, and, above all, the risk the writer takes daily. "If you decide to enter the page," she warns in a piece called "The Page," "take a knife and some matches, and something that will float. Take something you can hold onto, and a prism to split the light and a talisman that works, which should be hung from a chain around your neck: that's for getting back." What she calls "the full horror of a journey into the page" — in which the writer makes a "thin incision" which lets the "darkness" beneath the page "well through" — is fraught with greater risk than any descent into Mexican tombs. It calls for the courage of desperation, lies, a plot.

In the last section, Atwood turns theory to practice, sketching incisively a series of pieces that let the darkness through. Some treat literary subjects: "Mute," for example, which describes the state of indecision before embarkation, "waiting for the word, the one that will finally be right. A compound, the generation of life, mud and light." But most cover a range of familiar Atwood subjects: the difficulty women have liking men, the opposition of the sexes ("He's a carnivore, you're a vegetarian. That's what you have to get over"), the complex nature of human beings, the limbo between sanity and madness, the hot fact of rage. In each can be felt the whiplash of tension generated by Atwood's determination to get the right words to make her version of reality seem true. The section closes with "Instructions for the Third Eye," an appeal to intuition over reason.

Atwood unites these four sections poetically through recurrent images and words. The African cave and tunnel from *Boy's Own Annual* becomes the pyramid and tunnel in Mexico and later the "darkness" that lies beneath the page; the pink "princess line" dress of adolescence becomes the costumed romantic heroine of women's fiction; the magical objects of childhood reappear as Mexican tomb carvings, then as the woman herself worshipped by men, and finally as the "talisman" the writer must wear to get back safely from that journey into the page.

This collection will undoubtedly arouse the anti-Atwoods to redouble their attacks. What, no plot? Just those same dreadful opinions about everything? More nasty feminism? Self-examination? Does she think *writing* is all there is to life? To some extent her critics will be right; the book could have been called *Atwood's Sketch Book* or *Themes and Variations*. Often there seems little reason for the juxtaposition of the pieces. Some — "Before the War," for example — are not as memorable as they might be.

But other readers will hear the subtle resonances that occur as Atwood recasts her images in clean new forms. The effect resembles the strange phenomenon that occurs when a note played exactly true on one violin string causes another string an octave away to vibrate in sympathy. The resulting sound is as penetrating and eerie as the voice of a boy soporano or the laughter of a loon. It sounds like a refined scream.

Charms and Riddles
[*Bluebeard's Egg*]
Magdalene Redekop*

"Sally stands at the kitchen window . . ."; "Loulou is in the coach-house, wedging clay . . ."; "this is Joseph, in maroon leather bedroom slippers . . ."; Father "spreads a tarpaulin beneath a likely-looking tree, striped maple let us say . . .": these are the people who inhabit the eternal

*From *Canadian Forum*, January 1984, 30–31. Reprinted by permission of the journal.

present of Atwood's fictional world. "This is the freedom of the present tense, this sliding edge." The last line is from a story called "The Sunrise" but it could stand as an apt description of Atwood's craft. Yvonne, skating on thin ice, looks into store windows, hoping always to discover behind them "something that will truly be worth seeing." That hope seems to be the motivating force in these stories. They have an improvisational quality which is belied by the careful craftsmanship, the exquisite control of the edge of that blade, the uncanny balancing of, on the one hand, our fear that we are on thin ice and, on the other, our hope for vision.

The story-telling voice, while it involves us in the "let's imagine that" process, is also eerily alienating. Like the wilderness, the stories are haunted by the "ghosts of those not yet dead," including that of the narrator. The result is that monotone two-dimensionality which has earned Atwood a certain notoriety. Like all her fiction, this collection is about the human need to reduce reality by making it into a manageable, flattened picture. One character's severely reduced version of another often acts as a prison. The poets assembled in Loulou's kitchen are reassured when she returns — after a frightening lapse into intelligence — to her pose of stupidity. By means of Atwood's ironic inversion we feel the claustrophobia that Loulou ought to feel. The same goes for the painfully happy Betty: the more vehemently she insists that we should colour her kitchen bright yellow, the more we sense the darkness in the corners. In "Bluebeard's Egg," Sally clings to the illusion that her control over her mental "Polaroid print" of her husband is as complete as her power over the story of Bluebeard. She loves Ed for his stupidity, his "innocence, lamb-like, shining with the light of (for instance) green daisied meadows in the sun." Her shattering discovery of his duplicity makes it impossible for her to complete the fiction written from the point of view of Bluebeard's egg.

Heather Cooper's poster of woman and egg adorns the dust-jacket of this book, realizing one among many paper images within the book. "Animated valentines," "Kate Greenaway greeting cards," the "sickly Rosetti madonna," the "lady on a chocolate box" — a host of women are squashed to fit into the framed flatness of glossy pop art. If we take these paper dolls at face value, we ignore the often horrific three-dimensional world that lurks behind the flimsy constructs. A rhythmic alternation between surface and depth is characteristic of Atwood's art. The more demonic and threatening the background, the flatter the characters. But if there is a hell behind the paper dolls, there is also a heaven of sorts. There is here an exuberance that comes from the energy necessary to repudiate the horrors confronted. Like Loulou's poet-friends, Atwood's readers might laugh at the suggestion that she is a "raving optimist" but she is — in a way.

It is true that in Atwood's version of gothic we witness characters figuratively chopped up like the beloved sisters in the Bluebeard tale. We also see the sisters reassembled by Sally, but that wholeness has a specious quality. In the end, there is no discovered truth that can be gingerly handed to the reader like Bluebeard's egg made whole again. Rather, the very self-consciousness of the fiction makes us aware that we are, willy-nilly, involved in the process of murdering to create. We know that the egg can never be put together again. On the other hand, there is an affirmation that comes through loud and clear in the last story—"Unearthing Suite"—the narrator's moving and complex tribute to her parents. This story *has* to be the last one. It's not as if we have not seen splendid "sights" along the way, but everything seems to move towards this final revelation of what is truly "worth seeing."

When it comes, however, the vision is not witnessed directly. By a curious inversion, the adult daughter cannot enter fully into what is revealed to her child-like parents. She can only approximate the revelation through her own unearthing, story-telling activity. The most poignant image in the book is oblique: "Look, my father has unearthed a marvel: a slug perhaps, a snake, a spider complete with her sack of eggs? . . . You can't see it from here: only the backs of the children's heads as they peer down into his cupped hands." Here, where she might easily abandon the "sliding edge" of the present tense and adopt a comfortable, retrospective stance, Atwood sustains the tension to extraordinary effect. Oddly enough, we feel most included at the moment when we are explicitly excluded. One with the ghostly voice of the narrator, we are unable to re-enter the paradisal world of our first parents. When they play their ancient guessing game, we cannot guess the answer and we share the daughter's feeling of loss.

This loss, however, like the word "vacancy," holds a special charm because it is a sign signifying that "there is room." What we do *not* see—but what we know is *worth* seeing—is the ultimate focus of hope, the window opening out of the claustrophobic world portrayed in the preceding stories. The oblique answer to the parent's riddle turns out to be a discovered dropping which tells of the recent rare presence of a fisher. Surely this "deposit of animal shit" brings with it the smell of a three-dimensional, earthy reality. The answer to the riddle, however, is not a final answer. The classification of the dropping breaks the spell for a moment, but it does so only to put the artist on firm ground, ready to start creating again. It is the mother who restores the charm of "vacancy." For her, this dropping is "something else:" it is a "miraculous token, a sign of divine grace. . . ."

This is the stuff that stories are made of. Look, Margaret Atwood has unearthed another marvel.

Pandora's Box and Female Survival: Margaret Atwood's *Bodily Harm*

Roberta Rubenstein*

Margaret Atwood's *Bodily Harm* (1981) is a feminist, existential study of the relation between women and patriarchy. Having recently undergone a partial mastectomy, the protagonist Rennie Wilford is vulnerable and disaffected. She becomes unwittingly involved in political events on Caribbean islands where she goes to escape from her deteriorating personal life in Canada. The narrative is structured through parallels in event and symbol, including doubled figures of doctors and grandmothers. Hands and "faceless strangers" are other important images of both connection and alienation between people. Cancer functions as a scourge of the body and a metaphor for such diseases of the body politic as violence, pornography, and sadism. Through these doublings as well as allusion to the mythical Pandora, Atwood establishes correspondences between female guilt, power, victimization, and moral responsibility. Ultimately, Rennie discovers her complicity in female victimization and transcends her crippling self-contempt.

I

Margaret Atwood's first three novels (*The Edible Woman*, 1969; *Surfacing*, 1973; *Lady Oracle*, 1976) focus on the quest for unified female selfhood. In each narrative, problems related to ego boundaries, merging, and separation form a cluster of psychological issues that are ultimately clarified for the protagonist as she comes to understand her relationship to her parents (particularly her mother), with a man, or both. *Life Before Man* (1979) moves closer to a kind of existential reality: the void is not just the inner vacuum that precedes autonomy or follows separation from the parents. Rather, it is the void in which we are all suspended as part of our solitary humanness; one becomes more acutely aware of it in direct proportion to one's sense of separateness and isolation from others.

The author's most recent novel, *Bodily Harm* (1981), develops these thematic concerns in even more global dimensions, in both figurative and geographical senses. On the one hand, it is Atwood's most politically feminist novel, immediately concerned with such issues as body image, female sexuality, male-female relationships, and male brutality in a patriarchal society. One might even conclude that the novel is an angrily anti-male work. In a certain sense it is so, although the object of Atwood's anger is less the male sex per se than the patriarchal establishment and value system that continue to endow it with excessive privileges and powers, both personal and political.

*From *Journal of Canadian Studies* 20, no. 1 (Spring 1985):120–35. Reprinted by permission of the *Journal of Canadian Studies/Revue d'études canadiennes*.

On the other hand, *Bodily Harm* is a deeply existential novel, focusing on the relation of the individual woman to society: her sense of connectedness to the major moral conflicts of her time, to the issues of power and powerlessness; the illusion of exemption from evil; and the necessity for being politically and personally engaged. Additionally, it examines the nature of moral responsibility for both the individual and the group in a world they never made. The novel is what I would term a truly feminist existentialist text: a novel about "power politics" that not only connects the female world meaningfully to the real structures of power but insists that they cannot be understood separately. Thus, male aggression and female passivity are seen not only in their immediate, private forms but also through their major consequences upon political or public reality—and vice versa. The body politic is the form writ large of the individual body, in this instance the female body; bodily harm in one domain is directly felt in the other.

II

Like each of the four novels that precedes it in Atwood's canon, *Bodily Harm* is narratively segmented, in this case into three distinct story strands which constitute the experiences of Rennie (Renata) Wilford of Ontario, Canada, who tells her story in retrospect: "This is how I got here. . . ."[1] In interweaving Rennie's recent experiences with those of childhood, and in turn with the surprising sequence of events on a pair of islands in the West Indies that literally change Rennie's life, Atwood illustrates that each person contains several "stories" which must somehow be synthesized for coherence of personality. In college Rennie had believed that "there was a real story, not several and not almost real" (p. 64). Later in the novel, Paul, an American loner in the islands who figures centrally in the narrative, reiterates, "In this place you get at least three versions of everything, and if you're lucky one of them is true" (p. 150). Only at the very end of the novel does Rennie understand how the fragments of her experience are organically connected. In finding that truth, she discovers her freedom and thereby achieves wholeness at a time in her life when, given the circumstances, she might be least expected to do so.

The three strands of Rennie's story which organize and advance (or flash back) the narrative are: (1) the remote past, including her childhood in the deadening environment of a prim matriarchal family in a small Ontario town; (2) the recent past in Toronto, including Rennie's destructive relationship with her aggressive lover, Jake, and her discovery of breast cancer followed quickly by surgery; and (3) the immediate past, retracing Rennie's unwitting involvement in a political intrigue taking place on a pair of small Caribbean islands recently freed from colonial rule. The three stories intertwine both narratively and thematically; flashbacks to the first two (retold in the present tense) are interpolated at associatively significant moments in the more straightforwardly chronological narrative of Rennie's adventures in St. Antoine and St. Agathe.

Moreover, the narrative advances through a series of significant parallels. Both the details of Rennie's life in Toronto and the events that take place in the West Indies commence just before a major crisis: Rennie's cancer operation and the political scramble on the islands following independence from Britain. Parallels between the two sets of events proceed through a number of resonating images and motifs, until the split within Rennie — if not within the leadership of the islands — is progressively resolved.

The novel opens with an event that foreshadows the insidious links among sex, power, violence, and death that bind the narrative. Rennie returns one afternoon to her Toronto apartment to find a broken door through which an intruder has crashed. Two bullying policemen remind her how lucky she is that she was not there when the apartment was forcibly entered; the sinister evidence is a rope lying coiled like a snake on her bed, intended for her. In her absence, her living space has been invaded, just as her body recently has been invaded by malignant cells. Moreover, the break-in alters Rennie's perception of herself. Afterwards, she "couldn't shake the feeling that she was being watched. . . . She began to see herself from the outside, as if she was a moving target in someone else's binoculars" (p. 40). Thus, both the "invasion" of cancer and the invasion of her dwelling space precipitate Rennie's incipient self-estrangement.

Like her mother (who had made Rennie feel responsible for accidents that happened to her during her childhood), the policemen investigating the forced entry make Rennie feel as if she invited such an assault. Throughout the novel policemen play a sinister role: as agents of authority, they are neutral when they should be involved and involved when they should be neutral. They become symbols for institutionalized brutality, sanctioned by the patriarchal powers and by the impersonality of their uniforms.

The detail of the rope is left deliberately unexplained. It comes to assume a variety of meanings, from the echo of "rape" which the word resembles, to the image of something coiled like the original mythical snake, ready to tempt the female into knowledge of evil (or good), or to bring bodily harm with its sting. Gradually we learn that Rennie's former lover, Jake — a man with canine teeth and predatory desires — prefers sex that includes bondage and sadism. For example, he would sometimes arrive at Rennie's apartment by surprise, through a window or fire escape, and enjoyed overpowering Rennie sexually with such prescriptions as "Pretend you're being raped" (p. 117). He views Rennie as a body whose mind is of little consequence; he makes her feel like a "small malicious animal" (p. 199) to match his own animalistic sexuality. In their bedroom — *her* bedroom — he hung two provocative posters, one showing a "brown-skinned woman wound up in a piece of material that held her arms to her sides but left her breasts and thighs and buttocks exposed" (p. 105). The other poster displays a woman lying feet first on the sofa; her head, "up at the other end of the sofa, was tiny, featureless, and rounded like a doorknob. In the foreground there was a bull" (pp. 105–06). Though the posters had made Rennie uneasy, she had failed to challenge Jake's aggressive possession of her space (and body).

In their first and last attempt at lovemaking after the partial removal of her left breast, Rennie senses Jake's awkwardness and resistance; later, remembering it (like most of the Toronto flashbacks) in the present tense, she recalls the way he had concentrated on the lower half of her body. She had seemed so vulnerable that Jake could not make love to her at all. "[H]e liked thinking of sex as something he could win at" (p. 207). In such an imposition of submission, Rennie had felt even more alienated from her own body. She had watched Jake with detachment "from her head, which was up there on the pillow at the other end of her body" (p. 199), in unconscious imitation of the poster above them on the wall.

Even though Jake is implicated as the intruder who left the rope in Rennie's apartment, the identity of that "faceless stranger" who haunts her broadens to become not only several actual men in her life but also a term reflecting a particular psychic orientation to experience. In St. Antoine and St. Agathe there are a number of actual and symbolic "faceless strangers," including the unknown person who breaks into Rennie's hotel room during her absence—in sinister repetition of the event in Toronto not long before.

Some of Rennie's anxieties about invasion and violation can be understood through the cultural attitudes toward both the female flesh and cancer; Rennie is a double victim, of both disease and male exploitation. Men worship the breast, and women internalize the male overvaluation of this aspect of their anatomy. Because it is also associated with the actual and symbolic qualities of nurturance, the loss of part or all of a breast affects a woman's sense of her procreative capabilities; after her operation, Rennie wonders and worries whether she will be able to bear a child.

Moreover, cancer itself is the most dread disease of the twentieth century. It is intrepid for Atwood to use it so centrally in her fictional world, articulating a fear that is perceived particularly by women as threatening to their very sense of selfhood and relationship.[2] In *Illness as Metaphor* Susan Sontag has observed: "Nobody conceives of cancer the way TB [tuberculosis] was thought of—as a decorative, often lyrical death. Cancer is a rare and still scandalous subject for poetry; and it seems unimaginable to aestheticize the disease."[3] Elsewhere Sontag adds that such a radical disease metaphor is used "to propose new, critical standards of individual health, and to express a sense of dissatisfaction with society as such."[4] Clearly, this latter point is precisely Atwood's intention.

As a corollary issue, Rennie is also a stranger to her own body. She thinks of it as a "sinister twin, taking its revenge for whatever crimes the mind was supposed to have committed on it" (p. 82). When she had first learned of her disease, she had been so devastated that her perception had split in two; "she believed two things at once: that there was nothing wrong with her and that she was doomed anyway, so why waste the time [on an operation]?" (pp. 22–23). As she later confesses: "Nothing had prepared her for her own outrage, the feeling that she'd been betrayed by a close friend. She'd given her body swimming twice a week, forbidden it junk food and cigarette smoke, allowed it a normal amount of sexual release. She'd trusted it. Why then had it turned against her?" (p. 82).

Compounding Rennie's inner division is the fact that conventional attitudes toward the male and female sex roles of active/passive or aggressive/receptive are reinforced at every level of culture. Rennie herself both participates in and perpetuates them. A journalist who writes about "radical chic" and "life style" subjects—fads in fashion, new styles of clothing or ornamentation, and other trends of interest to readers of women's magazines—she has written more than one article reiterating the traditional receptive role for women in relationships with men.

III

Rennie flees Canada to escape the overwhelming pressures on her physical and mental integrity: not only Jake, but also the intruder in her flat and the even more insidious intruder in her body. Her journalistic pose is partly a pretext for travel, partly a neutral mask to provide anonymity and distance from whatever she might see or encounter. In what later proves to be a sharply ironic detail, Rennie feels both invisible and safe in the foreign environment of the islands. In fact, everyone else is in disguise, too. As Paul later tells her, " 'almost nobody here is who they say they are at first' " (p. 150).

Though islands typically suggst separation and isolation, the "Twin Islands in the Sun" (p. 67) that Rennie visits are emblematic of the doubled imagery that structures the text. For example, "terminal" is both the point of departure and the name for her fear of dying from her disease; during the course of the novel she moves from "terminal, the end of the line, where you get off" to terminal as a place "where you can get on, to go somewhere else" (p. 299) in more than one sense. Sontag has noted that the metaphors associated with cancer "refer to topography (cancer 'spreads' or 'proliferates' or is 'diffused' . . .)."[5]

Significantly, the first person Rennie meets en route to the "twin islands" is a doctor, Dr. Minnow, one of the islands' three candidates for the first election since independence from Britain one month earlier. Minnow regards Rennie as an innocent, a representative of the "sweet Canadians" whose well-intentioned political efforts never achieve their aim because of Canada's political naiveté. Before Minnow's assassination during the bloody aftermath of the elections, the doctor "imposes" on Rennie, hoping to show her the true corruption in the government and thereby move her to expose it through her writing. Rennie resists Minnow's urgings, insisting that she is a different kind of journalist; rather than politics, she writes about "what people wear, what they eat" (p. 136). Dr. Minnow reminds her that he is interested in those same problems—but from a deeper political and humane perspective to which Rennie is blind at that point in her life.

Rennie recalls another doctor, her own grandfather, a country physician of violent temperament whose primitive life-saving methods (as Rennie describes them) uncannily resemble torturous mutilations of the body: "he drove a cutter and team through blizzards to tear babies out through holes he cut in women's stomachs and then sewed up again, he amputated a man's leg with an ordinary saw . . ." (p. 55). By contrast, Dr. Daniel Luoma, Rennie's breast surgeon (with a name that sounds almost like a variety of cancer) is a model of male normalcy and decency. She feels that he has power over her because he "knows something about her she doesn't know, he knows what she's like inside" (p. 81). Further, "he's the only man in the world who knows the truth, he's looked into each one of us [his patients] and seen death. He knows that we've been resurrected, he knows we're not all that well glued together, any minute we'll vaporize. These bodies are only provisional" (pp. 142–43).

Yet like Rennie's grandfather, Dr. Luoma has performed a mutilating operation (one generally practiced by men upon women's bodies) to save Rennie from her own disease. Each of the doctors in the narrative thus embodies the paradoxes of patriarchy: the opposing stances of healing and destruction as practiced in the characteristically male institutions of medicine and politics. Even when they are humane people, the doctors participate in the structure of power that presides over violence, manipulation of opinion, and life itself. "*Doctored*, they say of drinks that have been tampered with, of cats that have been castrated," Rennie remarks (p. 101, emphasis in original).

Like doctors, grandmothers appear as central—and doubled—figures in the narrative. Rennie has a haunting recurrent memory of her senile grandmother, in whose home she lived as a child in Griswold, Ontario, with her mother (and without her father, who lived in Toronto with another woman). In this memory fragment, the elderly woman keeps wailing that she's lost her hands and cannot locate them. The parallel figure on the islands is ancient Elva, grandmother of Prince, one of the other two political candidates in the election. Elva's status is deliberately ambiguous: on the one hand, she is a link in the subversive chain of illegal gun shipments to the islands; on the other, she is also a "doctor"—one gifted with healing hands. She cures a German woman's acutely painful reaction to a sea urchin sting by laying on hands, a gift she has inherited from her own grandmother, just as Rennie eventually inherits a gift of healing from hers. At one point during the confusing events on the islands Rennie wishes that she could "put herself into the care of [Elva's] magic hands" (p. 194).

Concerning the power of grandmothers, late in the novel, Lora Lucas tells Rennie, "This whole place [the islands] runs on grandmothers" (p. 231). When the two women are in jail together, Lora gives the guards her sexual favours in return for improvements in their accommodation, and challenges Rennie's disgust with " 'You wouldn't put out to save your granny, would you?' " (p. 285). Ironically—as the reader subsequently learns—it is Rennie's "granny" who, through the link of female generations, saves her.

Similarly, hands are central to the meaning of the novel, referred to more than fifty times in the text. (An analysis of *Bodily Harm* could be constructed from the imagery of hands alone.) They are consistent emblems for both tangible and symbolic connections between human beings. When Rennie had first awakened from her operation, for example, Dr. Luoma (later Daniel) had gripped her arm with his hand, forming an "odd growth" in opposition to the "odd growth" in her body (p. 32). Their slight relationship exists primarily through hand-holding and pats of the hand. Rennie believes that Daniel's soul is literally "in his hands" (p. 198), just as in another sense her own is. She desires his touch not as her surgeon but as her lover, believing that his hands on her body could transform more than her medical fate.

In the islands, hands grab Rennie's shoulder (p. 176) or shake hers. A deaf mute beggar pursues Rennie, who fears his advances until she is told that he only wishes to shake her hand to bring her good luck; later the man is gratuitously beaten up by the police, presumably for vagrancy. Rennie's own hands frequently shake or are pressed together in moments of tension. Late in the novel, when she talks to Dr. Minnow on the eve of the election, she notices his tense hands: "it's as if he has to hold onto them to keep them from moving, lifting, striking out" (p. 228). On another occasion, Lora tells Rennie that making love with Paul is like "shaking hands" (p. 217).

Intending to remain a detached journalist on her vacation, Rennie initially resists the pressures put on her by Minnow and various other people she meets in St. Antoine and St. Agathe who intrude or impose upon her psychologically to try to use her for their own diverse purposes. The most significant of these are Paul, an American loner who, Rennie eventually learns, is the "connection" in an illegal gun-running operation; and Lora Lucas, a big-breasted Canadian drifter with a sordid past. Rennie's innocence and uninvolvement are quickly compromised; barely two days into her stay, she agrees to retrieve a parcel from the airport on St. Antoine as a favour for Lora, whom she scarcely knows.

The box reputedly contains medicine for the grandmother, Elva, who lives on the twin island of St. Agathe. Without knowing its contents,

Rennie hides the box under the bed in her hotel room. After the room is forcibly entered in her absence, she looks into the box and discovers that it contains a weapon. Only much later, after she has conveyed the box to its recipient, does she realize that she has been the go-between for the delivery of a machine-gun that may subsequently be employed in the assassination of two of the three political candidates, Dr. Minnow and Elva's grandson, Prince.

This sequence of events also alludes to the story of Pandora who, like Rennie, was an innocent young woman entrusted with an important container whose contents she could not resist knowing. According to the legend, when she opened the container evil and and disease were released into the world; only hope remained in the container. Significantly, Rennie once wrote for a journal named *Pandora* (p. 43); by the end of the novel she has discovered that saving capacity, hope. Other images of boxes and packages in the novel build upon this allusion. Jake, Rennie's erstwhile lover before her operation, is a package designer who creates "the label, the container, the visuals for the advertising" (p. 103). As Rennie later sees, "she was one of the things Jake was packaging" (p. 104).

Moreover, Jake views her as a "box" in the obscene sense. "You're so closed, Jake said once . . . I want to be the one you open up for. But she could never remember afterwards what he had actually said. Perhaps he'd said, I want to be the one who opens you up" (p. 106). Still later Rennie recalls Jake's exploitative and debased view of the female sex: "What is a woman," Jake said once. "A head with a cunt attached or a cunt with a head attached? Depends which end you start at. It was understood between them that this was a joke" (p. 235).

In the more remote past, Rennie's grandmother and mother had displayed a stern sense of decency and propriety, classifying certain kinds of unacceptable behaviour: "They all have the category, it gets passed down like a cedar chest, though they each put different things into it," Rennie reflects (p. 156). Rennie's own chest is also a kind of container; its alteration by breast surgery alters, for a time, her sense of the boundaries between inside and outside. After her operation she "no longer trust[ed] surfaces" (p. 48), since they betray what lies beneath.

When she sees insects and other repugnant creatures, she imagines them having exuded from her scar; she dreams she's full of "white maggots eating away at [her] from the inside" (p. 83). When the healing scar tissue aches, she is afraid to look at it, fearing that she'll see "blood, leakage, her stuffing coming out" (p. 22). Elsewhere she worries that the scar will "split open like a faulty zipper, and she will turn inside out. Then she would see what Daniel saw when he looked into her, while she herself lay on the table unconscious as a slit fish . . . he knows what she's like inside" (pp. 80–81). Even intimate relationships give another person power over Rennie's boundaries: love "made [one] visible, soft, penetrable" (p. 102). These images of boundary violation and decay also convey Rennie's sense of having been physically violated, exposed while she was incapable of defending herself, like the forced entries into her living spaces.

Like several of Atwood's earlier protagonists who experience blurred body boundaries and a division between their physical entity and the self or mind (particularly Elizabeth Schoenhof of *Life Before Man*, who experiences occasional moments out of her body), Rennie dreams of herself in such states: "There's a line between being asleep and being awake which Rennie is finding harder and harder to cross. Now she's up near the ceiling, in the corner of a white room . . . her body is down there on the table, covered in green cloth, there are figures around her, in masks, they're in the middle of a performance, a procedure. . . . It's the heart they're after. . . . she doesn't trust them, she wants to rejoin her body, but she can't get down" (pp. 172–73). Significantly, in this context, "immunologists class the body's cancer cells as 'nonself,' " Sontag notes.[6]

The self-consciousness about physical boundaries extends to Rennie's perceptions of other people. Once regarding Lora's fingernails bitten below the quick, she is repulsed by the "sight of ravage, damage, the edge between inside and outside blurred like that" (p. 86). Later, in jail with Lora for her presumed connection to the pervasive political intrigue on the islands, Rennie visualizes a "jigsaw puzzle, in her head, the top border, the ones with the flat edges, it's always the sky, one piece fits into another . . ." (p. 280). While in prison, she is understandably totally disoriented, feeling as if "she has been turned inside out, there's no longer a *here* and a *there* (p. 290, emphasis in original). By this point in the novel, the boundaries of Rennie's world, both physical and psychological, have been radically altered.

Rennie's most overwhelming exposure to the extreme form of boundary-violation has already occurred earlier in her life, in Toronto, when her editor gave her an assignment to do a piece on pornography from the female point of view. The editor of *Visor* (the magazine's title alludes both to a mask and to an object that frames and thereby limits vision) believed that the existing articles he had seen on the subject in women's magazines "missed the element of playfulness" (p. 207). The section describing Rennie's research is itself Atwood's own extremely powerful condemnation of pornography.

In researching material for the article, Rennie views the works of a pop sculptor who uses life-sized mannequins of both sexes, which he twists into utilitarian objects like chairs and tables. In its debasement and manipulation of the body (primarily the female form), his "art" underscores the images and experiences of female powerlessness and male manipulation and exploitation that recur throughout *Bodily Harm*. The sculptor argues, in defense of his bizarre work, "What art does is, it takes what society deals out and makes it visible, right?" (p. 208). Against such irony, the novel itself accomplishes this goal with especial force.

The additional "raw material" that Rennie views is far more graphic and shattering. With her friend Jocasta (whose name alludes to unnatural sexual acts) as her companion, she views the police collection of seized obscene objects. The two women make their way easily through the first room full of "ordinary" sexual appliances. In another room Rennie watches "with detachment" (p. 210) a series of film clips of women in positions of intercourse with a variety of animals, and even sits impassively through several "sex-and-death" pieces which she assures herself must be faked with ketchup. The grand finale, however, destroys her neutrality entirely: a picture of a woman's vagina with a live rodent exiting from it shocks her into emotional involvement. "Rennie felt that a large gap had appeared in what she'd been used to thinking of as reality. What if this is normal, she thought, and we just haven't been told yet?" (p. 210). After viewing the pornography exhibit, she had been understandably reluctant to make love with Jake; she had dimly felt that "he thought of her as the enemy" (p. 211), when of course it is Jake who is the enemy. For the first time Rennie understands that she has been Jake's "raw material" (p. 212), a mannequin he has manipulated and debased according to his own impoverished values. Jake's very insistence upon the normalcy of his perverted view of Rennie and of women reinforces Atwood's point.

Such shocks form the backdrop for Rennie's reluctant growth from the "visored" perspective of journalistic (and personal) detachment to a political awareness that she must be involved, must take a position against the exploitation and degradation of women. Moreover, in implicitly pairing cancer (Rennie's) and pornography as twin forms of corruption — one in the body, the other in the body politic — Atwood emphasizes a striking cultural equivalence. As Sontag has pointed out, to many people the disease of cancer is felt to be "obscene — in the original meaning of that word: ill-omened, abominable, repugnant to the senses."[7] Bodily Harm thus juxtaposes two forms of physical outrage and violation to the boundaries of the body.

Images of abuse and violation of women are doubled in the island thread of Rennie's experiences. Lora Lucas recapitulates to Rennie her life of continuous victimization. Like Rennie, she suffers from low self-esteem and insecurity about her own rights. Lora is a more obvious victim of male use and abuse than Rennie, however. As a child she was virtually raped by her step-father; more recently, in her job as a cook on boats captained by men of the islands, it was understood that she would also be available for sexual pleasures. The evidence is all around Rennie: she hears of a woman prisoner "chop[ping] up another woman" (p. 131), which resonates with her own horror of someone "cutting some of her off" (p. 23), and her present sense of mutilation. She learns from Paul that, in the curious logic of the islands, "chopping up a woman" in a fit of anger is considered a lesser crime than stealing, for the former is a crime of passion while the latter is premeditated.

Naively and desperately, Rennie clings to her mask of detachment, believing that because she is a tourist and a journalist who is, additionally, harbouring a potentially terminal disease, she is somehow "exempt" (pp. 78, 81, 203 and passim). She tries several times to get "off the hook" of involvement or responsibility (pp. 185, 230). Ironically, it is one of the "faceless strangers" — that image which trails her throughout the novel — who helps her finds her way to human connection.

Paul, himself a "connection" in the political sense, is another disaffected man, in many ways the least likely person to aid in the restoration of Rennie's selfhood or womanhood. Yet on a symbolic level he functions as Rennie's alter ego or double. Recalling some of the more literal grotesques of *Lady Oracle* and *The Edible Woman*, both Paul and Rennie are "freaks": Paul is a "danger freak" who deliberately seeks situations of great personal risk (p. 239); Rennie thinks of herself as an "event freak," always waiting passively for something to happen to her. She adds, "Experiences were like other collectables, you kept adding them to your set" (p. 143). Paul is a true mercenary, as detached and neutral in his political and gun smuggling activities as Rennie is (initially) about sexual politics and island politics. Even at the end, it is unclear which side, if any, Paul has been working for. Rennie has frequently seen him (like the island policemen) wearing mirror glasses which reflect the observer rather than reveal the wearer. Symbolically, she has looked into the detached, objective face of Paul (or of the policemen) and seen the image of the "faceless stranger": not male but female — the alien dimension of her own being.

As if enthralled by that very alienness, Rennie goes with Paul to his impersonal shell of a house, where he leaves her while he pursues his own questionable political errands. While waiting for him to return, Rennie reads old Dell mystery books that amplify the novel's counterbalancing images. The descriptions of the female victims in the stories suggest rape; further, Rennie identifies with the victims, imagining the method of death as strangulation or "a wound still oozing, preferably in the left breast" (p. 246). As in her own earlier experience with the Toronto police, the private detectives in these stories "[express] outrage at the crime, even though the victim provoked it" (p. 246).

Before she and Paul make love, Rennie wonders whether she should warn Paul that a part of her is "missing." But Paul is "missing something" too (p. 214). Moreover, at the time, Rennie does not care what he thinks; she believes that "nothing can touch her. . . . She's exempt" (p. 203). She feels as detached from her physical self "as if she's died and gone to heaven and come back minus a body" (p. 203) — another of the several images of resurrection and body-mind division in the novel, but this time ambiguously evoking both death and renewal.

After their first lovemaking, Paul becomes once again remote, warning Rennie against involvement. Yet the very fact that he accepts the "missing place" naturally allows her to begin to accept herself and allow the severed parts of herself to come together again. In contrast to Jake, who wanted to force the "box" of Rennie's sexuality, Paul enables her to give herself willingly: "She's open now, she's been opened, she's being drawn back down, she enters her body again and there's a moment of . . . incarnation. . . . she can still be touched" (p. 204).

The word "incarnation" of course carries with it associations of resurrection and renewal of the flesh; Paul literally "[gives] her back her body" (p. 248). Thus, "massive involvement" is not the invasive cancer from which Rennie fears she will die, but the commitment to her life experiences that will save her. The restoration of touch that Paul provides Rennie — even in his detachment — resonates at every level of the novel, as the reader recalls the earlier imagery of hands in all of their possible literal and figurative functions and meanings. When Paul rescues Rennie and Lora by boat from the riots that ensue after the election on St. Agathe, they touch hands one last time before he vanishes forever from Rennie's life.

IV

The incipient and implied violence depicted thus far in the novel becomes explicit in the political machinations on the islands. In the public brutalizations that follow the election, two of the three contenders for office are assassinated by gunshot, including Prince, Lora's lover. Rennie realizes how important it is to understand victimization, to learn the difference between what Paul has observed as "people with power and people without power" (p. 240). In the confusion of Minnow's death, she begins to see the full import of power games and the consequences of neutrality practiced on a massive scale, as hers has been on a personal scale.

However, her first consideration is to flee from the chaotic place she has stumbled into as a "tourist." Thinking that she is safe when she reaches the airport of St. Antoine, Rennie finds instead that the terminal is shut down and no flights can leave the islands, which are in a state of civil insurrection. Soon afterwards she is taken into custody by the police, along with Lora Lucas, because of her presumed political activities (some people even think she is a CIA agent). The English hotel manager who has expressed her disapproval of Rennie's activities from the day she arrived in the islands (like a spectre of Rennie's conventional mother and grandmother) smiles at her "malignantly" (p. 262), as if to say "I told you so."

The final segment of the novel takes place in an atmosphere of pure paranoia, an intensification of the "alien reaction paranoia" (p. 76) experienced in an unfamiliar place when one does not know what the actual dangers are. When Rennie finds herself in jail, she is still "strangely uninvolved in her own fate" (p. 258); her attitude towards her cancer affects and infects her relation to the world. Marsdon, the power-mad islander who plays all sides to gain his own questionable ends, had looked at Rennie earlier and seen "fragmentation, dismemberment" (p. 258).

With Lora Lucas in such close proximity in a single jail cell, Rennie decides that she does not even like the woman. Believing that they have nothing in common but their physical circumstances, she fails to see that Lora resembles her profoundly in emotional circumstances. Instead, she retreats to memories of loving and being loved as escape from her sense of helplessness and from the actual squalor of her immediate environment. Many of her recollections focus on hands, bodies, and endings. In particular she remembers a girlhood moment in the autumn with her grandmother and mother, when her hands had been numb with cold. She recalls feeling something "missing" from them (p. 274). Her last time with Paul had evoked a similar sense of absence: "Acts of the body, acts of love, what's left? A change, a result, a trace, hand through the sea at night, phosphorescence. . . . Possibly she is the last person [Paul] touched. Possibly he is the last person who will ever touch her. The last man" (p. 283). She remembers Daniel in surgery, his hands "poised for incision" (p. 283), his image "a talisman [of normalcy] she fingers, over and over, to keep herself sane" (p. 284).

Momentarily she puts her life in context: in this chaotic place, others are dying more rapidly by accident or violence than she is with a known fatal disease. Lora disappears with one of the guards, and her long absence worries Rennie; she tries not to imagine the things that can be done to either of them. When her cell-mate returns with chewing gum, Rennie is disgusted that Lora sells her body so cheaply. Sexually abused since childhood, Lora regards her body as an object — but so does Rennie, in her own detached way. Only later does Rennie appreciate that Lora has used the only lure she has that can help both of them: an appeal to the male animal's base appetites.

In the cell, Rennie feels the deprivations of the flesh as an intensification of the cell disease already within her. In such a condition of acute powerlessness, the boundaries of selfhood are threatened to the extreme: "She's been invaded, usurped, germs taking over, betrayal of the body" (p. 286). She dreams of food and water, imagines her head "swelling up, she's going to burst open, she's going to die . . ." (p. 286). Envisioning even greater violations and mutilations of her mind and body, she is grateful that "no one has done anything to her yet" (p. 287).

When Rennie dares to look out the sole barred window of their cell, with Lora's hand-hold to support her, she watches in horror the abusive and sadistic torture of prisoners by policemen and guards. The horror is the pleasure that the administrators of the abuse derive from it. A policeman in her direct line of sight is "not doing this [torturing the prisoners] just because he's been ordered to: he's doing it because he enjoys it. *Malignant*" (p. 289, emphasis in original). Thus is the violence of pornography linked with the pornography of violence; both are society's cancerous growths.

What Rennie witnesses also shocks her into a realization that power does corrupt in exactly this way. It is the greater ability of males, Atwood implies, to detach themselves from feeling in order to assume power positions, where they may be tempted to objectify or perpetrate violence upon others. As Rennie later admits, "She's afraid of men and it's simple, it's rational, she's afraid of men because men are frightening. She's seen the man with the rope, now she knows what he looks like. She has been turned inside out, there's no longer a *here* and a *there*. . . . She is not exempt. Nobody is exempt from anything" (p. 290, emphasis in original).

In absolute terror and anxiety, Rennie confronts the "faceless stranger," the rope man who, in her mind, has trailed her all the way from Canada—the man whom she cannot escape. But he is not Jake, not Daniel, not Paul, "not anyone she's ever seen before. . . . [She] can't see him, this is what is so terrifying, he isn't really there, he's only a shadow, anonymous, familiar, with silver eyes that twin and reflect her own" (p. 287). Indeed, he *is* her dark shadow, her double, her denied self—and the form of her deepest recognition of submission to male power. The faceless stranger is both the anonymous lust for power and domination and the dark side of every person. While that urge to power is more easily identified and located in men—it is in them that power resides in patriarchy—Rennie discovers that she is not simply their victim; she, too, has taken part in events for which she was not prepared to accept responsibility, acts which "she doesn't want to see" that have caused others harm (p. 293). Wearing the "visor" or mask of a journalist does not permit her to withhold judgment; failure to act is a form of action. When she looks into the face of evil she sees that everyone is a complicitor; there is no escape. Like Kafka's Joseph K, she is condemned by the fact of being alive, guilty of being human, despite her protestations of innocence.

V

Before Rennie achieves "massive involvement," Atwood diverts the narrative direction (and tension) with one of the novel's two flash-forwards. Two sections, narrated in the future tense, describe what "will happen" to assure Rennie's release from prison and from the country. The conference between Rennie and the representative of the Canadian government recapitulates some of the same power manipulations drama-tized earlier in the novel. Mirroring Rennie's own earlier position of moral neutrality, the Canadian official argues that their country does not "interfere in internal matters" (p. 295) or "make value judgments" (p. 296). Rennie signs a false release that will facilitate her exit, a note indicating to the Canadian official that she will not write about what she has seen. For her, it is one final—but this time, chosen—act of capitulation made in the name of her newly-won inner freedom and knowledge. Yet, in agreeing to such censorship, she sees for the first time the terrible consequences of neutrality or objectivity practiced on a national scale. From her experience she has learned that to remain "objective" in the face of what she has witnessed and participated in is a crime of collaboration. In the presence of injustice, one must take a stand.

The final pages of *Bodily Harm* reiterate this knowledge on the personal, private level, as Atwood once more intertwines the threads of Rennie's memories of childhood with her immediate situation and the reader's knowledge that Rennie will escape. Lora has by then been gun-whipped and beaten (for lashing out at the guard who had deliberately misled her with the lie that her lover, Prince, was still alive). Rennie, wondering what to do with Lora's bruised body, recalls the final piece in the fragmentary recollection of her grandmother whose hands were "missing." At the time, her mother, she now remembers, had shown her what to do to assuage her grandmother's anguish: she "[took] hold of her grandmother's dangling hands, clasping them in her own" (p. 298).

The power of the "mothers" prevails. Recovering this crucial memory of human touch and connection, Rennie is at last aware of what has been "missing" in herself; only now can she reach beyond her sense of detachment to "connection" with another human being. Gently, she takes one of Lora's cold but unlacerated hands and administers comfort to her battered face and body, slowly bringing her back to consciousness. At first Rennie is repelled by the sight of the battered flesh; "it's no one she recognizes, she has no connection with this, there's nothing she can do, it's the face of a stranger . . ." (p. 298). But finally the bond of human contact alters both of them, as Rennie moves beyond her self-alienation to admit that "there's no such thing as a faceless stranger, every face is someone's, it has a name" (p. 299).

In this recognition, the sinister symbolism of the faceless stranger shifts to a positive acknowledgement of mutuality. Lora is Rennie's own darker double, the other face of her own being, the woman whose exposure to violent sexual abuse from childhood makes her the symbolic female scapegoat for patriarchal exploitation. Rennie, having too readily defined herself as a victim, saves Lora in order to save herself, to oppose the world that has made the battered woman who and what she is. Her "gift" to Lora is another instance of the laying on of hands that connects people in the novel: echoing her mother's crucial act of connection with her grandmother, Rennie literally pulls the body of Lora through "an invisible hole in the air" (p. 299) back to consciousness, at the same time pulling her own denied self into awareness.

At last she knows that the ability to identify oneself with another woman, to connect to another person in empathetic touch, is the only real antidote to what she has seen and experienced: the deadening objectification that allows one person to see others as mere bodies to which violence may be done. Lack of meaningful, respectful touching is the corollary of the diverse acts of animalistic and opportunistic violence depicted throughout the novel — from Jake's lustful and exploitative possession of Rennie's body to Marsdon's murderous monomania, from pornography to the anonymous torture of political prisoners.

Like the characters in Albert Camus' *The Plague*, who discover that no one can remain exempt from evil, Rennie learns that the battle against the forces of death and dehumanization is not hers alone, but one in which everyone, regardless of gender, must participate. In Rennie's case, cancer is a disease not only of the breast but of the chest — the heart; and not only of her body but of the social body. Ironically, the ability to oppose it is the life-saving "massive involvement" which can restore both. If, like Pandora, Rennie has innocently contributed to the proliferation of violence through her own actions, she must use her new awareness to prevent such complicity in the future. This is the "hope" that remains in Pandora's box.

Only with this awful knowledge about personal responsibility, female alliance, and the terrible consequences of their abdication can Rennie Wilford be truly redeemed and whole. On the airplane trip back to Canada after her release from custody, she determines her new role as a "subversive" (p. 301), one who opposes patriarchy's concentration of power and domination in men. She is "flying" in more than the literal sense: even with death waiting in the wings, so to speak, she has reason for joy. As she reflects:

> Zero is waiting somewhere, whoever said there was life everlasting; so why feel grateful? She doesn't have much time left, for anything. But neither does anyone else. She's paying attention, that's all.
>
> She will never be rescued. She has already been rescued. She is not exempt. Instead she is lucky, suddenly, finally, she's overflowing with luck, it's this luck holding her up.
>
> (p. 301)

The future is literally in her hands.

Notes

1. Margaret Atwood, *Bodily Harm* (Toronto: McClelland and Stewart, 1981), p. 11. All subsequent quotations are indicated by parenthetical page numbers in the text.

2. Two other novels of which I am aware concern a woman who has undergone a mastectomy: Penelope Mortimer's *My Friend Says it's Bullet-Proof* (New York: Random House, 1968) and Joan Winthrop's *Underwater* (New York: G.P. Putnam's, 1974). Like Atwood, Winthrop uses her female protagonist's disfigurement symbolically, but in this case to suggest Kate Stevens' bisexuality. Unhappily married to dull Harry and the mother of a baby daughter, Kate finds her true sexuality in her first lesbian relationship. The flat side of her chest is, symbolically, her "male" side, an alter ego named Valery St. John, who "drove a yellow convertible, kept gin in the dashboard, and climbed up the gutters of the snug dormitories and into the beds of exciting women" (p. 14).

Mortimer's character resembles Rennie Wilford more directly, and may even have influenced Atwood. Also a journalist, Muriel Rowbridge leaves her lover (because of her own self-disgust) and travels to the United States on a journalistic assignment. Through relationships she enters during the course of her travels, she gains a more positive perspective on herself and her condition.

3. Susan Sontag, *Illness as Metaphor* (New York: Farrar, Straus and Giroux, 1977), p. 20.

4. Sontag, pp. 72–73.

5. Sontag, p. 15.

6. Sontag, p. 67.

7. Sontag, p. 9.

Journey to Light [*Interlunar*]   Anne Blott*

With her ten books of poetry, in addition to prose fiction and criticism, we have come to expect control and deftness from Margaret Atwood. What is particularly striking in this collection is the arrangement of the poems into a pattern of thought and of discovery. The main body of the poems is in three groups of "Interlunar" poems, beginning with "Doorway" and ending with the title poem. These lead the reader through a process of encounter, descent, and re-emergence, a movement keyed in part by Atwood's reshaping of the myths of Orpheus, Euridice and Persephone. Introducing these groups are eleven "Snake Poems," which anticipate many of her themes, cast in a sardonic naturalist's tour of the snake: myths, truths, and lies. *Interlunar* displays fully the range of Atwood's skills with the language, her wit and control of the tone especially. In "Singing to Genghis Khan," for instance, the tone modulates from the opening lyric suggestion of Scheherezade through the bite of the unexpected into a conversational kicker — the final note of menace:

> In the plum-coloured tent in the evening
> a young woman is playing a lute,
> an anachronism,
> and singing to Genghis Khan.
>
> It is her job. It is her intention
> to make him feel better.
> Then maybe she can get some sleep
> and will not be murdered.

Again, the sound patterns of the poems and their precise diction are remarkable, as in this series of images defining the snake in "Bad Mouth":

> Each one is a hunter's hunter,
> nothing more than an endless gullet

*From *Fiddlehead*, no. 146 (Winter 1985):90–95. Reprinted by permission of the author.

> pulling itself over the still-alive prey
> like a sock gone ravenous, like an evil glove,
> like sheer greed, lithe and devious.

On the cover of *Interlunar*, forms are reflected like land masses in water. In the water also is a sun, but its real body does not appear in the sky above. This cover art is Atwood's own, and as the collection reveals itself, the visual imagery evokes with increasing power a sense of the permanence both of states of being and of potentiality. The book explores many phases of growth and movement working through to recognition that nothing is ever lost, for all things are part of a continuum. Atwood situates herself along this continuum, at once child and parent, with the contrary pulls of isolation and desire inscribing an arc on the larger-scale cycle of life, death, and rebirth. "It is touch I go by," she states in one of the last poems,

> the boat like a hand feeling
> through shoals and among
> dead trees, over the boulders
> lifting unseen, layer
> on layer of drowned time falling away.
> ("A Boat")

The concept of the cycle is dominant in the collection, a symbol of wholeness that contains and shapes the stresses and fractures of all the separate phases. In the same poem, the cover image is developed, as "the water stills itself, / a sunset shivering in it. / One more going down to join the other." The term "interlunar" itself means the period between the old and the new moon, a period of waiting that bridges the sinister and demonic waning moon and the regenerative and creative waxing moon. Thus the moon is both constant and changing, as in the Buddhist truth, "One moon appears reflected in all waters / Wherein all moons from the one moon derive." (Yang Chia's *Song of Enlightenment*).

Heraclitus stated that all things are one and are in flux: we can and cannot step in the same river twice. In her "Snake Poems," Atwood invokes both renewal through transmutation and the acceptance of unacknowledged contraries:

> Unfurling itself from its cast skin,
> the snake proclaims resurrection
> to all believers
>
> though some tire soon of being born
> over and over. . . .
> ("Metempsychosis")
>
> But pick it up and you would hold
> the darkness that you fear

> turned flesh and embers,
> cool power coiling into your wrists
> and it would be in your hands
> where it has always been.
> ("After Heraclitus")

This key concept of power links all the poems. Variously, it means control, destruction, and creation, all manifested in isolated statements. But "Doorway," which opens up the three sets of "Interlunar" poems, gives it its most resonant meaning, that of inherent potential. In November, "month of entrances," Atwood feels only the power of waiting as life outside retreats to the roots:

> Power of the grey stone
> resting inert, not shaping itself.
> Power of the murdered girl's
> bone in the stream, not yet a flute.
> Power of a door unopened.

Immediately following, "Before" reinforces this awareness that one form matter takes is the transformation from another and the anticipation of yet a third. Atwood's probing of isolated elements from a whole pattern can be read in the related motifs of fragmentation and singleness: "One Species of Love," "It's only one version," and "This is only one kind." In several poems the motif of a journey through several phases further defines the theme of unity through change.

But such unity comes only through struggle against outside forces and inner ignorance. Atwood's poems evoke states of physical and psychological menace, a *frisson* of the skull beneath the skin which sharpens the reader's wits, blocking a too-facile entry into the world of the poetry. Some poem titles work counter to their content: "The Healer" cannot heal, and "Harvest" looses rape and ritual slaughter on a female scapegoat. Awareness of death is telescoped backwards in time through a sequence of poems. In "A Holiday," the poet describes her own daughter's "playing at barbarism," unaware of the possibility of future starvation — nuclear winter, say — when all experience and language itself may be reduced to mere survival. But in the present, mother and daughter foraging in the woods are at play:

> So far we do it
> for fun. So far is
> where we've gone
> and no farther.

In her second poem, "Lunchtime During a Peak Year in the Yellowjacket Cycle," Atwood herself is the daughter, camping out with her mother. "Her nomadic children ignore her. / Every year she is shorter / and we are more oblivious." Wasps try to feed off the child Margaret Atwood while she squats by the stewpot eating meat:

This is the summer I am going to devour
everything I can dig up or strangle,

. . . .

. . . ferocious
with hunger for every untried
food, dazed by the sunlight
and abundance, knowing nothing about death.

This pair of poems is preceded by "Bedside," in which the poet's father is dying, hands emptying of power while Atwood holds his feet, as she had done as a child. Only now he is walking with no shadow, where she cannot follow.

In addition to these poems of mortality and child-parent relations, a group of poems focusses on the gaps, contact, and dead ground between male and female. Here again, the postures are varied and none is definitive. Some of Atwood's male personae are threatening, like the Robber Bridegroom: "Why do the women fail him and die badly?" In the first Orpheus poem, his "flesh voice" seeks to dominate, while other men are uncomprehending, fixed in another mode of perception, as in "Precognition": "You did not consider me a soul / but a landscape, not even one / I recognize as mine." The men in "The Words Continue Their Journey" are icons, "with their moustaches / and passwords and bravado," clichés of *machismo*. Some of Atwood's female voices rail against the roles they play: the batterings of sex, the invalid mothers, the failure of healing, "boredom / and the enraged sheen of your floors." The powerful persona of "Snake Woman," the first poem in the book, has backed off into the wings, with only the cool and controlled tone of the poet herself as its echo. In "Three Denizen Songs," Atwood's female persona shifts from "the energy of an open socket," fearsomely all knowing, through the male perspective of female as "curved space," velvet, milky, pendulous, a lush moon, a meat egg, and finally to a frightened alien in a pink print dress, cornered and probed by scientists.

After some knowledge, what response? Given these roles and stereotypes, Atwood's first "Interlunar" poems spiral down through bleak interactions between men and women. In "Valediction, Intergalactic," the tone is self-mocking: all men are less perfect than my expectation, so I am abnormal — a creature from distant space. "Goodbye / earthling, you were more perfect / than anyone, though far from it." In "Hidden," the woman is resigned and despairing. "I doubt that I ever loved you. / I believe I have chosen peace." She weeds in a June garden, closing herself up instead of opening out:

and I'm too close to the ground, to those
who have faded and merged, too close
to contagion . . . .

. . . .

> Think of this as the dormant phase
> of a disease.

The final poem of this first group, with the treacherously-soothing title "A Sunday Drive," presents the waste and rot of humanity in the streets of Bombay and ends with another valediction: *The desire to be loved is the last illusion: / Give it up and you will be free.*" Yet this does not yet stand as the final phase, and "Interlunar II," containing the Euridice poems, presents the nightmare vision of the poet's complete absence of response. Again it is spring, in a recurring dream that a dying man has come to be comforted, to be touched. But no response is possible in this surreal atmosphere of isolation, "No Name." Focussed unblinkingly on the poet's subconscious, unredeemed by humour or the ironic treatment of a parodic male, this poem is the nadir of the relations between the sexes in Atwood's book. The dreamer finds no point of contact and cannot even wake up from the dream.

From this dark night, the final group, "Interlunar III," presents a succession of poems to return to the light. The tone is increasingly sure, the tensions held in balance. There is nothing to fear: not death, not life, neither permanence nor impermanence; and the distance between the lovers has become a space rather than a void. "What can I offer you," Atwood asks in "The White Cup,"

> This is the one thing I wanted to give you,
> this quiet shining
> which is a constant entering,
> a going into

In this open-ended poem, Atwood has brought the reader through to affirmation, and in the final poem of the book, the title-poem "Interlunar," she completes the process of working through change to a state of peace:

> Trust me. This darkness
> is a place you can enter and be
> as safe in as you are anywhere;
> . . . .
> . . . the darkness
> that you can walk so long in
> it becomes light.

"Reading a Political Thriller Beside a Remote Lake in the Canadian Shield," Atwood contrasted the ancient rock at her back, the forest, the sunset and the moon with the cardboard emotions of characters still locked at each other's throats in attitudes of spurious passion. Few readers could close *Interlunar* without feeling Margaret Atwood's crystalline intelligence still resonating in their minds.

Control and Creativity: The Politics of Risk in Margaret Atwood's *The Handmaid's Tale*

Lucy M. Freibert*

At the end of *Lady Oracle* (1976) Margaret Atwood's author/narrator declares, "I won't write any more Costume Gothics. . . . But maybe I'll try some science fiction."[1] In *The Handmaid's Tale* (1985) Atwood makes good that promise in what one might call "political-science fiction" but what she calls "speculative fiction."[2] This boldly political and darkly comic novel illustrates Atwood's grasp of the cultural, historical, philosophical, and literary facets of Western tradition, and the role of woman within that frame. Atwood demonstrates the absurdity of Western patriarchal teleology that views woman's biology as destiny and exposes the complicity of women in perpetuating that view. She also ridicules the mental gymnastics of academics, specifically those bent on establishing "the text." Instead of a modest proposal, her Swiftean serio-comic vision comprises an ironic indictment of a society that treats woman's body as a pawn and her life as an academic question. Ultimately, Atwood, with a bow to *écriture féminine*, suggests that even in such a context an imaginative woman willing to improvise and take risks can beat the system and savor a measure of joy in the process.

Although more overtly political than her previous work, *The Handmaid's Tale* is no departure from Atwood's system. As Sherrill E. Grace has pointed out, Atwood's vision has not essentially changed, but has expanded and deepened.[3] The political component in her poetry and prose, respectively, from *The Circle Game* (1966) and *The Edible Woman* (1969) onward, intensified in their counterparts, *Power Politics* (1971) and *Bodily Harm* (1982). In *The Handmaid's Tale* the context is essentially political, and, as the protagonist remarks, "Context is all."[4]

In a 1985 interview, several months before *The Handmaid's Tale* appeared, Atwood addressed the matter directly: "the political to me is a part of life. It's part of everybody's life."[5] "What we mean [by political]," she continued, "is how people relate to a power structure and vice versa. And this is really all we mean by it. We may mean also some idea of participating in the structure or changing it. But the first thing we mean is how is this individual in society? How do the forces of society interact with this person?"[6] The protagonist Offred in *The Handmaid's Tale*, struggling against oppressive structures, embodies Atwood's definition. Moreover, Offred promises to come off a winner: "I intend to last," she says (17).

Set within this political context, Atwood's novel, as the following analysis demonstrates, deconstructs Western phallocentrism and explores

---

*This essay was written especially for this volume and is published here for the first time by permission of the author.

those aspects of French feminist theory that offer women a measure of hope.

I

Atwood's design alerts the reader to the novel's satiric mode. The title, along with the biblical, Swiftean, and Sufi epigraphs and the final "Historical Notes" that frame the tale, focuses attention on form and tone.

The Chaucerian ring of the title sets up expectations of a medieval setting with lords and ladies, retainers and handmaids, a recounting of the battle of the sexes from top to bottom of a hierarchal range, a latter-day Canterbury saga. The title dictates an intimate first-person narrative yet evokes a sophisticated courtly detachment. Atwood does not disappoint these expectations but essays a bizarre satire that even Chaucer would not have dared.

The dual effect of the double-entendre in the pun on the word *tale*, as literary creation and anatomic part, combines humor and denigration that Atwood maintains throughout the work. Thus the pun sets up the basic conflict between the protagonist and the society that regards her as a sexual object. The resulting irony works simultaneously on multiple levels. The structural looseness allowed by the tale's literary conventions permits the narrator innumerable digressions, spanning her entire life.

Atwood projects the tale into the end of the twentieth century, when the United States has suffered a right-wing takeover that has produced the Republic of Gilead, a monolithic theocracy more oppressive even than Puritan rule.[7] The central aim in Gilead is to increase population in a society where nuclear radiation, chemical pollution, abortion, and other sexual and surgical processes have made sterility the norm. This condition in the Republic of Gilead ironically approximates what Jeremiah prophesied for its biblical namesake. When the Israelites had worn His patience to the limit, God called forth Jeremiah and through his mouth foretold the desolation of the Promised Land. Aghast that Gilead, the most fertile area, might be included, Jeremiah cried out, "Is there no balm in Gilead; is there no physician there? why then is not the health of the daughter of my people recovered?"[8] Silence suggests Gilead's fate.

Atwood's Gileadians design a system that recognizes divine power but relies heavily on human control. The system brooks no resistance or dissent. A military hierarchy—Commanders, Eyes, Angels, and Guardians—maintains surveillance through the use of electronic devices, a network of checkpoints, and an ubiquitous fleet of multipurpose vans, agents of both life and death. Menials not engaged in this chain of command serve as chauffeurs (often also Eyes), shopkeepers, and service personnel. Ironically, in the process of fostering new life and claiming to protect women, the officers carry out abductions, hangings, and batterings that turn the society into a fascist state hazardous to life, particularly for women.

The rigid political system blights both private and public sectors. Women find themselves relegated to one of eight categories. The blue-clad Wives of the Commanders preside over their homes and gardens, and attend public functions such as the Prayvaganzas, Salvagings, and birthings. Sexual duties fall to the red-clad Handmaids, drilled in self-denial and renunciation and reduced to fertility machines. The green-clad Marthas clean and cook. The Econowives, married to upper-level menials, combine the functions of the other groups and consequently wear striped blue/red/green dresses. At the Rachel and Leah Center, the Aunts use electric cattle prods to keep the Handmaids in line. The black-clad Widows, a rapidly diminishing group, live in limbo. The gray-clad Unwomen, those who refuse to cooperate with the system, work in the Colonies, cleaning up city ghettoes, toxic dumps, and radiation spills, and watch their bodies disintegrate before their eyes. Finally, the unlabeled women hidden from public view inhabit a Bunny Club where a few hours each day they serve the pleasure of the Commanders and visiting businessmen, and the rest of the time their own.

To identify the source of this dystopia's[9] obsession with progeny and sex, Atwood draws her first epigraph from the story of the biblical Rachel. This choice establishes the idea that long ago religio-political pressure to procreate set society on a collision course with personal autonomy, and will continue that oppression into the future. The epigraph on page 7 tells its own story:

> And when Rachel saw that she bare Jacob no children, Rachel envied her sister; and said unto Jacob, Give me children, or else I die.
> And Jacob's anger was kindled against Rachel; and he said, Am I in God's stead, who hath withheld from thee the fruit of the womb?
> And she said, Behold my maid Bilhah, go in unto her; and she shall bear upon my knees, that I may also have children by her.
> — Genesis 30:1–3

This is not, of course, the only biblical instance of sexual substitution. Sarah gave her handmaid Hagar to Abraham and Rachel's sister Leah gave her handmaid Zelpha to Jacob.[10] The custom of using the handmaid for progeny permeated Israelite history and custom. Legal documents dating from the fifteenth century B.C. supplement biblical records of the practice and cite the protective measures for both handmaid and offspring.[11] Against this background Atwood's handmaid appears as the heir and counterpart of millions who have preceded her.

The Republic of Gilead, with headquarters in Cambridge, Massachusetts, has institutionalized the Handmaid's function. The young women given to the Commanders and their wives assume their owners' names, thus Of-fred, Of-glen, Of-warren.[12] The treatment of the individual Handmaid by both husband and wife reinforces the concept of person as property: the Commander uses Offred for his private as well as public service, ordering her to visit him in his study whenever his wife is away, and the wife Serena Joy secretly "gives" Offred to the chauffeur Nick when the Commander seems unable to get her pregnant.

The biblical epigraph not only suggests the violation of individual autonomy—the central focus of *The Handmaid's Tale*—it also foreshadows the female envy and male/female enmity that form the inner tension of the novel. In Atwood's tale envy is pervasive: "In this house we all envy each other something," says Rita, one of the Marthas (57). The same may be said of the whole society. Serena Joy and the other Wives vie with one another for the fertile Handmaids and envy their fortunate rivals as Rachel envied Leah. The Handmaids suffer from the resentment of the Wives, the Econowives, and the Marthas. "How she must hate me" (101), Offred says of Serena Joy, "I am a reproach to her; and a necessity" (23). "The Econowives do not like us," Offred reports, "Beneath her veil the first one scowls at us. One of the others turns aside, spits on the sidewalk" (54). The Marthas think the Handmaids' task is "not that bad. It's not what you'd call hard work" (20). The enmity between the Commander and Serena Joy parallels Jacob's anger at Sarah. Observing the Commander's obvious affront to Serena Joy, Offred remarks, "Who knows what she said to him, over the silver-encrusted dinner table? Or didn't say" (97). Serena Joy's anguish lies in her inability to adapt to the wifely role she had so ardently advocated as a national TV personality (55–56). Phyllis Schlafly comes to mind.

The most humorous correspondence between the biblical account and Atwood's tale stems from the passage in which Rachel expresses the hope that Bilhah will "bear upon my knees." In Gilead protocol for the periodic impregnation of the Handmaid requires that the Wife arrange herself at the head of her bed with legs outspread, the Handmaid lying between them with her head on the Wife's stomach. Thus positioned the two form one body as Offred receives the Commander (104). A comparable scene occurs at the birth of a Handmaid's child, when the Wife reclines at the head of the bed on which the Handmaid lies in labor, and during delivery sits on the upper portion of a double-decker birthing stool. In both crucial moments, the Handmaid is between the Wife's knees. The control exerted through both rituals provokes rollicking laughter, yet stifles fulfillment. As Offred comments about the impregnation ceremony, "There's something hilarious about this, but I don't dare laugh" (106). Neither does the reader, aware of the comic yet demeaning implications of the arrangement, paralleled in current legalistic maneuvers of medical and judicial "experts" to control women's bodies.

The religious trappings that pervade the political structure foster the idea that the primary purpose of the system is to protect women, while the actual purpose is to control them and reinforce the notion that their biology is their destiny. At lunchtime in the Rachel and Leah Center, the Handmaids listen to the Beatitudes: "Blessed be this, blessed be that. They played it from a disc, the voice was a man's" (99). The formulaic speech patterns imposed on the Handmaids, "Blessed be the fruit," "May the Lord open," "Praise be" (29), "Under His Eye" (54), "Let that be a reminder to us" (295), serve to perpetuate the religious nature of their role and to prevent practical conversation. The prayer sessions that precede each impregnation form high burlesque. The household assembles: Serena Joy sits in her chair with a footstool for her feet. Offred kneels beside her and the Marthas and the chauffeur Nick stand behind them. The Commander enters, unlocks the box containing the Bible, reads "the usual stories. God to Adam, God to Noah. *Be fruitful, and multiply, and replenish the earth"* (99).[13] Although the scene is potentially explosive, no one dares to snicker, for the Angels wait to take the blaspemer to the gibbet.

The second epigraph, taken from Jonathan Swift's *A Modest Proposal*, predicts the political depth Atwood plumbs. In seeking to relieve Irish poverty, Swift suggested facetiously that select young children be fattened and eaten, thereby providing succulent fare for those who could afford it, relieving parents of the need to provide for them, and alleviating the unemployment problem resulting from overpopulation.

Atwood, writing about a time of underpopulation, does not offer a satiric political proposal but rather pushes late twentieth-century ideological conflicts to what she considers their logical conclusions. "There's not a single detail in the book that does not have a corresponding reality, either in contemporary conditions or historical fact," she said in an interview.[14] Military buildup makes a coup d'etat possible. Government failure to prevent wholesale plunder of natural resources and to monitor chemical pollution produces an unsafe environment. Right-wing attempts to control sexuality clash with feminist and gay interests. Feminist campaigns against rape, child abuse, and pornography inadvertently give credence to right-wing calls for sexual control and book burnings. Atwood blames no one group, but indicts, by sheer exposure, those who espouse simplistic solutions that deny the rights and welfare of others.

The Swiftean exaggerations Atwood calls logical consequences reach a climax in the Prayvaganzas, Salvagings, and similar events: "Women's Prayvaganzas are for group weddings. . . . men's are for military victories. These are the things we are supposed to rejoice in the most, respectively" (232). The group weddings reward the warriors with virgin brides. Salvagings, public executions of either sex, produce the Wall hangings for what was once Harvard Yard. Included among the trophies are abortionists, priests, homosexuals, and recalcitrant Handmaids.

Although daily acquiescence implies consent to one's own and others' oppression, the festival fever of these public events intensifies the horror of women's complicity in their subjugation. At the hangings each Handmaid must touch the rope in assent to the murders. At Particicutions the

Handmaids ritually dismember any man accused of rape. The Aunts supply the rhetoric that arouses the women to savagery.

Not all the women succumb to the system gracefully. The Handmaid Moira, while yet a novice, escapes from the Rachel and Leah Center and when caught chooses posting at the brothel. Ofglen becomes a member of Mayday, an underground group that helps people escape to Canada. Her courageous attempt to assist a Guardian unjustly accused of rape (his real crime was being a member of Mayday) leads her to suicide lest she betray any of her friends. Janine, another Handmaid, retreats into the past to escape the present. The openly defiant, particularly former nuns, choose banishment to the Colonies as Unwomen. Although forced into complicity by fear during her three postings, Offred, once freed, threatens the system by telling her tale.

The third epigraph, the Sufi proverb "*In the desert there is no sign that says, Thou shalt not eat stones*" (7), epitomizes Atwood's view of social control. It implies that on the most basic level of survival human beings instinctively know what to do and what to avoid; it suggests the corollary that authorities should avoid unnecessary regulation. Sufi simplicity counterpoints the outrageous legalism of Gilead's political structure and pleads for human freedom and survival. The proverbial desert evokes the sterility and isolation in which Offred must compose her being. The title and epigraphs together tense the critical antennae for the tale.

II

In satirizing, and thereby demystifying, Western phallocentrism in this worst of all possible contexts, Atwood also tests the viability of French feminist theory. She does not, of course, set out methodically to incorporate French feminist principles, but eclectically draws on the most useful. She sets Offred, body and voice, against the body politic and through her condemns the patriarchal tradition. What is more important in terms of *écriture feminine*, Atwood demonstrates through Offred that women, able to take risks and to tell stories, may transcend their conditioning, establish their identity, joyfully reclaim their bodies, find their voices, and reconstruct the social order.[15]

Atwood portrays Offred as a bloody Mary—a contemplative, both virgin and magdalen, a "handmaid of the Lord" in New Testament terms. In her red dress, sandals, and veil with its white wimple ("wings") that hides her face, she looks like a nun. Like a nun she sleeps in a cell-like room that has no mirror, goes out only with a companion, and converses in formulaic phrases reminiscent of the antiphonal chant of the Divine Office. By conflating the traditional images of wife and handmaid, handmaid and virgin, virgin and harlot, Atwood asserts that whatever her station woman has been and still is sexual, bloody, the producer of children, the servant, "A Sister, dipped in blood" (19).

Atwood rotates Offred through three psychological states: fear, despair, and boldness. Fear frequently paralyzes Offred, keeping her obedient to the rules. She fears the Aunts, Angels, Eyes, other Handmaids, Marthas, Nick, Serena Joy, and the Commander—everyone who might report her conduct and put her in jeopardy. She lives in boredom and despair, continually searching for a means of suicide, aware that every effort has been made to prevent her ending her life through external means or through those "other escapes, the ones you can open in yourself, given a cutting edge" (18). The boldness that stimulates her creativity and risk-taking comes slowly. On an early adventure she reports: "I like this. I am doing something, on my own. The active tense. Tensed. What I would like to steal is a knife, from the kitchen, but I'm not ready for that" (108).

While Offred's fear, despair, and boldness evoke the reader's empathy, it is Atwood's attention to voice that creates the illusion of reality and elicits pity and fear for Offred despite the high burlesque of the tale. Offred is, indeed, a voice crying in the desert. Atwood gives her the same low-keyed voice that B. W. Powe derides as "virtually interchangeable" in all the previous novels.[16] But that voice, approximating the limited scope of Offred's life symbolized by the blinkers on her veil, is precisely what makes *The Handmaid's Tale* credible. At times tentative, at others defiant, it persists to the end, giving force and direction to the tale.

Offred literally *tells* her story, recording it on tape instead of writing it down:

> I would like to believe this is a story I'm telling. I need to believe it. I must believe it. Those who can believe that such stories are only stories have a better chance.
>   If it's a story I'm telling, then I have control over the ending. . . .
>   It isn't a story I'm telling.
>   It's also a story I'm telling, in my head, as I go along.
>
> (49)

The method, ancient in form but contemporary in technique, replicates the tenuousness of woman's condition. Having experienced an uncomfortable relationship with an activist mother, survived two marriages of questionable compatibility, and suffered the loss of her mother, husband, and daughter, Offred finds herself in a void: "I'll pretend you can hear me. But it's no good, because I know you can't" (50). Atwood creates this sense of isolation in order to emphasize that Offred's invention of her risk-filled story becomes the source of her freedom.

The only support Offred receives from other women comes from furtive nighttime sharings in the dormitory at the Center, brief exchanges with Ofglen while shopping, conversations with Moira at the Center and at the brothel, and one brief moment of verbal rapport with Serena Joy. Moira, a role model of resistance, brings Offred word about her mother. Serena Joy, an unlikely ally, procures Offred a momentary look at a picture of her lost daughter. Ofglen, shopping companion, friend, and member of Mayday, serves Offred in one sense as an ideal but also as a warning that sacrificing for others diminishes one's own life. For the most part, Offred learns that she must make decisions from moment to moment on her own, thereby building her interior strength and eventually generating her story.

At the outset Atwood draws on centuries-old conditioning that convinces woman that her body is her only means of survival. Offred muses over the possibility of negotiating an escape from the Rachel and Leah Center: "The Angels stood outside it with their backs to us. They were objects of fear to us, but of something else as well. If only they would look. If only we could talk to them. Something could be exchanged, we thought, some deal made, some trade-off, we still had our bodies. That was our fantasy" (14). The idea that she might use her body for negotiation is pure bravado, however, for later, when she learns about the Commanders' hotel, she makes no effort to change her posting. Nevertheless, through responding to her body, she comes to realize her power with words and develops her voice.

Offred takes her first risks to satisfy bodily urgings. Once when a guard bends down to see her face, she raises her head: "I raise my head a little, to help him, and he sees my eyes and I see his, and he blushes. . . . He is the one who turns away" (31). Another time when passing a guard, she moves her hips as she walks away — "It's like thumbing your nose from behind a fence or teasing a dog with a bone held out of reach. . . . I find I'm not ashamed after all. I enjoy the power; power of a dog bone, passive but there" (32).

As she tells her tale, Offred realizes that an embodied imagination, not body alone, offers the real potential for freedom. She speaks of creating her stories as she creates herself: "I wait. I compose myself. My self is a thing I must now compose, as one composes a speech. What I must present is a made thing, not something born" (76). This self-generation frees her from the limitation of biological determinism.

Offred gets the chance to develop both aspects of her being through her association with the Commander — the head — and Nick — the heart. *conclusion* From the first, being with the Commander is a kind of intellectual game that activates Offred's imagination. It holds just enough risk and fear to keep her adrenalin flowing. When she begins her visits to his study, where he wants her to play Scrabble with him, allows her to read books and magazines, and shares with her the schoolboy's joke *"Nolite te bastardes corborundorum,"* she begins to see the value of her own way with words. When the Commander gives her a pen with which to write the quotation, she exults: "The pen between my fingers is sensuous, alive almost, I can feel its power, the power of the words it contains" (196). Later discussions with him lead her to analyze old concepts such as romance and love, the relation of love to sexual abuse (237–38). Atwood even allows Offred to revel in her power over the Commander. Offred manipulates him to get the hand lotion, the magazines, etc. She boasts of that power and admits enjoying it and trading on it, all the time realizing the emptiness of her gains. Even when the Commander asks her to kiss him as if she means it and when he takes her in his Whirlwind[17] to the hotel for the night out, including sex, her mind is racing. Like the French feminist Luce Irigaray's "she," Offred "goes off in all directions."[18] No risk is too great for her, even though she is shaking with fear. In the womb Offred developed an affinity with risk—her mother risked everything by conceiving her at thirty-seven (130).

Delight in manipulating language and sensing its power leads Offred to expand her self and perfect her tale. Failing to recognize this achievement, Mary McCarthy faults Atwood for not inventing "a language to match the changed face of common life."[19] Although Offred uses the oppressor's language, she uses it to her advantage and fits it to her needs. She learns to adapt stories to her physical condition. When tired, she chooses one about someone else: "I'm too tired to go on with this story. I'm too tired to think about where I am. Here is a different story, a better one. This is the story of what happened to Moira" (138). Offred learns to reconstruct stories and to plan for the future; she examines the creative process. For her, as for Scheherazade, the tale becomes a means of survival:

> This is a reconstruction. All of it is a reconstruction. It's a reconstruction now, in my head, as I lie flat on my single bed rehearsing what I should or shouldn't have said, what I should or shouldn't have done, how I should have played it. If I ever get out of here—
> Let's stop there. I intend to get out of here. It can't last forever.
>
> (144)

Offred's real breakthrough to her courageous sexual self comes not with the Commander, who soon bores her, but with Nick. When she first encounters Nick and he winks, she does not dare respond. However, when they meet in the sitting room where she has gone to steal a flower to press, she reacts readily to his embrace and kiss: "I want to reach up, taste his skin, he makes me hungry" (109). Her joyous reaction to her desire embodies precisely the French *jouissance*. As their relationship develops, with Serena Joy's blessing, it matters little whether Nick is the Tempter in the Garden or the Delivering Angel who arrives in the nick of time, for he serves to release Offred to sexual abandon and freedom to record her tale. Through her friendship with Nick she even discovers satisfaction with her life. Thus, when she might have changed this her third (and last) posting by choosing to move to the brothel, she risks staying where she can continue her affair with Nick: "I said, I have made a life for myself, here, of a sort. That must have been what the settlers' wives thought, and women who survived wars, if they still had a man" (283). The risk-filled spirit of adventure permeates Offred's actions and choices, turning her into a perfectionist. She creates and recreates accounts of her meetings with Nick, each time making them more intense, more precise. To him she entrusts her real name; his using it reinforces her sense of continuity and inspires hope.[20]

That Nick serves also as Offred's physical liberator is not surprising. He and Ofglen and Moira—honest rogues who also know how to feel for others—have influenced Offred, have given her the support she needed at various stages in her development, and have taught her by example that risk is inseparable from creativity. But this time when Offred listens to Nick's "trust me"—the traditional patriarchal ploy for co-opting women— Offred hears with an experience and knowledge that enable her to speak out, tell her tale, and perhaps precipitate the action that will bring Gilead to an end.

Although Atwood as speculator draws from the French feminists, as realist she questions their ultimate success. While Offred's tapes may have helped bring about the demise of Gilead, they do not bring about Atwood's ideal society. In the "Historical Notes," which follow the transcription of Offred's tapes, Atwood satirizes the academics of 2185, little different from those of two centuries earlier, who argue about "the text." Historical mystery buffs may find in the appendix delightful confirmation of their own intuitions that the Aunts Sara, Lydia, Elizabeth, and Helena were really pseudonymic adaptations for Sara Lee, Lydia E. Pinkham, Elizabeth Arden, and Helena Rubenstein (321). But "serious" academics will turn bloody as they hear themselves echoed in the pedantic analysis of the scholarly Professor James Darcy Pieixoto, who attempts fruitlessly to fill in the minute details indicated by the text, particularly to identify the Commander, Serena Joy, Nick, and Offred herself. Further embarrassments will emerge at the conference chair's recounting of all the extracurricular diversions that the conferees will not want to miss and her urgings that speakers keep within the time allotted for the papers so they will not miss dinner again. Although the satire of "Historical Notes" goes easier on occupants of the ivory tower than the tale does on the socio-religious Western patriarchy, the small-mindedness of academe in dealing with reality cannot be missed.

How Atwood will top this indictment of Western society and its clash of ideologies over women's experience, one can only conjecture. Novels are not expected to change society. *The Handmaid's Tale*, however, will surely embarrass many in high places and could bring some response. Whatever else she has accomplished in this novel, Atwood reaches the goal set by Hélène Cixous when she wrote "a feminine text cannot fail to be more than subversive. . . . If she's a her-she, it's in order to smash everything, to shatter the framework of institutions, to blow up the law, to break up the truth with laughter."[21] Intent—political or literary—aside, this, at least, Atwood achieves.

[September 1986]

Notes

1. Margaret Atwood, *Lady Oracle* (New York: Simon and Schuster, 1976), 345.

2. Atwood has on two occasions referred to *The Handmaid's Tale* as "speculative fiction": in an interview on the Fred Fiske Show, "Author Margaret Atwood on *The Handmaid's Tale*," WAMU, 88.5 FM, 5 March 1986, 8:00–9:00 P.M., and in an interview with Cathy N. Davidson, "A Feminist '1984': Margaret Atwood Talks About Her Exciting New Novel," *Ms.* (February 1986), 26. In addition to the obvious meanings of speculative — contemplative or conjectural or risky — Atwood may also have had in mind the speculum, or mirror, literature of the Middle Ages and Renaissance; for example, the *Mirror for Magistrates*, the *Speculum Meditantis*, and similar works. On pages 13, 19, and elsewhere in *The Handmaid's Tale*, mirrors and reflecting glass serve important functions; for example, the window at Soul Scrolls (p. 176) allows Offred and Ofglen to see each other's faces for the first time.

3. See Sherrill E. Grace, "Articulating the 'Space Between'; Atwood's Untold Stories and Fresh Beginnings," *Margaret Atwood: Language, Text, and System*, ed. Sherrill E. Grace and Lorraine Weir (Vancouver: University of British Columbia Press, 1983), 4. Grace quotes Atwood on the subject of artistic growth: "If you look at what most writers actually do, it resembles a theme with variations more than it does the popular notion of growth. Writers' universes may become more elaborate, but they do not necessarily become essentially different." Grace then applies the view to Atwood.

4. Margaret Atwood, *The Handmaid's Tale* (Toronto: McClelland and Stewart, 1985), 154, 202. Pagination for subsequent quotations from this volume is cited in the text.

5. Margaret Atwood, "An Interview with Margaret Atwood," conducted by Elizabeth Meese, University of Alabama, April 1985, *Black Warrior Review* 12, no. 1 (Fall 1985):96. See also Jo Brans, "Using What You're Given: An Interview with Margaret Atwood," *Southwest Review* 68, no. 4 (Autumn 1983):312 for a related discussion. The content of the Brans interview is interesting particularly because it suggests that Atwood was working on *The Handmaid's Tale* as early as 1983.

6. Meese interview, 100.

7. Atwood dedicated *The Handmaid's Tale* to Mary Webster, a Puritan ancestor, and to Perry Miller with whom she studied at Harvard and from whom she learned that "the classical tradition in America is political." Meese interview, 100.

8. Jeremiah 8:22. The Book of Jeremiah provides background for Atwood's story. Gilead is mentioned repeatedly in the Old Testament as particularly desirable. See James Strong, *The Exhaustive Concordance of the Bible* (New York: The Methodist Book Concern, 1890, 1936), 385.

9. In an interview, "Margaret Atwood: 'There's nothing in the book that hasn't already happened,'" *Quill & Quire* 51, no. 9 (September 1985):66, Atwood comments that *The Handmaid's Tale* could be called science fiction, "but it's not science fiction of the classic kind. There are no martians. There are no space machines. I would say instead that it is a dystopia, a negative utopia." More recently, she has referred to it as "speculative fiction," as cited in note 2 above.

10. The *Concordance* cites over fifty entries for *handmaid* and its variants.

11. *Ancient Near Eastern Texts Related to the Old Testament*, 3d ed., ed. James B. Pritchard (Princeton, New Jersey: Princeton University Press, 1969), passim 159–227.

12. *Offred* is also a pun on the protagonist's unorthodoxy, her desire to take off the red robes of her role.

13. On the Fred Fiske Show, Atwood spoke of the Bible's being locked up the way people kept tea locked up, and referred to the way slaves in the southern United States had only selected parts of the Bible read to them.

14. Le Anne Schreiber, "Female Trouble: An Interview," *Vogue*, January 1986, 209.

15. Ann Rosalind Jones, "Writing the Body: Toward an Understanding of *l'Écriture féminine*," *The New Feminist Criticism*, ed. Elaine Showalter. (New York: Pantheon Books, 1985), 361–77, discusses the works of Julia Kristeva, Luce Irigaray, Hélène Cixous, and Monique Wittig, including such topics as rejection of phallocentrism, reclaiming one's body, finding one's speaking voice, the context of women's discourse, *jouissance*, etc.

16. B. W. Powe, " 'How to Act': An Essay on Margaret Atwood," *Antigonish Review* 52 (1983): 134–35.

17. Atwood seems to be recalling Jeremiah when choosing the brand name—Whirlwind—for the Commander's car. She writes: "The car is a very expensive one, a Whirlwind; better than the Chariot, much better than the chunky, practical Behemoth" (27). Jeremiah 4:13 reads: "Behold, he shall come up as clouds, and his chariots shall be as a whirlwind. . . ." Jeremiah 23:19 reads: "Behold, a whirlwind of the Lord is gone forth in fury, even a grievous whirlwind. . . ." See also Jeremiah 25:32; 30:23.

18. Luce Irigaray, *"Ce sexe qui n'en est pas un,"* in *Ce sexe qui n'en est pas un* (Minuit, 1977). Quoted in *New French Feminisms: An Anthology*, ed. Elaine Marks and Isabelle de Courtivron (Amherst: University of Massachusetts Press, 1980), 103.

19. Mary McCarthy, "Breeders, Wives and Unwomen," *New York Times Book Review*, 9 February 1986, 35.

20. Atwood teases by placing a list of Handmaids' names at the beginning of the novel, leaving it to the reader to eliminate them one by one as Offred's former name. Finally *June* alone remains unidentified. Aunt Lydia comes near to a revelation: "No mooning and Juneing around here, girls," she warns (232).

21. Hélène Cixous, "The Laugh of the Medusa," *Signs*, Summer 1976. Quoted in *New French Feminisms*, 258.

PRIMARY BIBLIOGRAPHY

Poetry

Double Persephone. Toronto: Hawkshead Press, 1961. [Self-published chapbook, out of print.]

The Circle Game. Toronto: Contact Press, 1966; House of Anansi Press, 1967, 1978.

The Animals in That Country. Toronto: Oxford University Press, 1968; Boston: Little, Brown, 1968.

The Journals of Susanna Moodie. Toronto: Oxford University Press, 1970.

Procedures for Underground. Toronto: Oxford University Press, 1970; Boston: Little, Brown, 1970.

Power Politics. Toronto: House of Anansi Press, 1971; New York: Harper & Row, 1973.

You Are Happy. Toronto: Oxford University Press, 1974; New York: Harper & Row, 1974.

Selected Poems. Toronto: Oxford University Press, 1976; New York: Simon & Schuster, 1978.

Two-Headed Poems. Toronto: Oxford University Press, 1978; New York: Simon & Schuster, 1980.

True Stories. Toronto: Oxford University Press, 1981; New York: Simon & Schuster, 1981; London: Jonathan Cape, 1982.

Interlunar. Toronto: Oxford University Press, 1984.

Selected Poems II: Poems Selected and New 1976–86. Toronto: Oxford University Press, 1986; Boston: Houghton Mifflin, 1987.

Fiction

The Edible Woman. Toronto: McClelland and Stewart, 1969; Boston: Little, Brown, 1969; London: André Deutsch, 1969.

Surfacing. Toronto: McClelland and Stewart, 1972; New York: Simon & Schuster, 1973, c. 1972; London: André Deutsch, 1972.

Lady Oracle. Toronto: McClelland and Stewart, 1976; New York: Simon & Schuster, 1976; London: André Deutsch, 1977.

Dancing Girls and Other Stories. Toronto: McClelland and Stewart, 1977; New York: Simon & Schuster, 1982; London: Jonathan Cape, 1982.

Life Before Man. Toronto: McClelland and Stewart, 1979; New York: Simon & Schuster, 1979; London: Jonathan Cape, 1980.

Bodily Harm. Toronto: McClelland and Stewart, 1981; New York: Simon & Schuster, 1982; London: Jonathan Cape, 1982.

Murder in the Dark: Short Fictions and Prose Poems. Toronto: Coach House Press, 1983.

Bluebeard's Egg. Toronto: McClelland and Stewart, 1983; Boston: Houghton Mifflin, 1986.

The Handmaid's Tale. Toronto: McClelland and Stewart, 1985; Boston: Houghton Mifflin, 1986; London: Jonathan Cape, 1986.

Nonfiction

Survival: A Thematic Guide to Canadian Literature. Toronto: House of Anansi Press, 1972.

Days of the Rebels: 1815/1840. Canada's Illustrated Heritage. Toronto: Natural Science of Canada, 1977.

Second Words: Selected Critical Prose. Toronto: House of Anansi Press, 1982; Boston: Beacon Press, 1984.

Books Edited

The New Oxford Book of Canadian Verse in English. Toronto and London: Oxford University Press, 1982.

The Oxford Book of Canadian Short Stories in English, selected by Margaret Atwood and Robert Weaver. Toronto and New York: Oxford University Press, 1986.

INDEX